The ONE-ELEVEN Story

by Richard J Church

Published by   Air-Britain (Historians) Limited

Registered Office   1 East Street, Tonbridge, Kent, England

Sales Department   5 Bradley Road, Upper Norwood, London SE19 3NT

Membership Enquiries   1 Rose Cottage, 179 Penn Road, Hazlemere, Bucks
                        HP15 7NE

© Air-Britain (Historians) Limited

Users of this publication are advised that the data contained herein cannot be reproduced, stored in a retrieval system or transmitted in the form in which it appears by any means, electronic copying, recording or otherwise, without the express permission of the copyright owner, Air-Britain (Historians) Limited. Individual items of information may be used in other publications with due acknowledgment to Air-Britain (Historians) Limited.

ISBN 0 85130 221 1

Cover photographs:

Front cover: A Faucett One-Eleven operating a typical Andean gravel strip
               sector   (Brooklands Museum)

Rear cover: C/n 119 - Srs.422EQ This fine study of an executive One-
               Eleven shows N114M of Montex Drilling in front of one of its
               Vickers Viscount predecessors   (BAe)

               C/n 251 - Srs.485GD 1003 of the Air Force of the Sultanate
               of Oman with its main deck cargo door open   (BAe)

CONTENTS

	Page
Introduction	3
General History	5
Technical Description	59
Structure	59
Corrosion Protection and Finish	61
Flight Deck Layout and Controls	62
Interior Accommodation	62
Powerplant	64
APU	65
Fuel	65
Systems	66
Electronic Equipment	67
Overall Dimensions	68
Internal Dimensions	70
Weights and Loadings	71
Performance	72
Maintenance	74
Product Support	74
Flying the One-Eleven	76
Annual Delivery Summary	80
Series Identification System	81
United Kingdom Production Totals with Engine Type	83
Operators of the One-Eleven	84
Scheduled Route Maps	127
Individual Aircraft Histories	156
Registration and Serial/Constructor's Number Cross-References	204
Abbreviations	211

INTRODUCTION

The year 1993 saw the thirtieth anniversary of the first flight of the One-Eleven airliner. The type will probably be the last all-British jet airliner ever to be built in the United Kingdom. It was also one of the most successful types ever produced in this country, and although not selling in the numbers of its predecessor, the Viscount, it far exceeded it in the value of sales. Like its predecessor, it also sold well in the United States market. Although production has long since ceased in the United Kingdom, production in Romania may well get under way again if the latest agreement with Kiwi International Airways Inc of the USA is finalised. Should this take place, the Series 2500 would be the version involved, which it is proposed to power with the Rolls-Royce Tay 650 engine. This is basically a re-engined version of the Series 500 with modernised cockpit equipment.

With major longterm users of the type recently retiring their aircraft, it seemed a logical time to produce a Monograph on this most successful airliner. Other publications on the One-Eleven have been produced, but none has previously gone into such detail on the individual aircraft histories or operator information. Unfortunately, many of the historical records of the type have been lost with the closure of most of the former British Aircraft Corporation sites in Southern England. Sources of information have been many and varied; Air-Britain's own publications have produced much of the information, while other sources include ABC World Airways Guide, Aeroplane, Aircraft Illustrated, Air International, Air Pictorial, Australian Aviation, Aviation Letter, Flight International, Flying Review International, Jane's All the World's Aircraft, UK Independent Airlines and various BAC technical publications. Airline operators who have assisted with detailed information on their aircraft include Air Malawi, Austral Lineas Aereas, British World Airlines, British Airways, European Aviation, Ladeco, Maersk Air, Philippine Airlines, SARO Airlines, TACA International and the ever-helpful staff of the sadly lamented Dan-Air Engineering at Manchester. Additionally, FLS at Manchester and Lovaux of Hurn have been particularly helpful.

Many individuals have also helped in the research; special thanks must go to J A K Travers for his in-depth research into Nigerian operators, to Elliot Greenman for his considerable assistance with the Mohawk/USAir fleets, to Dave Wilkinson for access to his extensive records of the early One-Eleven days and to the engineering and flying crew staff of British Airways who have assisted during the preparation of this publication. Special thanks must also go to Wayne Barker, Fred Barnes, Richard Collishaw (and for access to his father Denys' collection of One-Eleven paperwork, photographs and slides), M D Harries, Ray Hoddinot, John Roach and Ray Turner for their help, while British Aerospace Airbus at Filton have provided some technical details, drawings and access to their utilisation records. Paul Taylor and Alan Miles of European Aviation have been most helpful with the latest UK developments, and Avro International at Woodford have kindly allowed access to what remains of the former BAC/BAe Photographic Section negative archives. Malcolm Fillmore and Bernard Martin, Air-Britain's United Kingdom register specialists, have provided much detailed information on British registered examples of the aircraft, while Donald M Hannah has provided access to his details of BEA and British Airways One-Eleven fleets. Mike Goodall and the team at the Brooklands Museum have been extremely helpful with access to their extensive archives of photographs and BAC manuals. Lyn Buttifant, Chris Chatfield and Jenni Phillips have helped transform the manuscript into this landmark Air-Britain publication.

An unusual and most welcome addition to this Air-Britain Monograph is the contribution by Captain Douglas Brown, British Airways Flight Manager Birmingham, who gives a fascinating insight into the flying characteristics of the aircraft and to the affection the type generated with those who flew it. Douglas Brown's contribution, "Flying the BAC One-Eleven", is much appreciated and included much additional information which is contained in other parts of this book.

Any corrections, amendments or additional information would be greatly appreciated at the address shown below.

Richard J Church

November 1994

44 South Street
Epsom
Surrey KT18 7PQ

GENERAL HISTORY

Conceived as a jet successor to the Vickers-Armstrongs Viscount, the origins of the One-Eleven can be traced back to two separate design studies. Vickers had been working on proposals which had been designated the VC11, while Hunting Aircraft had been working on their H.107. The former was proposed as a scaled-down Vickers VC10 with four Rolls-Royce RB163 turbo-fan engines seating approximately 140 passengers. It was however to be the latter type which was eventually developed into the One-Eleven.

The Hunting 107, when first proposed in 1956, was to have been a four abreast 32 seat short field turbojet airliner with a low set wing and two rear fuselage mounted Bristol Orpheus 12B engines and was to have had a range of 1,000 statute miles. The project was later shelved pending the availability of a more suitable turbo-fan rather than pure jet powerplant. In 1959 the project was reactivated, but with capacity increased to 48 passengers. After consideration of the various engines then on offer, including the Rolls-Royce RB149 and the Bristol BE.61, it was decided to adopt the new Bristol Siddeley BS.75. The marks G-APOH were registered for the first airframe with c/n H.107.

The aircraft and guided weapons interests of the Bristol Aeroplane Company, the English Electric Company and Vickers Ltd came together in February 1960 to form the British Aircraft Corporation. A controlling interest was also taken in Hunting Aircraft Ltd at the same time. The new corporation took a long, hard look at the commercial aircraft prospects and decided to conduct a comprehensive market survey of approximately 100 leading airlines throughout the world to ascertain the most promising type to develop. The results of this survey indicated that an aircraft with a capacity of at least 60 passenger seats and a range of between 100 and 1,000 statute miles stood the most chance of selling in large numbers in the world market. It would be targeted as an economic jet replacement not only for Vickers Viscounts, but also for the Convair 240/340/440 range and the Martin 202 and 404 types. An increase in cruise speed of approximately 180 mph over the fastest of the Viscount series, the 810, was possible.

The Hunting 107 went some way towards filling these requirements. BAC renamed the project the BAC.107 and, with the experience of the Vickers design team behind them, proceeded to make several changes to the aircraft. Retained were the four abreast cabin layout and the Bristol Siddeley BS.75 engines rated at 7,350lb static thrust. The tailplane was relocated to the top of the fin from the mid position of the original aircraft, while the passenger capacity was increased to a high density figure of 59, to be carried over a range of approximately 500 miles (804km). Cabin windows were increased to 26 each side. Although fulfilling many of the requirements of the market survey, the BAC.107 remained somewhat basic for the sophisticated United States market and fell short on both capacity and range. BAC continued to market the BAC.107 in its current form but set about introducing major improvements to the aircraft.

It was apparent from the market survey that if the aircraft was to sell well in the United States, which was to be the prime target of the sales team, certain criteria would have to be met. A capacity of between 60 and 80 seats would be the ideal, while the aircraft would have to be self-sufficient at the smaller, less well equipped, airfields which it would be likely to serve. For these reasons it was essential that the aircraft should be fitted with a reliable auxiliary power unit to provide engine starting, electrical and hydraulic power and cabin air-conditioning/heating on the ground. It would also have to be configured with internally fitted powered airstairs. A relatively high maximum landing weight in relation to the maximum take-off weight was essential in order that the aircraft could be fuelled at the start of multi-sector short stage flights for the entire journey. It was also considered that waist-high access to cargo holds would be ideal to facilitate quick off/onloading of luggage and freight. With all these design features, minimal turnrounds would be achievable at transit stations. The proposed fuselage diameter was increased to accommodate a five-abreast cabin layout, and the project was renumbered the BAC.111. For such an aircraft the power output of the BS.75 engine was insufficient since a thrust rating of approximately 10,000lb was required. Rolls-Royce was developing such an engine at the time in the shape of the RB163 Spey for installation in the Hawker Siddeley Trident airliner, and it was decided to adopt this engine for the BAC.111. The new project was designed to incorporate all of these requirements and was a much more sophisticated aircraft than the BAC.107.

The British Aircraft Corporation decided to proceed with the detailed design and manufacture of the BAC.111 project in March 1961 and to lay down an initial production batch of 20 aircraft. This total was to include two static test airframes and a flying prototype. The first static test airframe would be used for fail-safe tests in which the structure would be deliberately weakened before being subjected to representative flight loads with wing bending through hydraulic jacks. The second fuselage would be pressure tested in a water tank at Filton. A full-scale hydraulic and flying control rig would also be built to check out these systems. Production was to be shared amongst four BAC plants; Hurn was to be the location for production of the forward and mid fuselage sections and also the centre for final assembly, Filton would construct the rear fuselage and tail section, while Luton would manufacture the wings, ailerons and flaps. Finally, Weybridge would build the centre section, undercarriage and wing skins and would later take over the Luton allocation of work when that site was closed down.

The public launch of the project came on 9 May 1961, when the manufacturer announced a launch order for ten aircraft from British United Airways to serve their domestic and European schedules; options on a further five aircraft were placed at the same time. The type was to be marketed as the "One-Eleven". As detailed design proceeded apace, the company's marketing team was able to report considerable interest in the aircraft, especially from the United States of America. Ozark Airlines placed a Letter of Intent for the purchase of five aircraft at the time of the launch, while Frontier Airlines followed suit in June with a commitment for six aircraft. Problems with the US Civil Aeronautics Board, which threatened the withdrawal of both companies' local service route subsidies if the contracts were finalised, led to both deals coming to nought. On 23 October 1961, however, a firm order for six aircraft was announced for Braniff Airways, with options placed on an additional six aircraft. This was the first time that an American airline had ordered a non-American airliner off the drawing board. Unlike all the other airline One-Elevens ordered, the Braniff contract specified that the ventral airstairs and rear access were not fitted to their aircraft.

At the time of the launch of the One-Eleven it was announced that development of the VC11 had been abandoned. This aircraft would have had a maximum take-off weight of approximately 170,000lb (77,110kg), a length of 136ft (46.25m), a wing span of 103ft (31.40m) and a capacity payload range of approximately 1,800 miles (2,895nm). It would have been more of a Vickers Vanguard replacement in size. At the press conference at the launch of the One-Eleven programme Sir George Edwards, BAC's Executive Director, stated that "..it was BAC's intention to continue with the BAC.107 project because first indications showed a market for a lighter, more austere aircraft than the One-Eleven". By this time the BAC.107 had a maximum take-off weight of 48,500lb (22,000kg), an overall length of 84ft 11in (25.88m), a wing span of 81ft 8in (24.90m), a height of 23ft (7.01m) and a wing area of 825 sq ft (76.64 sq m). It was anticipated that development of this programme would follow about one year behind the One-Eleven, but by the end of 1961 the programme was abandoned and the Bristol Siddeley BS.75 engine programme put on hold. From now on, all BAC's efforts in developing short haul airliners would be concentrated on variants of the One-Eleven.

Other orders were soon placed by Mohawk Airlines of the USA for four aircraft on 24 July, by Kuwait Airways for three aircraft with an option on a fourth on 9 August, and by Central African Airways Corporation for two aircraft on 26 September, all in 1962. The first, a local service carrier based at Utica-Rome in New York State, was prepared to forego its subsidy in order to upgrade its service to jet operation in the belief that such a move would be profitable. Bonanza Airlines in the USA also ordered three aircraft in November 1962, but this was cancelled in February of the following year after the CAB refused the airline a loan guarantee for the purchase. Surprisingly, this decision was later reversed when the same airline proposed the purchase of DC-9 equipment. In January 1963 Hawaiian Airlines announced that it intended to order three One-Elevens, but no order was finalised. On 5 March 1963 Braniff Airways converted its earlier placed option and doubled its commitment to 12 aircraft, while Aer Lingus placed an order for four aircraft on 3 May to supplement its Vickers Viscount fleet on its European network. An order for eight aircraft, later increased to ten, for an undisclosed customer (now known to be Western Airways Ltd - no connection with Western Airlines of the USA) was also included in the order list at this time, but the order was cancelled in 1964.

All orders so far received had been for the Series 200 aircraft, which was to be powered by Rolls-Royce RB163 Spey 2 Mk.506-14s of 10,410lb (4,722kg) static thrust. Maximum take-off weight was set at 73,500lb (33,339kg). A Series 200 cutaway drawing is shown overleaf. In May 1963 BAC announced two heavier and longer range versions of the aircraft; these were the Series 300 and 400. The new types were to be powered by the higher rated Spey 25 Mk.511-14, with the option of a water injection system to maintain take-off power in hot/high conditions. The water injection system was also an option on Series 200 aircraft and was taken up by British United Airways in order that economic payloads could be carried on its more demanding West African routes. Helmut Horten's later ordered aircraft was also delivered with the system installed. All Spey 2 powered Series 200s were later demodified, and none is now believed to have the system operational.

Overall dimensions of the Series 300/400 aircraft were to be the same as the Series 200, although the engine nacelles would be 4in (10cm) longer due to the addition of a fifth stage to the low pressure compressor on the Spey 25. A further refinement on the Series 400 was the installation of lift dumpers, the Series 300 having provision for this addition. The Series 400 was specifically designed for operation within the USA and was restricted to a maximum gross take-off weight of 80,000lb (36,282kg) in order to comply with the restriction then imposed on two crew operated aircraft. The MTOW was initially set at 78,500lb (35,607kg) to comply with these rules; the Series 300 was for operation where these restrictions did not apply and had an MTOW of 82,000lb (37,195kg). The first customer for the Series 400 was American Airlines, which placed on order for 15 aircraft on 17 July 1963 at a cost in excess of £14 million. This was the first time that American Airlines had purchased a foreign aircraft and was a major success for the sales team, especially since the home-built Douglas DC-9 had recently been launched.

The prototype, resplendent in British United Airways' colour scheme and registered G-ASHG, was rolled out at Hurn on 28 July 1963 with much publicity. For a new British airliner to be rolled out for its first flight with an order book for 60 aircraft already outstanding was a great achievement for the British Aircraft Corporation. Furthermore, none of these orders was for the two nationalised state corporations, British European Airways and British Overseas Airways Corporation, or their subsidiaries. It was evident

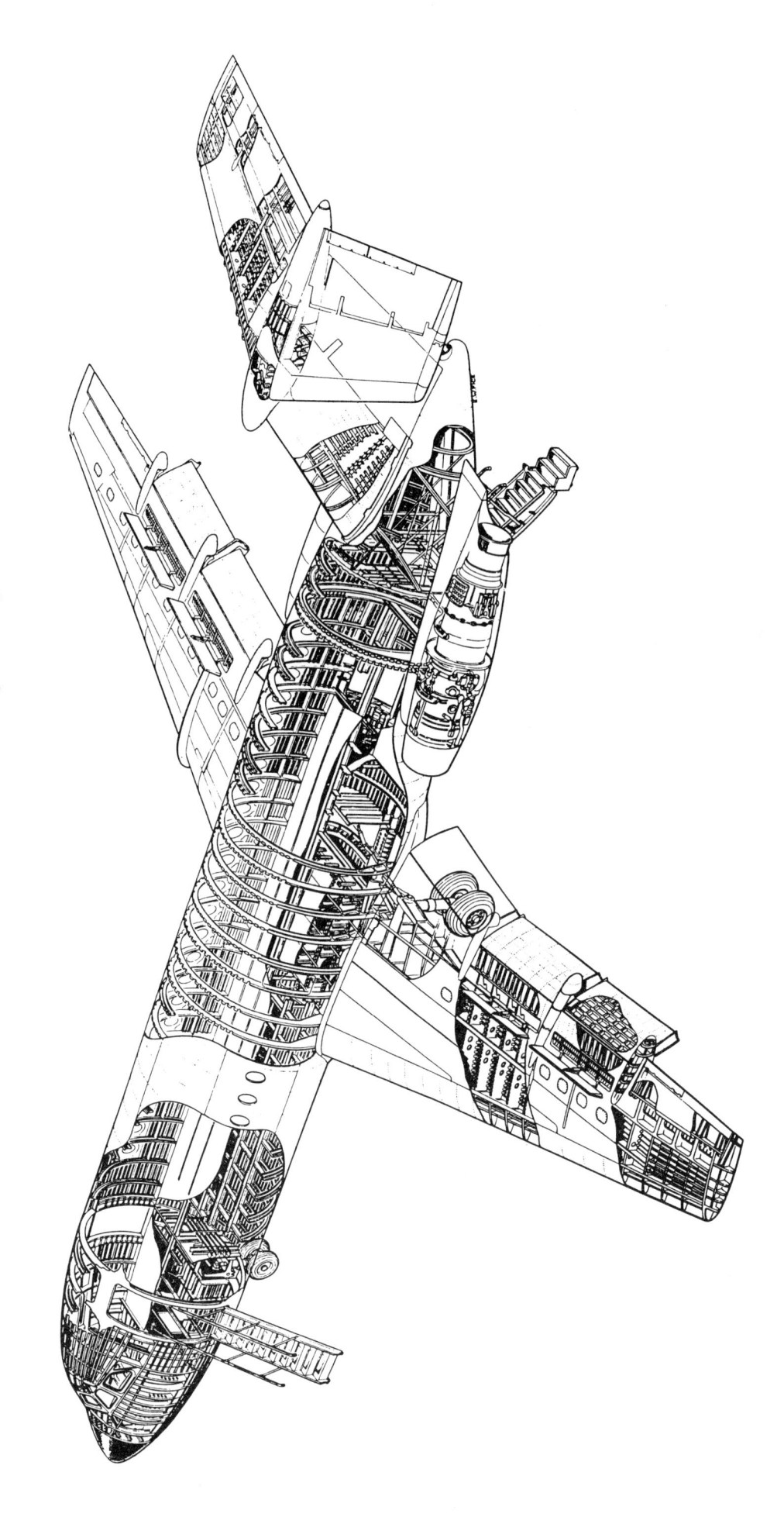

BAC One-Eleven Srs.200 cutaway drawing

at this time that the manufacturer had a potentially very successful product. BAC was now ready to fly the prototype, while the only direct competition, the Douglas DC-9, had only been launched four months earlier.

The first flight took place on 20 August 1963 at 7.42pm and lasted 27 minutes, with G R (Jock) Bryce, BAC's Chief Test Pilot, in command. In the first 28 days thirty and a half flying hours were completed in 19 flights, during which general handling trials were conducted. Total hours flown had risen to 70 by 14 October. A major setback to the programme occurred on 22 October when the prototype failed to recover from a deep stall and crashed at Chicklade in Wiltshire, killing all on board. All but the tail of the aircraft was destroyed by fire, and this disaster sadly killed seven of the Vickers and Hunting development team. These were Lt-Cdr M J Lithgow (Pilot), Capt R Rymer (Co-Pilot), Ben J Prior (Assistant Chief Aerodynamicist Vickers), C J Webb (Assistant Chief Designer Hunting), R A F Wright (Senior Flight Test Observer 1-11), G R Poulter (Flight Test Observer Vickers) and D J Clark (Flight Test Observer Hunting).

At the time of the accident the aircraft was involved in a programme to assess its stability and handling characteristics as it approached the stall, together with measurements of the lift coefficient of the wing. Tests had already been completed satisfactorily at various flap settings, gradually moving the position of the centre of gravity (CofG) from a forward position to a rearward one. It was on the fifth approach to the stall with an 8° flap setting and with the CofG at its rearmost position that the accident occurred. The two flight recorders indicated that the stall was reached very abruptly in this configuration, causing downward acceleration and an unexpected and rapid increase in incidence. The elevator trailed up as these two conditions rapidly increased; this was momentarily arrested by the crew, but with the aft CofG and a rapidly decreasing forward speed, the incidence further increased reducing the effectiveness of both the tailplane and the elevator. The force required to stop the elevator trailing up became too strong, and it soon reached the stop. The aircraft continued to descend rapidly with the fuselage in a horizontal position until it hit the ground with the engines still rotating. BAC quickly appraised the situation and set about a programme of modifications to rectify the problems which had led to the accident.

The flight test programme restarted at the Wisley Flight Test Centre after the first production aircraft first flew on 19 December 1963. The crash of the prototype did not affect customer confidence, which was soon indicated by re-orders received from American Airlines for ten Series 400s and from Braniff Airways for two Series 200s, both placed in February 1964. Other orders placed during the year were for one Series 200 with options on two further aircraft from Mohawk Airlines in March, the first order for an executive Series 200 from Helmut Horten of West Germany in June, two Series 400s from Philippine Airlines with an option on a third in November and a further five Series 400s from American Airlines in December. Page Airways International, who were appointed exclusive sales agents for newly built executive versions of the aircraft in the USA, also ordered two aircraft for potential customers in November of the same year. During the year Kuwait Airways took advantage of the improved performance offered by the Series 300 aircraft and upgraded their order from Series 200 aircraft.

By the end of July 1964 the sixth production British United Airways aircraft had joined the test programme. G-ASJA was used for systems testing and evaluating airfield performance, while G-ASJB was the first aircraft to fly with a modified wing leading edge introduced after the accident to the prototype. This was designed to improve the nose-down pitching characteristics of the aircraft. The aircraft was employed on handling trials until it was involved in a heavy landing while crew training at Wisley on 18 March, which eventually led to its write-off.

C/n 004 - Srs.200AB G-ASHG, the original prototype, photographed on a test flight on 04Oct63, less than a month before its unfortunate demise (Brooklands Museum)

An early photograph of production at Hurn; aircraft for Mohawk Airlines, Austral and the Força Aerea Brasileira (Brooklands Museum)

The fourth production aircraft, G-ASJD, was the first to be flown with a fully powered elevator (replacing the earlier used servo-tab control) and also had the modified leading edge enabling slow speed handling trials to be resumed. This aircraft made a precautionary forced landing on Salisbury Plain on 28 August after streaming the tail parachute whilst taking part in stalling trials. The pilot took this precautionary action after sensing impending trouble. Subsequent analysis of the flight data recorder traces and instruments was to show that all was normal and that the pilot's action had not been necessary. A parachute had been fitted to some of the aircraft involved in the certification programme after the prototype accident; this was designed to raise the tail of the aircraft in the event of a deep stall being entered and to give the aircraft a nose-down attitude enabling it to gain forward speed, effective elevator control and recovery from its predicament. The aircraft was not seriously damaged and was dismantled and returned by road to Hurn, where it was rebuilt. This particular aircraft still flies in the United Kingdom with the Defence Research Agency.

The third production aircraft, G-ASJC, which had been used earlier for handling trials, resonance testing and for tropical trials in Madrid, was fitted with fully powered elevators in August 1964 and continued the work previously done with G-ASJD. G-ASJE was used for systems testing and took part in many overseas demonstrations, as did G-ASJF. During the early stages of flight testing several of the aircraft were fitted with temporary large tail skids mounted on the underside of the ventral door. The contour of the nose cone was also changed to give the aircraft a more streamlined shape, and the wing fence was relocated further inboard. A stick shaker/pusher system was incorporated to avoid any chance of the type entering a deep stall in service; as the aircraft approaches the stall, the control stick shakes as a warning to the crew of the impending situation. If this warning is overlooked, the control stick moves forward, pitching the aircraft nose down, thus eliminating the danger (assuming the aircraft has sufficient altitude to recover).

Part of the final stages of flight testing was carried out by G-ASJA when it was used for performance testing at maximum weights at hot and high airfields. The aircraft left Wisley for Dakar, Senegal via Madrid and Las Palmas on 16 October. After nine days of measurements at Dakar the aircraft returned to Torrejon, Madrid for a further two weeks of tests. During this time the aircraft was demonstrated to Aviaco and visited La Coruna (the first jet airliner to visit this location), an airfield with a 5,000ft (1,524m) runway and a difficult approach. A team of technicians from the manufacturer, the Air Registration Board and equipment suppliers who travelled with this aircraft throughout the tour found all aspects of its performance and the engineering reliability excellent. This same aircraft was to return to Africa in January 1965, this time to Johannesburg, for a further series of hot and high trials and measurements. By 23 October the type had amassed 1,000 hours in the air, and G-ASJG joined the certification programme. The first export aircraft, for Braniff Airways, was rolled out on 24 May 1964 and was used subsequently on customer variation trials while their third aircraft was later used for acceptance tests.

In July 1964 the British Aircraft Corporation was able to announce improvements in the operating weights and range for all currently offered marks of aircraft. This was as a result of the structural testing to destruction of one of the two static test airframes. Failure of the wing did not occur until reaching 117% of the design load. The Series 200 MTOW was increased by 500lb (227kg) to 74,500lb (33,793kg), the MLW by 1,000lb (454kg) to 66,000lb (29,937kg) and the MZFW to 59,000lb (26,762kg). The Series 300 MTOW was increased by 3,000lb (1,361kg) to 85,000lb (38,555kg), and the MLW of both Series 300 and 400 aircraft was increased by 7,000lb (3,175kg) to 76,000lb (34,473kg). The maximum payload of both the last two Series was increased to 19,200lb (8,709kg). Progressively higher weights were later certified as tests and experience were gained. The ultimate weights are shown in the tabulated figures.

Prior to the granting of a full United Kingdom Type Certificate of Airworthiness on 9 April 1965, British United Airways took delivery of G-ASJI on 22 January for 200 hours of intensive route proving, which was completed on 14 February. On 9 April 1965 the world's first revenue passengers were carried on a One-Eleven when British United's G-ASJJ departed London-Gatwick for Genoa in Italy, the aircraft having been delivered to them three days earlier. The FAA type certificate for the Series 200 was granted on 16 April 1965, which led to Braniff International inaugurating service with the type on 25 April on a multi-sector flight between Corpus Christi and Minneapolis-St Paul. Mohawk Airlines closely followed them with their inaugural service on 15 July, and Aer Lingus commenced service with the type on 3 June. During 1965 all 14 of Braniff's fleet were delivered, with the last few arriving in the company's new highly visible colour scheme. All ten British United Series 200 aircraft were also delivered during that year, as was the four strong Aer Lingus fleet and the first five aircraft for Mohawk Airlines. By the end of the year total hours flown by One-Elevens had exceeded 35,000 and an estimated one and a quarter million passengers had flown in the type.

During 1965 orders continued to be received. Mohawk Airlines took up their option on two aircraft in February, while at the same time placing options on three additional aircraft. A new American customer was Aloha Airlines, which ordered two Series 200s in March and placed an option on a third. In the same month TACA International of El Salvador was the first of several Central American carriers to order the type when it placed an order for two Series 400s with an option on two additional aircraft.

An order for two Series 300s was received from British Midland Airways in November, but this was later cancelled. British Eagle International Airways ordered two Series 300s in December with an option on a third, while Philippine Airlines took up their option on a third Series 400 and placed an option on a fourth in the same month. The Royal Australian Air Force ordered two Series 200s for VIP duties in December, powered by the higher rated Rolls-Royce Spey Mk.511-14 engines.

Competition

Although the British Aircraft Corporation had taken the lead in developing a shorthaul jet, the American competition was soon evident. First on the scene was Douglas, who had been promoting shorthaul jet projects from early 1957 under the designation Douglas 2000. Initial studies were for a scaled-down four-fifths size DC-8 with four underslung wing-mounted Pratt & Whitney JTF10A-1 engines with a capacity similar to that of the Boeing 727-100. The idea did not come to fruition because of the lack of interest amongst prospective customers, who were not yet ready for jet aircraft for this sector of the market. By 1962 DC-8 production had passed its peak, and Douglas was looking for work to fill the void in its plants. The company had come to the same conclusions as the British Aircraft Corporation about customer requirements and redefined the project around two rear fuselage-mounted jet engines, calling the project Model 2086. Size and general arrangement were almost identical to the One-Eleven, and the company even considered the Rolls-Royce Spey engine throughout the early definition stage, but eventually settled on the higher powered Pratt & Whitney JT8D as the powerplant but in a de-rated form.

The project was officially launched on 8 April 1963 as the Douglas DC-9, some two years after the One-Eleven go-ahead. Orders were received from Delta Airlines some three weeks later for 15 aircraft with a further 15 on option. Bonanza Airlines, which had earlier placed an order for three One-Elevens and was later forced to abandon the deal because of a Civil Aeronautics Board ruling, was the next to order with a three aircraft commitment on 1 July 1963. This time the CAB was to sanction the order. Douglas was very disappointed with

C/n 055 - Srs.401AK N5015, the first of 30 such aircraft for American Airlines (Brooklands Museum)

C/n 085 - Srs.301AG G-ATPL in SAS c/s while on lease from British Eagle (Brooklands Museum)

C/n 087 - Srs.401AK G-AXCP The first of many One-Elevens received by Dan-Air; this shows the original c/s used on the type
(Brooklands Museum)

sales of the aircraft up to this time, especially when American Airlines selected the One-Eleven on 17 July 1963. Foreign sales came with orders for eight aircraft from Air Canada in November 1963 and from Swissair with an order for 12 aircraft in May 1964. All these orders were strongly contested by the British Aircraft Corporation with its One-Eleven. The next major success for Douglas was when Trans World Airlines selected its product with a 20 aircraft order on 20 July 1964. Two other large United States carriers had still not selected shorthaul jets, these being Eastern Airlines and United Airlines. Eastern could have gone for either the One-Eleven or the DC-9 but finally selected the Douglas aircraft when the manufacturer agreed to develop a stretched version, initially known as the Series 20. All previously ordered aircraft had been Series 10s, which were only marginally larger than the One-Elevens then on offer. This deal was sealed when Douglas agreed to lease Eastern Airlines Series 10 aircraft pending the availability of a stretched version. It was to be the even further stretched Series 30 which would eventually be ordered by Eastern. It is believed that Swissair's decision to opt for the DC-9 was mainly based on the early availability of a stretched version of the type.

The first DC-9 flew on 25 February 1965, some 18 months after the first flight of the One-Eleven prototype. It is interesting to note that, following the crash of the One-Eleven prototype, Douglas immediately took advantage of the knowledge gained from this incident and commenced new wind tunnel tests to overcome the deep stall problems prevalent with aircraft in this configuration. This led to increasing the tailplane area by some 20% and adding vortilons beneath the wing. The passage of time shows how Douglas has reaped the benefits of an early decision to offer a range of models of varying capacity, range and performance with its DC-9 project; this has clearly led to its huge sales success.

The other main competitor in the short range jet arena was Boeing, which did not enter the race until their Boeing 737 was launched on 19 February 1965, initially in its Series 100 form. The first aircraft did not fly until 9 April 1967 and, unlike the One-Eleven and DC-9, had a six-abreast cabin layout rather than the two/aisle/three scheme of the competition. Typical One-Eleven cabin layouts are shown opposite. Boeing used a cabin width common to that of their Boeing 707/720 and 727 range of aircraft. Launch customer was Deutsche Lufthansa with an order for 21 aircraft announced at the time of the launch. Very few of the Series 100 were to be built, the higher capacity Series 200 being the popular version in the type's early days and the version which received United Airlines' endorsement.

Returning to the BAC One-Eleven, two Series 400 development aircraft were built in advance of the first American Airlines Series 401AK. The first of these flew on 13 July 1965, with the second following in September of that year. The first aircraft was used for tropical trials at Madrid-Torrejon from 11 September, while the second was prepared for a programme of intensive demonstration flights throughout the world. This entailed the fitting of an executive forward cabin and airline seating in the rear cabin by Marshalls of Cambridge (Engineering) between 5 and 12 November. The executive cabin was designed by Charles Butler Associates of New York to the requirements of Page Airways International.

The first tour departed Wisley on 17 November and was to Central America and the United States. Thirty-three cities were visited in the USA, Nassau in the Bahamas, Mexico City, Guatemala City, San Salvador, Tegucigalpa, Managua and San Jose in Costa Rica. A three and a half week break in the tour took place in December to enable American Airlines to use the aircraft for crew training. The American FAA type certificate for the Series 400 was granted earlier on 22 November. The aircraft returned to Wisley on 8 January 1966, having flown 50,000 miles.

15

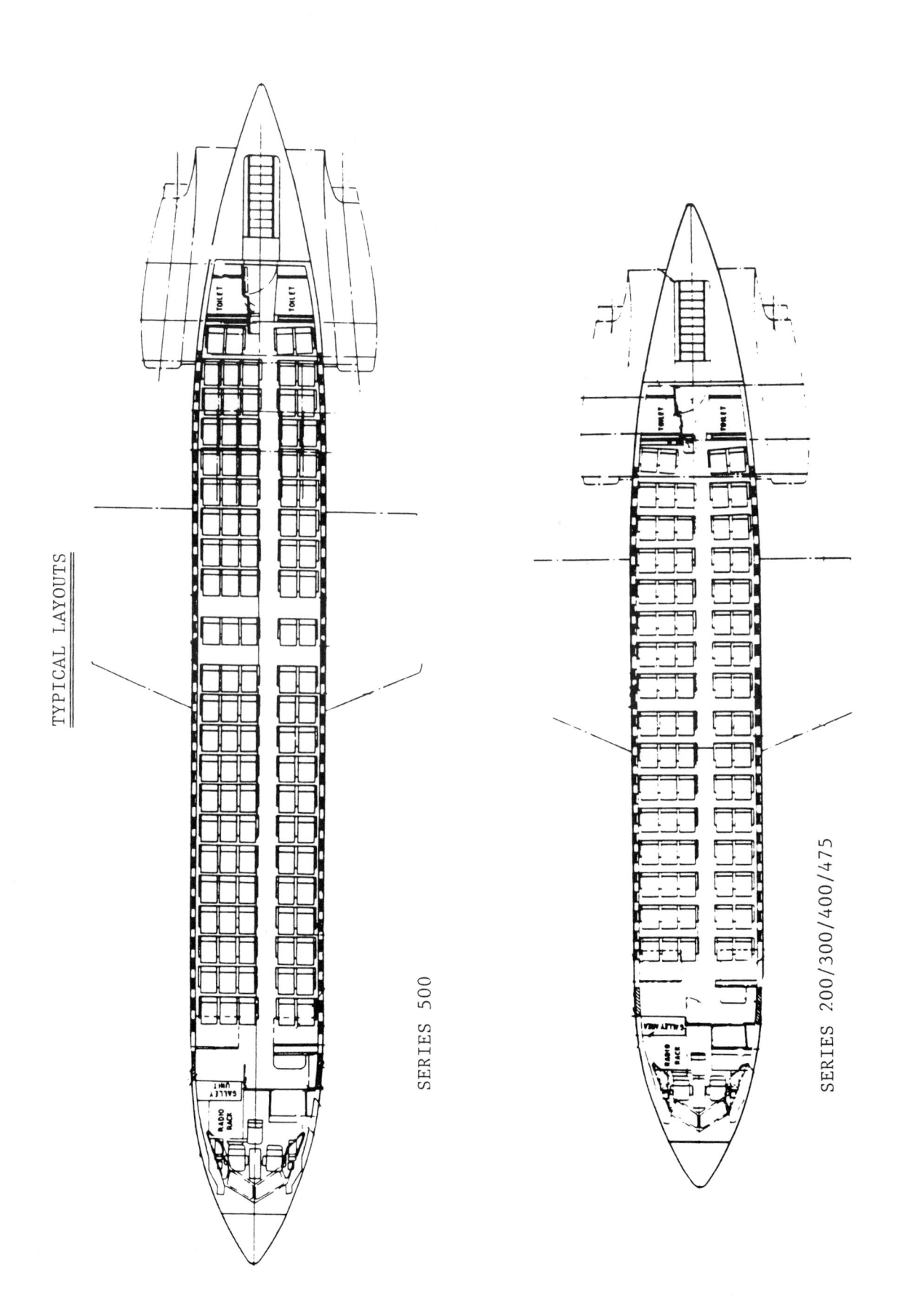

TYPICAL LAYOUTS

SERIES 500

SERIES 200/300/400/475

The second tour departed Wisley on 21 January and after flying to Rome, Damascus, Bahrain, through India to Bangkok, Singapore, Bali, Darwin, Townsville and Sydney, it finally arrived in Christchurch, New Zealand, on 26 January. It was demonstrated for a week in New Zealand, during which time it visited Dunedin, Wellington, Auckland and Whenupai. Australia was the next country to receive a week's demonstration, with the aircraft shown in Melbourne, Canberra and Sydney. On 9 February the aircraft left for the Philippines via Townsville and Biak. Six days of flying here saw the aircraft visiting Bacolod, Cebu, Davao and Manila before it left for Japan, with demonstrations in Taipei en route. After three days of demonstrations in Tokyo, the aircraft left via Taipei for Hong Kong, where both the aircraft and crews were rested for three days. From Hong Kong the aircraft flew to Bangkok, Rangoon and Colombo, with demonstrations at all points. The tour then continued to India, where G-ASYE was shown in Benares, Bombay, Calcutta, Delhi, Hyderabad and Madras over a four day period. From India the aircraft continued to Teheran via Sharjah and then to Istanbul and Rome before returning to the UK on 8 March. In this tour 70,000 miles were flown.

Less than a month later G-ASYE left Wisley on 5 April 1966 via Keflavik, Gander and Bermuda for Nassau in the Bahamas, where the first demonstrations were carried out with visits to Freeport and Miami. From there the aircraft left for Port of Spain, Trinidad, and onwards to Brazil, where the aircraft was shown in Belem, Brasilia, Rio de Janeiro, Sao Paulo, Urububunga, Londrina, Porto Alegre and Curitiba. The tour then continued to Asuncion (Paraguay), Montevideo (Uruguay), Buenos Aires, Santiago and to Lima in Peru. The aircraft was flown to Cuzco and Arequipa in Peru before leaving for Quito (Ecuador), Bogota (Colombia) and Caracas in Venezuela. The aircraft was also flown to Barquisimeto in Venezuela before returning to Port of Spain for further demonstrations and finally returned to Wisley via Nassau, New York, Chicago, Montreal, Goose Bay and Keflavik, arriving back in the UK on 1 May, completing another 40,000 miles of flying.

In the 334 flights of these three tours G-ASYE had flown 160,000 miles from Arctic cold to tropical heat and had visited airfields with elevations as high as 9,000 feet (2,745 metres). Over 100 guest pilots flew the aircraft on these tours, which added 396 hours to the aircraft's logbook total. Only three minor technical delays were recorded throughout the duration of the tours, proving conclusively that the aircraft was both rugged and reliable and could achieve all that the manufacturer claimed of it. On 7 July the sister development aircraft, G-ASYD, commenced lower weather minima flight trials aimed at achieving Category 2 clearance for the type.

An additional final assembly line was set up at Weybridge to cope with increased demand for One-Elevens. Six aircraft were completed and flown from here during the first half of 1966.

During 1966 the Series 400 entered service with the launch customer, American Airlines. This company inaugurated service with the type on 6 March and had received all 30 aircraft ordered by the end of that year. Aloha Airlines launched services with its first Series 200 on 27 April, linking several islands in the Hawaiian group. Philippine Airlines commenced service with its first Series 400 on 1 May, flying from Manila to Cebu, Bacolod and Davao and internationally to Hong Kong and Taipei.

Although completed for Central African Airways, this company's two Series 200s were refused an export licence after Southern Rhodesia's unilateral declaration of independence and the order was taken over by Zambia Airways Corporation. This company was not yet ready however to put the type into service and chose to lease the aircraft to British Eagle International Airways, who inaugurated service with the aircraft on 9 May. Although

C/n 008 - Srs.201AC XX105 in early BLEU titles with the RAE (Brooklands Museum)

C/n 029 - N2111J - The first of 18 Srs.204AFs for Mohawk Airlines (Brooklands Museum)

C/n 040 - Srs.207AJ 9J-RCI Zambia Airways at Heathrow (P R Keating via Andy Heape)

C/n 042 - Srs.203AE N1548 Allegheny at Pittsburgh in May77 (Andy Heape)

One of the two Srs.207AJs built for Central African Airways which were not del because of Rhodesia's Unilateral Declaration of Independence (Brooklands Museum)

C/n 054 - Srs.410AQ N3939V of Victor Comptometers (Brooklands Museum)

certificated at Series 200 weights, these aircraft were powered by the higher rated Spey 25 Mk.511-14 engines of the Series 300/400 and also had provision for the use of a water injection system, which made them unique amongst airline users of Series 200s. (The Royal Australian Air Force One-Elevens were also fitted with this mark of Spey but did not have water injection systems.) The variation gave the aircraft a quite spirited performance and still does to this day, the aircraft currently flying with Ladeco in Chile. British Eagle also leased the three Series 300s ordered by Kuwait Airways, which no longer had a use for so many different types in its fleet. By late July British Eagle were flying all five aircraft on their international and domestic schedules, together with some charter work.

During the year Mohawk Airlines took delivery of another four aircraft, raising their fleet to nine, while Aloha Airlines took its second aircraft on strength.

The year 1966 saw repeat orders received from Mohawk Airlines for two aircraft in February (these being delivered later in the year) and for their tenth aircraft in May, while placing an option on a further five. From Mohawk's tenth aircraft all were fitted with brake cooling fans, which further assisted short turnround capability. Aloha Airlines ordered its third Series 200 in October and placed options on a further two. A round of orders for Series 400s from Central America included one for LACSA of Costa Rica with a second on option in January, one for LANICA of Nicaragua with an option on a second and one for Aerocondor of Colombia, both in April. This last order was subsequently cancelled. European charter operators announced several orders during the year; the first was Laker Airways, which ordered three Series 300s in February, followed by Channel Airways, which ordered four Series 400s in September with an option on two more. Bavaria Fluggesellschaft Schwabe & Co of West Germany ordered two Series 400s with an option on a third in November.

It was during 1966 that the upper weight limit for two crew operation was lifted in the United States and from this time Series 400 aircraft were certificated at the earlier approved higher weights enjoyed by Series 300s in other parts of the world. All new aircraft in this configuration from this time were classified as Series 400s and the Series 300 became redundant apart from those already contracted for.

It was not only airline versions of the One-Eleven which were to enter service during 1966. The first executive version to be handed over to a customer was a Series 200 which was delivered to Helmut Horten of West Germany on 29 January. A further Series 200 was delivered to Tenneco in April; this, like the Braniff aircraft, was not fitted with ventral airstairs. Tenneco had previously been known as the Tennessee Gas Transmission Company and was eventually to fly three One-Elevens in its executive fleet. These two executive Series 200s were the first two One-Elevens to be assembled at and flown from Weybridge. In September Victor Comptometer of the USA took delivery of the first Series 400 executive One-Eleven; this aircraft had been the previously much-travelled second Series 400 development machine which had taken part in the intensive series of worldwide demonstration flights.

Reports from the USA, where the type was now well established in service with four airline operators, indicated that the aircraft was performing well. Braniff reported that it was the most reliable type in its fleet and that each aircraft was flying on average 14 sectors and nine and three-quarter hours per day. With no back-up aircraft, the fleet was flying one and a half million miles per month. Aloha's single aircraft was initially flying 20 sectors per day over an average sector length of only 124 miles (200km), which took only 24 minutes to fly. Mohawk's five aircraft were flying an average 14 sectors per day and were regularly achieving ten minute turnrounds. This latter company had noted a 27% increase in

C/n 053 - G-ASYD in the process of being stretched into the Srs.500 prototype from its earlier Srs.400 form (BAe)

C/n 053 - G-ASYD as the Srs.500 prototype in a rare shot in British United's c/s (note non-standard test equipment beneath the fuselage) (via D Slack)

passenger boardings over the first three months of the year and believed that this was mainly due to the introduction of the One-Eleven fleet.

During the early stages of development, British European Airways had been involved in discussions over the aircraft with the manufacturer, but these had not led to an order. The airline had expressed a preference for a mixed fleet of Boeing 727-200s and 737-200s, in a statement made on 1 June 1966. The British Government rejected this request and directed the airline to look at home-produced alternatives and talks over a version of the One-Eleven to fill the need in the smaller aircraft category were resumed with BAC. This type was required to replace the large Vickers Viscount fleet, with particular reference to the Internal German Services based at Tempelhof Airport in Berlin. By September 1966 a specification had been agreed for a stretched version of the One-Eleven to be known as the Series 500, which would fly 97 passengers over a range of 950 miles (1,528km) and would have a full tanks range of 1,650 miles (2,654km).

Initial plans for a stretched version of the aircraft had been floated as early as the summer of 1963; although the manufacturer had received positive interest from several operators, up to this time it had been considered commercially imprudent to proceed without a large order base. In retrospect, it would seem that it was the lack of different capacity versions of the One-Eleven which lost BAC several important orders to its main competitor. The DC-9 was being marketed in several versions of different capacities and range. Because of this Douglas was struggling to come to terms with the additional costs involved and to maintain the planned production schedule. Major orders were won by Douglas, however, due to the prospect of larger capacity versions being available in the immediate future.

The Series 500 was launched on the strength of an order placed on 27 January 1967 by British European Airways for 18 aircraft with an option for six additional aircraft. Total cost of the development of this new version was £9 million and was to be borne by the British Government. This investment by the Government was to be recovered from a levy on all future sales of the aircraft.

The new version had the fuselage extended by 13ft 6in (4.11m) made up of two plugs. One plug forward of the wing was 8ft 4in (2.54m) long, while one aft of the wing was 5ft 2in (1.57m) long. This enabled four additional seat rows to be fitted, increasing the passenger capacity by 20. Total seating at 34in (0.86m) pitch was set at 97. To cope with the additional seating, overwing emergency exits were doubled to four (two each side). Total underfloor hold volume was also increased from 534ft^3 (15.12m^3) to 687ft^3 (19.45m^3). MTOW as originally planned was set at 91,000lb (41,277kg), an increase of 4,000lb (1,831kg) over that of the Series 400. At these higher weights structural changes were necessary; these included thicker integral stiffeners on the machined panels on the top and bottom wing surfaces and a beefed-up undercarriage. The capacities of the air-conditioning system and the APU were increased to cope with the increased cabin volume, and the wing span was increased by 5ft (1.52m) by the addition of wing tip extensions. Rolls-Royce Spey 25 Mk.512-14E engines of 12,000lb (5,493kg) static thrust were to be the uprated powerplants. The following four pages show the design development from the Hunting 107 project to the projected Series 800 One-Eleven.

The conversion of the first Series 400 development aircraft, G-ASYD, was started at Hurn on 4 February 1967. The aircraft was rolled out on 22 June 1967 and first flew in its new guise as the Series 500 prototype on 30 June 1967. This flight lasted 74 minutes and was flown by Brian Trubshaw, the then Manager Flight Operations BAC Weybridge/Filton Division, who was later to fly the first British Concorde on its maiden flight. The prototype Series 500 initially flew at sub-standard operating weights compared with production aircraft

Design evolution of the One-Eleven

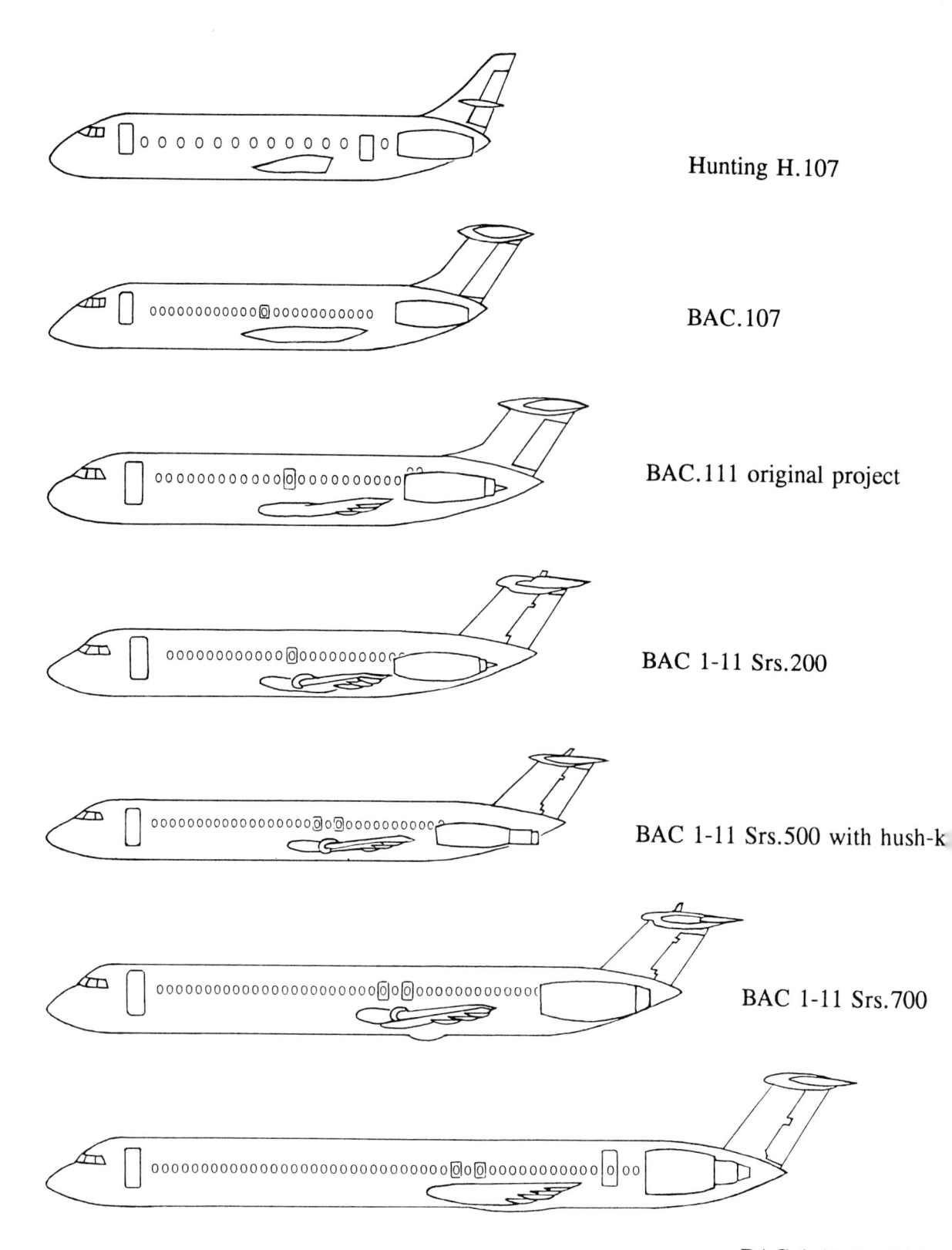

Hunting H.107

BAC.107

BAC.111 original project

BAC 1-11 Srs.200

BAC 1-11 Srs.500 with hush-k

BAC 1-11 Srs.700

BAC 1-11 Srs.800

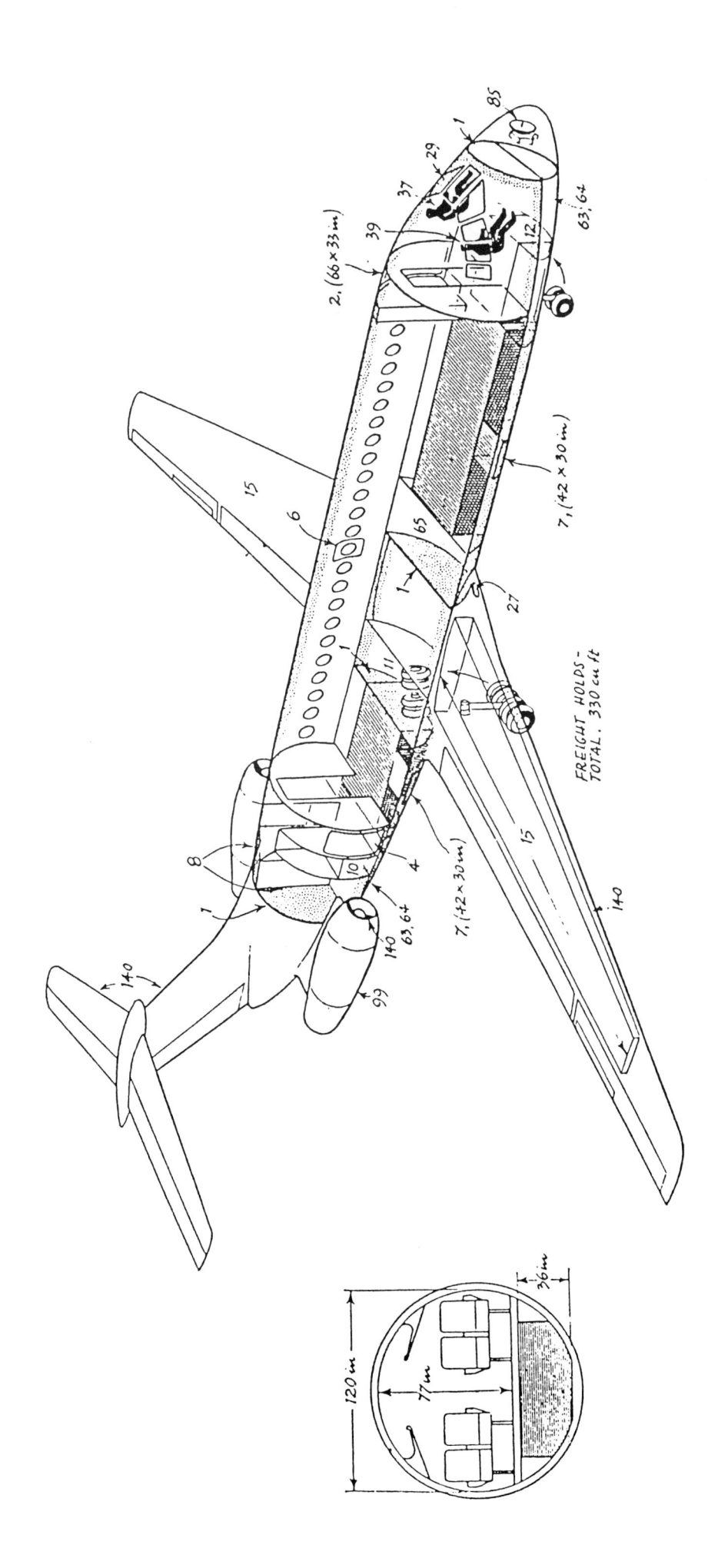

BAC.107 project drawing (key not included)

BAC One-Eleven Srs.400

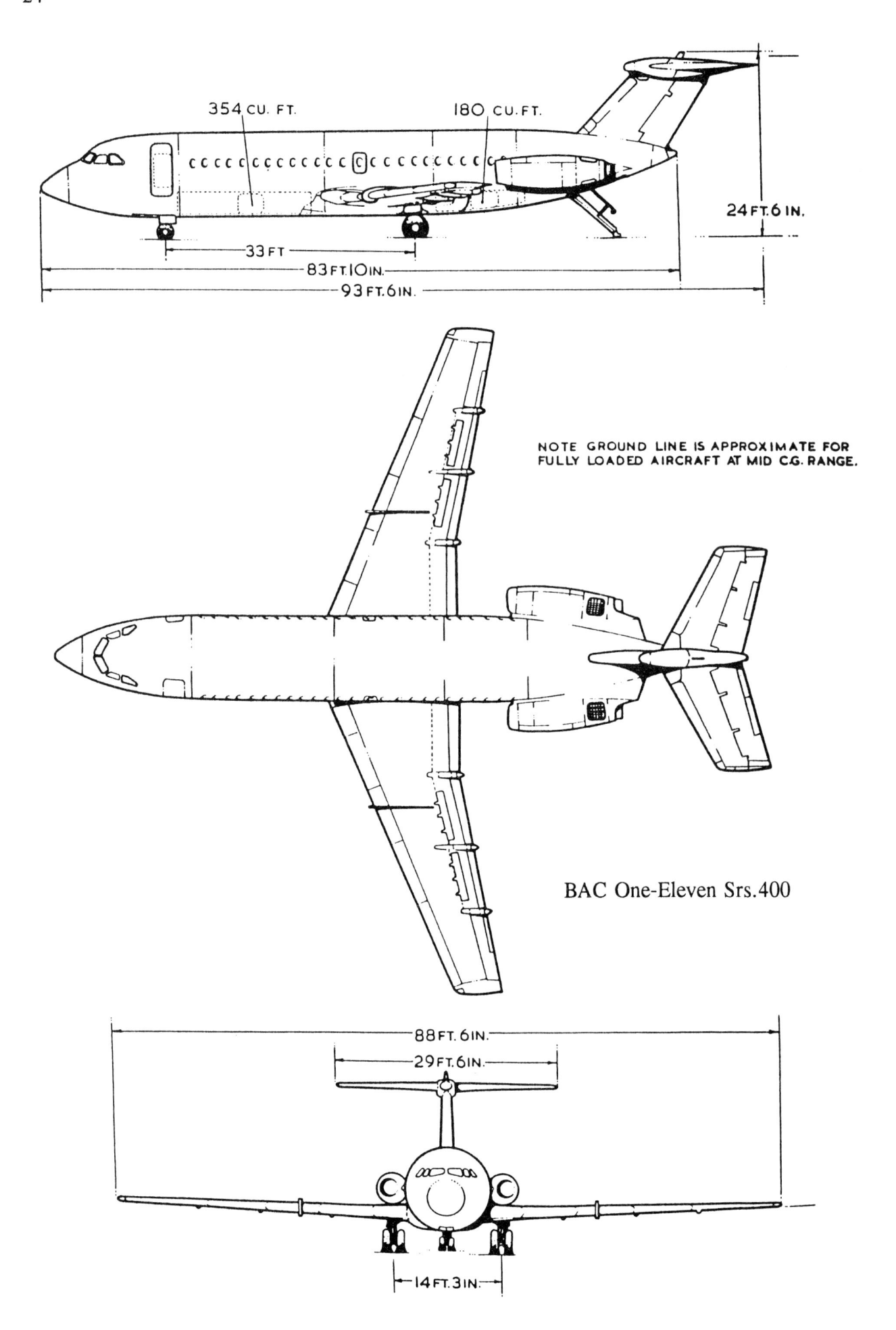

NOTE GROUND LINE IS APPROXIMATE FOR FULLY LOADED AIRCRAFT AT MID C.G. RANGE.

BAC One-Eleven Srs.500

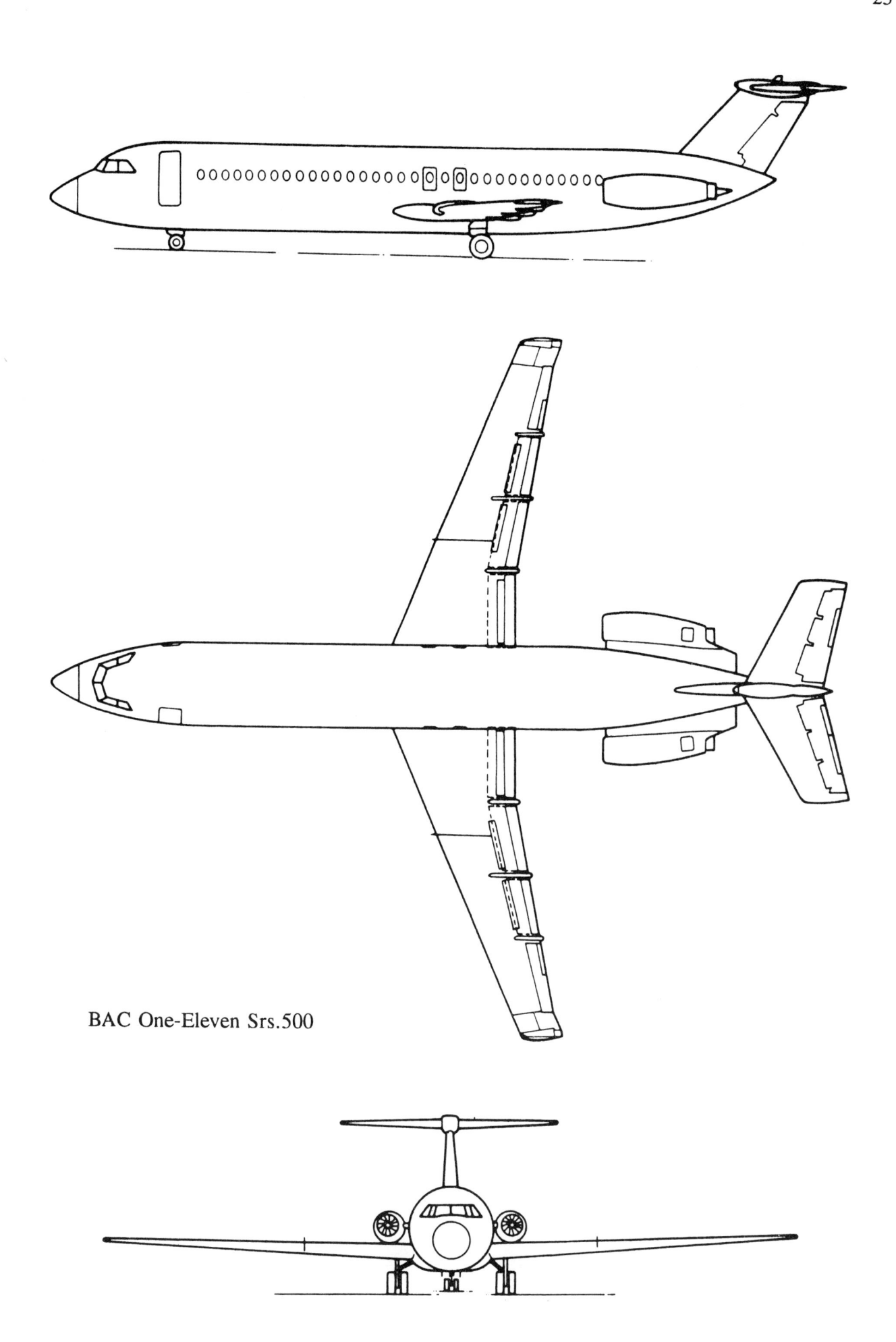

C/n 093 - Srs.407AW YS-17C of TACA International (BAe)

C/n 107 - Srs.320L-AZ G-AVBW of Laker Airways (BAe)

C/n 114 - Srs.408EF G-AVGP in its short-lived Channel Airways livery (BAe)

and still had the Rolls-Royce Spey Mk.511-14 engines installed for the first few weeks of flight testing. The aircraft was however aerodynamically similar to production aircraft and would contribute much to the certification programme prior to the first flight of the first BEA aircraft.

Orders continued to be received during 1967, although none was signed for the stretched version. In February Autair International Airways ordered two Series 400s, increasing this to three later in the year. On 3 May BAC announced the following contracts: Austral Compania Argentina de Transportes Aereos and its sister company, Aerotransportes Litoral Argentino, jointly ordered four Series 400s and at the same time placed options on two Series 500s, this being the first of several sales to South America. Mohawk Airlines raised their firm order total to 14 with a repeat order for four Series 200s, Philippine Airlines took up their option on a third Series 400 and placed an option on a fourth, and finally Channel Airways ordered two more Series 400s, although these were subsequently to be cancelled. The following March Laker Airways ordered its fourth Series 300, and later in the year two orders were to come from Brazil; these were both for Series 400s and comprised two aircraft for Viaçao Aerea Sao Paulo (VASP) in June and two VIP versions for the Força Aerea Brasileira in November.

It was in July 1967 that BAC learned that it had been unsuccessful in its bid to supply the United States Air Force with One-Elevens for use in the aero-medical transport role to the AX2 specification. A version of the Series 400 had been submitted with a large main deck freight door similar to that later fitted to the Air Force of the Sultanate of Oman One-Eleven fleet. This contract was awarded to McDonnell-Douglas for a version of the DC-9, later to be known as the Nightingale.

Central America was an area in which BAC had particular success. In February 1967 TACA International Airways took delivery of its second Series 400, while LACSA accepted its first Series 400 in April. LANICA received its Series 400 in April, which replaced a Series 200 which the company had been leasing from Aer Lingus from October 1966. TAN Airlines of Honduras later shared the operation of this aircraft following the signing of an agreement on 19 October.

The European airline scene was further expanded with British Eagle International Airways taking delivery of two Series 300s in April and May. This company took advantage of the late delivery of Douglas DC-9 aircraft to Swissair and Scandinavian Airways System and leased one aircraft to each of these carriers from April 1967 to April 1968 and from August 1967 to March 1968 respectively to help to fill the shortfall. In mid-December the Zambian Airways Corporation lease of two aircraft to British Eagle came to an end and they started flying schedules throughout East Africa for the parent company. Laker Airways took delivery of its three Series 300s in February, April and May, with the last being delivered directly to Air Congo on lease to operate its schedules within Africa. Channel Airways took delivery of its first Series 400 in June, and Bavaria Fluggesellschaft leased a Series 400 from BAC from March to October before taking delivery of its own aircraft in December.

In October and November Austral of Argentina received its two Series 400s and inaugurated service on 23 October. In the USA, a new executive Series 400 was delivered to Engelhard Industries during September. Aloha Airlines took delivery of its third aircraft in May, whilst Mohawk Airlines received three aircraft during the year with delivery in January, August and December. This last aircraft, a Series 204AF registered N1123J, was both the last aircraft delivered in 1967 and also the one hundredth One-Eleven to be delivered to a customer. This event took place on 30 December.

By the end of the year 60 One-Elevens were operational with four airlines in the USA, flying in the central, eastern and northern states and Hawaii. Three of this total were with corporate customers. In Europe 24 aircraft were in service flying with four UK carriers, one Irish, one in West Germany, one in Switzerland and one in Scandinavia, while a corporate aircraft was based in West Germany. Zambia Airways were flying two aircraft in East Africa, and Air Congo was operating its leased Laker Airways aircraft. In Central America four aircraft were flying for four airlines and in South America Austral of Argentina and VASP in Brazil were each flying two aircraft. Finally, Philippine Airlines were now flying three aircraft in Asia.

The next year saw the first flight of the first production Series 500 aircraft, a Series 510ED for British European Airways registered G-AVMH. This took place on 7 February 1968, after which the aircraft joined the certification programme at the Wisley, Surrey, test centre. This aircraft was fully instrumented like the prototype, G-ASYD, and was used to confirm the latter's performance figures and to cover operations at the higher weights. The second production aircraft, G-AVMI, first flew on 13 May and joined the certification programme when not employed on crew training duties. BEA's aircraft were fitted with a Smiths Industries SF5 flight director and compass system, unlike all other One-Elevens built, and instrument layout was also non-standard. This was apparently to create some commonality with the company's HS Trident fleets. Each was also fitted with a Decca Harco Omnitrac moving map display for more precise navigation in the restricted corridors over East Germany en route to Tempelhof, Berlin. Strangely, BEA opted to have no forward airstairs fitted to its aircraft. These were the only Series 500s not fitted with forward airstairs, and this was to be a major problem in later years when trying to dispose of the aircraft to third world countries. Certification of the new variant was eventually obtained on 15 August 1968.

On 4 March British United Airways ordered five Series 500s, primarily for inclusive tour work within Europe. This was followed by an order from Caledonian Airways on 14 March for three Series 500s with an option on a fourth for similar work. These aircraft were to be powered by the higher rated Rolls-Royce Spey 25 Mk.512DW engines with a water injection system to maintain maximum power output on take-off at hot and high airfields. This new version of the engine was to be rated at 12,550lb (5,580kg) static thrust and would power all Series 500 aircraft produced except the Srs.510EDs of BEA. Both carriers specified one class seating for 109 passengers.

These new Series 500s had new flap track fairings which reduced drag together with improved brakes and anti-skid systems. Later in the year Autair International Airways Ltd ordered five Series 500s with a further two on option. In order to secure this order BAC developed a refined wing leading edge which was generally known as the "New Leading Edge". Autair was unable to lift a full charter load out of Luton, its home base, even with water injection on the then current Series 500. The re-contoured leading edge with more camber and a bigger nose radius, together with a new range of flap settings, generated more lift at lower airspeed. Approximately 4,400lb (2,000kg) of additional payload could be carried out of limiting airfields, while approach speed could be reduced by about three knots for the same weight. This was achieved at the expense of a small increase in cruise fuel consumption. All future orders were to incorporate the New Leading Edge with the exception of the Series 530FXs. Other new orders received at this time included two Series 500s for Bahamas Airways Ltd with an option on a third and a single Series 500 for Panair of West Germany with a second on option. Pending delivery of its newly ordered aircraft, Bahamas Airways would lease two new Series 400s from BAC. It was to be Panair's first Series 515 aircraft which would be the first to fly with the New Leading Edge and would

C/n 120 - Srs.419EP N270E of Engelhard Industries (Brooklands Museum)

C/n 121 - Srs.432FD VP-BCY of Bahamas Airways (Brooklands Museum)

C/n 131 - Srs.416EK G-AVOF in Cambrian/British Air Services c/s (Brooklands Museum)

lead to the type being certificated for an MTOW in excess of 100,000lb, actually 104,500lb (47,400kg) and enabled the aircraft to carry 119 passengers.

The last Series 200s contracted for were ordered in 1968. Two separate repeat orders for firstly three and then a single aircraft came from Mohawk Airlines, bringing their total order to 18 aircraft. Tenneco also ordered their second new Series 200.

A major breakthrough came on 26 February 1968 with the announcement of the sale of six Series 400s to Romania. This was the first sale of new Western-built shorthaul jets to the Communist Bloc and was to herald further sales to Transporturile Aeriene Romane (TAROM) and a licence production deal in years to come.

Twenty-three aircraft were delivered to customers in 1968. Of these, seven were Series 510EDs for British European Airways with the first, G-AVMJ, going to them on 29 August. First revenue passengers were carried on 1 September on the internal German network (IGS) on ad hoc substitutions. Four aircraft had been received by the time the type was introduced into regular service on 17 November. From 1966 competition on the IGS routes had been difficult to combat after Pan American introduced 127 seat Boeing 727-100s into service and as a stop gap measure BEA Vickers Viscount 800s were reconfigured with 53 first class seats and marketed as "Silver Star" flights. From the beginning of August 1968 HS Comet 4Bs had been operated on some of the IGS routes, but these aircraft were hardly suited to low level flying down the Berlin corridors. The arrival of the One-Elevens was clearly not before time. From Tempelhof the One-Elevens initially served Bremen, Cologne, Dusseldorf, Frankfurt, Hamburg, Hanover, Munich and Stuttgart on the IGS services. The aircraft flew up to 12 sectors per day with scheduled 20 minute turnrounds throughout the day and achieved a remarkable degree of reliability for a new type with BEA.

Flights into Berlin were restricted to carriers from France, the UK and the USA at this time; Air France was unable to operate its Caravelle IIIs into Tempelhof's short runway, as this mark of Caravelle was not fitted with thrust reversers and the regular use of braking parachutes was not viable. Consequently this carrier was forced to operate from Tegel Airport, which is situated somewhat further from the city centre than Tempelhof, losing Air France much business. When its market share had dropped to 4%, the company entered into negotiations with BEA which culminated in an agreement finalised on 24 September. Under this deal, One-Eleven services would be jointly marketed by the two carriers and operated from Tempelhof to Frankfurt (ten times daily) and Munich (five times daily), flight deck crews would be from BEA, but a cabin crew member from each operator would be carried on these services. To avoid embarrassment to Air France, One-Elevens so used would be painted in a neutral colour scheme. This arrangement was to start at the commencement of the summer schedules in 1969.

Other operators to receive aircraft during 1968 were Autair International Airways, which took delivery of three Series 400s in February, March and May, while a fourth was leased from the manufacturer in December. Channel Airways exchanged its Series 400 for a new aircraft in May; this aircraft was fitted with no fewer than 99 seats, two seat rows more than fitted to any other short fuselage One-Eleven. To comply with emergency evacuation procedures an additional overwing emergency exit was installed on each side (standard on Series 500s). This airline was famed for high density seating on its aircraft, having installed no fewer than 139 seats in its HS Trident 1E fleet and 88 seats in its one and only Douglas DC-4. Laker Airways took delivery of a fourth Series 300 in April. All three of these UK carriers were to use their aircraft in the lucrative inclusive tour market. This sector of the market had previously been mainly served with written-down propeller-driven types retired from service by the major scheduled carriers.

C/n 119 - Srs.422EQ PP-SRT of VASP (Brooklands Museum)

C/n 154 - Srs.423ET VC92-2110 of the Força Aerea Brasileira seen at Wisley (Brooklands Museum)

C/n 136 - Srs.510ED G-AVMH The first production Srs.500 aircraft in its short-lived BEA 'Red Square' c/s

(BAe)

C/n 188 - Srs.517FE VP-BCN of Bahamas Airways (Brooklands Museum)

C/n 161 - Srs.402AP EC-BQF of TAE; the only One-Eleven to be registered in Spain (Brooklands Museum)

Mohawk Airlines received four more aircraft during the year, while Bahamas Airways' lease of two Series 400s started in November and December. TAROM received its first Series 400 in June 1968 and inaugurated service with the type on the 20th of the same month. The company's second aircraft was delivered in December of that year. Another airline to introduce the type during the year was ALA of Argentina, who did so on 29 September. This company too accepted its second aircraft in December.

The air forces of two nations took delivery of new aircraft in 1968 for VIP duties. These were Australia, which accepted two Series 200s in January and February, and Brazil, which received its first Series 400 in October.

One-Elevens appeared in two other airlines' colours during 1968. KLM Royal Dutch Airlines leased one of British Eagle's Series 300s from March to August to operate its Rotterdam to Heathrow schedules, while a Series 400 was painted in the colours of Compania Dominicana de Aviacion for a deal which, in the end, did not take place.

The first of the higher weight Series 500s, a Srs.509EW for Caledonian Airways registered G-AWWX, took to the air for the first time on 11 February 1969. The Spey 25 Mk.512DW engine with water injection had earlier flown in the prototype during August 1968. The first aircraft to be certificated at the increased MTOW of 104,500lb (47,400kg) and incorporating the new wing leading edge first flew on 22 May and was destined for Panair of West Germany.

Once again, with a high level of activity on the production front, BAC laid down a final assembly line at Weybridge for Series 400 aircraft. Another seven aircraft were assembled here during 1969 and 1970. The last Hurn built Series 200 was the eighteenth and final Mohawk Airlines aeroplane, which took to the air for the first time on 12 May 1969. This was closely followed by the last Hurn built Series 400, which first flew on 26 June and was destined for TAROM.

New orders received during the year for Series 500s came from Germanair for three (with the lease of a Series 400 from August 1969 pending the first delivery of new aircraft), two for British Midland Airways with an option on a third, which was taken up later in the year, and three for the Austral/ALA combine. Both Caledonian Airways and Autair International took up their options for one and two aircraft respectively, as did Panair for a single aircraft. Bavaria Fluggesellschaft and LACSA each took up their options on single Series 400s, with the former ordering its fourth at the end of the year. A new customer was Gulf Aviation Co, who placed an order for a single Series 400 with an option on a second on 29 July.

No fewer than 41 new aircraft were delivered to customers during 1969; these comprised 28 Series 500s, the last three Series 200s and ten Series 400s. BEA received ten of its aircraft, leaving G-AVMR with BAC for autoland development. Caledonian Airways and British United Airways took three and five Series 500s respectively in time for the peak summer package holiday business. Panair of West Germany received its first aircraft in June, while Germanair took delivery of two Series 500s in October and December. Court Line Aviation, as Autair was now known, received its first two Series 500s at the end of the year; this company adopted a spectacular colour scheme for its new fleet, with each aircraft being painted in one of four colours. These were orange, pink, turquoise and lilac. Prior to receipt of these aircraft one of Autair International's Series 400s achieved a utilisation record during the month of August, having flown 402 hours 36 minutes during the month, which averaged out at over 13 hours' flying per day. For a shorthaul aircraft this was most impressive and indicated the level of technical and operational reliability which the One-Eleven could achieve.

C/n 187 - Srs.515FB D-ALAT in Panair's c/s (Brooklands Museum)

C/n 193 - Srs.523FJ G-AXLL awaiting delivery to British Midland Airways (Brooklands Museum)

C/n 208 - Srs.515FB D-ALAS of Paninternational (Brooklands Museum)

With aircraft in the maximum 119 seat inclusive tour configuration galley space was at a premium. This led to the adoption of an unusual seat-back catering system by Court Line for its aircraft. The original Caledonian Airways also used this system for a short while when they too fitted their aircraft with 119 seats. This system entailed the installation of two slots in the back of each passenger seat which were loaded with round trip catering at the UK base prior to departure. Each slot had a lockable door which remained locked until the aircraft was in the cruise. The cabin crew released the catering for the appropriate sector by using an Allen Key. Package tour-wise passengers presumably came prepared with their own Allen Keys and consumed both lots of catering on the outbound sectors.

The Austral/ALA combine added three Series 500s to its Series 400 fleet in November, while Bahamas Airways took delivery of two Series 500s in July to replace the leased Series 400s. Mohawk Airlines accepted its last two new Series 200s in January and May, while Tenneco received its second executive Series 200 in July; this was the last Series 200 to be delivered. Four Series 400s were delivered to TAROM, two in July and the others in November and December. Single Series 400s were also delivered to Trabajos y Enlaces (TAE of Spain) in March and to Gulf Aviation in November. The Brazilian Air Force took its second Series 400 in May, LACSA its second in November and Bavaria Fluggesellschaft its second in April. Channel Airways received its third Series 400 in October 1969, but this was immediately leased to British United Airways.

Secondhand Sales

In April 1969 American Airlines sold one of its Series 400s to Magnolia Homes as an executive aircraft, while in October British United Airways sold one of its Series 200s to Barwick Industries of the USA, also for executive use. These were the first of many airline short fuselage One-Elevens which would eventually find their way into the executive aircraft market. In March and April Mohawk Airlines received all three Aloha Airlines Series 200s, which brought the Mohawk fleet up to 20 by the summer of 1969.

Following the collapse of British Eagle International Airways at the end of 1968, five Series 300 aircraft came on to the used aircraft market. Two of these were sold to Quebecair in April; this company immediately put the aircraft into service on its scheduled routes throughout eastern Canada and on charter flights. Another of the British Eagle aircraft was sold to Dan-Air Services in October, joining two Series 400s which the company had bought from American Airlines in March. The latter two aircraft were used for flying inclusive tour charter flights, initially out of Luton, to many European destinations and were the first of many One-Elevens to see service with this carrier. BAC leased a Series 400 aircraft to Philippine Airlines in October to replace an aircraft lost in an accident.

By this time the Rolls-Royce Spey had really reached the peak of its development for power output in its commercial form without major changes. Without the considerable expense of a powerplant type change, BAC saw some potential for further sales by developing a rough field version of the One-Eleven. Utilising the Spey Mk.512DW with water injection and the later new leading edge extended wing of the Series 500 aircraft but employing the short fuselage of the Series 400, the project was designated the Series 475. Larger low pressure tyres were adopted for the main undercarriage, which necessitated a redesign of the main gear wheel bay, actuation jacks, doors and underbelly fairing. The nosewheel tyres were slightly wider and used marginally reduced pressures. One optional extra was a gravel runway kit to protect the aircraft from debris thrown up when operating from secondary unpaved airfields; this included a glassfibre coating on vulnerable areas of the underbelly, wings and flaps and additional protection for the nose gear, radio antennae, rotating beacon and water drain masts. Deflector plates were also fitted between the wheels.

C/n 228 - Srs.520FN PP-SDQ of Sadia (Brooklands Museum)

An historical line-up at Gatwick in 1970 - a BEA Srs.510ED in the c/s adopted when used on the joint BEA/Air France services out of Tempelhof, G-AWYS (c/n 175), a Srs.501EX of British United when operated on behalf of Swissair, a Laker Airways Srs.320L-AZ and a British United Srs.501EX (Brooklands Museum)

Once again, the first Series 400/500 development aircraft was modified as the prototype for the new version. The fuselage plugs which had been inserted in G-ASYD when it was converted to the Series 500 prototype were now removed, bringing the fuselage of the aircraft back to its original Series 400 length. In its new form, G-ASYD first flew from Hurn on 27 August and Faucett of Peru was the first customer for this type, with an order for a single example placed in June.

Other orders placed in the first half of 1970 were for a third Series 500 for Paninternational (the former Panair) and a third Series 500 for Bahamas Airways with extra tankage for a proposed route to New York. Although built and painted for Bahamas Airways, this aircraft was never delivered to them before the airline ceased trading. On 6 August BAC announced orders for a further ten aircraft; these comprised four Series 500s for Philippine Airlines, two more Series 500s for Court Line Aviation, a fourth Series 500 for Paninternational and a fifth Series 400 (the last production Series 400) for Bavaria Fluggesellschaft. The latter carrier also ordered two Series 500s at the same time. The end of the year saw the second customer for the Series 475, Air Pacific, the former Fiji Airways, which announced its intention of ordering a single aircraft. East-West Airlines of Australia was also reported to have ordered a Series 475 for 1972 delivery, but this deal was never finalised. Aviateca of Guatemala announced an order for a Series 500 in November and immediately leased a similar aircraft from Court Line Aviation pending delivery of their own aeroplane.

Deliveries of new aircraft during the first half of 1970 were four Series 500s to Court Line Aviation, three Series 500s to British Midland Airways, the last two Series 400s to be built to Bavaria Fluggesellschaft, Caledonian's fourth Series 500, Germanair's third Series 500, two Series 500s to Paninternational, three Series 500s to British United Airways and the eighteenth Series 500 to BEA. All these aircraft were with their operators in time for the peak summer operations. Sadia of Brazil took delivery of two Series 500s in October and at the end of December, having earlier gained experience with the type by leasing an aircraft from Austral of Argentina from mid September 1970. This company flew its One-Elevens on an extensive domestic network which entailed a very high utilisation with aircraft flying during the day and night. Finally, in December, Bavaria Fluggesellschaft took delivery of one Series 400 and one Series 500, its first extended fuselage version.

On receipt of its first Series 500s Court Line Aviation disposed of all but one of its Series 400s. Three of these were sold to Cambrian Airways, which introduced them into service in January 1970 on domestic and Irish Sea schedules together with charter work. Lufthansa made use of one of Bavaria Fluggesellschaft's Series 400s on domestic schedules from Mondays to Fridays throughout the year, while Swissair leased a British United Airways' Series 500 to cover European schedules from April to October. Bahamas Airways bought a Series 300 previously operated by British Eagle to join their two Series 500s in April and Dan-Air Services took a second aircraft from the same source in March. In the USA Mohawk Airlines added three ex-Braniff Airways Series 200s in September, raising their fleet to 23 One-Elevens. In November, Air Malawi took a longterm lease on one of Zambia Airways' two Series 200s to operate on its schedules within East Africa and to South Africa. Bavaria Fluggesellschaft leased a Series 400 from BAC in August 1970 to replace one of their own aircraft which was badly damaged in a take-off accident in July. During 1970 LACSA operated a three times weekly schedule on behalf of Cayman Airways between Grand Cayman and Kingston, Jamaica.

In 1971 there was a marked downturn in orders received for One-Elevens. Faucett of Peru ordered its second Series 475 at the beginning of the year and Air Pacific confirmed its order for one Series 475 in April. A third customer for this variant was Air Malawi, which ordered one aircraft in September. New orders for Series 500s came from Germanair for

An unidentified Srs.500 of Transbrasil (Brooklands Museum)

C/n 237 - Srs.531FS TI-1084C of LACSA (Brooklands Museum)

C/n 243 - SRs.481FW 7Q-YKF of Air Malawi (Brooklands Museum)

its fourth, Court Line for two more and Phoenix Airways of Switzerland for a single aircraft. A second Series 400 was sold to Gulf Aviation and a similar aircraft to a corporate customer in Singapore.

Fourteen aircraft were delivered in 1971. Bavaria Fluggesellschaft, Paninternational and Germanair each received a single Series 500 during the first half of the year. Court Line Aviation received two Series 500s in March, while Phoenix Airways took delivery of one Series 500 on 1 April.

Empresa Guatemalteca de Aviacion replaced the leased Court Line Series 500 with its own aircraft in March to join the many One-Elevens in Central America, and LACSA took delivery of its first Series 500 in May 1971. In May Faucett received the first Series 475 to be delivered to any customer and introduced the type on to its domestic network, replacing unpressurised Douglas DC-4s; this coincided with the Peruvian nation celebrating its one hundred and fiftieth anniversary. The aircraft was immediately pressed into service, flying to gravel strips high in the Andes Mountains.

In October and November Philippine Airlines accepted three Series 500s, for which the company traded the three Series 400s it was then operating. The last of these Series 500s was the two hundredth One-Eleven to be delivered to a customer; this took place on 5 November 1971. Two other aircraft delivered during 1971 were Gulf Aviation's second Series 400 and a similar type to an executive customer in Singapore; both of the aircraft had been earlier leased by BAC to other operators prior to these sales.

Further Used Aircraft Movements

In January 1971 Cambrian Airways obtained its fourth Series 400 which, like its other aircraft, had operated previously with Autair International/Court Line. Laker Airways added a fifth One-Eleven to its fleet in February when it obtained a Series 300 formerly operated by Bahamas Airways. Court Line Aviation obtained two Series 500s in September and October 1971 from the same source and was also involved in several leasing deals during the year. It leased a Series 500 from Austral of Argentina for the summer peak from April to October, while come the winter decline in business the company leased single Series 500s to Leeward Islands Air Transport Services and Lineas Aereas de Nicaragua (LANICA). These were from November 1971 to July 1972 and from December 1971 to March 1972 respectively, the latter replacing LANICA's Series 400 damaged in a hijack attempt. British United Airways sold one of its Series 200s to the Royal Aircraft Establishment in September 1971 and this aircraft was initially used by the Blind Landing Experimental Unit.

In the USA, Braniff Airways leased a Series 200 to Flamingo Airlines of the Bahamas from July 1971 to May 1972, while American Airlines started to retire its Series 400s, finding the capacity of the aircraft insufficient for the market which the type had helped to develop. Lastly, Dan-Air Engineering purchased the wreckage of a damaged German One-Eleven and had it flown to Hurn in the world's only Canadair CL-44-0; it was slotted into the Hurn production line in mid-1971 and rebuilt using new components where required. The aircraft, c/n 127, was reflown in December and put into service with Dan-Air Services. It is still flying to this day with ADC Airlines of Nigeria.

In January 1971 the two Argentinean airlines, Austral and ALA, were merged completely to form Austral Lineas Aereas and continued to operate their four Series 400 and three series 500 One-Elevens. During January 1971 the One-Elevens of British United Airways and Caledonian Airways first appeared with Caledonian//BUA titles after the merger of these two carriers. At the end of 1971 the name was changed again and the title British Caledonian

Airways was adopted. The West German charter airline, Paninternational, ceased trading on 6 October 1971 and its three remaining One-Eleven 500s came on to the used aircraft market.

Orders received in 1972 included a third Series 500 for Bavaria Fluggesellschaft in January, while in June Court Line Aviation purchased the undelivered third Series 500 for Bahamas Airways. September saw orders for two more Series 500s for LACSA of Costa Rica, a third Series 500 for Transbrasil (previously known as Sadia) and a second Series 475 for Air Pacific. Although BAC carried out a sales and demonstration tour of South America with a Series 475 in May and June 1972, no new orders resulted from it.

New aircraft deliveries during 1972 amounted to only seven aircraft. These were single Series 475s to Air Malawi in February and to Air Pacific in March. In March BAC also delivered single Series 500s to British Caledonian Airways and to Bavaria Fluggesellschaft. In June Court Line Aviation accepted its ninth Series 500, which was immediately leased to Leeward Islands Air Transport Services. September saw Transbrasil taking delivery of its third Series 500, while LACSA accepted its second and third Series 500s in November 1972 and May 1973. The only other delivery to take place in 1973 was the second Air Pacific Series 475 in August.

Although there was little movement in new aircraft during 1972 and 1973, the used market was very active. In the USA, Mohawk Airlines merged into Allegheny Airlines on 12 April 1972; with this merger Allegheny received Mohawk's 23 One-Eleven 200s. This fleet was expanded to 31 aircraft with the purchase of the eight remaining Braniff Airways' airline configured Series 200s by September 1972. This large fleet continued to serve the northern and eastern states of the USA based on Pittsburgh. Braniff's only other remaining airline configured One-Eleven had been sold to Qualitron Aero as the first aircraft in a programme to convert them for the corporate market. Only the one aircraft was converted in the end, and the aircraft was repossessed by Braniff in August 1972, being sold into the corporate sector two months later. A few of the retired American Airlines' Series 400s were disposed of during 1972. One was delivered to Hurn for preparation by BAC for a new British airline to be based in Berlin called Orientair. Although the aircraft was painted and received its Certificate of Airworthiness in the United Kingdom, the new company was still-born and the aircraft remained in storage at Hurn.

LANICA of Nicaragua took a short term lease of an American Airlines aircraft in March to replace a Series 500 which the airline had previously been leasing from Court Line Aviation. In June 1972 Transporturile Aeriene Romane (TAROM) purchased a Series 400 from American Airlines, followed by a used Series 400 from BAC in August. In Europe, following the collapse of Paninternational, two of their Series 500s were purchased by Germanair in May, while the remaining aircraft was leased to British Caledonian from August to October 1972. Court Line leased two Series 500s to Leeward Islands Air Transport in June and November, the first replacing a similar aircraft which they had earlier leased to them. Channel Airways ceased trading on 1 February 1972, and their two Series 400s were put into store. In the Far East, Robin Loh leased his Series 400 to Air Siam Air Company, which put the aircraft into service between Bangkok and Hong Kong from May to December 1972.

In January 1973 National Aircraft Leasing of Los Angeles took delivery of its first Series 401AK from American Airlines. This company, a member of the Tiger Leasing Group, was eventually to purchase 16 of these aircraft for conversion to executive configuration and ultimate sale or lease to major corporations. Under the agreement American Airlines would virtually zero-time the aircraft before handover; this work entailed a complete major overhaul of the undercarriage with new wheels, brakes, tyres and anti-skid systems. Cold Air Units were replaced and new ducting and valves installed. All radios, electronics and autopilots were removed, serviced and bench-tested, while all the flying controls and flaps were overhauled. X-ray inspections were carried out where necessary and the aircraft weighed. Hot and cold sections of the engines were completely overhauled and all the latest modification states incorporated, while the Auxiliary Power Unit and its generator were also fully overhauled. Each aircraft was then flight tested before handover to the new owner.

On receipt from American Airlines the aircraft were flown to The Dee Howard Company at San Antonio for the next stage of the work. This company was contracted to carry out the conversions designed by National Aircraft Leasing. Each aircraft was fitted with a de luxe interior in colours and fabrics chosen by the customer. The new interior comprised 11 individual fully reclining and adjustable 360° swivelling chairs, one four-seat and two three-seat couches (the latter converting to provide sleeping accommodation), two toilets and a separate dressing room, an executive desk complete with telephone, calculator and provision for an electric typewriter, a centrally located bar complete with lighting and cabinet stowage, a fully equipped galley with lighting and ventilation isolated from the main cabin, cabin overhead lighting, table lamps and reading lights, a four-place conference table with provision for a slide or film projector, video tape system and an eight track stereo system. Finally, the exterior was painted to the customer's choice.

The aircraft were wired for the installation of a dual Delco Carousel IVa inertial navigation system and a dual HF system. A NAL designed long range fuel system was installed, which entailed the fitting of either seven or ten extra fuel cells in the rear of the forward freight hold area. These increased the fuel capacity by 4,618 litres (1,220 USG) or 6,056 litres (1,600 USG), giving the aircraft a range with 45 minutes' reserve of 3,753 miles (6,040km, 3,259nm) or 3,950 miles (6,357km, 3,431nm) with ten or eight passengers respectively. With seven cells fitted, there is still 137cu ft of underfloor hold space.

The last of these 16 aircraft was delivered to NAL for conversion in April 1975. These immaculate aircraft were shown at both Farnborough and Paris Air Shows for several years, and customers were found for them in both the USA and the Middle East.

Other American Airlines Series 400s were sold during 1973. Jet Travel took three of the aircraft and converted them for corporate use, while two others were sold direct to executive customers during the year. Four aircraft were sold to the Bahamas, with two going to Out Island Airways in March and June and two going to Bahamasair in November and December. Quebecair took delivery of a third aircraft in March 1973, this time a Series 400 formerly operated by Philippine Airlines. TACA International increased its fleet of Series 400s to three in April 1973 when it acquired an aircraft from LACSA. In December 1973 LACSA purchased the third Paninternational Series 500, for which they traded their last Series 400 to BAC. LACSA now had a fleet of four Series 500s, one of which was leased to Cayman Airways and painted in that company's colours for operation between Grand Cayman and Miami as well as to Kingston, Jamaica.

British Midland Airways sold its three Series 500 aircraft to Transbrasil, with the first two being delivered to Brazil in May and November 1973; the third was to follow in April 1974. Two of these aircraft had been leased to Court Line at different times between February 1972 and April 1974. A Series 500 which had been leased to Court Line from new in April 1971 was returned to Hurn at the end of 1972 and reconfigured as a Series 530FX for British Caledonian Airways, to whom it was delivered in March 1973. A third Series 500 was leased to Leeward Islands Air Transport by Court Line in December 1973. British European Airways purchased three used Series 400s from various sources for operation by its Birmingham based regional division. From September 1973 the soon to be merged British European Airways, British Overseas Airways Corporation and British Air Services were marketed as British Airways, and the first of these three aircraft was painted in British Airways colours and entered service at the end of October. The other two aircraft entered service in April and August 1974. Cambrian Airways leased one of its aircraft to Gulf Air from October 1973 to July 1974.

In February 1974 Philippine Airlines ordered another two Series 500 aircraft, which were delivered in June and July of the same year. The Air Force of the Sultanate of Oman ordered three Series 475s in July of that year, one of which was delivered in December 1974. These aircraft were to be fitted with a quick change passenger/cargo interior layout and also a large upward opening main deck cargo door forward of the wing on the port side. This option had been available to customers for some time, but this was the first occasion on which it had been taken up. The door, measuring 10ft 0in x 6ft 1in (3.05m x 1.85m) is hydraulically operated, and to complement the door a readily removable freight handling system is installed, comprising a freight floor overlay fitted with longitudinal roller sections and ballmats in the door area. The first two aircraft for the SOAF were delivered initially without the cargo door and handling system and were returned to Hurn later for conversion.

During 1974 the Series 475 development aircraft, G-ASYD, was fitted with hushkits in an effort to reduce the engine noise levels. First flown on 14 June 1974, the kit comprises intake duct linings, acoustically lined jet pipes and a six chute exhaust silencer. The kit, weighing 400lb (181kg), has a performance penalty but brings the aircraft noise levels within ICAO Annex 16 requirements. The engine silencing, developed as a collaborative effort between Rolls-Royce and BAC, creates an increase in fuel consumption of 2% and a thrust loss of 0.75%. Most airline-configured and several executive One-Elevens have now been fitted with these hushkits.

By July 1974 British Airways' One-Eleven fleet had risen to 25 with the recently purchased three Series 400s and the ex-Cambrian Airways four Series 400s. Series 400s continued to be transferred to the corporate market during the year; VASP's two aircraft were sold as executive aircraft in June, while one of the former Channel Airways aircraft (after initial sale to Air Hanson in January) was finally sold to the Philippines for government use in July 1974. A former Philippine Airlines Series 400 was sold to the Royal Aircraft Establishment in May, doubling this government agency's One-Eleven fleet. Gulf Air raised its fleet to three with the purchase of an ex-LACSA Series 400 in February. Philippine Airways added two ex-Germanair Series 500s in April and November, raising its fleet to seven. Germanair leased a Court Line Series 500 from May to October 1974, while another Court Line Series 500 was leased to Cyprus Airways in May. This aircraft became stranded in Nicosia after the Turkish invasion in July and consequently saw little use. Court Line had the three aircraft which had been on lease to its subsidiary in the West Indies returned in March and April.

On 15 August 1974 Court Line ceased trading after the collapse of the Clarksons Group. Another One-Eleven operator to collapse in 1974 was Phoenix Airways of Switzerland, which shut down on 17 March. British Caledonian leased two aircraft to South America during 1974; the first Series 500 was leased to Austral Lineas Aereas in January, whilst a second went to Transbrasil from February to December. This latter carrier leased two further used Series 500s from BAC in October and December 1974. In July Air Pacific leased one of its Series 475s to Air Malawi in a deal which was to continue until November 1975.

In May 1975 BAC received an order from Technoimportexport, the Romanian State Enterprise for Foreign Trade, for five Series 500 aircraft. These were to be operated by TAROM and were for delivery in 1977. Part of the deal was for IRMA to build a further 100 Britten-Norman Islanders in Romania and for the same company to construct parts for all future One-Eleven production. On the strength of receiving this order, BAC laid down a further batch of ten One-Elevens. Production had earlier stopped after the last SOAF aircraft was completed, the 217th One-Eleven built. Authorisation of this new batch gave the programme a new lease of life.

Around the time of the announcement of the Romanian order BAC revealed details of various One-Eleven developments which it was studying. The first, designated the One-Eleven 700, was a stretched Series 500 powered by re-fanned Rolls-Royce Spey 606s rated at 16,900lb (7,665kg) static thrust and seating between 119 and 134 passengers. The aircraft, 12ft (3.66m) longer than the Series 500, would have had a maximum range of 2,000 miles (3,360km) and an MTOW of 117,000lb (53,070kg). It was also proposed that existing Series 500 airframes be brought up to Series 700 standard, which would have been done by inserting one fuselage plug of 8ft 4in (2.54m) forward of the centre section and one of 3ft 10in (1.12m) aft of it. Local strengthening of the centre section, wing and rear fuselage would also have been required. It would have had a revised underbelly fairing and a new main undercarriage.

The second proposal, designated the One-Eleven 800, would have been 32ft 6in (9.90m) longer than the Series 500 and seated between 144 and 161 passengers. It would have been re-engined with General Electric/SNECMA CFM56s of 22,000lb (9,979kg) static thrust, giving the aircraft an MTOW of 137,000lb (62,142kg) and a range of 2,400 miles (3,840km). Wing span of this variant would have been increased by 10ft (3.05m).

The first variant had initially aroused interest in Japan but as a Series 700J with a new technology high lift wing as a replacement for NAMC YS-11 airliners on domestic routes. It was proposed that this type might be jointly developed by both countries, but in the end neither of these two proposals was developed.

Dan-Air Services considerably expanded its fleet of One-Elevens during 1975, adding four ex-Court Line Series 500s between January and March, two ex-Zambia Airways Series 200s at the end of March and finally, an ex-BCAL Series 500 in October. BCAL also sold a Series 500 to Monarch Airlines in November 1975. Monarch also bought an ex-Court Line Series 500 in March and leased a further Series 500 from February 1975, which extended to October 1976. Austral Lineas Aereas leased single Series 500s from BCAL in January 1974 and December 1975 before purchasing the first aircraft in October 1975; this Argentine airline also purchased the former Phoenix Airways Series 500 in January 1975. The lease of the second BCAL aircraft would extend to April 1976.

In September and November Philippine Airlines further expanded its One-Eleven fleet with the purchase of two ex-Court Line Series 500s. BCAL leased two Series 500s in the summer of 1975, one to Air Malta from the beginning of May to the end of October and the other to Austrian Airlines from the beginning of April to early September. BAC leased a Series 500 to Aviateca of Guatemala in September (the aircraft having previously been on lease to Transbrasil), which doubled this carrier's fleet. Bavaria Fluggesellschaft sold one of its Series 400s to a corporate user in December and leased a similar aircraft to Gulf Air in November. In September 1975 Tenneco increased its corporate fleet of One-Eleven 200s to three with the purchase of Helmut Horten's aircraft. TAROM leased a Series 400 to Liniile Aeriene Romane from December 1975.

C/n 231 - Srs.527FK RP-C1193 Philippine Airlines penultimate One-Eleven photographed prior to delivery in Jul80
(Brooklands Museum)

Activity at Hurn during 1976 was at a very low key. The Air Force of the Sultanate of Oman's first two Series 475s were returned for the fitting of cargo doors and cargo handling systems. In February one of Philippine Airlines' Series 500s was redelivered to them after a six month repair following a bomb explosion in the port rear toilet. This explosion had killed one passenger and injured several others and had torn a large hole in the cabin roof. The aircraft, RP-C1184 c/n 190, suffered a similar fate two and a half years later; surprisingly, the second incident happened in the same toilet, causing similar damage and killing another passenger. Once again a hole was torn in the roof and the aircraft was returned to Hurn for permanent repair. On both occasions the aircraft was in flight when the explosion took place and on both occasions the aircraft had temporary repairs actioned in the Philippines, enabling it to ferry to the UK for permanent repair. The strength of the airframe was clearly a major reason for the survival of this particular aircraft in these two identical incidents. This aircraft was finally retired by Philippine Airlines in January 1992, by which time it had flown over 42,000 hours and carried out over 38,500 landings. Several other aircraft were returned to Hurn over the years for repair or rebuild by the manufacturer after bomb, fire or crash damage; these came from Costa Rica, Cyprus, Nicaragua, West Germany, the UK and Oman.

The Series 475 development aircraft, G-ASYD, was flown to Japan in October 1976 for demonstrations to TOA Domestic Airways and All Nippon Airways and to prove its suitability for operations at the more restricted Japanese airfields. BAC was hopeful of selling this version to Japan as a NAMC YS-11 replacement. Many of the airfields visited had only 4,000ft (1,219m) runways, and the aircraft coped with these conditions to British landing and take-off performance criteria. The Japanese authorities, however, insisted on a greater than usual fuel reserve and greater performance margins if the type was to be certificated in that country.

To cope with these requirements the Series 475D was proposed, which incorporated a further wingtip extension which raised the span to 96ft 10in (29.51m). An extension of the trailing edge flap chord by 4.65% and further re-profiling of the wing leading edge was also proposed. It was found that the aircraft would have achieved the required field performance improvements with these modifications but with a restricted maximum zero fuel weight due to increased wing bending moments with the increased span. Increased loads on the flaps would also have restricted maximum weights usable when fully extended. It was therefore decided to carry out a further series of wind tunnel tests with modifications to the wing leading edge alone in an effort to bring the performance up to Japanese requirements. It was found that these could be met by modifying the wing leading edge from the wing root to the wing fence alone. It was also found in these tests that rather than redesign the whole area with the increased costs of a re-tooling programme, the desired effect could be obtained by affixing a small triangular fillet to this section of the leading edge. Further refinements were proposed, including the use of the advanced Hytrol Mk 111A anti-skid system, together with automatic braking and deployment of lift dumpers triggered by a combination of the compression of the main oleos on touchdown together with wheel spin-up. A further improvement in the silencing of the exhaust area of the engines was proposed, which incorporated an eight lobe exhaust nozzle and an ejector cowl which moved aft behind the thrust reverser cascades for take-off and landing. Total weight of this last modification was put at 750lb (340kg) but was more than made up for by the thrust improvement.

All but the ejector cowl modification were built into the prototype, with work starting in April 1977. The aircraft was then re-designated as a Series 670; it was thought that a new Series number would identify the improvements over the original Series 475 more clearly to prospective customers. The aircraft was first flown as a Series 670 on 13 September 1977, after which a comprehensive flight trial programme was carried out. It was found that the pilot workload was much reduced, braking was smoother and brake life increased and distance limited landing weights could be increased by 5,000lb (2,268kg). Unfortunately, neither the Japanese or any other customer could be found for this version, and none was built.

At the end of the year the first of the new production batch was rolled out. This aircraft, YR-BCI destined for TAROM, was the first production aircraft to be built with hushkits fitted as standard and first flew on 20 December 1976.

There were no new aircraft deliveries in 1976, and there was also little activity in the used aircraft market. BCAL sold one of its Series 500s to Dan-Air Services in April, while BAC sold a used Series 500 to Monarch Airlines in October. In December the Força Aerea Brasileira sold its two Series 400s to the Ford Motor Company; these were to be based at Stansted in the UK and used for corporate communications between the many Ford plants throughout Europe. In the same month National Aircraft Leasing leased two of its Series 400s to Austral Lineas Aereas of Argentina for four months prior to their executive conversion. The manufacturer leased a Series 500 to Bavaria Fluggesellschaft from April to September before leasing the same aircraft to Cyprus Airways for one year from October. TAROM leased a second Series 400 to Liniile Aeriene Romane from April 1976.

Two major events were to take place during 1977; the first of these was the setting up of British Aerospace. Effective at midnight on 29 April, the assets of the British Aircraft Corporation, Hawker Siddeley Aviation, Hawker Siddeley Dynamics and Scottish Aviation were purchased by the British Government and merged into the new nationalised corporation. On 28 May a co-production agreement was signed between British Aerospace and the Romanian Government, which was expected to lead to the gradual transfer of technology and the ultimate complete manufacture of One-Eleven aircraft in the Romanian Government Aircraft Factory at Baneasa Airport, Bucharest. It would be another two years before contracts would be signed sealing this deal.

During 1977 all five Series 500s ordered by TAROM were delivered between March and August, while the first of Cyprus Airways' new Series 500s was delivered in December. British Aerospace purchased three of Transbrasil's Series 500s; the first of these was leased to Cyprus Airways from January until the receipt of its own aircraft, while the second was leased to Compania de Aviacion Faucett in August where it joined that company's two Series 475s flying domestic schedules in Peru. The third aircraft was sold to Arkia Inland Airways of Israel in August, where the aircraft entered service on 2 August flying charter flights to European destinations and also operating El Al Israel Airlines' schedules between Tel Aviv and Larnaca. In March BCAL sold one of its Series 500s to Philippine Airlines, raising that company's fleet to nine. Bavaria/Germanair sold the last two Series 400s it had in service; both of these went to corporate users in November, one of them being the third aircraft for the Ford Motor Company in the UK. Bavaria/Germanair had been formed out of the merger of these two One-Eleven operators on 1 March 1977. BCAL leased a Series 500 to Air Malawi for one month in November, while British Airways leased a Gulf Air Series 400 from August to November 1977.

With the re-launch of the British Aerospace 146 shorthaul airliner in July 1978, any further development of the One-Eleven within the United Kingdom was clearly at an end. With BAe now nationalised and these two types competing over much of their operational range, all effort and available development funding would now be devoted to the new type. In June 1978 the co-production agreement of the previous year between Romania and the UK was further endorsed with the signing of another agreement. The signatories of this new agreement were Nicolae Ceaucescu, the Romanian President, and Lord Beswick, Chairman of British Aerospace.

In January 1978 Cyprus Airways' second Series 500 was delivered. The same company took delivery of a third aircraft in October, with this aircraft immediately being leased to British Airways. In May 1978 a Series 475 was purchased by a Saudi Arabian private customer, this being the only export sale of an executive version of the 475 Series.

In the used aircraft sector, Bavaria/Germanair sold its last Series 400 to Air Pacific of Fiji, where it joined that company's two Series 475s. This aircraft had previously been on lease to Gulf Air. British Aerospace was busy during the year disposing of used aircraft; the first of these was a Series 500 which had been on lease to Transbrasil, which was sold to Austral Lineas Aereas in January. Another ex-Transbrasil Series 500 was leased to Aviateca of Guatemala for one month in April before it was sold to Cayman Airways at the end of May. Cayman Airways returned to One-Eleven operations on 29 June 1978 after an eight month break, during which time Douglas DC-9s were used. A second used Series 500 was sold to Arkia Inland Airways in May following its earlier lease to Cyprus Airways. The second Series 500 which had been on lease to that company was sold to Philippine Airlines in August, raising this airline's fleet to ten aircraft. At the end of October BCAL leased a Series 500 to British Airways, which joined the aircraft leased from Cyprus Airways until April 1979. In June all three Gulf Air Series 400s were bought for the use of British Island Airways on European charter flights. They were to be delivered after refurbishment by British Aerospace.

On 9 June 1979 contracts were finally signed for licence manufacture of One-Elevens in Romania. This followed the earlier signing of the co-production agreement on 28 May 1977. The deal included three new Hurn-built aircraft which would serve as pattern aircraft for One-Elevens built in Romania. These three aircraft comprised two Series 500s and one freight door equipped Series 475. Production in Romania was to be at the Intreprinderea de Reparat Material Aeronautic factory at Baneasa and would take place alongside Britten-Norman Islander production. The plan was to use British produced sub-assemblies or kits for the aircraft and gradually increase the Romanian content until, when aircraft number 22 had been completed, all future production would be completely Romanian built. Production jigs were to be transferred from Hurn to Bucharest; the Rolls-Royce Spey Mk.512DW was also to be produced in Romania, but this time by the Turbomecanica company. Similar technology transfer would gradually be built into the engine manufacture as with the airframe.

At the beginning of the year British Airways was confirmed as purchasing three additional Series 500s, but unlike their Series 510EDs these aircraft would be standard production aircraft with the usual Mk.512DW engines and cockpit instrumentation.

There were no new One-Eleven deliveries during 1979, but construction was well under way on the three aircraft for British Airways. In the USA Allegheny Airlines was renamed USAir on 28 October and continued to fly its 31 One-Elevens. BAe bought one of TACA's Series 400s in January and fitted the aircraft with a main deck cargo door similar to those fitted to the Sultan of Oman's aircraft. This was the first and so far only Series 400 to be so equipped; the aircraft was sold to Turbo-Union and entered service in August 1979 and was used for the transport of engines and personnel between various plants in connection with the Tornado programme. BAe delivered the second and third ex-Gulf Air Series 400s to British Island Airways in January and February. This company was merged into Air UK later in the year and took a fourth used Series 400 on strength after its refurbishment and repaint in the company's shortlived dark blue colour scheme. In March BAe sold a used

Series 500 to Austral Lineas Aereas which had previously been on lease in Guatemala, while in November the same company took delivery of the first of three Series 500s which it purchased from Hapag-Lloyd of West Germany. Arkia returned its two Series 500s to BAe in September, one of which was sold to Dan-Air Services the following month. In November LACSA sold one of its Series 500s to Cayman Airways, doubling the latter's fleet.

British Airways took delivery of their three Series 500s in March, June and August 1980 and immediately based them at Birmingham. These aircraft replaced two Series 400s which were traded in part exchange to BAe. Evidence of the gathering momentum of the Romanian deal was apparent when the first complete fuselage was flown out of Hurn on 26 January 1980 in one of the French registered Guppy aircraft. On 13 November, the first of the two Series 500 pattern aircraft flew from Hurn.

In January 1980 the second and third Hapag-Lloyd Series 500s were delivered to Austral, increasing that company's fleet of Series 500s to nine. Austral was still operating two Series 400s, though these were sold to BAe in October 1980 and February 1981. Hapag-Lloyd also sold a Series 500 to Air Malawi in October 1980, joining that airline's single Series 475. BAe sold two used Series 500s (the second ex-Arkia aircraft and an ex-Aviateca aeroplane) in July to Philippine Airlines, the last One-Elevens to be received by this carrier. Their fleet now numbered 12 and enabled the company to dispose of the last of its NAMC YS-11 fleet. USAir started the slow rundown of its One-Eleven 200 fleet with the disposal of one of its aircraft into the corporate market in May 1980.

TAROM took delivery of its sixth Series 500 in January 1981 and in late August accepted a Series 475 pure freighter with a large main deck cargo door. This aircraft, the second pattern aeroplane, proved extremely useful in transferring jigs and parts from the UK to Romania as the production line was set up at Baneasa.

The last German registered One-Elevens were disposed of in 1981. One of Hapag-Lloyd's Series 500s was leased to Dan-Air from April 1981, and the remaining two aircraft were sold to BCAL at the end of October. The leased Dan-Air aircraft was sold to BCAL in the spring of 1982. BCAL's fleet of seven Series 200s was sold to a new California based airline at the end of the year; this company, Pacific Express, received the first of these aircraft in December 1981 and took delivery of the last in June 1982. They were used on a scheduled network throughout the west coast and were expected to be replaced with a fleet of British Aerospace 146s at some later date. In November LACSA sold another Series 500 to Dan-Air and at the same time leased an aircraft to TACA International. This latter lease continued until March 1982, when this aircraft also found its way to Dan-Air. BCAL leased a Series 500 to Austrian Airlines in April and May 1981.

TAROM's seventh Series 500 was delivered in March 1982, which left two Series 475s on the production line with no customer. These two aircraft had been expected to go to the Queen's Flight of the Royal Air Force as VIP transports, but this was not to be and the aircraft remained in store at Hurn until flown in 1984. They were eventually sold to McAlpine Aviation for executive charter work after fitting out in the USA. Total United Kingdom One-Eleven production amounted to 235 aircraft, of which 232 were delivered to customers. These comprised 56 Series 200s, nine Series 300s, 69 Series 400s, 12 Series 475s and 86 Series 500s, of which 161 were exported.

Components were supplied to Romania for the production of a further 22 aircraft. After the last Series 475s departed Hurn, British Aerospace withdrew from the Hurn complex. It was not long before they also abandoned the old Brooklands site at Weybridge, having closed down its satellite airfield at Wisley some time before. This was the end of an era.

Between the first flight of the first Vickers Viking on 14 June 1945 and the first flight of the last British-built One-Eleven on 1 May 1984 940 airliners had been built at the former Vickers-Armstrongs plants at Brooklands, Hurn and Wisley. These comprised 163 Vikings, 444 Viscounts, 44 Vanguards, 32 VC-10s, 22 Super VC-10s and 235 One-Elevens. In addition to these some 252 Valettas, a military version of the Viking, were built together with 163 Varsities, which were much modified derivatives of the Valetta with a nose wheel undercarriage.

The prototype of a four engined longrange turbojet airliner, the Vickers 1000, was also partially completed at Wisley before the project was abandoned.

With the closure of all these sites great design, engineering, flight testing and sales teams which had taken many years to build up were dismembered and lost for ever. The speed with which the One-Eleven was progressed from an idea to full production and the competence of the company in overcoming the traumatic deep stall problem so quickly was evidence of the skills, knowhow and experience held by these teams of professionals. Had the threat of nationalisation not stopped further private investment in new developments of the One-Eleven, the story could well have ended differently.

Meanwhile, although production had come to an end in the UK, in Romania it was just beginning. The first Rombac One-Eleven, a Series 561RC, was rolled out from the IRMA factory at Baneasa on 27 August 1982; it took to the air for the first time on 18 September and was delivered to TAROM on 24 December 1982.

There was plenty of activity in the used aircraft market during 1982. Apart from the continued delivery of Series 200s to Pacific Express by BCAL, USAir sold a Series 200 to Air Illinois in July to operate their scheduled routes out of Chicago. It also leased a Series 200 to Pacific Express in November and another aircraft to Quebecair from May to January 1983, joining their two Series 300s and one Series 400. Quebecair added two further Series 400s, previously operated by Austral, in September. Laker Airways ceased operations on 25 February, and their four Series 300s were sold to BCAL in time for the summer season. Air Manchester was a new British carrier which started operations with a Series 400 in May, and although two other One-Elevens appeared in their colours only the one aircraft was ever used and the company ceased operations just six months after start-up. Dan-Air leased a Series 400 to British Midland Airways from October to January 1983 for use on the company's schedules out of Heathrow. Dan-Air bought LACSA's last One-Eleven in May 1982, raising their Series 500 fleet to ten. At the very end of 1982 Cayman Airways retired their two Series 500s and put them in store.

USAir leased a second Series 200 to Pacific Express in May 1983 until December of the same year. They also leased a second aircraft to Air Illinois in October, which was sold to them in January 1984. The four ex-Laker Series 300s which had been bought by BCAL were all sold to Okada Air of Nigeria, with two delivered in September and the rest following in November. These were the first of many One-Elevens to see service in Nigeria and were put into service on scheduled domestic routes competing with Nigeria Airways. BAe leased single Series 400s to Dan-Air from May to September, to British Island Airways (re-formed on 1 January 1982 after breaking away from Air UK) from May to November 1983 and to BCAL from the end of November 1983 to January 1984. Dan-Air Services also leased a Series 500 from Monarch Airlines in March, which they finally purchased at the end of October, increasing their Series 500 fleet to 11. Dan-Air also disposed of one of their ex-American Airlines' Series 400s to the Westinghouse Electric Corporation in the USA, which was to be used for research purposes.

USAir disposed of another five aircraft in 1984 to Florida Express, this new company inaugurating services on 26 January from Orlando. The first four aircraft were delivered between January and March, while the fifth arrived in October, two of these being initially on lease. A sixth aircraft, which had previously been in corporate use, was purchased in July. The company very rapidly built up a network of scheduled services hubbing on Orlando, Florida. Two other USA carriers which started One-Eleven operations during 1984 were Cascade Airways and Britt Airways; the former, based at Spokane, Washington, leased three Series 200s from September and October 1984 to operate on schedules in the western USA and to Canada. These aircraft had formerly been operated by Pacific Express, which had ceased operations on 2 May 1984. Later in the year Cascade Airways obtained two Series 400s to add to their fleet. Britt Airways purchased their first Series 400 in June to operate on schedules based on Chicago. Other United States airlines to start One-Eleven operations during 1984 were Atlantic Gulf Airlines and Wright Airlines, both of which leased a Series 200 from Air Illinois. The former took delivery of its aircraft in November and eventually flew schedules with the type from Tallahassee and Miami to the Dominican Republic and to the Turks & Caicos Islands. The Wright Airlines' lease only lasted until September 1984.

In the UK another new airline to operate the type was Airways International Cymru, which purchased Quebecair's two Series 300s with delivery in March and November. A Series 400 was leased from British Island Airways pending delivery of the second aircraft. These aircraft were used on charter and inclusive tour flights to Europe. Dan-Air Services leased two aircraft for the summer season; a Series 400 was leased from May to October, while a Series 500 was leased from TAROM from March 1984 through to December 1985. In January 1984 BCAL bought a Series 500 formerly operated by Faucett of Peru, while British Island Airways received two Series 500s the following month; these had been stored at Miami since being withdrawn by Cayman Airways in December 1982.

During 1985 Florida Express further expanded its fleet with the purchase of two Series 200s from USAir in February and a third from the same source in December. Air Wisconsin leased four Series 200s, formerly operated by Pacific Express, with delivery in January and February. These aircraft operated scheduled routes based on Chicago pending delivery of further new British Aerospace 146s. Britt Airways bought its second Series 400 in March 1985. In Europe, Lauda Air of Austria leased two Series 500s from TAROM for charter flights with delivery in March and April; these leases continued until November 1985 and July 1986. TAROM also leased single examples of Series 500s to both Dan-Air and Inex-Adria Airways of Jugoslavia for the summer of 1985. Air UK leased two Series 400s from British Island Airways to use on their scheduled services, these being delivered in May and November. Monarch Airlines sold one of its Series 500s to British Island Airways in October, while Quebecair sold three Series 400s to Okada Air of Nigeria at the very end of the year. Dan-Air Services added a Series 300 to its large One-Eleven fleet in April 1985.

Florida Express added the seven aircraft to its fleet which BCAL had earlier sold to Pacific Express. These aircraft, which since the collapse of Pacific Express had been leased to Air Wisconsin and Cascade Airways, were delivered to Florida Express between January and July 1986. This company also took delivery of two Series 400s in June and July which had previously been operated by corporate users. Atlantic Gulf Airlines tripled its One-Eleven fleet with the delivery of two Series 400s in May and June; one of these was operated on behalf of Grenada Airways for a short while. Atlantic Gulf ceased trading on 1 September 1986.

TAROM was once again a major lessor of Series 500s for the 1986 summer season in Europe. Istanbul Hava Yollari leased three aircraft, Adria Airways leased two and British Island Airways one. TAROM also leased their one and only Series 475 pure freighter to Anglo Cargo Airlines from March 1986 and a further Series 500 to Ryanair of the Irish Republic in November 1986. This last aircraft inaugurated jet service by this carrier on the Dublin-Luton route on 1 December 1986. From November 1986 to April 1987 Air UK subleased one of the two Series 400s it was leasing from British Island Airways to British Airways.

During 1987 Okada Air further expanded its One-Eleven fleet with the addition of four Series 400s. Two of these came from Britt Airways in May and August, while the other two came from corporate users in May and September. Another Nigerian operator to start service with the type in 1987 was GAS Airlines, which by June was using a Series 400 leased from TAROM. A new airline in the UK, Mediterranean Express, purchased the two ex-Faucett Series 475s which had been stored for some years. These arrived in the UK in March and December 1987, but the second was found to be beyond economic restoration. The remaining aircraft was put into service in June on European charter flights. In 1987 Pertamina of Indonesia based a Series 400 in Cairns, Australia, which was used to fly workers between the Queensland city and Timika in West Irian; the aircraft continued to ply this route until January 1992.

Once again TAROM was busy during the year leasing out its Series 500s. Summer leases included two aircraft to British Island Airways, one to Anadolu Hava Yollari and one to Adria Airways of Jugoslavia. Longterm leases by TAROM were a second aircraft to Ryanair in April and another to Ryanair's UK based subsidiary, London European Airways, from May 1987. This latter aircraft was put into service on scheduled routes from Luton to Amsterdam and Brussels.

Major changes to One-Eleven operators took place during 1988. On 14 April BCAL merged into British Airways, and with the merger came a fleet of 13 Series 500 One-Elevens, which led British Airways to retire its last Series 400s at the end of the summer season and put them in store. Another merger took place in the USA one month earlier, on 1 March, when Florida Express merged into Braniff Airways. With that merger came 15 Series 200 and three Series 400 One-Elevens, making Braniff a One-Eleven operator again after a 16 year break. Twelve of these aircraft were sold to Guinness Peat Aviation between June and September 1988 and leased back by Braniff. Florida Express had earlier sold one of its Series 400s to Westinghouse Electric in January for research work, doubling that organisation's One-Eleven fleet.

On 1 June 1988 TACA International withdrew its last One-Eleven after over 21 years' service with the carrier; this company had been the first to order the type in Central America when it placed its order for two Series 400s on 18 March 1965, and at the time of withdrawal it was the last airline operating One-Elevens in Central America.

In January 1988 Airways International Cymru ceased trading, but one of its two Series 300s was operated on lease by Dan-Air from May to November. During the first half of the year Flightways Air Services operated a Series 400 on a schedule between Singapore and Christmas Island, an Australian Protectorate in the Indian Ocean. Ryanair expanded its Series 500 fleet by leasing another three aircraft from March and a fourth from May 1988; all were leased from TAROM and operated over both an expanded scheduled network and on charter work.

Braniff Airways ceased operations on 6 November 1989, which marked the end of airline operations of One-Elevens in the USA. USAir had withdrawn the last of their fleet in the summer of that year; this company and its predecessors, Mohawk Airlines and Allegheny Airlines, had operated the type for 24 years and had a peak fleet of 31 aircraft. Twenty years earlier, over 60 aircraft were in airline service in the USA with American Airlines, Mohawk, Braniff and Aloha Airlines.

British Island Airways leased two of its Series 400s to Transport Aerien Transregional (TAT) from March and April 1989 to February 1990. These aircraft operated scheduled services throughout France and to Corsica. BIA sold two of its Series 400s to Okada Air in October, while GAS Airlines purchased two similar aircraft from Romania in April and November. In March London European Airways obtained the ex-Mediterranean Express Series 475 and immediately leased it to Baltic Airlines for a new scheduled route from Malmo in southern Sweden to Southend; this route was only flown for two months. London European also leased a Series 500 to Loganair from March 1989. This was replaced by the Series 475 in early June, with that aircraft flying Loganair's domestic routes until October 1989. The second Mediterranean Express Series 475, which never saw service, was dismantled in June 1989 and the fuselage transported to Hurn, where it is used for watermisting fire retardant trials by AIM Aviation.

Only three TAROM Series 500s were taken on summer lease in 1989. Two aircraft went to Jugoslavia, one to Jugoslovenski Aerotransport (JAT) and the other to Adria Airways. The third aircraft was leased to Dan-Air Services from March to October.

Following the collapse of Braniff Airways, Guinness Peat Aviation soon started placing the aircraft which had been on lease to them. Two of the Series 200s were leased to British Air Ferries in March and May 1990, with a third arriving at Southend in October for spares use only. BAF used these aircraft for ad hoc charter work alongside their large fleet of Vickers Viscount 800s. Another Series 200 was leased to a new Nigerian carrier, ADC Airlines, in December 1990, and one of the Series 400s was leased to Shabair of Zaire in September, where it joined that company's two Hawker Siddeley 748s on domestic scheduled and charter work. A second Series 400 went to the Detroit Redwings as a team transport in July 1990.

The International Lease Finance Corporation, which had earlier purchased Dan-Air's short fuselage One-Elevens and leased them back to Dan-Air, leased the two Series 300s involved to Linea Aerea del Cobre (Ladeco) of Chile in November and December 1990. These two aircraft, which had been used on Dan-Air's scheduled routes, are operated on Ladeco's one-class domestic schedules and on charter flights after inaugurating service on 7 December 1990.

During the year Classic Air leased four of the former USAir fleet on passenger charter work, and Kabo Air took delivery of the first of a large fleet of One-Elevens when it received an ex-USAir Series 200 in November. British Airways sold its five stored Series 400s to Birmingham European Airways, with delivery during the first half of 1990. These aircraft were immediately put into service on an expanded scheduled network of services from their Birmingham base to European destinations and to Belfast. British Island Airways ceased operations on 1 February 1990, and its large One-Eleven fleet was soon disposed of. Two more Series 400s were sold to Okada Air in June and October, while three Series 500s went to London European Airways in April and May, where they were used for European charter and inclusive tour flights. Dan-Air also took one of the Series 500s on lease from April to October 1990. The first of London European's Series 500s was transferred to Ryanair in June 1990; two others followed in December, where they replaced leased TAROM aircraft.

The Dee Howard Company, having signed agreements with Rolls-Royce and British Aerospace in February 1986, proceeded to develop a prototype conversion of a Series 401AK airframe to take Rolls-Royce Tay 650 turbofans at its San Antonio, Texas, headquarters. The company was no stranger to the One-Eleven, having earlier converted 16 similar aircraft from airline to corporate configuration on behalf of National Aircraft Leasing. The prototype was in fact one of these earlier converted aircraft. The prime intention of the conversion was to extend considerably the life of the airframe by installing much quieter and more fuel-efficient engines and, at the same time, to give the aircraft a much greater reserve of power over the original Rolls-Royce Spey 25 Mk.511-14 engines. The mark of Tay installed was rated at 15,100lb (6,717kg) static thrust. The aircraft type was redesignated the One-Eleven 2400 and first flew on 21 January 1990. The prototype's certification programme was interrupted in order that the aircraft could be shown at the Farnborough Air Show in September 1990. It was noticeably quieter than the standard One-Elevens and gave a most impressive performance. Unfortunately the project was abandoned later that year with the certification 90% complete, reportedly due to a disagreement with British Aerospace. The company then concentrated on its Tay conversion programme for the Boeing 727, for which it had received a large order from United Parcel Services.

There was a major exodus of One-Elevens to Nigeria during 1991. Kabo Air took delivery of eight former USAir Series 200s between February and October and also purchased a Series 400 from TACA International, which was delivered in November. Okada Air obtained the first Series 500s to be operated in Nigeria when they bought two aircraft from British Airways in July. In May that year they received two Series 300s formerly operated by British Island Airways, a similar aircraft from Dan-Air and a Series 400 from TAROM. Two other aircraft were also delivered to Okada Air in 1991; these were a Series 200 in December which had previously been operated by the Royal Australian Air Force and an ex-Birmingham European Airways Series 400 in August. Hold-Trade Air Services was another Nigerian airline to start One-Eleven operations with the delivery of three Series 200s between June and September from Aer Lingus through Guinness Peat Aviation. Aer Lingus had been flying its fleet of four Series 200s for over 25 years when its last service was flown with the type on 3 March. ADC Airlines added a second Series 200 and a Series 400 to their fleet in April, both leased from Guinness Peat Aviation. All these Nigerian operators use their aircraft on both scheduled and charter flights within Nigeria. Shabair of Zaire took delivery of its second aircraft in March, this time a Series 200.

SARO Airlines of Mexico leased a Series 200 from Guinness Peat Aviation and put the aircraft into service on 18 March 1991. At the time, this was the only One-Eleven in airline service in North and Central America and flew both scheduled and charter flights from the company's base at Monterrey. In Chile, Ladeco doubled its One-Eleven fleet with the delivery of two Series 200s to Santiago during November and December on lease from ILFC.

The last two London European Airways' Series 500s were transferred to Ryanair in April and May 1991, where they replaced leased TAROM aircraft, and on 31 May London European was put into receivership. The airline's Series 475 was leased to British Air Ferries by a Swedish leasing company and became the only Series 475 left in passenger service after Air Malawi withdrew its One-Eleven fleet in June. BAF put this unique aircraft into service on 30 June. GEC Ferranti Defence Systems purchased a Series 500 from British Airways in June to use as a radar testbed for the Eurofighter 200 programme.

In the UK the Royal Aircraft/Aerospace Establishment was merged into the Defence Research Agency in April 1991 and continued to fly its three One-Elevens in various research programmes.

Philippine Airlines flew its last service with a One-Eleven on 31 May 1992 when RP-C1185 flew into Manila from Legaspi as the PR278. PAL was the first airline outside the USA to have ordered the uprated Series 300/400 version when it placed its initial order for two aircraft on 2 November 1964. Its first aircraft was delivered on 19 April 1966 and entered service on 1 May the same year, when it replaced the company's Vickers Viscounts in service. In the intervening 26 years, Philippine Airlines operated 17 different examples of the type and also maintained the Series 400 which was operated on behalf of the Philippine Government. The Series 500 aircraft alone flew over 368,700 hours and made nearly 400,500 landings in Philippine Airlines' service.

On 31 December 1992 British Airways flew its last service with a Series 510ED when - G-AVMS flew to Birmingham from Glasgow as flight BA5382. This 18-aircraft fleet carried its first revenue passengers on 1 September 1968 and over the years flew 720,593 hours and carried out 809,165 landings with BEA and British Airways without a single major accident. Probably the most serious incident was when an aircraft was crew training at Teesside; while carrying out flapless landings, the crew managed to put the aircraft down on the runway with the undercarriage still stowed. There was undoubtedly more damage done to the Training Captain's pride than to the aircraft, which was soon flying again. British Airways continued to fly Birmingham schedules with its ex-British Caledonian Series 500s, but these too were to be withdrawn during the summer of 1993.

Another major event during 1992 was the last flight of a Dan-Air Services One-Eleven. This took place on 6 November when G-BCWA flew into Gatwick from Toulouse as flight DA910. Two days later the company was officially taken over by British Airways, and another famous name had departed. Dan-Air had received its first One-Eleven from American Airlines in March 1969 and had operated 27 different aircraft during their service period with the carrier on both charter and scheduled services.

Anglo Cargo Airlines ceased trading on 13 January 1992, and its unique Series 475 pure freighter was subsequently returned to TAROM. Brymon European Airways was formed on 25 October from the merger of Birmingham European Airways and Brymon Airways. The four Series 400s continued to operate scheduled services out of Birmingham, and an ex-British Airways Series 500 joined the fleet in late March 1993. The company's twice daily Bristol to Paris schedule was upgraded to a One-Eleven at the start of the summer schedules in 1993. The "new" Series 500, G-AWYS, has won some notoriety among airline staff; an elderly lady passenger who died of a heart attack on the aircraft when it overran the runway into the sea at Corfu on 19 August 1972 has reportedly haunted it ever since and has been seen sitting in the same seat on numerous occasions by crew members.

The entire Dan-Air fleet of 11 Series 500s was passed to British Air Ferries in November 1992, and three of these aircraft were immediately pressed into service. The aircraft had been sold to ILFC by Dan-Air and leased back by them prior to the demise of the airline.

Four more aircraft joined the Nigerian One-Eleven fleets during 1992. These were a second ex-Royal Australian Air Force Series 200 and an ex-Air Malawi Series 500 which were delivered to Okada Air in January and July, a second ex-TACA International Series 400 to Kabo Air in February and a fourth ex-Aer Lingus Series 200 to Hold-Trade Air in March. Ryanair leased two Series 500s from TAROM for the summer season, and Air Malawi's Series 475 was reportedly leased in September to a cargo operator in Malaysia named Wirakris Udara. Romavia leased the first of two Series 500s to Citylink Airways of India in November 1992, this being the first Romanian lease of Series 500s outside Europe. Another new operator to start service in 1992 was National Aviation of Egypt, which leased a Series 400 to operate on cargo charter work.

On 6 April 1993 British Air Ferries was renamed British World Airways, with a new colour scheme being introduced at the same time. At the time of launch four of the ex-Dan Air Series 500s were in service, with a fifth being prepared for service; the two Series 200s and the Series 475 had been withdrawn in December 1992. The company soon announced that it intended to start scheduled services with the One-Elevens between Stansted and Bucharest. After initial delays because of licensing problems, service was inaugurated on this route on 28 June.

A new carrier named Aero Asia started scheduled service in May 1993 on two domestic routes within Pakistan with two Series 500s leased from TAROM, while Citylink Airways of India ceased operating in October of the same year.

Although officially withdrawn from regular scheduled service on 31 May 1993, two One-Elevens remained in service with British Airways Regional Division operating flights on an ad hoc basis from the Birmingham base.

At the time of the withdrawal from service of British Airways' last One-Eleven after operating the last revenue service with the type on 1 July 1993, some 30 Series 500s were known to be in storage awaiting new users or breaking up. Over 800,000 hours were flown by British Airways and BEA with its Series 500 aircraft (this includes the hours flown by the ex-BCAL fleet after its absorption into British Airways and those flown by the two leased aircraft). Actual totals were 880,914 hours and 966,651 landings; the total hours flown are further increased to well over one million if the flying of the Series 400 fleet is included. Not a single fatality among passengers and crew was recorded in just two months short of 25 years' service - not a bad record for a type which BEA had originally stated did not form part of its fleet requirements.

On 1 August Brymon European Airways was de-merged and the One-Eleven operations of the former Birmingham European Airways became a wholly owned subsidiary of Maersk Air of Denmark. The company was renamed Maersk Air Ltd and the aircraft repainted in full British Airways' colours with small "Operated by Maersk Air" titles; scheduled services were flown from this date with British Airways' flight numbers. It had been barely a month after the retirement of One-Elevens from British Airways' service before the type was once again flying in British Airways' colours.

It was during 1993 that British Airways started disposing of its One-Eleven fleet after donating two of its Series 510EDs to museums at Cosford and Duxford in March. On 7 May the remaining 16 Sereis 510EDs were sold to European Aviation; the majority of these aircraft remain in store, although two are leased to a new United Kingdom operator, Air Bristol, which commenced operations in October operating a Monday to Friday communications flight between Filton and Toulouse on behalf of British Aerospace. British Airways leased four Series 501EXs to Ryanair in June and sold a further aircraft to Oriental Airlines of Nigeria in July. Two aircraft were later sold to JARO International of Romania in October. In early August the Ford Motor Company sold two of its three Series 400s to Kabo Air of Nigeria, while Aero Asia of Pakistan had doubled its Series 500 fleet to four by the end of the year by leasing further Romanian aircraft.

On 16 February 1994 European Aircharter commenced charter work with the first of four Series 510EDs leased from the parent European Aviation for summer 1994 operations. The company announced that it had contracts to operate inclusive tour programmes over its first season. Ad hoc charter work included operating schedules on behalf of both Maersk Air and Ryanair from Birmingham and Stansted respectively.

After the Rolls-Royce flying unit at Filton was closed down at the beginning of 1994 the only Series 400 to be converted with a main deck large freight door, which had been flown on behalf of Turbo-Union for 15 years, was sold to Nationwide Air Charter of South Africa with delivery in April. In March 1994 JARO International leased one of its Series 500s to Air Alfa of Turkey, while in June 1994 European Aviation purchased two of British Airways ex BCAL Series 500s. The same company has procured the remaining four stored Series 500s of British Airways.

By June 1994 airline users of the One-Eleven were reduced to Air Alfa, Air Bristol, British World Airlines, Cyprus Airways, European Aircharter, JARO International, Maersk Air, Romavia, Ryanair and TAROM in Europe, Austral Lineas Aereas and Ladeco in South America, Aero Asia in Pakistan, ADC Airlines, GAS Airlines, Hold-Trade Air Services, Kabo Air, Okada Air and Oriental Airlines in Nigeria, National Aviation in Egypt, Nationwide Air Charter in South Africa and Shabair in Zaire.

Executive use of the type continues, although to date only with the short fuselage versions. Over 40 aircraft are operated in this configuration, while the SOAF still operates its three Series 475s in the military transport role. Three of the corporate aircraft are currently employed flying sports teams around the USA and Canada. Most of the executive versions are based in the USA, the United Kingdom or Middle East, but several have recently appeared in Nigerian use. The Defence Research Agency and GEC Ferranti Defence Systems in the United Kingdom operate single examples of all versions except the 300 Series in various research programmes, while two Series 400s are used in similar work with Westinghouse Electric in the USA. The UK Empire Test Pilots' School employs a single Series 475 for experience in flying commercial airliners by its students.

British Aerospace continued to fly the much modified G-ASYD both in the communications and development roles. Based at Filton, it regularly flew to Toulouse in connection with the Airbus programme, whilst one of its last development tasks entailed the flight testing of a Lucas Fly-by-Light spoiler actuation system. The aircraft was retired in October 1993 and on the morning of 14 July 1994 was flown into Weybridge, where it landed on the much shortened runway after donation to the Brooklands Museum. Here it joined examples of its stablemates, which include an early production Vickers Viking, a Viscount 800, a Varsity and a standard VC10. This fascinating museum is located on the site of one of the original Vickers-Armstrongs plants where some of the One-Elevens were completed. The factory was built within the original Brooklands banked motor-racing circuit.

Lead aircraft for hours and landings achieved are tabulated below and are the latest figures available at the time of writing. The highest flown aircraft, c/n 043, a former Braniff Series 203AE, is flown by ADC Airlines of Nigeria and leads the rankings on both achieved hours flown and landings performed; this aircraft is one of a fleet of three flown by the carrier. These superbly maintained and painted aircraft are regular visitors to the United Kingdom for Check Cs. Two of the former USA based Series 200s are known to have exceeded 60,000 flying hours, while a further 21 aircraft have attained over 50,000 hours. Indicating the kind of schedules they once operated, two of these aircraft have carried out over 80,000 landings, while at least 23 others have exceeded 70,000 landings.

Two Series 300s and at least 15 Series 500 aircraft have exceeded 50,000 hours flown, with several of these approaching the 60,000 hour mark. Average sectors flown by the Series 500s have however been somewhat longer than was the case with Series 200s in the USA, and it is believed that only one of the aircraft has surpassed the 50,000 landing threshold. Unfortunately accurate updates of flying hours/landings are not obtainable from some operators, which makes statistical data somewhat unreliable.

Type	Regn	C/n	Operator	Total
Series 200	5N-AYY	043	ADC Airlines	62,050 hours 80,672 landings
Series 300	CC-CYF 5N-IVE	033 112	Ladeco Okada Air	52,436 hours 55,836 landings
Series 400	N162W G-BBME	087 066	Westinghouse Electric Maersk Air	48,228 hours 47,420 landings
Series 475	7Q-YKF OB-R-953	243 239	Air Malawi Faucett	32,503 hours 29,218 landings
Series 500	G-OBWB LV-JNS	202 194	British World Airlines Austral Lineas Aereas	58,951 hours 52,842 landings

ROMANIAN PRODUCTION

Following the previously-mentioned first flight and delivery of the first Romanian assembled One-Eleven to Transporturile Aeriene Romane (TAROM) in December 1982, production progress was painfully slow. This was mainly due to the lack of hard currency to procure the necessary items and the lack of commitment to the project by the government of the day. It was anticipated that the Baneasa factory would produce some six aircraft per year, but in the event only one aircraft per year on average was completed, and to date only nine aircraft have flown, these all being Series 500s. All but one of these were delivered to TAROM, with the last going direct to Romavia. IRMA was left to fend for itself when President Ceausescu was ousted in the revolution of 22 December 1989; production had virtually ceased and a capital injection was required to set the line working again. The company has since been renamed Romaero, and the tenth aircraft, ordered by the Romanian Army, was being built as a Series 475 with a large forward main deck freight door. The order was cancelled following the revolution because of the lack of funds for the purchase. The aircraft remains 85% complete, and aircraft number 11, a Series 500, is 70% completed. Many of the components for the remainder of the 22 aircraft are complete, while components for the required Rolls-Royce Speys for these aircraft are available.

Romaero was hopeful of completing the remainder of the 22 aircraft and laying down production of all new Romanian produced aircraft when a company called Associated Aerospace announced that it was ordering 50 aircraft from Romania to be powered by Rolls-Royce Tay 650 engines. This pronouncement took place in April 1990 with the statement that the company would be marketing the aircraft worldwide. The aircraft would be fitted with modern glass cockpits and fitted out by AIM Aviation at Hurn after ferry from Romania. Unfortunately this ambitious project was soon to founder when the company ceased trading.

On 9 February 1993 it was announced that Kiwi International Airlines of Newark, New Jersey, was purchasing 11 Series 2500 Rolls-Royce Tay 650 powered aircraft from Romaero with an option on a further five. If this deal is to be completed the co-operation of British Aerospace, Alenia and the Dee Howard Company in the USA will be required. First deliveries are due to take place in late 1995, by which time it is hoped to have the aircraft certificated in both the UK and the USA. The option on five aircraft was taken up in June 1993, which should lead to the building of the first all-Romanian One-Eleven airframes. The type will be known in Kiwi International service as the "Airstar 2500".

Many of the Romanian produced Spey powered aircraft have been leased to foreign carriers in Europe over the years, and recently two were leased to a new Indian carrier, Citylink Airways, and a further five to Aero Asia of Pakistan.

TECHNICAL DESCRIPTION

Brief details are provided in the following sections of the structure, flight deck, interior layout, powerplant and other operational systems.

STRUCTURE

The primary structure is designed on "fail-safe" principles. Alternative paths for structural loads are provided so that either a failure or partial failure of a single main structural member does not induce a total collapse of the entire structure or reduce the strength of the structure to below that required to sustain design flight loads. The structure is designed to have a minimum crack-free period of 40,000 flights, with further life extension after the minimum of attention. The airframe is designed so that maintenance and/or repair can be completed with the minimum of specialised equipment. Numerous inspection panels are provided to assist in monitoring wear and/or corrosion in otherwise inaccessible areas.

Fuselage

Conventional circular-section all-metal semi-monocoque structure built on fail-safe principles with continuous notched light alloy frames and stringers with riveted connections. Copper-based aluminium alloy skin. The fuselage is built up from three major sub-assemblies consisting of forward, centre and rear sections. The centre fuselage contains the wing centre section. Beams across each frame form the floor supports and substantial main frames attach the wing centre section to the fuselage. The cabin floor consists of replaceable sandwich panels supported by a grid formed by the seat rail support beams and the transverse floor beams and is flat throughout the cabin. Seat rails are secured to the floor beams and run the length of the cabin floor. These are in detachable sections for replacement purposes and are suitable for the installation of either forward or rearward facing seats with an incremental pitch variation of one inch. All exposed rails have plastic capping. The floors in the galley and toilet areas are sealed, while the floor between the two galley areas is drained to avoid fluid seepage into the underfloor compartment. Series 200/300/400 and 475 aircraft have 24 elliptical windows, each side measuring 14in (0.35m) high by 9.5in (0.24m) wide. Series 500 aircraft have 33 identical windows each side. Average window pitch is 20in (0.51m).
All passenger windows are triple-paned. The inner pane is a separately removable scratch pane, while the two outer panes can withstand the maximum pressure differential. Electrical de-icing and hydraulically powered windscreen wipers are provided to the two front windshield panels, while electrically heated glass is used for all cockpit windows with a demisting facility. The entire fuselage, including the freight holds, is pressurised excluding the nose cap, undercarriage bays, wing centre section and tail portion. The cabin is not encumbered by any structural bulkhead.

Engine Mountings

The Rolls-Royce Spey mounting attaches directly on to the engine frames and rear pressure bulkhead and consists of a pair of steel beams from which the engine is suspended. A trunnion mounted on the front beam picks up a spherical bearing on the engine, and thrust loads are transmitted by a tubular strut to the rear pressure bulkhead, whence they are reacted into the fuselage by a machined beam on the outside of the fuselage between the two engine frames.

Wings

Cantilever low-wing monoplane. All-metal structure of copper-based aluminium alloy built on fail-safe principles. Aspect ratio of 8 (Series 200/300/400), 8.5 (early Series 500), 8.65 (Series 475/500) and a sweepback of 20° at quarter chord. Thickness/chord ratio 12.5% at root, 11% at tip. Dihedral 2°. Incidence 2°30'. The wing panels are machined from solid metal. The main torsion box is built up from three shear webs - a front, centre and rear web - and is a continuous structure from wing tip to wing tip. In addition, the leading edge is capable of carrying the front web loads. Nearly all skin panels are integrally machined. The greater part of each wing comprises an integral fuel tank. The aircraft has manually operated aerodynamically balanced Redux bonded light alloy honeycomb ailerons with spring tabs, the port tab also being used for trimming. These are assisted by hydraulically operated spoilers through Dowty Boulton Paul actuators (two on each wing forward of the flaps), which also serve as air brakes. Hydraulically operated three-piece light alloy Fowler flaps on each wing are activated through Hobson screw jack actuators, which are enclosed in three flap track guide rail housings on each wing plus single units in the wing roots. Hydraulically operated lift dumpers are employed inboard of the spoilers (not fitted to Series 200/300 aircraft). Double skinned (the inner of which is corrugated) leading edges are de-iced by hot air, which passes between them, bled via a perforated distribution duct from the engine compressors and are removable in five sections for maintenance. The leading edges can be illuminated from fuselage-mounted lamps for inspection for ice build-up. The outer wing box is butt-jointed to the centre section, held by internal and external butt straps in short sections.

Tail Unit

Cantilever monoplane type with tailplane mounted on top of fin. All-metal light alloy structure. The variable incidence tailplane is controlled through a Hobson screw-jack driven by duplicated hydraulic motors. The fin is integral with the rear fuselage. The elevators and rudder are of light alloy construction and are actuated hydraulically through Dowty Boulton Paul tandem jacks. Leading edges of the fin and tailplane are de-iced by hot air bled from the engine compressors in the same manner as the wing leading edge.

Landing Gear

Retractable tricycle type with twin wheels on each unit. Nosewheel retracts forward, while mainwheels retract inwards, actuated hydraulically. Emergency free-fall system available. All wheels stowed in unpressurised areas. The wheels are braked and the nosewheel centralised automatically at the start of the retraction cycle. Oleo-pneumatic shock absorbers. Hydraulically actuated nosewheel steering through 78° either side, while limited steering is available through the rudder pedals. The main undercarriage doors are closed after both extension and retraction for both nose and mainwheels.

	Wheels	Brakes	Anti-Skid System
Series 200 *	Dunlop or Bendix	HD or thin pad	Maxaret
Series 300	Dunlop	HD	Maxaret or Goodyear ABPC
Series 400 **	Dunlop or Bendix	HD or thin pad	Hytrol 11
Series 475/500 +	Dunlop	5 plate HD	Hytrol 111

*   Mohawk Airlines' Series 200s numbers 10 to 18 fitted with brake cooling fans
**   Philippine Airlines specified Maxaret, Hytrol 11 and Goodyear ABPC anti-skid systems on different Series 400 aircraft
+   British European Airways' Series 510EDs had HD modified brakes

Tyre Pressures	Mainwheels	Nosewheels	LCN*
Series 200	128psi (9.00kg/cm^2)	100 psi (7.03kg/cm^2)	36
Series 300/400	141 psi (9.91kg/cm^2)	110 psi (7.73kg/cm^2)	45
Series 500	160 psi (11.25kg/cm^2)	110 psi (7.73kg/cm^2)	53
Series 475	83 psi (5.83kg/cm^2)	105 psi (7.38kg/cm^2)	34
*at maximum all up weight			

Tyre Size	Mainwheels	Nosewheels
All version except Series 475	40 x 12	24 x 7.25
Series 475	44 x 16	24 x 7.70

Doors and Emergency Exits

Forward port passenger entry door opens outwards and forwards. Optional built-in hydraulically operated airstairs are stowed beneath the cabin floor at the forward passenger entrance. Rear passenger entry is through an inward opening door in the pressure bulkhead via hydraulically operated ventral airstairs (Series 203AE and 212AR not fitted with ventral entrance). Forward service door to starboard opens outwards and rearwards. Two overwing emergency exits (one each side) on Series 200/300/400/475 (except some Series 408EFs). Four overwing emergency exits (two each side on Series 500s and some Series 408EFs. The direct vision windscreen panels on the flight deck can be used as emergency exits, and escape ropes are provided for this purpose. Both forward doors and the ventral entrance are nominated emergency exits. All Series 200 and 301AG aircraft were delivered with two non-inflatable escape chutes, one located at each forward door. Series 304AX and 320L-AZ aircraft were delivered with a single non-inflatable escape chute at the forward passenger door. Series 400 aircraft were all delivered with either one or two non-inflatable chutes, with the exception of Series 401AKs, which were delivered with a single inflatable escape chute. All Series 475 and 500 aircraft were delivered with two inflatable escape chutes, with the exception of the Series 501EX (which had a single non-inflatable chute) and the Series 509EW and 510ED (which had two non-inflatable chutes).

CORROSION PROTECTION AND FINISH

All light alloy components, with the exception of castings (which are anodised) are treated with the Alocrom 1200 process, which makes their surfaces chemically resistant to corrosion.

They are then treated with epoxy/polyamide paint. Parts likely to be contaminated by water are then coated with primer which is stoved. Parts likely to be contaminated by more corrosive fluids such as oil, hydraulic fluid or toilet fluids have both a coat of primer and a stoved coat of gloss paint. Steel components are cadmium-plated prior to the application of epoxy primer and a finishing coat. After assembly parts likely to come into contact with hydraulic fluid are further coated with epoxy nylon lacquer.

After assembly the primer coat is touched up, particularly over rivet heads, before the customer's paint trim is applied. The leading edges of the wings and tail, the engine cowlings and the stub fairings are not painted and have clad-finished skins.

Aircraft skins and plating are generally flush-riveted, and all removable inspection panels are flush fitted.

FLIGHT DECK LAYOUT AND CONTROLS

The One-Eleven has a conventional cockpit layout. The aircraft can be flown from either the left or right hand seat. Air Speed Indicator/Machmeter, Altimeter, Vertical Speed Indicator, Turn and Slip Indicator, Flight Director Indicator, Course Indicator, clock, Compass Indicator and DME are all duplicated and positioned on the panels immediately in front of the pilots' seats. All engine instruments, hydraulic instruments and switches, fuel contents gauges, undercarriage indictors, fire test switches and flying control warning instruments are mounted in a central vertical panel. Autopilot, NAV/Comms, ADF, Weather Radar, Transponder and HF controllers are all mounted on a central pedestal.

The roof panel houses the electrics (including APU), fuel, air system, anti-ice and oxygen system indicators and switches. It also houses lighting switches for the instrument panels, together with navigation and landing lamp switches. Test switches for the stall warning and stick shaker systems are also mounted in the overhead panel.

The radio rack is mounted aft of the P2 seat and is directly accessible from the entrance way to the cockpit seating.

The flying controls are conventional with handwheel, rudder bar and pedals located in the Captain's and First Officer's positions. The rudder pedals are adjustable to suit individual pilots and carry independently toe-actuated wheel brake control pedals.

Throttle levers, undercarriage operating levers, flap controls and trim wheels are all mounted on the central pedestal. Nosewheel steering is controlled by a tiller mounted alongside each crew seat on the side wall beneath the window.

INTERIOR ACCOMMODATION

Entire accommodation air conditioned, pressurised, soundproofed and thermally insulated.

Flight Deck

Crew of two on flight deck. The two main crew seats are adjustable in height, slide fore and aft and are lockable in any position. A third crew seat, positioned between and behind the other two, stows flat against the radio rack bulkhead behind the starboard crew seat when not in use. All three seats are fitted with full shoulder harnesses with inertia reel type locking. A fourth crew seat situated immediately behind the captain's seat is optional. All instruments on the flight deck have variable intensity white integral lights. Additionally, variable intensity white and red general floodlighting is provided from lamps beneath the glare shield. These are all controlled from dimmer switches in the roof panel. Facilities in the cockpit area for both Captain and First Officer include a folding chart table, cup holder and ashtray together with stowage for briefcases, maps, torches, oxygen masks and headsets. Additional facilities include adjustable sun visors, anti-glare shroud for the instrument panel, oxygen bottle for the smoke mask set, three lifejacket stowages, a fire extinguisher, small mirror, waste bin and stowages for flight manuals, crew bags, fire axe and spare headset.

Cabin

Up to 89 passengers can be accommodated at 29in (0.74m) pitch five abreast in the short fuselage versions together with three cabin attendants. More typical for scheduled work is a 79 seat layout at 32in (0.81m) pitch. Typical mixed class layout is 16 first class (four abreast) and 49 tourist class (five abreast) seats. On the Series 500 aircraft up to 119 passengers can be accommodated in a five abreast layout at 29in (0.74m) pitch. More typical for scheduled work is a 97 seat one class layout five abreast at a 34in (0.86m) pitch. Typical mixed class layout is 12 first class (four abreast) and 74 tourist class (five abreast) seats. Three cabin attendant seats are fitted, a double unit which folds against the forward vestibule bulkhead by the forward passenger door and a single unit at the rear of the cabin which folds against the forward bulkhead of the right hand rear toilet.

Location of galleys, toilets, coat-space and cabin luggage stowage vary according to customer preference. All these services are located either between the cockpit and the main cabin or at the rear of the main cabin.

Specialist consultants, Charles Butler Inc, were retained by BAC to advise on the decor and furnishing design. Materials used are fire-resistant, rot-proof and pre-shrunk where practicable. The interior roof panels, upper walls and hatrack are of cotton-backed PVC. Side walls are of rigid PVC sheeting. Window blinds are of plasticised fabric, and carpets are of woollen material with foam underlay.

Rumbold was the recommended supplier of passenger seating with safety belts and lifejacket stowage, but the choice of manufacturer was at the purchaser's discretion. Overhead racks are fitted throughout the length of the passenger cabin. These also house flush-mounted passenger service units which incorporate individual reading lights, individual cold air outlets, individual attendant call buttons and drop-out oxygen masks if specified. A public address system which enables both technical and cabin crew to make announcements throughout the cabin is installed. The main cabin and vestibule are lit by ceiling-mounted fluorescent lamps for bright lighting, while incandescent lamps provide dim lighting.

Toilets

Two toilets are installed as standard. Usual layout was with two toilets at the rear of the cabin for all Series 400, 475 and 500 aircraft. The aircraft was plumbed for an alternate location of one of these units in the forward cabin; the only company to make use of this alternate location on these marks of aircraft was Air Malawi for their Series 481FW. Series 200 airline configured aircraft generally had one toilet forward and one to the rear of the passenger cabin, the only exceptions being Series 204AFs and 215AUs, which were delivered with single toilets to the rear of the cabin (British Airways, during the later years of operation of its Series 500 fleet, relocated one of the toilets to the forward part of the cabin when the aircraft were operated in a two class configuration). The toilets contain recirculating pneumatically operated chemical flushing closets, washbasins with hot/cold water supply, towel dispensers and the usual refinements. Fluorescent lighting is provided in the areas over the mirrors and along the side wall. Mirror lights are only illuminated when the toilets are in use, triggered by the door lock.

Galleys

Galley standards are to customer preference. These could include a refrigerator, water boiler, double oven, sink, trolleys, trays etc.

Holds

There are two underfloor baggage/freight holds, one positioned forward and the other aft of the wing centre section, with access by a single door to each hold to starboard. The doors are outward opening plug type and are stowed under the fuselage when open. The holds are in the pressurised area and are warmed by the air conditioning system, enabling the carriage of livestock. Numerous freight lashing points are provided, and nets are located at each door.

POWERPLANT

Two Rolls-Royce RB163 Spey 2 Mk.506-14 or 14AW turbo-fans, each rated at 10,410lb (4,425kg) static thrust mounted in pods on each side of the rear fuselage. This mark of engine applies to all Series 200 aircraft except the Series 207AJ and Series 217EA. The Series 300 and 400, together with the Series 207AJ and 217EA, are powered by the uprated Rolls-Royce Spey 25 Mk.511-14 or 14W rated at 11,400lb (5,069kg) static thrust. The W suffix indicates that the engine is fitted with an optional water injection system, with which demineralised water is sprayed into the combustion chambers during take-off at hot or high airfields. This enables maximum take-off power to be maintained by increasing the engine revolutions per minute but still within the turbine entry temperature limits. The water is contained in a 100 Imp Gall (500 litre) tank installed in the rear fuselage and is supplied to the engines by a turbine pump driven by air bled from the HP engine compressors. Series which used this option included the 201ACs, 207AJs, 211AH, the first 402AP, 407AWs, 409AYs, 412EB, 413FA, 414EGs, 420ELs, 422EQs, 423ETs and 432FDs.

The Series 510EDs built for British European Airways are powered by Rolls-Royce Spey 25 Mk.512-14E engines rated at 12,000lb (5,333kg) static thrust, while all other Series 500s and all Series 475s are powered by still higher rated Rolls-Royce Spey 25 Mk 512-14DW engines rated at 12,550lb (5,580kg) static thrust. All the Series 500 and 475 aircraft, with the exception of the Series 510ED, were delivered with a water injection system installed as standard.

The Spey is an axial flow turbo-fan with a twin spool compressor. The Spey 2 has a four stage low pressure compressor, while the Spey 25 has an additional fifth stage added. Both versions have 12 stage high pressure compressors. By-pass ratio is 0.7 to 1, with the by-pass air cooling the engine core and joining the hot gasses beyond the low pressure turbine. Ignition is induced by two 28 volt DC transistorised high energy units per engine producing 12 joules. Engine intake lips are protected from icing by air bled from the engine compressor. Fuselage mounted lights illuminate engine intakes for visible signs of icing. Pressure ratio 19 to 1.

Thrust reversers are standard on all versions. Internal clamshell doors, which in their stowed position lie along the jet pipe wall, hinge rearwards sealing the jet pipe and deflecting the exhaust gases through two banks of exhaust cascades positioned above and below the engines. These cascades, which are blanked off by the clamshell doors when stowed, deflect the gases forward via guide vanes.

The engines are designed to operate on either kerosene or wide-cut gasoline fuels.

Each engine is fitted with a complete fire detector and two shot extinguisher system as protection against inflight fires, using BCF as the retardant.

Hushkits (as described in the main text) were fitted as standard on all aircraft from c/n 252 onwards, including all Romanian production. Many earlier produced aircraft have since been fitted with similar kits.

AUXILIARY POWER UNIT

The APU is a Garrett AiResearch model GTCP 85-115 and is mounted in the tail cone behind the ventral airstairs tunnel within the unpressurised area. This unit provides electrical ground power and air conditioning together with air and electrics for engine starting. It is run during take-off to avoid the performance penalty of bleeding air from the main engines for cabin air conditioning at this critical stage of flight. It is started from the aircraft's internal batteries, and a fire warning system is installed. Operation of the fire controls shuts off the fuel supply to the APU and discharges a single shot BCF fire bottle.

FUEL

Integral wing tanks of 2,235 Imp Gall (10,160 litres) capacity are standard on all versions. A centre-section tank of 850 Imp Gall (3,864 litres) capacity is standard on all versions except the Series 200, where this is an option. Additional extra tankage of either 350 Imp Gall (1,591 litres) or 700 Imp Gall (3,182 litres) capacity is a further option. These further tanks are accommodated in the rear of the forward underfloor hold.

The National Aircraft Leasing modifications described in the main text gave even further fuel capacity. Once again, the extra tanks were accommodated in the rear of the forward hold. Additional capacity options available in this case were 1,015 Imp Gall (4,618 litres) or 1,332 Imp Gall (6,056 litres).

A single point pressure refuelling system (maximum pressure 50 psi, 3.52kg/cm^2) is installed with the access point on the lower fuselage wall just below the forward section of the starboard wing root. At maximum pressure the refuelling rate is 410 Imp Gall/minute (1,864 litres/minute). Defuelling can be accomplished at a rate of 130 Imp Gall/minute (591 litres/minute) at a pressure of 8 psi (0.56kg/cm^2). Provision for gravity refuelling is also available via three overwing fuelling points. Fuel is pumped to the engines and APU from the wing tanks, this being replaced by fuel transferred from the centre tank when in use. Each engine is fed by fuel from the wing tank on its own side, while the APU draws its fuel from the port wing tank through an electrically driven DC fuel pump. Each tank is fitted with twin AC electrically operated booster pumps. A cross-feed system is available to either or both engines from either wing tank. A Smiths Industries fuel gauging system calibrated in either kilograms or pounds is standard; on the Series 200 aircraft built for the United States market, however, a Simmonds system was fitted.

A fuel jettison system was an option available on Series 300/400/475 and 500 aircraft.

Oil capacity is 3 Imp Gall (13.66 litres) per engine.

SYSTEMS

Air Conditioning and Pressurisation

A fully duplicated Normalair-Garrett air conditioning and pressurisation system is fitted. High temperature air is bled from the final HP stage of the engine compressors and is ducted through individual main heat exchangers in the engine nacelle stubs. Cooling air is bled from the LP compressors for the main heat exchangers. The air is then passed through two stainless steel ducts beneath the cabin floor to the air conditioning bay in the wing centre section. The air conditioning system consists of a Cold Air Unit (CAU) or air cycle refrigeration machine with primary and secondary heat exchangers for each duct. The heat exchangers are cooled by ram air from under-fuselage intakes. An automatic temperature control valve allows controlled quantities of hot air to pass through the CAU to achieve the required temperatures in the aircraft compartments. Downstream of the CAUs is a water separator; any water extracted is drained overboard. One air system feeds the flight deck and the other the aircraft cabin. Temperature control switches for both cabin and flight deck are located in the roof panel on the flight deck. Maximum pressure differential is 7.5 psi (0.52 bars). Pressurised areas can be maintained at a pressure equivalent to an altitude of 8,650ft (2,636m) at an altitude of 37,000ft (11,285m).

Oxygen

Separate oxygen systems are provided for flight crew and passengers. On the short fuselage versions, one 1,870 litre bottle feeds the cockpit area, while a 3,200 litre bottle feeds the main cabin where a drop-out system is installed. Series 500 aircraft have a 2,100 litre bottle feeding the cockpit area; a similar bottle feeds the main cabin, while a third 2,100 litre bottle is fitted when a drop-out system is installed. In addition, three portable oxygen units of 120 litre capacity are provided and stored adjacent to the cabin attendants' seats, and a portable 310 litre capacity unit is stowed in the cockpit area. Apart from executive aircraft, no newly delivered Series 200 aircraft were fitted with drop-out oxygen systems except Series 203AEs for Braniff Airways. Of newly delivered Series 300 aircraft, only the Series 304AXs for British Eagle were fitted with a drop-out system. All Series 475s had drop-out oxygen systems installed except the Air Pacific Series 479FUs, which had provision for the fitment. Drop-out systems were not fitted to Series 509EW/510ED/537GF/539GL aircraft, while provision was made for the system to be installed on Series 501EX/527FK/530FX aircraft. All other Series 500 aircraft had a drop-out oxygen system fitted as standard. Charging point for replenishing the oxygen systems is beneath the forward fuselage.

Hydraulics

The hydraulic system operates wheel brakes, elevators, flaps, forward and ventral airstairs, landing gear, lift dumpers, nosewheel steering, rudder, spoilers/air brakes, tailplane incidence, yaw damper and windscreen wipers. The system pressure is 3,000 psi (207 bars). Two independent systems are provided, driven by pumps on each engine, and each system incorporates an accumulator to store system pressure. Standby pumps are provided on each system driven by an AC motor, while a further back-up is provided by a DC motor-driven pump powered by the aircraft batteries. The DC motor pump provides additional pressure to operate normal and emergency brake accumulators, captain's windscreen wiper, and the ventral and forward airstairs should both engine-driven and standby pumps fail. Each system provides power independently to tailplane incidence, wing flaps, rudder, rudder feel and elevator feel. Other hydraulically powered items are operated by either one system or the other.

Electrics

The aircraft uses a 115/200 volt three-phase 400Hz constant frequency AC generating system, fed by two 30kVa Plessey/Westinghouse AC generators (Series 203AE, 212AR, 401AK, 402AP, 410AQ and 527FK have 40kVa rated generators) driven by Plessey mechanical/pneumatic Constant Speed Drive and Starter units, one mounted on each engine. A similar generator is mounted on the Auxiliary Power Unit (APU) and is shaft driven. The two main generators supply two individual AC load bus-bars which are normally isolated but are automatically connected should one of the generators fail. They are also connected when the APU is the sole power supply or when an external power supply is connected. Should a complete main power failure occur, emergency power is provided through an inverter powered by two 24 volt lead-acid batteries. Each of these has a capacity of 25 ampere hours at the one hour rate. Electrically heated elements de-ice the pitot heads, water drains and stall warning sensors, while an automatic ice detector mounted below the cockpit window to port runs continuously in flight.

An independent emergency lighting system is fed by nickel/cadmium batteries, providing illumination of the passenger cabin, emergency exits, doors and essential notices.

A floor proximity lighting system has been fitted to many aircraft more recently to assist in the emergency evacuation of passengers should the cabin become filled with smoke (this is now mandatory with some licensing authorities).

Water System

Potable water is supplied for washing, galley and drinking purposes from a system supplied by a 20 Imp Gall (91 litres) tank which is pressurised at 10 psi (0.70kg/cm^2). Waste water is discharged overboard through heated drain masts.

ELECTRONICS AND EQUIPMENT

Communications and navigational equipment is generally to the customer's individual requirements. A typical customer fit would include dual VHF communications equipment to ARINC 546 supplied by Collins, Marconi or Bendix; Collins HF communications equipment; Collins or Marconi dual VHF navigational equipment to ARINC 547A including glideslope receivers and Bendix, Collins or Marconi marker receiver; single or dual Bendix DFA73, Collins DF203/DF206 or Marconi AD370 ADF; Bendix, Collins, Cossor or Wilcox ATC transponder to ARINC 532D; AWA, Collins, Marconi, Federal or RCA DME; Bendix, Collins or Ekco weather radar; flight data recorder, flight deck voice recorder to ARINC 557 and crew and service interphones.

An Elliott/Bendix 2000 series autopilot is fitted with an auto-throttle system available as an option on later production aircraft. A single or dual Collins FD105 (Series 200) or FD108 (all other Series) flight director system is installed on all One-Elevens with the exception of the Series 510ED. Bendix compass systems are fitted to all Series 200 (except 217EA) and 300 aircraft. Sperry C9 or CL11 compass systems are fitted to all other aircraft, with the exception of the Series 510ED. This last version was unique in being fitted with a Smiths

Industries SF5 flight director and compass system.

A Sundstrand Ground Proximity Warning System compatible to ARINC 594 was installed on late production aircraft, while a Bendix radio altimeter was an option on Series 475 and 500 aircraft.

The Series 485GDs were fitted with Marconi Omega Long Range Navigation Systems.

OVERALL DIMENSIONS

	Imperial	Metric	Type
Wing span	88ft 6in 93ft 6in	26.98m 28.50m	Series 200/300/400 Series 475/500
Wing chord at root	16ft 5in 16ft 9½in	5.01m 5.11m	All versions Series 500 (late production)
Wing chord at tip	5ft 3½in 5ft 5in	1.61m 1.65m	All versions Series 500 (late production)
Wing aspect ratio	8.0 8.5 8.65		Series 200/300/400 Series 500 (early production) Series 475/500
Sweepback at quarter chord	20 degrees		
Overall length	93ft 6in 107ft 0in	28.50m 32.61m	Series 200/300/400/475 Series 500
Length of fuselage	83ft 10in 97ft 4in	25.55m 29.67m	Series 200/300/400/475 Series 500
Maximum fuselage width/depth	11ft 2in	3.40m	All versions
Overall height	24ft 6in	7.47m	All versions
Tailplane span	29ft 6in	8.99m	All versions
Ground clearance to fuselage	2ft 7½in	0.80m	All versions
Wheel track	14ft 3in	4.34m	All versions
Wheel base	33ft 1in 33ft 0in 41ft 4in	10.08m 10.06m 12.60m	Series 200/300/400 Series 475 Series 500
Overall turning radius (measured to outer wing tip)	51ft 6in 56ft 0in	15.70m 17.07m	Series 200/300/400/475 Series 500

Overall Dimension; continued	Imperial	Metric	Type
Forward passenger door			
Height	5ft 8in	1.73m	All versions
Width	2ft 8in	0.82m	All versions
Height to sill	7ft 0in	2.13m	All versions
Ventral entrance			
Height	6ft 0in	1.83m	All versions
Width	2ft 4in	0.71m	All versions
Height to sill	7ft 0in	2.13m	All versions
Galley service door			
Height	4ft 0in	1.22m	All versions
Width	2ft 3in	0.69m	All versions
Height to sill	7ft 0in	2.13m	All versions
Overwing emergency exits			
Height	3ft 0in	0.91m	All versions
Width	1ft 8in	0.51m	All versions
Freight door (main deck)			
Height	6ft 1in	1.85m	Series 400/475
Width	10ft 0in	3.05m	Series 400/475
Height to sill	7ft 0in	2.13m	Series 400/475
Underfloor freight door (fwd)			
Height (projected)	2ft 7in	0.79m	All versions
Width	3ft 0in	0.91m	All versions
Height to sill	3ft 7in	1.09m	All versions
Underfloor freight door (rear)			
Height (projected)	2ft 2in	0.66m	All versions
Width	3ft 0in	0.91m	All versions
Height to sill	4ft 3in	1.30m	All versions

INTERNAL DIMENSIONS

	Imperial	Metric	Type
Cabin length (excluding flight deck)	56ft 10in 70ft 4in	17.31m 21.44m	Series 200/300/400/475 Series 500
Maximum cabin width	10ft 4in	3.16m	All versions
Maximum cabin height	6ft 6in	1.98m	All versions
Maximum floor width	9ft 6in	2.98m	All versions
Floor area (approx)	506ft^2 665ft^2	47.00m^2 61.78m^2	Series 200/300/400/475 Series 500
Forward freight hold Height Width Length Volume	 3ft 0in 7ft 5in 17ft 11in 22ft 10in 354ft^3 451ft^3	 0.91m 2.26m 2.46m 6.96m 10.02m^3 12.77m^3	 All versions All versions Series 200/300/400/475 Series 500 Series 200/300/400/475 Series 500
Rear freight hold Height Width Length Volume	 3ft 0in 7ft 5in 11ft 6in 10ft 0in 15ft 0in 180ft^3 156ft^3 236ft^3	 0.91m 2.26m 3.51m 3.06m 4.59m 5.09m^3 4.42m^3 6.68m^3	 All versions All versions Series 200/300/400 Series 475 Series 500 Series 200/300/400 Series 475 Series 500

EXTERNAL AREAS

	Imperial	Metric	Type
Gross wing area	980ft^2 1031ft^2	91.04m^2 95.78m^2	Series 200/300/400 Series 475/500
Ailerons (total)	30.8ft^2	2.86m^2	All versions
Flaps (total)	175.6ft^2	16.30m^2	All versions
Spoilers (total)	24.8ft^2	2.30m^2	Series 400/475/500
Vertical tail surface (total)	117.4ft^2	10.90m^2	All versions
Rudder (including tab)	32.8ft^2	3.05m^2	All versions
Horizontal tail surface (total)	257ft^2	23.9m^2	All versions
Elevators (including tab)	70.4ft^2	6.55m^2	All versions

WEIGHTS AND LOADINGS

	Imperial (lb)	Metric (kg)	Type
Typical Operating Weight Empty (varies with customer fit)	46,405 48,722 50,822 51,822 51,731 54,582	21,049 22,098 23,050 23,505 23,464 24,758	Series 200 Series 300 Series 400 NAL 400 Series 475 Series 500
Maximum Payload (typical figure)	17,595 20,025 21,269 26,418	7,981 9,083 9,647 11,983	Series 200 Series 300/400 Series 475 Series 500
Maximum Take-off Weight (typical figure)	79,000 88,500 98,500 104,500	35,833 40,142 44,678 47,400	Series 200 Series 300/400 Series 475 Series 500

The Maximum Ramp Weight figure for each model is 500lb (226.8kg) greater than the quoted MTOW figure shown above.

	Imperial	Metric	Type
Maximum Landing Weight	71,000lb 78,000lb 87,000lb	32,204kg 35,380kg 39,462kg	Series 200 Series 300/400 Series 475/500
Maximum Zero Fuel Weight (varies between customers - typical figure shown)	64,000lb 71,000lb 68,500lb 73,000lb 81,000lb	29,030kg 32,204kg 31,070kg 33,112kg 36,741kg	Series 200 Series 300/400 NAL 400 Series 475 Series 500
Maximum Wing Loading	78.3lb/ft^2 88.8lb/ft^2 89.2lb/ft^2 96.7lb/ft^2	382.0kg/m^2 433.6kg/m^2 435.5kg/m^2 472.0kg/m^2	Series 200 Series 300/400 Series 475 Series 500
Maximum Power Loading	3.82lb/lb st 3.96lb/lb st 4.16lb/lb st	390.1kg/kN 400.3kg/kN 424.7kg/kN	Series 300/400 Series 475 Series 500

PERFORMANCE

Maximum level cruising speed at 21,000ft (6,400m) TAS:		
	548mph (475kt, 882km/h)	Series 200/300/400
	541mph (470kt, 871km/h)	Series 475/500
Fuel economical cruising speed at 25,000ft (7,620m) TAS:		
	507mph (440kt, 815km/h)	Series 200/300/400
	461mph (400kt, 742km/h)	Series 475/500
Maximum never exceed diving speed (structural) EAS at sea level:		
	460mph (399kt, 740km/h)	Series 200
	472mph (410kt, 760km/h)	Series 300/400/475/500
Stalling speed (take-off flap setting) EAS:		
	125mph (109kt, 201km/h)	Series 200
	131mph (114kt, 211km/h)	Series 300/400
	114mph (99kt, 184km/h)	Series 475
	121mph (105kt, 195km/h)	Series 500
Rate of climb at sea level at 345mph (300kt, 555km/h) EAS:		
	2,500ft/min (762m/min)	Series 200
	2,580ft/min (786m/min)	Series 300/400
	2,480ft/min (756m/min)	Series 475
	2,280ft/min (695m/min)	Series 500
Maximum cruise height:	35,000ft (10,670m)	Series 200
	37,000ft (11,285m)	Series 300/400/475/500
	40,000ft (12,200m)	NAL 400
Still air range with maximum fuel, ISA, with reserves for 230 miles (200nm, 370km) diversion and 45 minutes hold:		
	2,130 miles (1,849nm, 3,430km)	Series 200 *
	2,250 miles (1,954nm, 3,620km)	Series 300/400
	2,300 miles (1,997nm, 3,700km)	Series 475
	2,165 miles (1,880nm, 3,484km)	Series 500
Still air range with capacity payload, ISA, reserves as above:		
	875 miles (759nm, 1,140km)	Series 200
	1,430 miles (1,241nm, 2,300km)	Series 300/400
	1,865 miles (1,619nm, 3,000km)	Series 475
	1,705 miles (1,480nm, 2,744km)	Series 500

Ferry range with zero payload, ISA, reserves as above:	
2,617 miles (2,272nm, 4,215km)	Series 200 *
2,477 miles (2,150nm, 3,988km)	Series 300
2,430 miles (2,109nm, 3,912km)	Series 400
2,339 miles (2,030nm, 3,766km)	Series 475
2,206 miles (1,915nm, 3,552km)	Series 500
3,950 miles (3,431nm, 6,357km)	NAL 400

Still air range with maximum standard fuel, ten passengers plus 45 mins reserve:	
3,753 miles (3,259nm, 6,040km)	NAL 400

Still air range with maximum optional fuel, eight passengers plus 45 mins reserve:	
3,950 miles (3,431nm, 6,357km)	NAL 400

Take-off run at sea level, ISA:	
6,500ft (1,981m)	Series 200
7,500ft (2,286m)	Series 300
7,450ft (2,270m)	Series 400
5,500ft (1,676m)	Series 475
6,500ft (1,981m)	Series 500

Balanced take-off to 35ft (10.70m) at sea level, ISA:	
6,850ft (2,088m)	Series 200
8,000ft (2,438m)	Series 300
7,800ft (2,377m)	Series 400
5,900ft (1,798m)	Series 475
7,300ft (2,225m)	Series 500

Landing distance (BCAR) at sea level, ISA, at maximum landing weight:	
4,720ft (1,439m)	Series 475

Flap operating speeds

	Setting	
Take-off	Approach	Landing
Series 200		
253mph (220kt, 408km/h)	207mph (180kt, 334km/h)	190mph (165kt, 306km/h)
Series 300/400		
276mph (240kt, 445km/h)	220mph (191kt, 354km/h)	207mph (180kt, 334km/h)
Series 475		
276mph (240kt, 445km/h)	220mph (191kt, 354km/h)	211mph (183kt, 339km/h)
Series 500		
276mph (240kt, 445km/h)	222mph (193kt, 358km/h)	211mph (183kt, 339km/h)

Landing gear operating speeds		
	253mph (220kt, 408km/h)	Series 200
	265mph (230kt, 427km/h)	All versions except Srs.200

* With optional centre fuel tank

MAINTENANCE

The maintenance programme for all versions of the One-Eleven was arranged from the outset in small packages of work which would take no longer than eight hours' elapsed time to accomplish and which, where possible, would avoid the use of specialised equipment. The original draft maintenance programme was set up by three committees, which consisted of representatives of customer airlines, BAC and Rolls-Royce. The three committees comprised one for structures, one for systems and the third for the powerplant. After the draft had been agreed it was presented in July 1964 to the US Federal Aviation Authority and to the UK Air Registration Board for their approval; the Maintenance Programme was given formal approval soon after this.

As originally proposed, the Maintenance Check cycles comprised a basic routine maintenance input at 500 flying hours, with minor inputs at 125 and 250 flying hours. Further tests and checks were to be carried out at 1,000 and 1,500 flying hours. Following continuous monitoring of in-service experience, this system was gradually modified until 1977, when a new system was adopted. This revolved around an annual base visit at 2,400 flying hours, which approximated to the average annual utilisation of the type by airline operators. Each operator has amended the basic maintenance cycle to fit in with its own requirements. The basic cycle is as follows and is repeated with the second Check C at 4,800 flying hours. This is known as the Check 2C, and the third at 7,200 is known as the Check 3C etc.

```
Check A        100 flying hours or one month
Check B1       300 flying hours or six months      or   300 flights
Check B2       600 flying hours or 12 months       or   600 flights
Check ½C     1,200 flying hours or two years       or 1,200 flights
Check C      2,400 flying hours or four years      or 2,400 flights
```

The figures quoted alternatively from flying hours are for use where utilisation is very low. This mainly applies to aircraft employed in the executive role.

The Maintenance Programme consists of recommended periods between repeated actions. These are controlled by accumulated flying hours and/or landings and/or elapsed calendar times. Some components have finite lives, while others have never exceeded inspection and/or service periods. Generally speaking, all such items are arranged in packages of work and are conveniently programmed into the above maintenance cycle.

PRODUCT SUPPORT

BAC's product support organisation provided its customers with comprehensive after-sales support. On the engineering side, the organisation had a team of fully trained service engineers who were available to go to the assistance of operators worldwide at short notice. The organisation also provided training courses for customer engineering staff at fully equipped schools at Weybridge and Hurn. Technical publications to ATA 100 specifications were supplied to customers and were regularly updated. These technical manuals were later transferred to a microfilm/reader system; microfilm readers with printer facilities saved considerable storage space and were much more efficient to use.

Weybridge was the original home of the spares provisioning service. A comprehensive stock of spares was maintained at this centre with a fully automated order processing system. For American customers a second customer support centre (including spares provisioning) is based at Arlington, Virginia, in the USA. The Weybridge centre was located conveniently close to London's Heathrow and Gatwick Airports for early despatch of AOG spares. These two centres had already been set up in support of Viscount, Vanguard and Britannia operators throughout the world. BAC organised regular Operators Conferences, where One-Eleven users were encouraged to send representatives; at these meetings mutual technical problems could be discussed and reviewed with the help of BAC's own service representatives.

When the Weybridge centre was closed, the customer support organisation was transferred to the Filton plant outside Bristol. This site was located close to the motorway system for early despatch of spares.

Customer aircrew were trained on their own aircraft at BAC's United Kingdom bases or at the airline's base if that was required.

The support organisation also provided route analysis and operations data for individual customers or prospective users of the type through the use of two Pegasus computers.

FLYING THE BAC ONE-ELEVEN

The BAC One-Eleven followed the practice established by the Vanguard and VC10 of providing a comfortable and well-designed workplace for its flight crew; it did so, however, in a flight deck which was much smaller than its two big brothers, being more reminiscent of the earlier Viscount. It also differed from the other Vickers/BAC products in introducing an American flight system in the form of the Collins FD105 on the earlier 200s and the more advanced FD108 on the later aircraft, including all the 400s and 500s with the exception of the 18 510 series for BEA, which uniquely were fitted with the Smiths Flight System developed for the De Havilland Trident.

As was common in British aircraft of the period, the pre-flight check list for the first flight of the day on the One-Eleven is lengthy, including many systems checks which would be more appropriate to an engineering input. I suspect that the only effect of this process is to wear out the back-up and standby systems much earlier than would otherwise have been the case. With this task out of the way, however, the remainder of the checks are straightforward and take little time.

The onboard Garrett APU can be started from the aircraft battery and provides air-conditioning and electrical power. With increasing demands over the years, however, especially from the galleys which were fitted into the aircraft in the 1980s, it can be necessary to have ground power plugged in to allow the galleys to function properly. Cabin crew checks also include much equipment which is a later addition to the aeroplane such as toilet smoke detectors and extinguishers, floor escape path lighting and inflatable escape slides.

Passengers can be boarded simultaneously through the forward and ventral airstairs, which makes the One-Eleven more independent of ground facilities than many more modern aircraft, and the APU provides all the facilities needed for engine starting, which involves a lot of switching of air and fuel supplies by the pilot. Many converting new Captains, more used to Pratt & Whitney "press the button and go" techniques, spent some time mastering the art of starting twin Rolls-Royce Speys, an action requiring 23 separate switch selections. If the air output from the APU is low or the outside air particularly hot, an element of juggling is required to feed the right quantity of fuel in to avoid exceeding the 600°C start limitation. Once running, however, a Jekyll and Hyde transformation takes place, as the Spey can now be slam accelerated, reversed and generally abused with impunity in a way an American engine would baulk at.

With both engines started the One-Eleven can, if desired, be reversed off the stand under its own power. The technique for this party trick involves first moving forward a short distance to remove flat spots from the tyres and free the brakes. Selection of idle reverse thrust will usually then move the aircraft backwards, and steering is effected through the normal tiller controls. Once taxying forward the provision of both pressure and temperature gauges for the brakes means that the pilot can avoid any overheating which can be a problem on short sectors with minimum turnround times. The normal means of achieving any cooling required is to leave the landing gear extended for a short time after take-off.

The actual take-off roll is very straightforward, with control of the nosewheel being available through the rudder pedals until sufficient speed is achieved for the rudder to become effective. Power settings up to full throttle are available on the Spey 511 engine fitted to the 400 series aircraft, though full throttle on the 500 series Spey 512 is only used in an emergency. Normally a significant amount of de-rating is used both to extend engine life and reduce noise.

Latterly the BAC One-Eleven became well known as one of the noisiest aircraft around. With the "dustbin" shroud fitted to the rear of the Spey the aircraft just crept into Stage 2 noise limits, and British Airways especially spent much time and effort in evolving flying techniques to reduce the noise nuisance as much as possible. Following trials in 1986 at Berlin, using the noise monitors installed at Tempelhof Airport, a procedure was adopted which involved rotating the aircraft at lift off to around 10° nose up, rather less than previously, and accelerating rapidly towards the minimum speed for retracting flap. At 500 feet above the airfield the flaps were retracted to the clean configuration and the power cut back a long way. This sequence gave rise to the classic "flat" take-off observed in the later days of British Airways' One-Eleven operation. At particularly noise sensitive airfields the technique was refined further by adopting a full power take-off and cutting the power back at 500ft by an addition 5%, the intention being to concentrate the noise on the airfield and thereby minimise the disturbance to outlying areas. All of this required very accurate flying from the crews and a high level of concentration, but its success could be seen in the statistics from airfields such as Dusseldorf and Frankfurt, where British Airways' One-Elevens were about three decibels quieter than those of other operators.

The flying controls of the One-Eleven are a little heavier than other similar types. This is because the aircraft was originally designed to have power assitance only for the rudder control. Following the crash of the prototype in a deep stall, however, a powered elevator was added, but the manually controlled ailerons were retained and, in order to keep the control forces in harmony, the elevator has been made heavier than would otherwise have been the case. Considering the aircraft comes from the same stable as the 66,000kg all-manual Vanguard, I suppose that it's a miracle that anyone under 15 stones can get it off the ground at all!

Engine malfunctions encountered during the take-off and early stages of the climb are easily contained, as the engine location at the rear of the fuselage does not lead to any large asymmetric forces in the event of a failure. Likewise the systems are well backed up, with an electric pump for each of the two hydraulic systems, as well as an engine-driven pump and the APU generator available to replace the engine-driven generators for the electrical system if required. The One-Eleven (with the exception of the 475), however, was never over-endowed with surplus power, and accurate control of pitch attitude is needed to maintain a steady single-engined climb.

In the event of a failure of one of the hydraulic systems the aircraft remains completely under control, with all powered flying controls being supplied by the working systems, and even with both systems failed a successful landing can be made flying initially in manual reversion but with emergency systems available to operate the elevator, flaps, brakes, nosewheel steering and landing gear. Likewise any one of the three available generators will automatically take over to provide power to almost all of the electrical system in the event of a failure. Should all three generators fail, then the aircraft battery will power most of the captain's flight instruments for 36 minutes to allow a successful landing to be made.

If the BAC One-Eleven has a weak link, it is in the area of the air-conditioning and pressurisation systems, which are a veritable Achilles heel. The loss of one of the two systems restricts the operating altitude and further despatch of the aircraft; for instance to allow a return to main base for repairs also requires that icing conditions are avoided as the same air systems also supply hot air de-icing to the wings and tailplane. The high pressure ducting from the engines, the pressure reducing valves in the system and the temperature control valves are all needed because the Spey contributes very hot high pressure bleed air to the system which must be controlled and cooled before it can be used. Each of these components has proved vulnerable to damage, especially the various valves in the system, which on many occasions had to be operated manually on the ground to allow air to reach the engine in order to start it.

In the early days of Spey operations the engineering staff were warned to be more discreet when freeing stuck valves prior to departure as the passengers were becoming concerned at the sight of a large amount of brute force being associated with an equally large amount of skill in knowing just where to hit the engine!!

Once cruising at the maximum altitude of 37,000 feet, the only difficulty is in following the navigation instructions given by ATC more used to dealing with a later generation of aircraft capable of finding any given spot on the globe with a little button-pushing to the flight management system. On aircraft of the One-Eleven's vintage, this is transformed into a flurry of maps, a guess at the wind and a rough DR (dead reckoning) heading which, strangely enough, usually managed to get us there. Often the most accurate way of finding points such as BARLU on the French coast was to use the weather radar tipped down to reflect the distinctive coastline, reminiscent of the "H2S" of wartime Lancasters.

The planning for the approach took advantage of the great flexibility of the aeroplane, which could maintain any speed between 210 and 350kt until quite close to the destination. Although not equipped with leading edge devices, the wing was quite sophisticated in its design and could be flown in the clean configuration as slow as 160kt. On the other hand, the 400 series and later 500 series aircraft had a maximum indicated speed of over 350kt, and the large speedbrakes mounted on the wing upper surface allowed the aircraft to be slowed rapidly to circuit and approach speeds. Where Air Traffic Control on occasion could not authorise descent until quite close to the airfield, either by virtue of conflicting traffic or terrain clearance, then the usual technique adopted was to slow to 220kt and then, with descent clearance obtained, to lower the landing gear and pull full speedbrake, at the same time lowering the nose and accelerating towards 300kt plus. The limit to the descent rate was usually that to which the Captain was willing to subject the passengers in terms of the nose-down attitude, but with an empty aeroplane on flight test I have seen instantaneous rates of descent approaching 20,000 feet per minute.

In bad weather conditions the well-harmonised controls, combined with the small tailfin and reasonably high wing loading, combined to give a relatively comfortable ride in all but the strongest turbulence. It has long been held that Vickers made their money building battleships and carried the same construction techniques into aircraft construction, and the reputation for them being carved from the solid seems to have been carried across to BAC with the One-Eleven, which knowledge certainly made the crews more comfortable when faced with a violent approach on a dark and dirty night, even if the passengers didn't share their feelings. Towards the end of the One-Eleven's career, an African-owned example succeeded in hitting a power cable on the approach to land; the subsequent damage to the local power supplies fortunately did not prevent the almost undamaged aircraft from making a successful landing. Similarly, when an Asian example overran the runway through a railway embankment and onto a road, the only casualties were in the truck which drove into the side of the aeroplane.

From the earliest days the BAC One-Eleven pursued an all-weather landing capability, with landings in fog to "Category 2" limits being demonstrated by the 400 series prototype in 1966. This made use of much work done by autopilot manufacturer Elliot Automation for the VC10 and was further refined by 1968 for the BEA order for 510 series aircraft, which were equipped for fully automatic landings in "Category 3" conditions. In British Airways' service these aircraft were eventually operated to a decision height of 60ft in a minimum visibility of 250 metres. Although this was a little more restrictive than the contemporary DH Trident's limits of 12ft and 75 metres, it was achieved with none of the complexity of the acknowledged pioneer of autoland and at a fraction of the cost; British Airways, British Caledonian and Maersk Air were however the only airlines to gain Cat 3 approval for their One-Elevens.

When operating to Cat 3 limits the whole process could appear deceptively peaceful, as fog conditions generally are accompanied by very light winds, and the capability of the autoland system required a slow approach to be flown with all configuration changes completed some distance from landing.

In British Airways operation the co-pilot would be controlling the aircraft through the autopilot, altering speed through the autothrottle and asking for flaps and landing gear to be extended at the appropriate moment. This freed the captain to negotiate an approach clearance with ATC, check the weather and monitor the conduct of the operation.

Approaching 1000ft above the airfield the visibility is checked, as is the autopilot status, and the final approach is commenced. Height checks from here on are from the dual indicators for the Radio Altimeter, and practically any failure will cause the autopilot to disengage automatically, in which case a go-around will be flown on instruments by the co-pilot, who remains flying on instruments throughout. At 400ft the final confidence checks on the autopilot are completed, and the annunciator for the autoland changes to "Flare Arm". Subsequent calls of "100 above" and "decide" come from the co-pilot at 160ft and 60ft. If at this point the captain is happy with what he can see of the runway lights, then a call from him of "land" signifies that he has taken control of the autopilot and is continuing with the autoland.

If the autopilot fails from this point on he will land the aircraft manually, with a slight flare to check the descent rate, close the throttles and check back slightly for touchdown. Normally, however, the autopilot will complete the autoland, although it uses a much higher nose-up landing attitude than its human counterpart and will often close the throttles at what seems to be a very early stage in the process. This can be a temptation for some manual intervention, though; with the limited visibility this often leads to an even more solid arrival than the aeroplane would have achieved if left to its own devices.

After touchdown the lift dump and reverse thrust are deployed manually and the excellent anti-skid brakes applied. Compared with the earlier Maxaret type of anti-skid system, the Hytrol electronic system fitted to most BAC One-Elevens is effective and reliable. It is very unusual to have a tyre burst unless there is a fault on the anti-skid itself, and it even allows touchdowns to be made with the brakes applied, though I have never met a One-Eleven pilot who was bold enough to find out if it worked!!

In summation, then, the BAC One-Eleven was a favourite with everyone who flew it, with well-harmonised controls and pleasant flying qualities. The flight deck was well laid out, although some of the systems were showing their age, and the lack of excess power could be distinctly embarrassing when "hot and heavy" out of Malaga, for instance, where a wide diversion over the sea was needed to get enough height to cross the coastal mountains. These little problems could all be forgotten, though, when making a gently curving approach to a short visual final, when the good points all combined to make flying a pleasure and landing a dream.

BAC ONE-ELEVEN DELIVERIES

Year	Series 200	Series 300	Series 400	Series 500	Series 475	ROMBAC 500	Total
1965	33	-	1	-	-	-	34
1966	10	3	33	-	-	-	46
1967	4	5	11	-	-	-	20
1968	6	1	9	7	-	-	23
1969	3	-	10	28	-	-	41
1970	-	-	3	19	-	-	22
1071	-	-	2	11	1	-	14
1972	-	-	-	5	2	-	7
1973	-	-	-	1	1	-	2
1974	-	-	-	2	2	-	4
1975	-	-	-	-	2	-	2
1976	-	-	-	-	-	-	-
1977	-	-	-	6	-	-	6
1978	-	-	-	2	1	-	3
1979	-	-	-	-	-	-	-
1980	-	-	-	3	-	-	3
1981	-	-	-	1	1	-	2
1982	-	-	-	1	-	1	2
1983	-	-	-	-	-	1	1
1984	-	-	-	-	2	1	3
1985	-	-	-	-	-	-	-
1986	-	-	-	-	-	2	2
1987	-	-	-	-	-	1	1
1988	-	-	-	-	-	1	1
1989	-	-	-	-	-	1	1
1990	-	-	-	-	-	-	-
1991	-	-	-	-	-	1	1
1992	-	-	-	-	-	-	-
Total	56	9	69	86	12	9	241

One-Eleven Series Identification System

Each aircraft produced was identified by a model number and generally a two-letter individual customer requirements code. As each prospective customer was identified, a two-number identity was added to the first number of the series type. As an example, the first prospective customer for the Series 200 was British United Airways, who were allocated the model number 201. Bonanza Airlines were allocated the model number 206 but in the event received no aircraft. It can be assumed that missing numbers in each series were allocated to prospective customers who failed to purchase aircraft. Research has revealed some of these numbers (such as Series 405 for Aviaco and Series 209 for Hawaiian Airlines), but unfortunately the full list has not been traced.

The two-letter code indicates the work package required to bring the aircraft up to that customer's individual requirements. The position and supplier of galley and toilet equipment, avionics fit, additional tankage, specific interior fit etc would be identified through the two-letter system. Thus Aer Lingus aircraft were built as Series 208ALs, being the eighth prospective Series 200 purchaser, and the 'AL' indicating that company's variations to the basic aircraft.

In some cases both numbers and two-letter codes were allocated to prospective customers where negotiations had reached an advanced level but which still failed to purchase. Examples of these are Series 511EY for BKS Air Transport and Series 538GG for Faucett of Peru.

Originally all aircraft were built to order; later aircraft were built in advance of orders, thus facilitating early delivery to new customers. These were built to a basic standard which could later be adapted to individual customer requirements. These basic standard aircraft were designated by the following model numbers; the Series 475s were identified as model 475EZs and the Series 500s as model 500ENs, while the equivalent Rombac basic aircraft are model 475RAs and 500RBs. There were no basic model numbers for Series 200, 300 or 400 aircraft, since all such aircraft were built to order.

The following lists show all known numerical and two-letter codes. Bracketed customer names indicate that no aircraft were actually built to these specifications.

200AB	British Aircraft Corp	320L-AZ	Laker Airways
201AC	British United Airways	400AM	British Aircraft Corp
202AD	(Western Airways Ltd)	401AK	American Airlines
203AE	Braniff Airways	402AP	Philippine Airlines
204AF	Mohawk Airlines	403	(Page Airways)
205AG	(Kuwait Airways)	405	(Aviaco)
206AH	(Bonanza Airlines)	406	(British Eagle Intl)
207AJ	Central African Airways	407AW	TACA International
208AL	Aer Lingus Teoranta	408EF	Channel Airways
209	(Hawaiian Airlines)	409AY	LACSA
211AH	Helmut Horten GmbH	410AQ	Victor Comptometer Inc
212AR	Tenneco Inc	412EB	LANICA
214	(Page Airways)	413FA	Bavaria Fluggesellschaft
215AU	Aloha Airlines	414EG	Bavaria Fluggesellschaft
217EA	Royal Australian Air Force	416EK	Autair Intl Airways
301AG	Kuwait Airways	417EJ	(United States Air Force)
303	(British Midland Airways)	419EP	Engelhard Industries
304AX	British Eagle International	420EL	Austral/ALA

81

422EQ	VASP	516FP	Aviateca
423ET	Força Aerea Brasileira	517FE	Bahamas Airways
424EU	TAROM	518FG	Autair/Court Line Avn
432FD	Gulf Aviation Co	520FN	Sadia/TransBrasil
475EZ	British Aircraft Corp	521FH	Austral/ALA
476FM	Faucett	523FJ	British Midland Airways
479FU	Air Pacific	524FF	Germanair
480GB	(Royal Air Force - Queen's Flight)	525FT	TAROM
481FW	Air Malawi	527FK	Philippine Airlines
485GD	SOAF	528FL	Bavaria Fluggesellschaft
487GK	TAROM	529FR	Phoenix Airways
488GH	Mouaffak al Midani	530FX	British Caledonian A/W
492GM	McAlpine Aviation	531FS	LACSA
496RD	(TAROM)	534FY	(LANICA)
500EN	British Aircraft Corp	537GF	Cyprus Airways
501EX	British United Airways	538GG	(Faucett)
509EW	Caledonian Airways	539GL	British Airways
510ED	British European Airways	561RC	TAROM
511EY	(BKS Air Transport)	562RC	Rombac (Customer)
515FB	Panair/Paninternational		

Additional two-letter codes have been identified which were not in fact used; these are as follows:

FZ	Series 500 proposed for Air Rhodesia
JA	Basic Series 670 proposed for the Japanese market
JB	Basic Series 600 proposed for the Japanese market
RE	Proposed Rombac Series 500 VIP layout

TOTAL UNITED KINGDOM PRODUCTION

Type	No	Engine
200AB	1	Spey 506-14
201AC	11	Spey 506-14A
203AE	14	Spey 506-14D
204AF	18	Spey 506-14D
207AJ	2	Spey 511-14
208AL	4	Spey 506-14
211AH	1	Spey 506-14A
212AR	2	Spey 506-14
215AU	3	Spey 506-14D
217AU	2	Spey 511-14
Total	58	Includes prototype w/o + one production a/c w/o before del

Type	No	Engine
400AM	1	Spey 511-14
401AK	30	Spey 511-14
402AP	4	Spey 511-14
407AW	2	Spey 511-14W
408EF	3	Spey 511-14
409AY	2	Spey 511-14W
410AQ	1	Spey 511-14
412EB	1	Spey 511-14W
413FA	1	Spey 511-14W
414EG	4	Spey 511-14W
416EK	4	Spey 511-14
419EP	1	Spey 511-14
420EL	4	Spey 511-14W
422EQ	2	Spey 511-14W
423ET	2	Spey 511-14W
424EU	6	Spey 511-14
432FD	2	Spey 511-14W
Total	70	

Type	No	Engine
501EX	8	Spey 512-14DW
509EW	4	Spey 512-14DW
510ED	18	Spey 512-14E
515FB	4	Spey 512-14DW
516FP	1	Spey 512-14DW
517FE	3	Spey 512-14DW
518FG	9	Spey 512-14DW
520FN	3	Spey 512-14DW
521FH	3	Spey 512-14DW
523FJ	3	Spey 512-14DW
524FF	4	Spey 512-14DW
525FT	7	Spey 512-14DW
527FK	5	Spey 512-14DW
528FL	3	Spey 512-14DW
529FR	1	Spey 512-14DW
530FX	1	Spey 512-14DW
531FS	3	Spey 512-14DW
537GF	3	Spey 512-14DW
539GL	3	Spey 512-14DW
Total	86	

Type	No	Engine
301AG	3	Spey 511-14
304AX	2	Spey 511-14
320L-AZ	4	Spey 511-14
Total	9	

Type	No	Engine
476FM	2	Spey 512-14DW
479FU	2	Spey 512-14DW
481FW	1	Spey 512-14DW
485GD	3	Spey 512-14DW
487GK	1	Spey 512-14DW
488GH	1	Spey 512-14DW
492GM	2	Spey 512-14DW
Total	12	

OPERATORS OF THE ONE-ELEVEN

Included in this section are all known airline operators of One-Elevens both past and present in alphabetical order. The various types and numbers of aircraft are detailed for each entry and the use to which each operator has put its fleet. At the end of each entry is a list of the registrations of aircraft used by that operator, together with the constructor's numbers where known. Bracketed registrations are those of aircraft which were identified as planned to be operated by that carrier but which, in the event, failed to do so. Each company's two-letter flight code and main base is shown where known (in some cases three letter codes are shown where a two letter one has not been identified). More detailed individual aircraft histories can be found by cross-reference to the section detailing these by constructor's number order. At the rear of the section is a selection of scheduled One-Eleven route maps grouped geographically.

Specialist non-airline users of the type are included in some instances, as are executive users who purchased new build aircraft. To include all executive users in this section would have been an impossible task; constant changes of ownership have taken place, and in many cases doubts exist over which company actually operated the aircraft. Many of the changes can be traced by reading the individual aircraft history section.

ADC Airlines (Aviation Development Company Limited), (ADK), Lagos, Nigeria

Obtained two Srs.203AEs and one Srs.414EG from Guinness Peat Aviation with one del in Dec90 and two in Apr91. Schedules are flown from Lagos to Abuja, Calabar, Kaduna and Port Harcourt, while charters are flown both domestically and to Conakry in Guinea.

5N-AYY 043   5N-BAA 041   5N-BAB 127

Adria Airways, (JP), Ljubljana, Jugoslavia

Known as Inex Adria Airways until 1986, this company leased one Srs.525FT for the summer season 1985, two Srs.525FTs for summer 1986 and three Srs.561RCs for summer 1987, all from TAROM. The aircraft were used to fly tourists on package holidays from many European countries to Jugoslavia.

YU-AKN 266   YU-ANM 266   YU-ANN 272   YU-ANR 401
YU-AN 403   YU-ANT 404

Aer Lingus Teoranta, (EI), Dublin, Eire

Ordered four Srs.208ALs on 03Mar63 laid out in a 74 seat one-class config. They were del between mid May and late Aug65. The first of the fleet entered service on 06Jun65, and the type was used over an extensive scheduled network from Dublin, Shannon and Cork to many UK points, which included Bristol, Cardiff, Edinburgh, Glasgow, Jersey, Liverpool, London (Gatwick and Heathrow) and Manchester. European destinations served included Amsterdam, Barcelona, Brussels, Copenhagen, Dusseldorf, Frankfurt, Lourdes, Madrid, Munich, Paris, Rome and Zurich. One aircraft was leased to LANICA from late Oct66 to late Apr67. The type was withdrawn after operating the last service on 03Mar91, ending nearly 26 years of continuous operation on both scheduled and charter flights.

EI-ANE 049   EI-ANF 050   EI-ANG 051   EI-ANH 052

Aeroamerica Inc, (EO), Berlin, West Germany

Operated a leased Srs.401AK on a programme of charter flights out of Berlin-Tegel from May to Oct76.

N5016   056

Aero Asia, (E4), Karachi, Pakistan

On 06May93 this company inaugurated scheduled services from Karachi to Islamabad and Lahore, both on a twice daily frequency, with two Srs.561RCs leased from TAROM. On 26Jul93 Pasni was added to the network, while Peshawar followed on 01Aug93. By early 1994 Faisalabad and Multan had been added to the destinations served and the fleet increased to five leased Romanian Srs.561RCs.

YR-BRA   401   YR-BRB   402   YR-BRD   404   YR-BRF   406
YR-BRH   408

Aeroflug, Dusseldorf, West Germany

Aeroflug was expected to use three Srs.402APs formerly operated by or on order for Philippine Airlines; although registration marks were reserved, the sale did not materialise.

(D-AFWA)   161   (D-AFWB)   094   (D-AFWC)   091

Aerolineas de Guatemala - Aviateca, (GU), Guatemala City, Guatemala

This company, known as Empresa Guatemalteca de Aviacion SA until 1974, leased a Srs.518FG from Nov70 until a newly ordered Srs.516FP was del in late Mar71, laid out with a 99 seat single class cabin. This was joined by a Srs.518FG which was taken on longterm lease from the manufacturer in Sep75. A further leased aircraft was a Srs.523FJ, which was in use from late April to late May78. The aircraft flew daily services from Guatemala City to Miami, Mexico City and San Pedro Sula (Honduras), with additional schedules to New Orleans and Merida (Mexico). The aircraft were disposed of in Mar79 and Apr80.

TG-ARA   205   TG-AVA   206   TG-AYA   211   TG-AZA   231

Aerotransportes Litoral Argentino - ALA, (SG), Buenos Aires, Argentina

Took delivery of two Srs.420ELs in Sep and Dec68 and one Srs.521FH in Nov69, which had been ordered in a combined deal with Austral Compania Argentina de Transportes Aereos. The Srs.420ELs were laid out in a 74 seat config, while the Srs.521FH was in a 104 seat config. Austral held 30% of the capital of ALA at this time. The two airlines additionally leased a Srs.413FA from late Nov68 until mid Apr69. The type was introduced into service on 29Sep68 on a scheduled network which concentrated on areas to the north of Argentina. Points served from Buenos Aires Aeroparque included Corrientes, Formosa, Parana, Posadas, Resistencia, Rosario, Salta, San Juan, Santa Fe and Tucuman within Argentina, while internationally Antofagasta (Chile) and Asuncion (Paraguay) were served. The airline maintained its identity until 23Jun71 when the two carriers were completely merged into a new airline named Austral Lineas Aereas.

G-AWWG 116   LV-JGX   117   LV-JGY   155   LV-JNT   196
LV-PKA   155   LV-PKB   117

Aerovias Condor de Colombia Ltda - Aerocondor, (OD), Barranquilla, Colombia

On 29Apr66 an order was announced by the British Aircraft Corporation for one Srs.400 aircraft for this operator which was due to be del in Oct67. No One-Eleven was however received by this airline.

Air Alfa, (LFA), Istanbul, Turkey

Lsd a Srs.528FL from JARO International by May94 to operate ad hoc charter flights within Europe.

YR-JBB   238

Air Bristol, (AZX), Filton Aerodrome, Bristol, UK

Two Srs.510EDs were leased from European Aviation Ltd, with the first painted in this company's colours by early Sep93. The company started operations on 11Oct93 flying a Monday to Friday "schedule" on behalf of British Aerospace Airbus Ltd between Filton and Toulouse; additional ad hoc charter work is also undertaken.

G-AVMT 147   G-AVMW 150

Air Congo, (QC), Kinshasa, Zaire

Leased a new Srs.320L-AZ through Laker Airways from May67 to the end of Feb68, followed by a second aircraft of the same type until May68; the aircraft entered service on 15May67. International schedules were flown from Kinshasa to Bujumbura, Entebbe, Lagos, Lusaka, Nairobi and Ndola, while Lubumbashi was also linked with the capital domestically.

G-AVBW 107   G-AVBY 113

Air Florida Inc, (QH), Miami, Florida, USA

British Island Airways Srs.400 One-Eleven aircraft operated from Gatwick to Amsterdam and Frankfurt four times weekly and to Brussels and Dusseldorf twice weekly on behalf of Air Florida, connecting with their six weekly DC-10 scheduled flights between Gatwick and Miami. The aircraft carried Air Florida stickers when so used from May83 until Air Florida ceased operations on 03Jul84.

Air Force of the Sultanate of Oman

Ordered three Srs.485GDs configured with a 79 seat single class cabin; these were del in Dec74, Jan75 and Nov75. The last was fitted with a main deck forward freight door before delivery, and the first two were returned to the manufacturer for similar fitment later on.

551	247	552	249	553	251	1001	247
1002	249	1003	251				

Air France, (AF), Paris, France

Joint services were flown from Apr69 until the end of Oct72 with British European Airways on the Berlin-Tempelhof to Frankfurt and Munich routes using the latter's Srs.510EDs painted in a hybrid colour scheme. Flown by BEA flight deck crews, the cabin staff were drawn from both carriers when so used. During 1986 a once weekly service was flown between Bucharest and Paris-Orly as a joint Air France/TAROM venture using TAROM One-Elevens and AF/RO flight numbers. British Airways One-Elevens have also been used to operate joint AF/BA flights from Nice to Manchester.

Air Illinois Inc, (UX), Carbondale, Illinois, USA

Purchased two Srs.203AEs from USAir with del in Jul82 and Oct83, the second aircraft being leased until purchased in Jan84. A Srs.401AK was leased in May86 to operate on behalf of Atlantic Gulf Airlines; this continued until Sep of the same year. The aircraft were used on schedules from Chicago-O'Hare to Evansville, Springfield and Champaign, all in Illinois and to St Louis until all scheduled services ended on 16Apr84. From this time only charter services were operated.

N217CA   063   N1542   016   N1547   041

Air Malawi Ltd, (QM), Blantyre, Malawi

Leased a Srs.207AJ from Zambia Airways from early Nov70 until the end of Mar72. A new Srs.481FW, laid out in a 74 seat single class config, was del in Feb72, and a Srs.479FU was leased from Air Pacific from Jul74 to Nov75. A Srs.501EX was leased from British Caledonian from late Nov to mid Dec77 and a Srs.530FX from the same source from Oct79 to the end of Apr80. In late Oct80 a Srs.524FF was purchased from Hapag-Lloyd. The aircraft were used on schedules from Lilongwe and Blantyre to Beira, Dar-es-Salaam, Gaborone (Botswana), Harare (Zimbabwe), Johannesburg, Lusaka (Zambia), Mauritius, Nairobi (Kenya) and the Seychelles. They were also used to fly migrant workers to and from South Africa on charter flights. The type was withdrawn from service on 13Jun91 and the aircraft offered for sale.

7Q-YKE   039   7Q-YKF   243   7Q-YKG   245   7Q-YKI   214
7Q-YKJ   240   7Q-YKK   235

Air Malta, (KM), Luqa Airport, Malta

Leased a Srs.530FX from British Caledonian in full Air Malta colours from late Apr to late Oct75. The aircraft was used on the company's schedules to European destinations after inaugurating service on 05May75.

G-AYOP   233

Air Manchester Ltd, Manchester, UK

Ordered two used Srs.416EKs, one of which was del in May82. The second, although painted in Air Manchester colours in Sep82, was not del. A third aircraft, a Srs.320L-AZ, was painted in the company's colours in Jun82 but was not del because of financing problems. The aircraft was mainly used in flying inclusive tour charters for Sureways Travel from Manchester to European holiday destinations. From Sep82 the aircraft was flown with British Air Ferries titles and flight numbers because of licensing problems in Spain. Operations had ceased by Nov82 and the aircraft was put in store.

(G-BKAU)   107   (G-BMAN)   131   G-SURE   129

Air Pacific Ltd, (FJ), Suva, Fiji

Ordered two Srs.479FUs, laid out in a 74 seat one class configuration, with del in Mar72 and Aug73. A used Srs.413FA was purchased in Jun78. The type inaugurated service on 02Apr72 and was used to operate schedules from Suva and Nadi to Tongatapu, Auckland, Port Moresby, Brisbane, Noumea, Port Vila, Apia, Honiara, Pago Pago and Papeete. The Nadi to Papeete flight was operated as a joint service with Union de Transport Aerien (UTA). One aircraft was leased to Air Malawi from Jul74 to Nov75. The type was withdrawn in Mar84.

DQ-FBQ 245   DQ-FBV 250   DQ-FCR 116

Air-Siam Air Company Ltd, (VG), Bangkok, Thailand

Leased a Srs.416EK from Mr Robin Loh of Singapore to operate scheduled flights between Bangkok and Hong Kong from May to Dec72.

9V-BEF 166

Air UK Ltd, (UK), Stansted, Essex, UK

Formed from the merger of British Island Airways and Air Anglia on 16Oct79, this company inherited two Srs.432FDs and one Srs.409AY from the former and continued to operate them on inclusive tour and charter flights to Europe and North Africa. One Srs.416EK was added in Dec79. The One-Elevens were withdrawn when a new airline was set up to operate these aircraft independently using the previously utilised British Island Airways name; this took place on 01Jan82. Air UK later leased the two Srs.432FDs from the new British Island Airways from May85 and Nov85 to Apr88 and Apr87 respectively. Earlier it had been anticipated that the airline might operate two ex-Braniff Srs.203AEs with registrations reserved for them, but this did not happen. The leased aircraft were operated on the Aberdeen to Amsterdam via Edinburgh schedules and from Glasgow to Amsterdam via Newcastle or Leeds. One of the aircraft was later subleased to British Airways from late Nov86 until the end of Apr87.

G-AXBB 162   G-AXMU 157   G-AXOX 121   G-CBIA 166
(G-BLVO) 041   (G-BLVP) 043

Airways International Cymru Ltd, (AK), Cardiff, Wales, UK

Purchased two Srs.304AXs from Quebecair with del in Apr84 and Nov84. A Srs.432FD was leased from Apr84 to Nov84. The aircraft operated inclusive tour and charter flights to European holiday destinations and were also leased to British Midland and Manx Airlines for varying periods of time. The company ceased operations in Jan88.

G-AXMU 157   G-WLAD 112   G-YRMU 110

Air Wisconsin Inc, (UA and ZW), Appleton, Wisconsin, USA

Leased four Srs.201ACs through British Aerospace from Jan85 until Apr86 pending del of new BAe146-200s. The aircraft operated schedules from Chicago-O'Hare to points including Appleton, Cedar Rapids, Green Bay, Kalamazoo, Mosinee, Rhinelander and Toledo.

N101EX	007	N104EX	011	N105EX	012	N107EX 085

ALA - see Aerotransportes Litoral Argentino

Alitalia - see Linee Airee Italiane

Allegheny Airlines Inc - see USAir

Aloha Airlines Inc, (TS), Honolulu, Hawaii, USA

Ordered two Srs.215AUs with an option on a third on 15Mar65, laid out in a 79 seat one class configuration. The option was taken up in Oct66, when two further aircraft were optioned; this last option was never taken up. The aircraft were del in Apr66, Jun66 and late May67 and were flown on inter-island schedules with effect from 27Apr66 linking Honolulu with points which included Hilo, Kauai and Maui. The aircraft were withdrawn from service in Mar69 and Apr69.

N11181	096	N11182	097	N11183	105

American Airlines Inc, (AA), New York, USA

Ordered 15 Srs.401AKs on 17Jul63; a further ten were ordered on 04Feb64 and another five on 01Dec64. They were laid out initially in a 63 seat mixed class config and later in a 69 or 74 seat one class configuration. Del took place from late Dec65 to mid Dec66 after the earlier lease of a development aircraft for crew training for three and a half weeks in Dec65. The type was introduced into service on 06Mar66, when it was known as the Astrojet 400. It was used on an extensive domestic network in the northeast and central USA and internationally served Toronto from New York, until finally withdrawn on 17Jan72. At the peak of operations 230 sectors a day were being flown over a network of 21 cities.

G-ASYE	054	N5015	055	N5016	056	N5017	057
N5018	058	N5019	059	N5020	060	N5021	061
N5022	062	N5023	063	N5024	064	N5025	065
N5026	066	N5027	067	N5028	068	N5029	069
N5030	072	N5031	073	N5032	074	N5033	075
N5034	076	N5035	077	N5036	078	N5037	079
N5038	080	N5039	081	N5040	086	N5041	087
N5042	088	N5043	089	N5044	090		

Anadolu Hava Yollari, Ankara, Turkey

Leased a Srs.525FT from TAROM in the summer of 1987 to operate on European charter flights. An airline with the same name had earlier been identified as negotiating for three new Srs.500 aircraft early in 1969.

TC-AKB   253

Anglo Cargo Airlines Ltd, (ML), Gatwick Airport, UK

Leased a Srs.487GK fitted with a forward main deck cargo door from TAROM from

17Mar86. This company specialised in ad hoc cargo charter flights and used the aircraft mainly within Europe. Operations ceased on 13Jan92.

G-TOMO 267   YR-BCR 267

APA International Air, (7P), Miami, Florida, USA

This company took over the Miami to Puerto Plata (Dominican Republic) schedule after Atlantic Gulf suspended operations on the route in Sep86. The service was operated thrice weekly with the two Srs.401AKs and one Srs.203AE formerly used by Atlantic Gulf until early 1987.

N217CA 063   N218CA 089   N1542 016

Arkia Inland Airways Ltd, (IZ), Tel Aviv, Israel

Purchased two used Srs.500s, a Srs.520FN in Jul77 and a Srs.523FJ in May78. The aircraft were used on charter flights to many European destinations and also flew some of El Al's schedules from Tel Aviv to Larnaca after the type inaugurated service on 02Aug77. Both aircraft were sold in Sep79.

4X-BAR 230   4X-BAS 199

Atlantic Gulf Airlines Inc, (ZY), Tallahassee, Florida, USA

Leased a Srs.203AE from Nov84 followed by two Srs.401AKs in early 1986. The aircraft were used on the company's schedules, which included a twice daily service between Tallahassee and Miami, one of which operated through West Palm Beach, a three times weekly service from Miami to Puerto Plata (Dominican Republic) and a five times weekly service from Miami to Providenciales, all but one of which operated via Grand Turk (both in the Turks & Caicos Islands). The company suspended operations on 01Sep86, and although it was planned to reform as Ocean Air, operation of the scheduled services was not resumed.

N217CA 063   N218CA 089   N1542 016

Austral Compania Argentina de Transportes Aereos, (AU), Buenos Aires, Argentina

Ordered four Srs.420ELs on 03May67 and at the same time placed options on two Srs.500s. These aircraft were ordered both for its own use and for that of Aerotransportes Litoral Argentino (ALA), which was 30% owned by the former from 1966. Two of these aircraft were del in Oct67 and Nov67 laid out in a 74 seat single class config, the other two going to ALA. A Srs.413FA was leased from late Nov68 until mid Apr69 and used by both airlines after initial use by ALA for crew training. Three Srs.521FHs were ordered in Nov69 laid out in a 104 seat one class config; two of these were del to Austral, while the third went to ALA, all in Nov69. The type was introduced into service on 23Oct67 over a network which mainly concentrated on schedules to the south and west of the country. Internationally, Montevideo was served from Buenos Aires, while a twice weekly schedule was also operated on behalf of LAN-Chile between San Carlos de Bariloche and Puerto Montt in Chile in 1970. Points served from Buenos Aires Aeroparque included Bahia Blanca, Comodoro Rivadavia, Cordoba, Mar del Plata, Mendoza, Mercedes, Neuquen, Rio Gallegos and San Carlos de Bariloche. A Srs.521FH was leased to Sadia from mid Sep70 to early Jan71 and the same aircraft to Court Line Aviation from mid Apr to mid Oct71.

Although both Austral and ALA maintained their individual identities, their routes were integrated from 1966, and on 23Jun71 the two airlines merged fully to form Austral Lineas Aereas.

G-AWGG	116	LV-IZR	122	LV-IZS	123	LV-JNR	192
LV-JNS	194	LV-PID	122	LV-PIF	123		

Austral Lineas Aereas, (AU), Buenos Aires, Argentina

This company was formed from the merger of Austral Compania Argentina de Transportes Aereos and Aerotransportes Litoral Argentino on 23Jun71. The former company had taken a 30% holding in the latter in 1966, and the routes and fleets were integrated from this time. The two airlines maintained their individual identities, however, up to the time of the complete merger. Austral is currently a subsidiary of Cielos del Sur SA. At the time of the merger seven aircraft were in service comprising four Srs.420ELs and three Srs.521FHs. The airline has obtained seven used Srs.500s since this time, a Srs.529FR in Jan75, a Srs.509EW in Oct75 (the aircraft having been leased from Feb74 prior to this), two Srs.518FGs from British Aerospace in Jan78 and Mar79 and three Srs.500s from Hapag-Lloyd in Nov79 and Jan80. An additional Srs.501EX was leased from British Caledonian for five months from Dec75, and two Srs.401AKs were leased from National Aircraft Leasing from Dec76 to Apr77. Following the complete merger of the two carriers a network of scheduled services throughout Argentina has been maintained. Points served have extended from Buenos Aires Aeroparque south to Bahia Blanca, Comodoro Rivadavia, Rio Gallegos and Trelew, west to Cordoba, Mendoza, Neuquen, San Carlos de Bariloche, San Juan and Villa Mercedes and north to Corrientes, Goya, Iguazu, Jujuy, Parana, Posadas, Reconquista, Resistencia, Rosario, Salta, Santa Fe and Tucuman, while a high frequency service was flown to Mar del Plata on the Atlantic coast. The following additional destinations were added to the scheduled network early in 1993: Esquel, Formosa, Rio Grande, San Luis, San Martin and Santiago del Estero. Under a government directive all international scheduled services were suspended in favour of Aerolineas Argentinas soon after the merger. The aircraft have also been used to operate charter flights throughout Argentina and internationally to points including Antofagasta, Punta Arenas, Puerto Montt and Santiago (Chile), to Asuncion (Paraguay), to Santa Cruz de la Sierra (Bolivia), to Florianapolis, Porto Alegre, Rio de Janeiro and Sao Paulo (Brazil) and to Montevideo (Uruguay). A Srs.521FH was leased to Court Line Aviation from mid Apr to mid Oct71. The last of the Srs.400s was disposed of in Jan82. During 1993 replacement of the One-Elevens began; by early 1994 only two aircraft remained in service, while new destinations served by the type were Rio Cuarto, Santa Rosa and Viedma.

G-AWWY	185	G-AXJK	191	LV-IZR	122	LZ-IZS	123
LV-JGX	117	LV-JGY	155	LV-JNR	192	LV-JNS	194
LV-JNT	196	LV-LHT	185	LV-LOX	212	LV-MEX	200
LV-MRZ	206	LV-MZM	187	LV-OAX	197	LV-OAY	227
LV-PEW	187	LV-PFR	197	LV-PID	122	LV-PIF	123
LV-PSW	185	N5039	081	N5042	088		

Austrian Airlines, (OS), Vienna, Austria

Leased a Srs.530FX from British Caledonian Airways from the end of Mar to early Sep75 and a Srs.501EX from the same company for the month of May81 to operate on some of its European schedules.

G-AXJK	191	G-AZMF	240

Autair International Airways Ltd - see Court Line Aviation Ltd

Aviateca - see Aerolineas de Guatemala

Aviation Development Company Ltd - see ADC Airlines

Bahamas Airways Ltd, (BH), Nassau, Bahamas

Leased two Srs.432FDs from Nov68 and Dec68 until Aug69 laid out in a 79 seat one class config. Two Srs.517FEs, laid out in a 99 seat one class config, were ordered with del in Jul69, and a used Srs.301AG was bought in Mar70. A third Srs.517FE was ordered fitted with long range tanks for operation on a proposed Nassau to New York route, but although painted in the company's colours it was not del. The aircraft were flown on the airline's schedules from Nassau and Freeport to Miami, Fort Lauderdale and West Palm Beach in Florida. The company ceased operations on 09Oct70.

VP-BCN	188	VP-BCO	189	VP-BCP	034	(VP-BCQ)	198
VP-BCY	121	VP-BCZ	157				

Bahamasair Holdings Ltd, (BH), Nassau, Bahamas

Trading as Bahamasair, this company was established on 01Jul73 as the national airline of the Bahamas from the merger of Out Island Airways and Flamingo Airlines. Two Srs.401AKs were inherited from Out Island, one of which was disposed of in Dec73. Two further Srs.401AKs were obtained from American Airlines in Nov73 and Dec73, one of which was sold in Oct76. The aircraft were used on routes from Nassau to Freeport and from these two points to Miami, while Atlanta was served from Nassau. The last aircraft were disposed of in 1984.

C6-BDJ	089	C6-BDN	062	C6-BDP	063	VP-BDI	074
VP-BDJ	089	VP-BDN	062	VP-BDP	063		

Baltic Airlines Sweden AB, (GP), Malmo, Sweden

Leased a Srs.476FM from Ryanair Europe/London European Airways, which was used to operate a scheduled daily service between Malmo and Southend, England, from 31Mar89 to 31May89, when the aircraft was returned to the lessor.

G-AZUK 241

Bavaria Fluggesellschaft Schwabe & Co KG, (BV), Munich, Germany

Ordered two Srs.414EGs with an option on a third on 29Oct66. The company leased a Srs.402AP from the manufacturer from Mar67 to the end of Oct67 prior to del of the first of its own aircraft. Its first Srs.414EG was del in late Dec67. Two Srs.400s were leased for the summer programme in 1968, firstly a Srs.408EF in mid May, replaced by a Srs.413FA from late Jun68 to Nov68. This last aircraft was later purchased as the second aircraft of the original order and re-del in Apr69. The option was taken up in 1969, and two further Srs.414EGs were ordered with del in Feb, Apr and Dec70, all fitted with 84 seat single class cabins. Following the loss of the company's first aircraft, a Srs.402AP was leased from the manufacturer from early Aug70 to early Jan71. Three Srs.528FLs, laid out in a 109 or a 114 seat single class configuration, were later ordered with del in Dec70, Feb71 and Mar72, and a Srs.518FG was leased from the manufacturer from Apr to Sep76.

The fleet was used on inclusive tour and charter flights throughout Europe and to North Africa, and one of the Srs.400s was leased to Gulf Air from Nov75 for 18 months. During 1970 a twice daily weekday scheduled service was flown between Hanover and Munich and a once daily weekday service between Hanover and Stuttgart on behalf of Lufthansa. The company merged with Germanair Bedarfsluftfahrt on 01Mar77 to form Bavaria/Germanair Fluggesellschaft, at which time it still operated three Srs.528FLs and two Srs.414EGs while the Srs.413FA was out on lease.

D-AILY 163	D-AISY 158	D-ALFA 234	D-ALLI 116
D-AMUC 227	(D-ANDI) 158	D-ANDY 127	D-ANNO 160
D-ANUE 238	G-AVEJ 094	G-AVGP 114	G-AWGG 116
G-AXMG 201	G-AYHM 161		

Bavaria/Germanair Fluggesellschaft GmbH, (BV), Germany

Formed on 01Mar77 from the merger of Bavaria Fluggesellschaft Schwabe & Co and Germanair Bedarfsluftfahrt, at which time three Srs.528FLs, two Srs.515FBs, two Srs.524FFs and two Srs.414FGs were in use, while a Srs.413FA was leased out. The two Srs.414FGs were sold to corporate customers in Nov77, and the last Srs.400 was sold to Air Pacific in 1978. The airline continued to operate its seven Srs.500 One-Elevens on similar work to that of the two founder companies until it was merged into Hapag-Lloyd Fluggesellschaft in Jan79.

D-AISY 158	D-ALFA 234	D-ALLI 116	D-AMAM 229
D-AMAS 187	D-AMAT 235	D-AMOR 197	D-AMUC 227
D-ANNO 160	D-ANUE 238		

Birmingham European Airways Ltd, (VB), Birmingham, UK

Purchased five Srs.400s from British Airways; these comprised two Srs.401AKs, two Srs.408EFs and one Srs.416EK. Del of these aircraft started in Jan90, and the first aircraft entered service on 01Feb90. British Airways' Srs.500s had earlier operated on the company's behalf from Birmingham to Milan and Copenhagen over the previous winter period. These services were not operated by dedicated aircraft but by any Srs.500 in the British Airways fleet available at the time (excepting Srs.510EDs). Following the receipt of the Srs.400s, the airline expanded its scheduled operations considerably. Destinations served from Birmingham included Amsterdam, Belfast, Copenhagen, Cork, Dublin, Geneva, Milan, Paris, Stockholm and Stuttgart. Schedules were also flown on behalf of British Airways from Monday to Friday between Oct90 and late Mar91. These were from Birmingham to Brussels and Frankfurt and from Newcastle to Frankfurt. One of the aircraft was sold in Aug91, after which British Airways Srs.500s operated some schedules in a manner similar to that used earlier. The company was merged with Brymon Airways to form Brymon European Airways with effect from 25Oct92.

G-AVGP 114	G-AWBL 132	G-BBME 066	G-BBMF 074
G-BBMG 115			

Bonanza Airlines Inc, Phoenix, Arizona, USA

Ordered three Srs.206AHs in Nov62 to replace Fairchild F-27s, but following the rejection of a loan guarantee by the US Civil Aeronautics Board in Feb63 the order was cancelled and the aircraft not built. Constructor's numbers 036 to 038 had been allocated.

Braniff Airways Inc, (BN), Dallas, Texas, USA

Marketing itself as Braniff International, this carrier placed its first order for six Srs.203AEs in a 63 seat two class configuration together with an option on six additional aircraft on 23Oct61. These options were taken up on 05Mar63 and a further two aircraft ordered on 14Feb64. An option was placed on 12 further aircraft on 30Sep64 but was not taken up. The aircraft were del between Mar and Dec65 and were unusual in being the only airline One-Elevens del without ventral airstairs fitted from new. Thirty cities in the central states of the USA, ranging from Minneapolis St Paul and Chicago to the north, Amarillo and Lubbock to the west, Brownsville and Corpus Christi to the south and Washington to the east were served on an extensive domestic network centred on Dallas. Service started on 25Apr65. Three of the aircraft were sold to Mohawk Airlines in Sep70, eight to Allegheny Airlines between Apr and Sep72 and two disposed of to executive users. One of these last two aircraft was converted to executive configuration during 1973 and retained by Braniff as a corporate aircraft until sold in Mar77. On 01Mar88 the company took over Florida Express and with it a fleet of 18 One-Elevens comprising nine Srs.203AEs (all previously operated by Braniff some 16 years earlier), six Srs.201ACs and three Srs.401AKs. Twelve of these aircraft were sold to Guinness Peat Aviation in 1988 and leased back by Braniff. The airline continued to maintain the Florida Express Orlando hub but with a much reduced One-Eleven operation. Destinations served through the hub were Fort Myers, Miami, Tampa and West Palm Beach in Florida and Nassau (Bahamas), Atlanta, Birmingham (Alabama), Cincinatti, Columbus (Ohio) and Indianapolis. A second hub was set up at Kansas City, which was linked with Atlanta, Cleveland, Houston, Indianapolis, Milwaukee, Minneapolis, Oklahoma City, Omaha, St Louis, San Antonio (Texas), Tulsa and Wichita. The company ceased all operations on 06Nov89.

EI-BWI	007	EI-BWJ	009	EI-BWK	011	EI-BWL	012
EI-BWM	013	EI-BWN	020	EI-BWO	041	EI-BWP	043
EI-BWQ	057	EI-BWR	061	EI-BWS	085	EI-BWT	127
N101EX	007	N102EX	009	N104EX	011	N105EX	012
N106EX	013	N107EX	085	N170FE	057	N171FE	061
N174FE	127	N541BN	015	N1135J	046	N1136J	071
N1541	015	N1542	016	N1543	017	N1544	018
N1545	019	N1546	020	N1547	041	N1548	042
N1549	043	N1550	044	N1551	045	N1552	046
N1553	070	N1554	071				

Brazil Air Force - see Força Aerea Brasileira

British Air Ferries Ltd, (VF), Southend, Essex, UK

Leased three Srs.201ACs from Guinness Peat Aviation with del in Mar, Apr and May90, one of which was obtained for spares use only. In Apr91 a Srs.476FM was added to the fleet, also on lease. In Dec92 the company leased the entire Dan-Air fleet of 11 Srs.500s, comprising four Srs.518FGs, two Srs.509EWs, two Srs.531FSs, one Srs.517FE, one Srs.515FB and one Srs.520FN. The two Srs.201ACs and the Srs.476FM were withdrawn from use with the arrival of the Srs.500 aircraft. One of the Srs.518FGs and the Srs.517FE were obtained for spares use only, and to date only five of the newly obtained aircraft have been operated commercially. They are either operated in a 119 seat all tourist or a 99 seat mixed class configuration and are used for ad hoc charter work throughout Europe and to the Middle East. From summer 1993 regular inclusive tour flights have been flown to Spain, Italy, Greece and France, with aircraft based at Stansted and Gatwick. The company's titles had earlier appeared on a Srs.416EK in Sep and Oct82 following licensing difficulties with

Air Manchester operations and the aircraft was flown with British Air Ferries' flight numbers. With effect from 06Apr93 the company was renamed British World Airlines after the operational base had earlier been moved to Stansted as from 01Feb93. A three times weekly scheduled service was inaugurated between Stansted and Bucharest on 28Jun93, but this, the only scheduled service operated, was abandoned in Mar94.

EI-BWI 007	G-AWWX 184	G-AXYD 210	G-AZUK 241
G-BCWA 205	G-BCXR 198	G-BDAS 202	G-BDAT 232
G-BEKA 230	G-BJMV 244	G-BJYL 208	G-BJYM 242
G-DBAF 011	G-OBWA 232	G-OBWB 202	G-OBWC 230
G-OBWD 203	G-OBWE 242	G-OBWF 210	G-OBWG 184
G-OBWH 208	G-OCNW 012	G-SURE 129	

British Air Services

This organisation was formed on 02Feb67 by British European Airways as a holding company jointly to manage Cambrian Airways and BKS Air Transport. One-Elevens of Cambrian Airways were flown with British Air Services titles before the fleet was fully integrated into that of British Airways.

British Airways Plc, (BA and BZ), London, UK

At the time of the complete merger of British European Airways, British Overseas Airways Corporation and British Air Services at midnight on 31Mar74 to form British Airways, the airline had on strength 18 Srs.510EDs, three Srs.416EKs, two Srs.408EFs and two Srs.401AKs. The various component parts of the eventual British Airways were marketed as British Airways with effect from 01Sep73. A Srs.432FD was leased from Gulf Air from Aug to Nov77, while a new Srs.537GF was leased from Cyprus Airways from Oct78 to Aug80 and a Srs.530FX from British Caledonian from late Oct78 to late Apr79, all three being operated out of Birmingham and Manchester. Three Srs.539GLs, laid out in a 99 seat single class configuration, were ordered with del in Mar, Jun and Aug80, with two of the Srs.416EKs being traded in part exchange in Jun and Aug of the same year. A Srs.432FD was leased from Air UK from Oct86 to the end of Apr87, mainly to fly Irish Sea services. The aircraft continued to fly numerous routes over the European and domestic network. Series 510EDs were progressively replaced in the German internal network as Boeing 737-236s came on strength, the last being withdrawn at the end of Mar86 when HS748s were deployed from Glasgow to cover the shorter or less densely travelled sectors. The aircraft were later used to operate shuttle back-up services from Heathrow to Belfast, Edinburgh, Glasgow and Manchester, replacing retired Trident aircraft in that role. The Srs.400s were mainly used to operate domestic and regional routes out of Birmingham, Manchester and Jersey. On 14Apr88 British Caledonian merged into British Airways, adding a further 13 Srs.500s of varying marks to the fleet. These were all deployed to Birmingham and Manchester by the end of the summer schedules in 1988, replacing the Srs.400 aircraft which were then retired. The three Srs.539GLs were withdrawn in Mar91 and subsequently sold. With effect from 13Jan92 One-Elevens were replaced in the Shuttle back-up role by Boeing 737-236s. Six Srs.510EDs were withdrawn from service on the same date, joining a seventh which had been withdrawn in Nov91. From this date all remaining Srs.510EDs were based at Manchester and all other One-Elevens at Birmingham. From 01Aug92 the type was progressively withdrawn from service in Manchester, with the last flight taking place on 24Dec92. The type was progressively withdrawn from Birmingham with effect from 01Dec92, with the last regular service taking place on 31May93. Two aircraft remained in service after this time for ad hoc substitutions for both British Airways and Brymon European Airways, culminating in the last revenue One-Eleven flight on 01Jul93.

On 08Nov92 Dan-Air Services was taken over, but the last of its fleet of 11 Srs.500s had been retired two days earlier and was not part of the agreement. See also Maersk Air.

G-AVGP 114	G-AVMH 136	G-AVMI 137	G-AVMJ 138
G-AVMK 139	G-AVML 140	G-AVMM 141	G-AVMN 142
G-AVMO 143	G-AVMP 144	G-AVMR 145	G-AVMS 146
G-AVMT 147	G-AVMU 148	G-AVMV 149	G-AVMW 150
G-AVMX 151	G-AVMY 152	G-AVMZ 153	G-AVOE 129
G-AVOF 131	G-AWBL 132	G-AWEJ 115	G-AWYR 174
G-AWYS 175	G-AWYT 176	G-AWYU 177	G-AWYV 178
G-AXJK 191	G-AXJM 214	G-AXLL 193	G-AXOX 121
G-AYOP 233	G-AZMF 240	G-AZMI 066	G-AZPZ 229
G-BBME 066	G-BBMF 074	G-BBMG 115	G-BFWN 261
G-BGKE 263	G-BGKF 264	G-BGKG 265	G-BJRT 234
G-BJRU 238	A40-BU 157		

British Caledonian Airways Ltd, (BR), London, UK

This company was formed from the merger of Caledonian Airways (Prestwick) and British United Airways on 30Nov70, although the company was initially marketed as Caledonian//BUA until 01Nov71. Inherited from these two companies were eight Srs.201ACs (one of which was sold in Sep71), eight Srs.501EXs and four Srs.509EWs. Two Srs.530FXs laid out in a 109 seat single class configuration were ordered with del in Mar72 and the second, after a year's lease to Court Line, in Mar73. A Srs.515FB was leased from mid Aug to mid Oct72 to cover a shortage following an accident to one of the Srs.501EXs in Greece. All the Srs.509EWs were disposed of, two in Oct75, one in Nov75 and one in May76, while one Srs.501EX was sold in Sep76. Following the sale of the seven remaining Srs.201ACs between Oct81 and Jun82 to Pacific Express, additional Srs.500s were procured to replace them. Two Srs.528FLs and one Srs.515FB were obtained from Hapag-Lloyd, with two del in Oct81 and the other in Mar82. Following operation of the last Srs.201AC service between Paris-Charles de Gaulle and Gatwick on 21Mar82, four ex-Laker Airways Srs.320L-AZs were operated between Apr82 until sold between Sep and Nov83, while a Srs.523FJ was bought in Dec83. The new company continued to operate the scheduled network built up by British United Airways, adding a Gatwick to Paris schedule in Nov71. An Edinburgh to Copenhagen via Newcastle route was added in Nov72, and a Gatwick to Brussels route in Jun74. With effect from 01Nov74, in a major cost-cutting exercise, service was withdrawn from Gatwick to Belfast, Gibraltar, Ibiza, Malaga and Palma, from Glasgow to Southampton and from Edinburgh to Copenhagen via Newcastle. A Gatwick to Algiers schedule was added in 1976. Charter and inclusive tour flights continued to be flown to Europe and North Africa, and aircraft were leased for varying periods to Transbrasil, Austrian Airlines, British Airways, Air Malawi and Air Malta. The company merged into British Airways on 14Apr88.

G-ASJC 007	G-ASJD 008	G-ASJE 009	G-ASJF 010
G-ASJG 011	G-ASJH 012	G-ASJI 013	G-ASTJ 085
G-AVOF 131	G-AWYR 174	G-AWYS 175	G-AWYT 176
G-AWYU 177	G-AWYV 178	G-AWWX 184	G-AWWY 185
G-AWWZ 186	G-AXJK 191	G-AXJL 209	G-AXJM 214
G-AXLL 193	G-AXYD 210	G-AYOP 233	G-AZMF 240
G-AZPE 208	G-AZPZ 229	G-BJRT 234	G-BJRU 238
G-BKAU 107	G-BKAV 109	G-BKAW 113	G-BKAX 133

British Eagle International Airways Ltd, (EG), London, UK

Leased two Srs.207AJs from Zambia Airways from Apr and May66 to mid Dec67 and three Srs.301AGs from the Kuwait Finance Company with del in Jun and Jul66. Two Srs.304AXs laid out in a 79 seat single class configuration were ordered with del in Apr and May67; the company inaugurated One-Eleven service on 09May66. The following destinations were served on a scheduled basis from Heathrow by the type: Dinard, Djerba, Glasgow, La Baule, Liverpool, Luxembourg, Newquay, Palma, Perpignan, Pisa, Rimini, Stuttgart and Tunis. The type was also used on charter work within Europe and to North Africa, and aircraft were additionally leased to KLM, Swissair and Scandinavian Airlines System. British Eagle ceased operations on 06Nov68.

G-ATPH 110	G-ATPI 112	G-ATPJ 033	G-ATPK 034
G-ATPL 035	G-ATTP 039	G-ATVH 040	

British European Airways Corporation, (BE), London, UK

Ordered 18 Srs.510EDs with options on a further six aircraft on 27Jan67; these options were not taken up. They were del in a 97 seat single class configuration between Aug68 and Aug69, except for one aircraft which was retained by the manufacturer for autoland development until May70. After ad hoc substitutions starting on 01Sep68, the type was introduced into regular service on 17Nov68 from Berlin-Tempelhof on the company's internal German network and on the Heathrow to Manchester route. As the fleet built up it took over most of the internal German network, much of the Manchester scheduled network and many of the Heathrow to Germany operations. A One-Eleven division was set up in Manchester during 1971; from here the aircraft were both maintained and controlled in their use on all Manchester international and domestic services except the Channel Islands routes together with the German internal network based on Tempelhof. From Apr69 until the end of Oct72 services were operated on joint Air France/BEA services from Berlin-Tempelhof to Frankfurt and Munich. All internal German services were operated by One-Elevens from 01Nov71 after the Viscounts were withdrawn from the region. Cambrian Airways Srs.400s were used to operate some Tempelhof-originating international German services between 1970 and Mar72 and also operated some Dublin to Birmingham and Manchester schedules.
All four Cambrian aircraft were used at various times. One used Srs.408EF and two used Srs.401AKs were purchased for operation on the Birmingham network, although only the first had entered service prior to the complete merger with BOAC and even then was painted in British Airways' new colours. This company officially ceased to exist on 01Apr74 after its merger with BOAC and British Air Services to form British Airways, although trading in the British Airways name had started on 01Sep73.

G-AVGP 114	G-AVMH 136	G-AVMI 137	G-AVMJ 138
G-AVMK 139	G-AVML 140	G-AVMM 141	G-AVMN 142
G-AVMO 143	G-AVMP 144	G-AVMR 145	G-AVMS 146
G-AVMT 147	G-AVMU 148	G-AVMV 149	G-AVMW 150
G-AVMX 151	G-AVMY 152	G-AVMZ 153	G-AVOE 129
G-AVOF 131	G-AWBL 132	G-BBMG 115	

British Island Airways Ltd, (KD and UK), London, UK

Purchased a Srs.409AY and two Srs.432FDs previously operated by Gulfair with del in Jun78 and Jan and Feb79 for operation on inclusive tour and contract charter flights within Europe. The company was merged with Air Anglia to form Air UK on 16Oct79 but was re-formed on 01Jan82 with the four One-Elevens which had been on strength with Air UK at that time. A fourth aircraft, a Srs.416EK, had been obtained in Dec79 by Air UK. The airline continued to operate inclusive tour and charter flights as before. A second Srs.416EK was leased from British Aerospace from May to Nov83. The company purchased a Srs.523FJ and a Srs.531FS from Cayman Airways in Apr and May84 and a Srs.518FG and a Srs.509EW from Monarch Airlines in May and Oct85. The airline later leased a single Srs.561RC during the summer of 1986 and two Srs.525FTs in the summer of 1987 from TAROM. Following delivery of the Srs.500s the Srs.400s were leased out to several operators for varying periods of time; these included Virgin Atlantic Airways, Air UK, Air Ecosse, Transport Aerien Transregional and Airways International Cymru. Services were also operated on behalf of Air Florida from Gatwick to Amsterdam, Brussels, Dusseldorf and Frankfurt. The company additionally flew scheduled services with the type from Gatwick to Catania, Palermo and Malta until all operations ceased on 01Feb90.

G-AVOF 131	G-AWWZ 186	G-AXBB 162	G-AXLN 211
G-AXMG 201	G-AXMU 157	G-AXOX 121	G-AYWB 237
G-CBIA 166	YR-BCL 255	YR-BCM 256	YR-BRA 401

British Midland Airways Ltd, (BD), East Midlands Airport, Derbyshire, UK

Initially ordered two Srs.303s on 20Nov65 for spring 1967 del, but the order was cancelled the following year. In mid 1969 the company ordered two Srs.523FJs, followed by a third two months later. Laid out in a 119 seat single class configuration, they were del in Feb and Mar70. The aircraft were used on the company's scheduled routes from East Midlands to Dublin, Jersey, Glasgow and Luton and from Jersey to Luton. A three-times daily service from Teesside to Heathrow was flown from 04May70. Service had previously been inaugurated with the type on the East Midlands to Jersey route on 24Feb70. European inclusive tour charter flights were also flown from East Midlands, Luton, Glasgow, Manchester, Belfast and Bristol. One aircraft was leased to Court Line Aviation from late Feb72 to Sep73, being replaced by a second until Apr74. The aircraft were sold to Transbrasil in Mar and Sep73 and Apr74. A Srs.401AK was leased from Dan-Air Services from Oct82 to Jan83 and two Srs.304AXs from Airways International Cymru for varying periods in 1985 and 1986 to operate schedules from Heathrow to Leeds/Bradford and Teesside.

G-AXCP 087	G-AXLL 193	G-AXLM 199	G-AXLN 211
G-WLAD 112	G-YMRU 110		

British United Airways Ltd, (BR), London, UK

The launch customer for the type ordered ten Srs.201ACs with options on a further five (which were not taken up) on 09May61. Laid out in a 69 seat single class configuration, they were del between Apr and Nov65. On 04Mar68 five Srs.501EXs were ordered, initially for use in the inclusive tour role, laid out in a 109 seat single class configuration with del between Apr and Jun69, and a further three of the same type were del in Mar70. A Srs.408EF was leased from Apr to Oct69 to cover the loss of an aircraft in an accident. The company inaugurated the world's first One-Eleven revenue service on 09Apr65 between Gatwick and Genoa and rapidly introduced the type on to its scheduled network between Gatwick and Amsterdam, Belfast, Edinburgh, Genoa, Gibraltar, Glasgow, Ibiza, Jersey, Le Touquet, Malaga, Palma, Rotterdam and Tunis replacing Vickers Viscounts and Bristol Britannias. The type was also used on schedules from Glasgow to Southampton and to Amsterdam via Newcastle. A weekly service from Gatwick to Lagos via Lisbon, Las Palmas, Bathurst, Freetown and Accra was operated with passengers and aircraft night-stopping at Las Palmas en route. The company merged with Caledonian Airways (Prestwick) to form Caledonian//BUA on 30Nov70.

G-ASJA	005	(G-ASJB)	006	G-ASJC	007	G-ASJD	008
G-ASJE	009	G-ASJF	010	G-ASJG	011	G-ASJH	012
G-ASJI	013	G-ASJJ	014	G-ASTJ	085	G-AWKJ	128
G-AWYR	174	G-AWYS	175	G-AWYT	176	G-AWYU	177
G-AWYV	178	G-AXJK	191	G-AXJL	209	G-AXJM	214

British World Airlines Ltd - see British Air Ferries Ltd

Britt Airways Inc, (RU), Danville, Illinois, USA

Obtained two used Srs.416EKs from British Aerospace in Jun84 and Mar85. The type was used on both charters and the company's schedules from Chicago to points which included Champaign, Evansville, Indianapolis and Terre Haute. The airline was bought by People Express in Feb86 but continued to fly services in its own name. The aircraft were sold in Aug87.

N390BA 129   N392BA 131

Brymon European Airways Ltd, (BC), Birmingham, UK

This company started operations on 25Oct92 following the merger of Birmingham European Airways and Brymon Airways of Plymouth. The four One-Elevens previously with the former carrier continued in service; these comprised two Srs.408EFs, a Srs.406EK and a Srs.401AK. A Srs.501EX was leased from British Airways in Mar93. The aircraft were flown on scheduled routes from Birmingham to Amsterdam, Belfast, Copenhagen, Dublin, Geneva, Milan and Stuttgart, and a Bristol to Paris schedule was started in Apr93. The merger was reversed on 01Aug93, and the former Birmingham European Airways was renamed Maersk Air Ltd after becoming a wholly-owned subsidiary of Maersk Air I/S of Denmark.

G-AVGP	114	G-AWBL	132	G-AWYS	175	G-BBME	066
G-BBMG	115						

Caledonian Airways (Prestwick) Ltd), (CA), Gatwick, UK

Announced an order for three Srs.509EWs laid out in a 109 seat single class configuration with an option on a fourth on 14Mar68; this option was taken up in 1969. Del of the first three took place in Mar and Apr69 and the fourth in Mar70. The aircraft operated inclusive tour flights from Gatwick, Glasgow and Manchester to European and North African destinations. The company merged with British United Airways to form Caledonian//BUA on 30Nov70.

G-AWWX	184	G-AWWY	185	G-AWWZ	186	G-AXYD	209

Caledonian//BUA - see British Caledonian Airways Ltd

Cambrian Airways Ltd, (CS), Cardiff, Wales, UK

This company, which was part of the BEA subsidiary British Air Services by the time One-Elevens were introduced, bought three used Srs.416EKs and one Srs.408EF which were del in Dec69, Jan and Apr70 and Jan71. The type inaugurated service on 15Jan70 between Heathrow and Liverpool. Schedules were flown from Heathrow to Cork, Isle of Man and Liverpool and from Dublin to Liverpool. In addition charters were flown from Bristol, Cardiff, Gatwick and Liverpool to European destinations. One aircraft at a time was rotated through Berlin to operate schedules on behalf of BEA on its internal German network between 1970 and Mar72, while Dublin to Birmingham and Manchester schedules were also operated on behalf of BEA in 1970. The Cambrian name ceased to be used with effect from 01Sep73; from this date all services were marketed in the British Airways name ahead of the complete merger of British Air Services with BEA and BOAC on 01Apr74.

G-AVOE 129   G-AVOF 131   G-AVGP 114   G-AWBL 132

Cascade Airways Inc, (CZ), Spokane, Washington, USA

Leased three Srs.201ACs late in 1984 and purchased two Srs.401AKs in late Nov84 and Feb85. The aircraft operated twice daily schedules from Seattle (Washington) via Portland (Oregon) to Boise, Idaho Falls and Pocatello in Idaho. Twice daily services were flown from Seattle to Spokane, of which one continued to Calgary (Alberta) in Canada. Seattle was also linked three times daily with Pasco, two of these flights continuing to Walla Walla and the other to Lewiston (Idaho). The company entered Chapter 11 bankruptcy on 21Aug85 and finally suspended operations on 07Mar86.

N102EX 009   N103EX 010   N106EX 013   N217CA 063
N218CA 089

Cayman Airways Ltd, (KX), Georgetown, Grand Cayman

One-Elevens were used on the Grand Cayman to Kingston (Jamaica) route from 1970, this being operated three times weekly on the airline's behalf by LACSA (which at the time was a 49% shareholder in Cayman Airways). Miami was an added destination from Apr72 under a similar arrangement. In 1973 a LACSA Srs.531FS was painted in full Cayman Airways colours and leased until Nov77. The aircraft operated twice daily from Grand Cayman to Miami and four times weekly to Kingston. The company returned to One-Eleven operations in Jun78 when a Srs.528FJ was purchased, followed by a Srs.531FS in Nov79. A daily Houston service was then operated, with the Miami service operating up to three times daily. The type was finally withdrawn in Dec82.

TI-LRJ 244   TI-1055C 162   TI-1095C 242   TI-1096C 244
VR-CAB 237   VR-CAL 211

Central African Airways Corp, (CE), Salisbury, Southern Rhodesia

Ordered two Srs.207AJs on 26Sep62 but, although completed in the company's colours, they were not del following the unilateral declaration of independence by Rhodesia on 11Nov65. This resulted in the refusal of an export licence following an international trade embargo. The order was taken over by Zambia Airways.

(VP-YXA) 039   (VP-YXB) 040

Challenge International Airlines Inc

Operated a Srs.401AK on behalf of Grenada Airways from Jun86 until early in 1987 on the latter's schedules between Miami and Grenada.

N218CA 089

Channel Airways Ltd, (CW), Southend, Essex, UK

On 05Sep66 this operator announced an order for four Srs.408EFs with an option on two more. Only three aircraft were eventually del, these being in either high density 99 or 89 seat configurations. The first aircraft, del in Jun67, was returned to the manufacturer on receipt of the second in May68. The third aircraft was leased to British Caledonian from del in Apr69 until Oct of the same year. The type entered service on 16Jun67 and was used on inclusive tour and holiday charter flights from Southend, Stansted, Bristol, Cardiff, East Midlands, Teesside, Manchester and Berlin to numerous European destinations. The type was occasionally used on scheduled services such as Southend to Rotterdam. The company entered receivership on 01Feb72, and the One-Elevens ceased flying on 15Feb72.

G-AVGP 114   G-AWEJ 115   (G-AWGG) 116   G-AWKJ 128

Citylink Airways, (XF), Delhi, India

Operated two Srs.561RCs leased from Romavia. The first entered service on 19Nov92. The aircraft were operated in a two class configuration on schedules from Delhi to Bombay and Calcutta. Operations ceased in Oct93, and the aircraft were returned to the lessor.

YR-BRH 408   YR-BRI 409

Classic Air Inc, Las Vegas, Nevada, USA

This passenger-carrying subsidiary of Buffalo Airways leased four Srs.204AFs from the International Leasing Group from Mar90. Operations were short-lived, and the aircraft were returned to the lessor in the same year the company was founded. It is doubtful if all four aircraft entered service.

N1120J 102   N1126J 179   N1127J 180   N1129J 182

Compania de Aviacion Faucett SA, (CF), Lima, Peru

Ordered two Srs.476FMs laid out in an 84 seat configuration which were del in Jul71 and Jul74. A used Srs.523FJ was leased from British Aerospace in Aug77 and was later purchased. The aircraft were used on scheduled services from Lima to numerous domestic points including Arequipa, Ayacucho, Chiclayo, Cuzco, Iquitos, Piura, Pucallpa, Puerto Maldonado, Tacna, Talara, Tarapoto, Tingo Maria, Trujillo and Tumbes. Many of these destinations had gravel strips in mountainous terrain, for which the Srs.475 had been specifically developed. The aircraft were withdrawn from service in Dec82.

OB-R-953 239   OB-R-1080 241   OB-R-1137 193   OB-R-1173 193

Compania Dominicana de Aviacion C por A, (DO), Santo Domingo, Dominican Republic

A Srs.408AF was painted in full Dominicana colours for lease to this carrier in Jul68; the deal was not completed and the aircraft not del.

(HI-148) 114

Court Line Aviation Ltd, (OU), Luton, Beds, UK

This company, known as Autair International Airways until 31Dec69, ordered two Srs.416EKs on 25Feb67 and a third later in the same year. Laid out in a high density 89 seat configuration, they were del in Feb, Mar and May68. A further Srs.416EK was leased from the manufacturer from Mar to Nov69 and a Srs.408EF from the same source from Dec68 to Feb70. The airline ordered seven Srs.518FGs, all of which were del from new in Court Line's new corporate colours in a high density 119 seat configuration. Del took place between Dec69 and Apr70, by which time all but one of the Srs.400s had been disposed of; the last Srs.400 was sold in Jan71. Two further Srs.518FGs were obtained, both being del in Mar71, one of these being on lease from British Caledonian until Dec72. Two used Srs.517FEs were bought in Sep and Dec71 and a third of the same type del new in Jun72. Leased aircraft operated were a Srs.521FH from Austral from Apr to Dec71 and two Srs.523FJs from British Midland, one from Feb72 to Sep73 and the other replacing it until Apr74. Four of the company's aircraft were operated by Leeward Islands Air Transport at various times from Nov71 to Apr74, Court Line being a 75% shareholder in that carrier at the time. Other single aircraft were leased to Cyprus Airways from May74, Aviateca from Nov70 to Apr71, Lanica from Dec71 to Mar72 and to Germanair from May74. The aircraft were used for intensive inclusive tour contract flights from Luton, Gatwick and several provincial UK airports to Europe and North Africa until the company ceased trading on 15Aug74.

G-AVGP 114	G-AVOE 129	G-AVOF 131	G-AWBL 132
G-AWXJ 166	G-AXLM 199	G-AXLN 211	G-AXMF 200
G-AXMG 201	G-AXMH 202	G-AXMI 203	G-AXMJ 204
G-AXMK 205	G-AXML 206	G-AYOP 233	G-AYOR 232
(G-AYSC) 235	(G-AYWB) 237	G-AYXB 192	G-AZEB 188
G-AZEC 189	G-BCCV 198		

CSA Ceskoslovenske Aerolinie, (OK), Prague, Czechoslovakia

During the period from Nov91 to the end of Mar92 a once weekly schedule was flown over the route Prague to Bucharest via Budapest using One-Elevens of TAROM on a service jointly operated by the two carriers.

Cyprus Airways Ltd, (CY), Nicosia and Larnaca, Cyprus

Started One-Eleven operations on 01Jun74 with a Srs.518FG leased from Court Line Aviation. The aircraft was stranded in Nicosia after the Turkish invasion of 20Jul74. Two aircraft were later leased from British Aerospace, a Srs.518FG from late Oct76 and a Srs.523FJ from late Feb77, pending del of the first two of three newly ordered Srs.537GFs. These were del in Dec77 and late Jan78 in a single class 104 seat configuration. The third aircraft was leased to British Airways from new in Oct78 until the end of Apr80. Destinations served from Larnaca (the new base following the partition of Cyprus) by these aircraft have included Athens, Heraklion, Munich, Paris, Rhodes, Rome, Salonica and Zurich in Europe and Amman, Bahrain, Beirut, Cairo, Damascus, Dhahran, Dubai, Jeddah, Kuwait and Tel Aviv in the Middle East. Paphos to the western end of the island had scheduled service added to Athens from the summer of 1984. From Oct92 twice-weekly services have been jointly promoted with Saudia to both Jeddah and Riyadh using CY/SV flight numbers.

G-AXLM 199	G-BCWG 204	5B-DAF 201	5B-DAG 257
5B-DAH 258	5B-DAJ 261		

Dan-Air Services Ltd, (DA), London, UK

First obtained two Srs.401AKs from American Airlines in Mar69, followed by two used Srs.301AGs in Oct69 and Mar70. A damaged Srs.414EG was purchased and rebuilt on the Hurn production line in Dec71. At the end of Mar75 two Srs.207AJs were obtained from Zambia Airways, and four Srs.518FGs (formerly with Court Line) were bought between Jan and Mar of the same year. Two Srs.509EWs were obtained from British Caledonian in Oct75 and May76, and a Srs.520FN was obtained from British Aerospace in Oct79. Three Srs.500s were later bought from LACSA; these comprised two Srs.531FSs and one Srs.515FB with del in Nov81 and Mar and May82. The last One-Elevens purchased were a Srs.517FE in Oct83 after earlier lease from Mar of the same year and a Srs.301AG in Apr85. Several aircraft were leased for short periods, mainly to cover summer peak traffic, coming mainly from British Aerospace, but a Srs.525FT was leased from TAROM from Mar84 to the end of Dec85 and a Srs.561RC from the same source in Sep and Oct88 and again from Mar to Oct89. The type was used on inclusive tour and charter services throughout Europe and to North Africa both from the UK and from Berlin. A network of scheduled services was built up with the type, starting in Nov74 on the route from Gatwick to Newcastle. Domestically Gatwick was also linked with Aberdeen, Belfast, Jersey and Manchester, Heathrow with Inverness (from 27Mar83) and for a short while Manchester, and from Manchester to Aberdeen and Inverness. Internationally the type operated schedules from Gatwick to Amsterdam, Berlin, Clermont Ferrand, Cork, Dublin, Ibiza, Lourdes, Madrid, Mahon, Montpellier, Nice, Paris, Perpignan, Rome, Toulouse and Zurich. Manchester was linked with Amsterdam, Berlin (via Amsterdam), Gothenburg and Oslo, while schedules were flown from Newcastle to Bergen and Stavanger. A Berlin to Amsterdam twice daily service was also flown with the type. The last of the short fuselage Srs.200/300/400s was disposed of in Nov91, leaving the airline with a fleet of 11 Srs.500 aircraft, two of which operated in a 119 seat charter configuration and the remainder in a 99 seat scheduled operation configuration. On 23Oct92 it was announced that the airline was to be taken over by British Airways. The last revenue One-Eleven flight took place when G-BCWA arrived at Gatwick from Toulouse as flight DA910 on 06Nov92 at 0937 in advance of the official takeover on 08Nov92.

G-ATPJ 033	G-ATPK 034	G-ATPL 035	G-ATTP 039
G-ATVH 040	G-AVOE 129	G-AVOF 131	G-AWWX 184
G-AXCK 090	G-AXCP 087	G-AXYD 210	G-AZED 127
G-AZPZ 229	G-BCWA 205	G-BCXR 198	G-BDAE 203
G-BDAS 202	G-BDAT 232	G-BEKA 230	G-BJMV 244
G-BJYL 208	G-BJYM 242	G-BPNX 110	G-BSYN 186
G-TARO 272	YR-BRD 404		

Defence Research Agency - see Royal Aerospace Establishment

Deutsche Lufthansa AG, (LH), Frankfurt, West Germany

Bavaria Fluggesellschaft Schwabe & Co was contracted to operate its Srs.400 One-Elevens on behalf of this operator during 1970. Weekday scheduled services were operated twice daily over the Hanover to Munich route and once daily over the Hanover to Stuttgart route.

Dimex - see Romavia

Dominicana - see Compania Dominicana de Aviacion C por A

East-West Airlines Ltd, (EW), Tamworth, New South Wales, Australia

Following a demonstration with a Srs.402AP which the manufacturer leased from Philippine Airlines in Jun69, an order was announced in Dec70 for one Srs.475 for this carrier, but no aircraft was subsequently del.

El Al Israel Airlines Ltd, (LY), Tel Aviv, Israel

Arkia Inland Airways Srs.500s were used to operate scheduled flights between Tel Aviv and Larnaca on behalf of this carrier in 1978 and 1979.

Emerald Air

Operated a Srs.204AF on lease from Pacific Express in Nov and Dec73.

N1120J   102

Empresa Guatemalteca de Aviation SA - see Aerolineas de Guatemala - Aviateca

Engelhard Industries Inc

Ordered a corporate Srs.419EP through Page Airways International with del in Sep67. It was initially laid out with a 74 seat cabin but was later converted into a corporate configurationuration and used worldwide on executive work until sold in Apr71.

N270E   120

European Aviation Air Charter Ltd, (EAF), Filton, Bristol, UK

Formed as a subsidiary and the operating arm of European Aviation Ltd, this company inaugurated service on 16Feb94 and currently operates five of the parent company's Srs.510EDs, with a sixth due to enter service in early 1995. All are op in 104 seat all-tourist configuration. A Srs.530FX in a 50 seat luxury configuration is due to enter service later in 1994 on executive charter work with a second Srs.530FX, a Srs.523FJ and a Srs.501EX due in service in early 1995. The company carries out ad hoc charter work trading as European Aircharter and has obtained contracts to operate inclusive tour charter work. Schedules have also been flown from Stansted on behalf of Ryanair Ltd and from Birmingham on behalf of Maersk Air Ltd.

G-AVMH 136	G-AVMI 137	G-AVMK 139	G-AVMN 142
G-AVMP 144	G-AVMS 146	G-AWYV 178	G-AXLL 193
G-AYOP 233	G-AZMF 240		

European Aviation Ltd, Warley, West Midlands, UK

This company initially purchased two former Royal Australian Air Force Srs.217EAs in Sep90, which were subsequently sold to Okada Air Ltd in Dec91. Later 16 Srs.510EDs were bought from British Airways, together with a comprehensive spares package, on 07May93. Two of these aircraft were leased to Air Bristol from Oct93, while a subsidiary company, European Aviation Air Charter Ltd, was formed in late Sep93 to operate a number of these aircraft on charter work from its base at Filton-Bristol. In Jun94 a Srs.530FX and a Srs.501EX were bought from British Airways, and it was anticipated that the final stored Srs.530FXs of British Airways and a Srs.523FJ of British Midland would also be purchased. At least one of these was due to be converted as a 50 seat executive aircraft for charter use by European Aviation Air Charter.

G-AVMH 136	G-AVMI 137	G-AVMJ 138	G-AVMK 139
G-AVML 140	G-AVMM 141	G-AVMN 142	G-AVMP 144
G-AVMR 145	G-AVMS 146	G-AVMT 147	G-AVMV 149
G-AVMW 150	G-AVMX 151	G-AVMY 152	G-AVMZ 153
G-AWYV 178	G-AXLL 193	G-AYOP 233	G-AZMF 240
G-EXPM 124	G-KROO 125		

Faucett - see Compania de Aviacion Faucett SA

Flamingo Airlines Ltd, (PL), Nassau, Bahamas

Leased a Srs.203AE from Braniff Airways from Jul71 to May72; this was used on routes from Nassau to Freeport and Port au Prince.

N1543   017

Flightways Air Services Pty Ltd, (FS), Perth, Western Australia

Operated a scheduled once-weekly service between Singapore and Christmas Island in the Indian Ocean with a Srs.401AK from Jan88. Service ceased by Jun of the same year.

N172FE   056

Florida Express Inc, (ZO), Orlando, Florida, USA

Obtained nine Srs.203AEs from USAir between Jan84 and Dec85, two of which were initially leased for six months before being purchased. From Jan to Jul86 the seven Srs.201ACs earlier operated by Pacific Express were procured. Between Jun86 and Feb87 five Srs.401AKs and one Srs.414EG were obtained from a variety of sources. The Srs.200 aircraft were operated in a 79 seat configuration, while the Srs.400s were fitted with 84 seats.   An extensive scheduled network hubbing on Orlando, Florida, was built up after inaugurating service on 26Jan84.   Clearwater/St Petersburg, Forts Lauderdale and Myers, Miami, Sarasota and West Palm Beach in Florida were fed through Orlando to points which included Akron, Birmingham (Alabama), Cincinatti, Columbus (Ohio), Dayton, Harrisburg, Huntsville, Indianapolis, Knoxville, Louisville, Milwaukee, Nashville, Norfolk and Richmond (Virginia). Nassau (Bahamas) was also served. The company was merged into Braniff Airways on 01Mar88, having earlier operated as a Braniff Express partner for a short while.

N101EX 007	N102EX 009	N103EX 010	N104EX 011
N105EX 012	N106EX 013	N107EX 085	N170FE 057
N171FE 061	N172FE 056	N173FE 087	N174FE 127
N179FE 075	N1135J 046	N1136J 071	N1543 017
N1544 018	N1545 019	N1546 020	N1547 041
N1548 042	N1549 043		

Força Aerea Brasileira

Ordered two Srs.423ETs on 19Nov67 which were del in Oct68 and May69. The aircraft were used for Government VIP transport, for which they were specially fitted out by Marshall of Cambridge (Engineering). Each aircraft was laid out with two cabins, one in an executive configuration and the other with 24 first class seats. They were disposed of in Dec76.

VC92-2110   154   VC92-2111   118

Ford Motor Company Ltd, Stansted, Essex, UK

Purchased two Srs.423ETs from the Força Aerea Brasileira in Dec76 and a Srs.402AP in Nov77 from Bavaria/Germanair Fluggesellschaft. These three aircraft were used to transport personnel between Ford's numerous car production plants in Europe. Two of the aircraft were advertised for sale in Mar93 and were eventually disposed of in Aug of the same year, leaving the company with a single Srs.423ET.

G-BEJM   118   G-BEJW   154   G-BFMC   160

GAS Airlines (General & Aviation Services) Ltd, (GR), Lagos, Nigeria

This carrier, which is administered from Ilorin, leased a Srs.424EU from TAROM in Jul87 until two aircraft of the same type were purchased from LAR with del in Apr and Nov89. A Srs.204AF was prepared and painted for this operator in May91 at Southend but was not del; a Srs.481FW was added in Mar93. The company flies both scheduled and charter flights within Nigeria. Points served include Ilorin, Kaduna, Kano, Lagos, Maiduguri and Yola. A three month experimental service was flown to Accra in 1990 but was abandoned as unviable.

YR-BCE   165   5N-AVX   167   5N-AXV   159   (5N-SKS)   100
5N-SKS   243

GEC Ferranti Defence Systems Ltd, Edinburgh, UK

This company purchased a Srs.539GL from British Airways in Jun91 to be converted as a testbed for the ECR-90 radar due to be installed in the European Fighter Aircraft. Due to the urgency of the programme and the earlier availability of an already modified One-Eleven airframe with the Defence Research Agency, however, the two aircraft were exchanged, and the flight testing has been carried out in the DRA's Srs.479FU.

G-BGKE   263   ZE433   245

General & Aviation Services Ltd - see GAS Airlines

Germanair Bedarfsluftfahrt GmbH, (DV), Frankfurt, West Germany

Initially ordered three, later followed by a fourth, Srs.524FFs in a high density 114 seat configuration, which were del in Oct and Dec69, Mar70 and May71. Capacity was later increased to 119 seats. Prior to the first del a Srs.409AY was leased from Aug to Oct69. Two used Srs.515FBs were purchased and del in May72. After the sale of one of its aircraft a replacement was leased in the form of a Srs.518FG from Court Line Aviation from May to the end of Oct74. The fleet was used on inclusive tour and charter work throughout

Europe and to North Africa. The company merged with Bavaria Fluggesellschaft Schwabe & Co on 01Mar77 to form Bavaria/Germanair Fluggesellschaft.

D-AMAM 229	D-AMAS 187	D-AMAT 235	D-AMIE 190
D-AMOR 197	D-AMUR 195	G-AXBB 162	G-AXMK 205

Grenada Airways Ltd, (GG), George Town, Grenada

Inaugurated a twice weekly schedule between Miami and Grenada on 11Jun86 with a Srs.401AK. The aircraft was operated on the company's behalf by Challenge International Airlines and did so until early 1987.

N218CA 089

Guinness Peat Aviation Group Plc

This company purchased 12 aircraft from Braniff Airways in 1988 and leased them back to that airline. They comprised six Srs.201ACs, three Srs.203AEs, two Srs.401AKs and one Srs.414EG. This lease continued until Braniff ceased operating in Nov89. Since that time three Srs.201ACs have been leased to British Air Ferries (one for spares use only), two Srs.201ACs and one Srs.414EG to ADC Airlines of Nigeria and one Srs.401AK and a Srs.201AC to Shabair of Zaire. Individual aircraft have also been leased to the Detroit Red Wings and to SARO Airlines of Mexico. The remaining two Srs.201ACs were broken up for spares in Orlando without further use. The four Srs.208ALs of Aer Lingus were purchased in 1991 and leased to Hold-Trade Air Services of Nigeria.

EI-BWI 007	EI-BWJ 009	EI-BWK 011	EI-BWL 012
EI-BWM 013	EI-BWN 020	EI-BWO 041	EI-BWP 043
EI-BWQ 057	EI-BWR 061	EI-BWS 085	EI-BWT 127
G-DBAF 011	G-OCNW 012	N682RW 061	XA-RTN 085
5N-AYY 043	5N-BAA 041	5N-BAB 127	5N-HTA 051
5N-HTB 052	5N-HTC 049	5N-HTD 050	9Q-CEH 057
9Q-CSJ 013	9Q-CUG 057		

Gulf Aviation Company Ltd, (GF), Bahrain

Ordered one Srs.432FD on 29Jul69 with an option on a second. This option was taken up and the aircraft del in Oct69 and Nov71. A used Srs.409AY was bought with del in Feb74. Two Srs.416EKs were leased from Cambrian Airways, one from Oct73 to the end of Jun74 and the other in Oct and Nov74, while a Srs.413FA was leased from Bavaria Fluggesellschaft in full Gulf Air colours from Nov75 to May77. One of the Srs.432FDs was leased to British Airways from Aug to Nov77. The aircraft were operated throughout the Gulf area and to Egypt, India and Pakistan. Points served from Bahrain included Abu Dhabi, Bombay, Cairo, Doha, Dubai, Karachi, Kuwait, Muscat, Sharjah and Shiraz. The type was finally disposed of in Nov77.

A40-BB 162	A40-BU 157	A40-BX 121	D-ALLI 116
G-AVOF 131	G-AWBL 132	G-AXBB 162	G-AXMU 157
G-AXOX 121			

Hapag-Lloyd Fluggesellschaft GmbH, (HF), Hanover, Germany

This company merged with Bavaria/Germanair Fluggesellschaft in Jan79, retaining Hapag-

Lloyd as the company name. With the merger came seven Srs.500 One-Elevens comprising three Srs.528FLs, two Srs.515FBs and two Srs.524FFs. The aircraft continued to be used on inclusive tour and charter flights, mainly within Europe. The aircraft were disposed of between Nov79 and Mar82.

D-ALFA 234	D-AMAM 229	D-AMAS 187	D-AMAT 235
D-AMOR 197	D-AMUC 227	D-ANUE 238	

Hawaiian Airlines Inc, (HA), Honolulu, Hawaii, USA

In Jan63 this carrier announced its plans to order three Srs.209 aircraft, but no order was finalised.

Hellenic Air, Athens, Greece

Obtained a Srs.215AU from the Aviation Leasing Group in Sep92. By mid Jan93 the aircraft had been painted in this company's colours.

SX-BAR 096

Helmut Horten GmbH, Dusseldorf, West Germany

On 10Aug64 this large department store company ordered a Srs.211AH fitted with a 34 seat executive cabin which was del in Jan66. The aircraft was used as a corporate aircraft until sold in Sep75.

D-ABHH 084

Hold-Trade Air Services Ltd, Kaduna, Nigeria

Leased four former Aer Lingus Srs.208ALs from Guinness Peat Aviation with del taking place between Jun91 and Mar92. A fifth aircraft, so far unidentified, was reportedly in service by Sep92.

5N-HTA 051	5N-HTB 052	5N-HTC 049	5N-HTD 050
5N-HTP ???			

Iberia Lineas Aereas de España SA, (IB), Madrid, Spain

Jointly marketed services were operated between 1984 and 1991 over the routes Bucharest to Barcelona and to Madrid both direct and via Zurich using TAROM One-Elevens flying with RO/IB flight numbers.

Inex Adria Airways - see Adria Airways

International Lease Finance Corporation

Purchased two Srs.207AJs in Dec89 and two Srs.301AGs in Jan90, all from Dan-Air Services. All four aircraft were immediately leased back to Dan-Air. The Srs.301AGs were returned to the lessor in Oct90 and immediately leased to LADECO. The Srs.207AJs were returned to ILFC in Oct and Nov91 and also leased to LADECO. This organisation later purchased 11 Srs.500s from Dan-Air and leased them back to the carrier. The entire fleet was leased to British Air Ferries when Dan-Air withdrew the type in Nov92.

CC-CYF	033	CC-CYI	035	CC-CYL	040	CC-CYM	039
G-ATPJ	033	G-ATPL	035	G-ATTP	039	G-ATVH	040
G-AWWX	184	G-AXYD	210	G-BCWA	205	G-BCXR	198
G-BDAE	203	G-BDAS	202	G-BDAT	232	G-BEKA	230
G-BJMV	244	G-BJYL	208	G-BJYM	242	G-OBWA	232
G-OBWB	202	G-OBWC	230	G-OBWD	203	G-OBWE	242
G-OBWF	210	G-OBWG	184	G-OBWH	208		

Istanbul Hava Yollari, (IL), Istanbul, Turkey

Leased three Srs.525FTs from TAROM during the summer of 1986 to operate on European charter flights to and from Turkey. A Srs.561RC was leased from the same source for similar work in the summer of 1988.

TC-AKA	255	TC-ARI	253	TC-JCP	254	YR-BRA	401

JARO International SA, (JT), Bucharest, Romania

This airline, which had previously leased aircraft from Romavia and TAROM for its charter operations, purchased two Srs.528FLs from British Airways in early Oct93. By May94 one of the aircraft was being flown on behalf of Air Alfa of Turkey.

YR-JBA 234   YR-JBB 238

Jugoslovenski Aerotransport - JAT, (JU), Belgrade, Jugoslavia

Leased a Srs.561RC from TAROM which was operated in full JAT colours during the summers of 1989 and 1990 on the company's European network.

YR-BRA 401

Kabo Air Ltd, (KO), Lagos, Nigeria

This carrier, which has its administrative headquarters at Kano and its maintenance base at Jos, obtained ten Srs.204AFs and one Srs.215AU formerly operated by USAir with del from Nov90. Two of these aircraft were reportedly used for spares only. Two Srs.407AWs were added in Nov91 and Feb92, and a Srs.414EG and Srs.423ET were added in Aug93. Scheduled services are flown from Lagos to Abuja, Enugu, Jos, Kaduna, Kano and Port Harcourt, while Abuja to Minna and Kano to Maiduguri schedules are also flown. Charter flights are undertaken domestically. The company has a contract with the Federal Government for the support of the ECOMOG (West African Military) force in Liberia.

5N-GGG	160	5N-KBA	179	5N-KBC	104	5N-KBD	102
5N-KBE	???	5N-KBG	082	5N-KBN	???	5N-KBM	105
5N-KBO	180	5N-KBR	093	5N-KBS	031	5N-KBT	100
5N-KBV	032	5N-KBW	106	5N-KKK	154	N1112J	030
N1122J	103						

Kiwi International Airlines Inc, (KP), Newark, New Jersey, USA

Signed an agreement to purchase 11 Rolls-Royce Tay powered Rombac One-Eleven 2500s on 08Feb93. Included in the deal was an option to purchase a further five aircraft; this option was taken up in Jun93. First deliveries are due to take place in late 1995.

N	411	N	412	N		N	
N		N		N		N	
N		N		N		N	
N		N		N		N	

KLM (Koninklijke Luchtvaart Maatschappij) NV, (KL), Amsterdam, The Netherlands

Leased a Srs.301AG from British Eagle International Airways in full KLM colours from late Mar to Aug68 for operation on the company's Rotterdam to London route.

G-ATPJ   033

Kuwait Airways Corporation, (KU), Kuwait

This company ordered three Srs.205AGs with an option on a fourth on 09Aug62; the order was amended to Srs.301AGs early in 1965. The option was not taken up, and the aircraft were never operated by Kuwait Airways but were initially leased to British Eagle International Airways laid out in a 79 seat single class configuration from Jun and Jul66 until that carrier ceased operations in Nov68. The aircraft were then sold.

(9K-ACI) 033   (9K-ACJ) 034   (9K-ACK) 035

LACSA - see Lineas Aereas Costarricenses SA

LADECO - see Linea Aerea del Cobre SA

Laker Airways Ltd, (GK), Gatwick Airport, UK

Ordered three Srs.320L-AZs on 08Feb66 laid out in an 84 seat single class configuration. They were del in Feb, Mar and May67, followed by a fourth aircraft in Apr68 which had been ordered on 28Jun67. One of these was del from new to Air Congo on lease from May67 to the end of Feb68, being replaced by a second aircraft of the same type until May68. A Srs.432FD was leased in Aug and Sep69 and a used Srs.301AG was bought in Feb71, this being sold in Feb81. The aircraft were used on inclusive tour and charter flights to European and North African destinations from many UK airports. The airline ceased trading on 25Feb82.

G-ATPK   034   G-AVBW   107   G-AVBX   109   G-AVBY   113
G-AVYZ   133   G-AXMU   157

LANICA - see Lineas Aereas de Nicaragua SA

Lauda Air Luftfahrt GmbH, (NG), Vienna, Austria

Leased two Srs.525FTs from TAROM with del in Mar and Apr85. The aircraft were operated on inclusive tour and charter flights throughout Europe until returned to the lessor at the end of Nov85 and Jul86.

OE-ILC   255   OE-ILD   256

Leeward Islands Air Transport Services Ltd, (LI), Antigua, West Indies

While under the control of Court Line this carrier initially leased a Srs.518FG from the parent carrier from late Nov71 to the end of Jun72. This was replaced by the first of three Srs.517FEs from the same source. The second following in Nov72 and the last in early Dec73. These last three aircraft had all originally been built for Bahamas Airways, but only two had actually seen service with that carrier. The type was first introduced into service on 01Dec71 on the company's schedules linking the Leeward and Windward chain of islands with other points in the West Indies. The aircraft were all returned to Court Line in Mar and Apr74.

VP-LAK   205   VP-LAN   198   VP-LAP   188   VP-LAR   189

Linea Aerea del Cobre SA - LADECO, (UC), Santiago, Chile

Leased two Srs.301AGs from the International Lease Finance Corporation with del in Nov and Dec90 and two Srs.207AJs from the same source in Nov and Dec91. The type was introduced into service on 07Dec90 and has been operated on single class domestic schedules from Santiago to Antofagasta, Arica, Balmaceda, Concepcion, Iquique, La Serena, Puerto Montt, Temuco, Valdivia and Vina del Mar and to Mendoza in Argentina. Charter flights are also flown, these having extended as far south as Puerto Williams in Chile.

CC-CYF   033   CC-CYI   035   CC-CYL   040   CC-CYM   039

Linea Aerea Nacional de Chile SA - LAN, (LA), Santiago, Chile

During 1970 a twice weekly schedule was flown on behalf of this carrier between San Carlos de Bariloche in Argentina and Puerto Montt in Chile by Austral Compania Argentina de Transportes Aereos with its One-Elevens.

Lineas Aereas Costarricenses SA - LACSA, (LR), San Jose, Costa Rica

Ordered one Srs.409AY with an option on a second on 19Jan66; this option was later taken up and the aircraft del in Apr67 and Nov69 laid out in a 74 seat single class configuration. Three Srs.531FSs laid out in a 99 seat single class configuration were later ordered with del in May71, Nov72 and May73. A used Srs.515FB was purchased in Dec73, when the second Srs.409AY was sold to the manufacturer, the first having been sold to TACA International Airlines in Apr73. The aircraft were used on scheduled routes from San Jose to Barranquila, Cartagina and San Andres Island (Colombia), Caracas and Maracaibo (Venezuela), Panama City, Grand Cayman, Miami and Mexico City. Service with the type was inaugurated on 14May67. The aircraft also operated on behalf of Cayman Airways between Grand Cayman and Kingston (Jamaica) and Miami. The last of the One-Elevens was disposed of in May82.

TI-LRF   237   TI-LRI   242   TI-LRJ   244   TI-LRK   208
TI-LRL   237   TI-1055C   162   TI-1056C   108   TI-1084C   237
TI-1095C   242   TI-1096C   244

Lineas Aereas de España SA - see Iberia, Lineas Aereas de España SA

Lineas Aereas de Nicaragua SA - LANICA, (NI), Managua, Nicaragua

A Srs.208AL was leased from Aer Lingus from late Oct66 pending del of a Srs.412EB ordered from the manufacturer on 04Apr66. An option was also placed on a second aircraft, but this was not taken up. The aircraft was del in Apr67 laid out in a 74 seat single class configuration but following an attempted hijack was returned to Hurn for repair in Jan72. A Srs.518FG was leased from Court Line to replace the damaged aircraft from Dec71, which in turn was replaced by a Srs.401AK leased from American Airlines in Mar72. The Hughes Tool Company took a 25% interest in LANICA in Jul72 while the damaged aircraft was being repaired and the decision was made to sell the One-Eleven and use surplus Hughes Tool owned Convair 880s on the company's routes. The One-Eleven had first been introduced into service on 01Nov66 on the Miami to Managua scheduled route, which was also flown via San Pedro Sula. The aircraft were also flown on scheduled services from Managua to Mexico City via San Salvador. Through an inter-governmental agreement the aircraft was also operated on behalf of Transportes Aereos Nacionales (TAN) both on their own services and over a pooled route between Miami and San Pedro Sula.

AN-BBI   111   AN-BBS   050   AN-BHJ   206   AN-BHN   074

Linee Airee Italiane - Alitalia, (AZ), Rome, Italy

A joint service was operated between London-Gatwick and Genoa by British Caledonian Airways' One-Elevens initially six and later seven times per week. This agreement had started by 1980 and continued until 1989, with British Airways taking over the operation from BCAL in Apr88. Through similar arrangements One-Elevens of British Airways were used on daily flights from Milan-Linate to both Birmingham and Manchester and on weekend flights from Rome to Manchester. Flights operated with AZ/BR or AZ/BA flight numbers. Joint services were also flown between Bucharest and Rome using TAROM One-Elevens, one of these flights operating via Tirana (Albania). These joint AZ/RO flights operated at various periods from Apr82 until late 1988.

Liniile Aeriene Romane - LAR, (QR), Bucharest, Romania

This operator, a subsidiary of TAROM, has obtained four Srs.424EUs from the parent company with the first two coming on strength in Dec75. Two of the aircraft were sold in Nigeria in Apr and Nov89.

YR-BCC   167   YR-BCD   159   YR-BCE   165   YR-BCF   168

Loganair Ltd, (LC), Glasgow, Scotland, UK

Leased a Srs.561RC from Ryanair Europe in Apr and May89, immediately followed by a Srs.476FM from the same carrier until early Oct89. The aircraft were mainly used in operating Manchester to Edinburgh schedules.

G-AZUK   241   G-BNIH   406

London European Airways Plc, (UQ), Luton, Beds, UK

Formed as a UK subsidiary of Ryanair, this company introduced a Srs.561RC leased from TAROM onto scheduled services from Luton to Amsterdam and Brussels on 22May87. From Jan88 the company was marketed as Ryanair Europe and the aircraft repainted accordingly. The scheduled operations ceased in Jan89, from which time the carrier concentrated on charter flights. A Srs.476FM was added to the fleet in Mar89, and three aircraft were added for operations during summer 1990, when the airline was once again marketed as London European Airways. These comprised a Srs.518FG and a Srs.531FS

Production of early Srs.200s for British United and Braniff Airways under way at Hurn

This immaculate executive interior of an unidentified US registered One-Eleven is typical of the fit which could be incorporated
(BAe)

A fine shot taken from the cockpit of TAROM's YR-BCI on finals into Hurn; instrument and cockpit layout are clearly shown   (BAe)

C/n 008 - Srs.201AC XX105 of the RAE/DRA on approach to Bedford in Sep91 (K Gaskell)

C/n 016 - Srs.203AE N1542 engineless in Atlantic Gulf c/s at Miami in Oct86 (K Gaskell)

C/n 039 - Srs.207AJ G-ATTP of British Eagle at Heathrow in Jul68 (J J Halley)

C/n 040 - Sr

C/n 014 -

C/n 066 - Srs.401AK G-AZMI in Orientair c/s without titles (R Collishaw)

C/n 015 -
c/s

C/n 042 - Sr

C/n 067 - Srs.401AK N109TH in Sep90 (Elliot Greenman)

C/n 074

C/n 050 - Sr

C/n 070 - Srs.203AE - The ill-fated Braniff N1553 seen in 1966 at Goose Bay on delivery; note lack of rear airstairs on this version (D Collishaw Collection)

C/n 056 - Srs.401AK N12CZ of Congoleum Aviation at Lasham in Mar86 (K Gaskell)

C/n 059 - Srs.401AK N650DH, the One-Eleven 2400 prototype with Rolls-Royce Tays (R J Church)

C/n 061 - Srs.401AK N682RW in Feb82 (Elliot Greenman)

C/n 066 - Srs.401AK G-AZMI in Orientair c/s without titles (R Collishaw)

C/n 067 - Srs.401AK N109TH in Sep90 (Elliot Greenman)

C/n 070 - Srs.203AE - The ill-fated Braniff N1553 seen in 1966 at Goose Bay on delivery; note lack of rear airstairs on this version (D Collishaw Collection)

in Apr and a Srs.523FJ in May, at which time the original Srs.500 was transferred to Ryanair. Two of the other Srs.500s were also transferred to Ryanair in Dec90, followed by the last of the type in May91. The aircraft were used on charter and inclusive tour flights throughout Europe and were also leased to Loganair for use on that company's schedules from Apr to Oct89. The company went into receivership on 31May91.

| G-AZUK | 241 | G-BNIH | 406 | G-DJOS | 237 | G-EKPT | 211 |
| G-FLRU | 201 | YR-BRF | 406 |

Lufthansa - see Deutsche Lufthansa AG

Maersk Air Ltd, (VB and BA), Birmingham, UK

With effect from 01Aug93 Brymon European Airways was broken down into its component parts of Birmingham European Airways and Brymon Airways. The former became wholly owned by Maersk Air I/S of Denmark and was renamed Maersk Air Ltd. The new airline continues to operate the four One-Eleven 400s and the single Srs.500 on the Birmingham originating schedules established by its predecessor. A second Srs.501EX was leased from British Airways in Aug94. Destinations served from Birmingham are Amsterdam, Belfast International, Copenhagen, Milan and Stuttgart. From late Mar94 Cork and Lyon were additional destinations served. The aircraft are now painted in British Airways colours with small Maersk Air titles and all scheduled services are flown as British Airways flights with BA flight numbers, while charter flights are flown with the VB flight prefix.

| G-AVGP | 114 | G-AWBL | 132 | G-AWYR | 174 | G-AWYS | 175 |
| G-BBME | 066 | G-BBMG | 115 |

Manx Airlines Ltd, (JE), Ronaldsway Airport, Isle of Man, UK

Leased a Srs.304AX from Airways International Cymru, which was introduced into service on the scheduled route from the Isle of Man to London-Heathrow on 16May87 in full Manx Airlines colours. The aircraft flew this route up to three times daily until replaced by a British Aerospace 146-100 on 04Dec87.

G-WLAD 112

Marmara Air, Istanbul, Turkey

Arranged the lease of two Srs.525FTs from TAROM for summer 1986 operations. The aircraft were painted in the airline's colours, but before delivery could take place the company was taken over by Istanbul Hava Yollari.

McAlpine Aviation Ltd, (RM), Luton, Beds, UK

Purchased the last two aircraft off the UK production line. These were built as Srs.492GMs, converted for executive charter work and del in Jul84. One was disposed of in Mar90 and the second in Oct92.

G-BLDH 262   G-BLHD 260

Mediterranean Express Ltd, (MEE), Luton, Beds, UK

Purchased two used Srs.476FMs with del in Jun and Dec87. The second had its overhaul abandoned and was never used. The remaining aircraft was operated until Jan88 on inclusive tour charters from UK provincial airports to mainland Europe.

G-AYUW 239   G-AZUK 241

PN Merpati Nusantara Airlines, (MZ), Jakarta, Indonesia

Leased a Srs.401AK, which was del from American Airlines in full Merpati colours, in Aug71. When no pure jet operating licence was granted by the Indonesian Government, the aircraft was returned to the lessor in Nov71 without seeing service with the airline. From mid 1977 a Srs.416EK of Pertamina/Pelita Air Service was used to operate a once weekly schedule on behalf of Merpati between Denpasar and Darwin; this continued until May78.

N5032   074   PK-PJC   166

Mohawk Airlines Inc, (MO), Utica-Rome, New York, USA

Placed the first order for four Srs.204AFs on 24Jul62. After eight repeat orders placed between 1964 and 1968, this carrier's final commitment for new aircraft was for 18 Srs.204AFs, which were del between May65 and May69. The aircraft were del in an unusual 69 seat single class configuration, which comprised alternating four and five abreast rows of seats with facing seat rows over the wing centre section. Two Srs.215AUs were bought from Aloha Airlines in Mar69, and a third was leased from the same source a month later. In Sep70 three Srs.203AEs were obtained from Braniff Airways. A comprehensive scheduled network was flown throughout the north-eastern states of the USA after inaugurating service with the type on 15Jul65. The points ranged from Boston and Providence in the east, New York (La Guardia, Kennedy and Newark), Pittsburgh and Washington in the south, Detroit, Cleveland and Minneapolis to the west and Burlington and Watertown in the north. Internationally, Toronto and Montreal in Canada were served. The company merged into Allegheny Airlines on 12Apr72.

N1112J   030   N1113J   031   N1114J   032   N1115J   082
N1116J   098   N1117J   099   N1118J   100   N1119J   101
N1120J   102   N1122J   103   N1123J   104   N1124J   134
N1125J   135   N1126J   179   N1127J   180   N1128J   181
N1129J   182   N1130J   096   N1131J   097   N1132J   105
N1134J   045   N1135J   046   N1136J   071   N2111J   029

Monarch Airlines Ltd, (OM), Luton, Beds, UK

Leased a Srs.518FG and a Srs.517FE from the manufacturer from Feb75 until Oct76 and from Mar75 until Mar83 respectively. A Srs.509EW was leased from British Caledonian Airways in Nov75 before being purchased outright in Jan77. A second Srs.518FG was leased from the manufacturer in Oct76 replacing a similar model. The three aircraft flew inclusive tour contract and charter flights to numerous points in Europe until the last aircraft was retired in Oct85.

G-AWWZ 186   G-AXMG 201   G-BCWG 204   G-BCXR 198

Mr Mouaffak Al Midani, Saudi Arabia

A corporate Srs.488GH was ordered by this customer with del in May78. It was then flown to Long Beach, California, for the installation of an executive interior and an avionics package prior to introduction into service. This, the only executive version of the Srs.475 to be exported new to a customer, was re-registered in Luxembourg in Dec85. It was mainly flown within Europe until it was disposed of in Jun93.

HZ-MAM 259   LX-MAM 259

National Aircraft Leasing, Burbank, California, USA

This organisation, part of the Tiger Leasing Group, purchased 16 Srs.401AKs from American Airlines, which were fitted out as luxury corporate aircraft with the option of additional fuel tanks installed in the forward underfloor hold to increase considerably the range of the aircraft. Conversion work was carried out under contract by the Dee Howard Company of San Antonio. The aircraft were either sold or leased to corporate users. Three of the aircraft were leased to airline operators pending executive conversion; two went to Austral Lineas Aereas from Dec76 to Apr77, and a third went to Aeroamerica from May to Oct76 and then to Pacific American Airlines from Jan to Jul77. Full details of the conversion work involved can be found in the main text.

N111NA	055	N111NA	060	N111NA	065	N112NA	059
N112NA	088	N5015	055	N5016	056	N5017	057
N5019	059	N5020	060	N5024	064	N5025	065
N5027	067	N5028	068	N5029	069	N5030	072
N5034	076	N5036	078	N5039	081	N5042	088

National Aviation Company (NC), Cairo, Egypt

By Jul92 this company was operating a leased Srs.401AK for cargo charter work.

N217CA   063

Nationwide Air Charter (Pty) Ltd, Lanseria, South Africa

Purchased a Srs.409AY fitted with a large main deck freight door in late Apr94. The aircraft had previously been flown by Rolls-Royce/Turbo-Union.

ZS-NNM   108

Okada Air Ltd, (9H), Lagos, Nigeria

This company, whose administrative and engineering base is at Benin, purchased four used Srs.320L-AZs with del in Sep, Oct and Nov83. Two Srs.420ELs were added in Nov85 and Feb86 together with a Srs.402AP in Jan86, all from Quebecair. In May and Sep87 two Srs.416EKs were bought from Britt Airways, while in May and Sep of the same year a Srs.401AK and a Srs.408EF were obtained from executive users. The first was retained as a corporate aircraft for the personal use of the owner of the airline. A Srs.409AY and a Srs.416EK were bought in Oct89 from British Island Airways, and two Srs.432FDs were obtained from the same source in Jul and Oct90. The year 1991 saw the addition of two Srs.304AXs, one Srs.424EU and one Srs.301AG in May, two Srs.539GLs from British Airways in Jul and one Srs.401AK in Aug. In Dec91 and Jan92 two Srs.217EAs were obtained, while a Srs.524FF was bought from Air Malawi in late Jul92. A contract was signed for the purchase of seven Srs.510EDs from British Airways, with the first due for del in Jun92; although these were painted in Okada Air colours, the deal was not completed and the aircraft not del. A scheduled network links Lagos with Abuja, Benin, Calabar, Enugu,

Jos, Kaduna, Kano, Port Harcourt and Yola (either via Kano or Kaduna). Charter flights are also undertaken, including executive work with the two Srs.217EAs which have retained the corporate configurations in use on the aircraft when they flew with the RAAF.

(G-AVMJ) 138	(G-AVML) 140	(G-AVMM) 141	(G-AVMR) 145
(G-AVMX) 151	(G-AVMY) 152	(G-AVMZ) 153	5N-AOK 113
5N-AOM 122	5N-AOP 109	5N-AOS 123	5N-AOT 133
5N-AOW 094	5N-AOZ 107	5N-AUS ???	5N-AYR 162
5N-AYS 129	5N-AYT 131	5N-AYU 062	5N-AYV 128
5N-AYW 166	5N-AXQ 157	5N-AXT 121	5N-BIN 265
5N-EHI 074	5N-MZE 110	5N-NRC 124	5N-OKA 168
5N-OMO 034	5N-ORO 264	(5N-OSA) 153	5N-OVE 112
5N-SDP 125	(5N-TOM) 125	(5N-USE) 151	5N-USE 235

Orientair Ltd, London, UK

This company arranged to buy two Srs.401AKs from American Airlines for operation on inclusive tour programmes from Berlin to Mediterranean holiday areas. The first aircraft was fully painted and readied for the company at Hurn by Oct72, but the company failed to start operations and the aircraft was not del.

(G-AXMI) 066

Oriental Airlines Ltd, (OAC), Lagos, Nigeria

Purchased a Srs.501EX and a Srs.515FB from British Airways, with the first aircraft handed over at the end of Jul93 and the second in Mar94.

5N-OAL 214   5N-IMO 229

Out Island Airways Ltd, (OE), Nassau, Bahamas

Purchased two used Srs.401AKs in Mar and Jun73 to operate on the carrier's inter-island routes. The airline was merged with Flamingo Airlines to form Bahamasair on 01Jul73. The aircraft continued to fly with OIA titles in addition to those of Bahamasair for some time after the creation of the new company.

VP-BDI 074   VP-BDJ 089

Ozark Airlines Inc, (OZ), St Louis, Missouri, USA

Placed a Letter of Intent for the purchase of five Srs.200 aircraft in May61; this was not followed up with a firm order.

Pacific American Airlines Inc, USA

Leased a Srs.401AK from National Aircraft Leasing from Jan to Jul77.

N5016   056

Pacific Express Inc, (VB), Chico, California, USA

This airline obtained the British Caledonian Airways seven strong fleet of Srs.201ACs between Dec81 and Jun82 and leased two Srs.200s from USAir from Nov82 and May83 to Dec83. A scheduled operation started on 27Jan82 and eventually linked Bakersfield, Chico, Fresno, Los Angeles, Modesto, Monterey, Palm Springs, Redding, Sacramento, San Francisco, San Jose, Santa Barbara and Stockton in California with Portland, Redmond, Medford and Klamath Falls in Oregon, Boise in Idaho and Reno and Las Vegas in Nevada. The company ceased operations on 02May84.

N101EX	007	N102EX	009	N103EX	010	N104EX	011
N105EX	012	N106EX	013	N107EX	085	N1120J	102
N1548	042						

Page Airways International Inc

This company was appointed exclusive sales agent in the USA for executive versions of newly built aircraft and was involved in the sale of two Srs.212ARs to Tenneco, one Srs.419EP to Engelhard Industries and one Srs.410AQ to Victor Comptometers.

Paninternational, (PE), Munich, West Germany

Known as Panair until 01Jan70, this airline initially ordered two Srs.515FBs, with two repeat orders for single aircraft being placed in 1970. The aircraft were del in Jun69, Mar and May70 and Mar71 laid out in a 109 seat single class configuration and were operated on inclusive tour and charter services throughout Europe until the carrier ceased trading on 06Oct71, going into liquidation on 31Dec71.

D-ALAQ   229   D-ALAR   207   D-ALAS   208   D-ALAT   187

People Express Inc - see Britt Airways Inc

Philippine Air Force

A Srs.408EF was obtained by the Central Bank of the Philippines on the used aircraft market in Feb74. After fitting out with an executive interior in the USA it was del to the Nichols Air Base near Manila in Jul of the same year. From here it was operated by the Philippine Air Force on Presidential and VIP flights by 702 Squadron of the 700th Special Mission Wing until it was disposed of in Feb84.

RP-C1   128

Philippine Airlines Inc, (PR), Manila, Philippines

Ordered two Srs.402APs on 02Nov64 with an option on a third to replace its Vickers Viscount 784 fleet. This option was taken up on 28Dec65, when a fourth aircraft was optioned. Although this latter option was taken up on 03May67, the aircraft was not del. The aircraft were del in Apr and Sep66 and Nov67 laid out in a 74 seat single class configuration. A Srs.432FD was leased from the manufacturer from Oct69 to Feb71 to replace one of the earlier del aircraft lost in an accident. Four Srs.527FKs laid out with 94 seat single class cabins were ordered on 06Aug70, of which only three were del, in Oct and Nov71. These replaced the Srs.400 aircraft, which were returned to the manufacturer in Jan and Feb72. Two further Srs.527FKs were ordered, with del in Jun and Jul74, while eight used examples of Srs.500s were purchased. These comprised two Srs.524FFs del in Apr and Nov74, two Srs.517FEs del in Sep and Nov75, a Srs.501EX del in Mar77 and a Srs.518FG del in Aug78. The last two aircraft were a Srs.516FP and a Srs.523FJ, both del in Jul80 to replace NAMC YS-11s, bringing the One-Eleven fleet up to 12. The Srs.402APs were introduced into service on 01May66 and were used internationally from Manila to Denpasar, Hong Kong, Saigon and Taipei, while domestically the capital was linked with Bacolod, Cebu, Davao and Iloilo. With the arrival of the Srs.500s the type was mainly used in flying domestic services among the many Philippine islands after introduction into service on 11Nov71. Destinations served from Manila included Bacolod, Cagayan de Oro, Cebu, Cotabato, Davao, Dumaguete, Iloilo, Kalibo, Laoag, Legaspi, Puerto Princesa, Roxas, San Jose, Tacloban, Tuguegarao and Zamboanga, while many of these points had direct flights between each other. Regional routes which did not justify widebody types were also served from Manila; these included Bandar Seri Begawan, Beijing, Ho Chi Minh City, Kota Kinabalu and Xiamen. With the introduction of leased Boeing 737-300s in Aug89, the One-Elevens were progressively withdrawn from service from Feb90. By mid May92 only one aircraft remained in service as a back-up to the Boeing 737 fleet. On 31May92 RP-C1185 operated the last One-Eleven service for Philippine Airlines when it flew into Manila from Legaspi as flight PR278, so ending 26 years of uninterrupted One-Eleven service with this carrier.

PI-C1121 091	PI-C1131 092	PI-C1141 094	(PI-C1151) 161
PI-C1151 157	PI-C1161 213	PI-C1171 215	PI-C1181 226
(PI-C1191) 231	RP-C1161 213	RP-C1171 215	RP-C1181 226
RP-C1182 246	RP-C1183 248	RP-C1184 190	RP-C1185 195
RP-C1186 188	RP-C1187 189	RP-C1188 209	RP-C1189 204
RP-C1193 231	RP-C1194 199		

Phoenix Airways AG, (HP), Basel, Switzerland

Ordered one Srs.529FR laid out in a high density 114 seat passenger configuration with del in Apr71. It was used on ad hoc charter and inclusive tour flights to European and North African destinations. The company ceased operations in 1974.

HB-ITL   212

Quebecair Inc, (QB), Quebec City, Quebec, Canada

Purchased two used Srs.304AXs with del in early Apr69 and a Srs.402AP with del in Mar73 following the earlier lease of a Srs.409AY for crew training from mid Mar to mid Apr69. A Srs.204AF was leased from USAir from May82 to Jan83, and two used Srs.420ELs were purchased in Sep82. The aircraft were used on schedules linking Quebec City, Montreal, Bagotville, Baie Comeau, Churchill Falls, Mont Joli, Rouyn, Schefferville, Sept Iles, Toronto, Val d'Or and Wabush and also on charter flights. The last One-Elevens were withdrawn in May85.

CF-QBN 110	CF-QBO 112	CF-QBR 094	C-FQBN 110
C-FQBO 112	C-FQBR 094	C-GQBP 122	C-GQBV 123
G-AXBB 162	N1117J 099		

Rolls-Royce Plc, Filton Aerodrome, Bristol, UK

Turbo-Union Ltd obtained a used Srs.409AY in Feb79 which was converted into a combi configuration by BAe at Hurn. The rear of the cabin from just ahead of the overwing emergency exits was initially fitted with 39 normal airline seats, while the forward section was stripped of seats and overhead racks. A large main deck cargo door measuring 10ft x 6ft 1 in (3.05m x 1.85m) was fitted, together with an additional 1in thick fire-resistant load-spreading plywood floor. This enabled a cargo load of 4,111kg to be carried on the main deck. The aircraft was operated on Turbo-Union's behalf by the Rolls-Royce Flying Unit carrying personnel, engines and equipment between plants in the UK, Germany and Italy, mainly in connection with the Panavia Tornado programme. The unit was closed down early in 1994 and the aircraft was sold.

G-BGTU   108

Romavia, (VQ), Bucharest, Romania

Obtained a Srs.561RC from TAROM in Mar90, followed by one used and a new Srs.561RC in 1992. This operator, which was known as Dimex until Feb91, was originally the Presidential and Government transport organisation but has more recently been licensed to operate both scheduled and charter flights in competition with the national carrier, TAROM.

In Nov92 the first of two aircraft entered service on lease to Citylink Airways of India, these being returned in Oct93.

YR-BRE   405   YR-BRH   408   YR-BRI   409

Royal Aerospace Establishment, Thurleigh, Beds/Farnborough, Hants and Boscombe Down, Wilts, UK

This research organisation, formerly called the Royal Aircraft Establishment, has obtained four used One-Elevens. The first, a Srs.201AC, was del in Mar73 and was initially used by the Blind Landing Experimental Unit at Thurleigh for the development of equipment to enable Category 3 approaches to be made. It was later used for investigation into steeper angles of approach in an effort to reduce the area over which noise nuisance was created. More recently it was used for flight control and navigation systems research. It is currently used as a flying laboratory in a contract from the UK Civil Aviation Authority for research into harmonising the various European Air Traffic Control Systems under the "PHARE" programme. It is fitted with an experimental Flight Management System which includes touch-screen computer controls and is the oldest One-Eleven still flying. The second aircraft, a Srs.402AP, was del to Farnborough in May74, where it was used by the Flight Management Department for research into communication and navigation systems and was fitted with externally mounted video cameras for monitoring control surfaces, engines etc which could not be observed from within the aircraft. It is still used in communications research as well as sonobuoy development work, for which it has been modified with a chute in the ventral entry area for launch purposes. The third aircraft, a Srs.479FU, was del to Thurleigh in Jun84, and the nose was considerably modified and recontoured to accommodate the Blue Vixen radar which was to be installed in the Sea Harrier FSR.2. The RAE was merged into a new body entitled the Defence Research Agency (DRA) with effect from Apr91. This third aircraft was exchanged for a Srs.539GL which GEC Ferranti Defence Systems Ltd had purchased from British Airways for flight testing the ECR-90 radar later to be installed in the European Fighter Aircraft. Since the flight testing of the Blue Vixen radar in the Srs.479FU had been completed and the aircraft was already modified to accept various fittings in the nose section, the exchange of aircraft took place in order that ECR-90 testing could be accomplished more quickly. The fourth DRA aircraft is to be used in radar research after it has been modified, replacing an earlier used Vickers Viscount and English Electric Canberra. All three flying laboratory One-Elevens were due to be based at Boscombe Down by 01Apr94, together with the Empire Test Pilots' School Srs.479FU.

XX105   008   XX919   091   ZE433   245   ZH763   263

Royal Air Force

The Queen's Flight of the Royal Air Force had originally considered the One-Eleven in 1971, but because of economy measures the type was rejected in favour of the HS Andover. The type was again considered in late 1977 as a replacement for the Andover and the specifications revised; this was done yet again in 1979 but this time with additional fuel tankage to increase the range to 2,400 miles. The Srs.475AM/670AM development aircraft was evaluated by the Flight for a week in Apr80, but capital sanction for a purchase was not forthcoming. Had it been adopted, the type would have been used worldwide for the transport of the UK Royal Household on official business. The last two Srs.475s off the UK production line had been earmarked for the Queen's Flight.

G-ASYD 053

Royal Australian Air Force

Ordered two Srs.217EAs on 01Dec65 which were del in Feb and Oct68. They were based at Fairbairn, Canberra, and operated in the VIP transport role by 34 (ST) Squadron, mainly flying longer domestic sectors. Overseas duties were also undertaken throughout Asia and Australasia, with one of the aircraft operating as far afield as Iran. The aircraft were initially each fitted with two executive cabins of 26 and 30 passenger seats, being later modified to seat only 28 passengers. Non-standard Rolls-Royce Spey Mk.511-14s engines were installed for improved airfield performance. They were eventually retired early in 1990, having flown over 28,000 hrs and 30,000 landings between them.

A12-124 124   A12-125 125

Ryanair Europe Ltd - see London European Airways Plc

Ryanair Ltd, (FR), Dublin, Eire

Leased its first aircraft, a Srs.561RC, from TAROM and introduced it into service on the company's Dublin to Luton schedule on 01Dec86. Two Srs.525FTs were leased from the same source in Mar and Apr87. For summer 1988 the fleet was doubled to six with the lease of two Srs.525FTs and a Srs.561RC in Mar, Apr and Jun, all from TAROM. Two Srs.525FTs were returned to TAROM in Nov89. In Jun90 a Srs.561RC was transferred from Ryanair Europe until it was returned to TAROM in Oct of the same year. In Dec90 a Srs.531FS and a Srs.523FJ were transferred from Ryanair Europe after another Srs.561RC was returned to TAROM a month earlier. A Srs.509EW previously operated by Dan-Air Services was taken on strength in Apr91, followed by Ryanair Europe's last Srs.500, a Srs.518FG, in May91. A previously used Srs.561RC and a Srs.525FT were once again leased from TAROM in Apr92 for the summer season. For summer 1993 the company initially leased an earlier used Srs.561RC from TAROM from Apr to Jun before leasing four Srs.501EXs from British Airways from early Jun after signing an agreement on 28May93. The last of the leased Romanian aircraft was returned to TAROM in Oct93. With the arrival of a fleet of used Boeing 737-200s in the spring of 1994, the One-Elevens were withdrawn from most scheduled services, and the four leased British Airways aircraft were returned to the lessor between Jan and Mar94. This was quickly followed by the withdrawal from service of two of the remaining One-Elevens in Apr94, leaving just two One-Elevens to carry out the Connaught/Knock and Cork schedules, some other offpeak schedules and ad hoc charter work. Once configurationured with 119 passenger seats, all aircraft were later fitted with either 104 or 109 seats. Over the years the One-Elevens were used on the company's scheduled routes from Dublin to Glasgow, Liverpool, Luton, Munich (both direct and via Stansted), Paris, Prestwick and Stansted, from Connaught/Knock to Birmingham, Coventry, Gatwick, Luton, Manchester and Stansted and from Cork and Shannon to both Luton and Stansted. The last new route to be inaugurated by the One-Eleven fleet was a twice daily schedule between Dublin and Birmingham on 08Nov93. The aircraft also carried out extensive charter work throughout Europe. The company controlled a UK subsidiary airline which operated the One-Eleven called London European Airways, which also traded for a while as Ryanair Europe.

EI-BSS	402	EI-BSY	266	EI-BSZ	272	EI-BVG	255
EI-BVH	407	EI-BVI	256	EI-CAS	406	EI-CCU	237
EI-CCW	186	EI-CCX	211	EI-CDO	201	EI-CIB	191
EI-CIC	177	EI-CID	174	EI-CIE	176	YR-BCI	252

Sadia SA Transportes Aereos - see Transbrasil SA Linhas Aereas

SARO Airlines (Servicios Aereos Rutas Oriente) SA de CV, (UF), Monterrey, Mexico

Leased a Srs.201AC from Guinness Peat Aviation in a deal dated 11Jan91. The aircraft was used on scheduled routes from the carrier's home base to Acapulco, Cancun, Leon-Guanajua, Mazatlan and Torreon and on charter flights, together with support flights for the airline's other types. The One-Eleven was introduced into service on 18Mar91 and was reported withdrawn from use and stored at Monterrey by Jul93.

XA-RTN   085

SAS - see Scandinavian Airlines System

Scandinavian Airlines System, (SK), Stockholm, Sweden

Leased a Srs.301AG from British Eagle International from Aug67 until it was replaced by a similar aircraft in Dec67. The first aircraft was painted in full SAS colours, and the second was returned to the lessor in Mar68. They were mainly used in operating schedules between Copenhagen and Zurich.

G-ATPJ   033   G-ATPL   035

Servicios Aereos Rutas Oriente SA de CV - see SARO Airlines

Shabair, (SS), Lubumbashi, Zaire

Leased a Srs.401AK from Guinness Peat Aviation in Sep90 and a Srs.201AC from the same source in Mar91. The aircraft have since been used on scheduled domestic routes from its home base to Mbuji-Mayi, Kalemie, Kananga and Kinshasa and from the latter point to Goma, Kisangani and Mbandaka. Charter flights are also flown.

9Q-CEH   057   9Q-CSJ   013   9Q-CUG   057

Sierra Leone Airways Ltd, (LJ), Freetown, Sierra Leone

The British United Airways/British Caledonian Airways One-Eleven multi-sector West African service was operated as a jointly marketed route with this operator over the Freetown to Lagos part of the journey.

Sultan of Oman's Air Force - see Air Force of the Sultanate of Oman

Swissair (Schweiz Luftverkehr AG), (SR), Zurich, Switzerland

Leased a Srs.207AJ from British Eagle International from Apr to Nov67, this then being replaced by a Srs.301AG from the same source until the end of Apr68. These aircraft were operated on scheduled routes from Zurich to Dusseldorf, Nice and Prague. The company later leased a Srs.501EX from British United Airways from Apr to the end of Oct70. This aircraft was used on scheduled routes from Zurich to Nice and Stuttgart and to Manchester via Rotterdam.

G-ATPK   034   G-ATVH   040   G-AWYS   175

TACA International Airlines SA (Transportes Aereos Centro Americanos), (TA), San Salvador, El Salvador

Ordered two Srs.407AWs with an option on two additional aircraft on 18Mar65. This option was not taken up, and the aircraft were del in Dec66 and Feb67 in a 74 seat single class configuration. A Srs.409AY was purchased from LACSA in Apr73 and a Srs.531FS leased from the same source from Nov81 to Mar82. The Srs.409AY was sold in Jan79. The type was flown on schedules from San Salvador to Belize City, Guatemala City, Houston, Kingston (Jamaica), Mexico City, Miami, New Orleans, Panama City, San Jose (Costa Rica) and Tegucigalpa after inaugurating service on 28Dec66. During the later years of service the type was used on charter flights throughout Central America and to Mexican destinations. The last aircraft was withdrawn from service on 01Jun88 and the aircraft put into store pending sale.

TI-LRI   242   YS-01C   108   YS-17C   093   YS-18C   106

TAE - see Trabajos Aereos y Enlaces

TAROM - see Transporturile Aeriene Romane

TAT - see Transport Aerien Transregional

Tenneco Inc, Houston, Texas, USA

Ordered one Srs.212AR through Page Airways International on 10Aug64, followed by a second in 1968 to add to the company's executive fleet. The aircraft were del in Apr66 and Jul69. A third aircraft, a Srs.211AH, was obtained secondhand in Sep75. The fleet was disposed of between Jan and Mar87 after use throughout the world.

N502T   083   N503T   183   N504T   084

Tiger Leasing Group - see National Aircraft Leasing Ltd

Trabajos Aereos y Enlaces - TAE, (JK), Bilbao, Spain

This operator ordered two Srs.402APs, of which only one was del in Mar69; this was used on inclusive tour and charter flights to Spain from many European points until the aircraft was repossessed and returned to the manufacturer in mid Feb70.

EC-BQF   161

Transbrasil SA Linhas Aereas, (QD), Sao Paulo, Brazil

Known as Sadia SA Transportes Aereos until Jun72, this airline ordered two Srs.520FNs which were del in Oct and Dec70 and a third which was del in Sep72, all in a mixed class configuration of 12 first and 74 tourist class seats. A Srs.521FH had earlier been leased from Sep70 to Jan71, initially for crew training. Three Srs.523FJs were bought from British Midland Airways, for which three Handley Page Heralds were exchanged as part of the deal. These were del to Transbrasil in May and Nov73 and Apr74. A Srs.530FX was leased from British Caledonian Airways from Feb to Dec74 after one of the Srs.520FNs was lost in a landing accident. Two Srs.518FGs were leased from BAC from Oct and Dec74 to Sep75 and Jan78 respectively. The aircraft were operated over an extensive domestic network from Sao Paulo and Rio de Janeiro northwards to Aracaju, Belem, Belo Horizonte, Brasilia, Fernando de Noronha, Fortaleza, Ilheus, Maceio, Manaus, Natal, Recife, Salvador, Sao Luiz and Vitoria and southwards to Campinas, Curitiba, Florianopolis, Iguassu Falls, Londrina and Porto Alegre. The last of the One-Eleven fleet was disposed of in Apr78.

PP-SDP	192	PP-SDQ	228	PP-SDR	230	PP-SDS	236
PP-SDT	193	PP-SDU	211	PP-SDV	199	PT-TYV	200
PT-TYW	206	PT-TYY	240				

Transport Aerien Transregional - TAT, (IJ and IO), Tours, France

Leased two Srs.432FDs from British Island Airways from Mar and Apr89 until Feb90. The aircraft were used on the company's scheduled domestic routes to Brest, Lille, Marseille, Mulhouse, Nantes, Nice, Paris-Orly and Figari in Corsica.

G-AXMU 157   G-AXOX 121

Transportes Aereos Centro Americanos - see TACA International Airlines SA

Transportes Aereos Nacionales SA - TAN, (TX), Tegucigalpa, Honduras

Following an inter-governmental agreement signed on 19Oct67, joint services were flown with LANICA's Srs.412EB with capacity shared on a 50/50 basis over the San Pedro Sula to Miami route three times weekly with effect from 01Nov67. The aircraft was also flown on TAN's own routes from Tegucigalpa to Miami via San Pedro Sula and/or Belize City five times weekly and to Mexico City three times weekly.

AN-BBI 111

Transporturile Aeriene Romane - TAROM, (RO), Bucharest, Romania

Ordered six Srs.424EUs on 26Feb68 in an 84 seat single class configuration with del between Jun68 and Dec69, while a Srs.409AY was leased from the manufacturer from May to Aug69. Two used aircraft were purchased in 1972, a Srs.401AK in Jun and a Srs.402AP in Aug. Five Srs.525FTs were later ordered with del from Mar to Aug77 and a further two of the same type with del in Jan81 and Mar82. These were fitted out in a 104 seat single class configuration. A Srs.487GK pure freighter with a large main deck cargo door was del in Jul81; this was used for transporting components from the UK to set up a One-Eleven production line in Romania until it went on longterm lease to Anglo Cargo Airlines from Mar86 to Jan92. Eight Romanian-built Srs.561RCs have so far been received since the first was del in Dec82. The aircraft have been used over the airline's comprehensive European international scheduled network and to the Middle East and North Africa, together with extensive holiday charter flights. Leases have been arranged to numerous operators in the UK, Eire, Jugoslavia, Nigeria and Pakistan. Other aircraft have been either sold or leased to LAR and Romavia in Romania.

YR-BCA	130	YR-BCB	156	YR-BCC	167	YR-BCD	159
YR-BCE	165	YR-BCF	168	YR-BCG	077	YR-BCH	161
YR-BCI	252	YR-BCJ	253	YR-BCK	254	YR-BCL	255
YR-BCM	256	YR-BCN	266	YR-BCO	272	YR-BCP	162
YR-BCR	267	YR-BRA	401	YR-BRB	402	YR-BRC	403
YR-BRD	404	YR-BRE	405	YR-BRF	406	YR-BRG	407
YR-BRH	408						

Turbo-Union Ltd - see Rolls-Royce Plc

Union de Transport Aeriene - UTA, (UT), Paris, France

Air Pacific Srs.479FUs operated over the Nadi to Papeete route as a joint venture on behalf of both carriers, using UT/FJ flight numbers.

USAir Inc, (AL and US), Arlington, Virginia, USA

This company, known as Allegheny Airlines Inc until 28Oct79, absorbed Mohawk Airlines Inc on 12Apr72. Included was that company's fleet of 22 Srs.203AE/204AF/215AUs and the continuation of the lease of one aircraft from Aloha Airlines, together with Mohawk's route network. A further eight Srs.203AEs were obtained from Braniff Airways between Mar and Sep72. The leased Aloha aircraft was finally purchased in Feb81. Between 1980 and 1983 the Srs.204AFs and Srs.215AUs all had the rear airstairs removed in common with the Srs.203AEs in a weight-saving exercise, and seating capacity was raised from 74 to 79 over the same period. The aircraft were used on a network much expanded from that of Mohawk Airlines; this extended southwards as far as Tampa, north to Toronto, Montreal and Ottawa in Canada, westwards to Chicago, St Louis and Evansville and eastwards to Boston and Providence. Pittsburgh was the major hub and operating base for the fleet and La Guardia, Newark and Kennedy were all served in New York. The aircraft were also used for charter work and were leased to several operators at various times in both the USA and Canada. The fleet was gradually reduced until by Jan89 only eight aircraft were still in service. By the summer of the same year all One-Elevens had been withdrawn.

N1112J	030	N1113J	031	N1114J	032	N1115J	082
N1117J	099	N1118J	100	N1119J	101	N1120J	102
N1122J	103	N1123J	104	N1124J	134	N1125J	135
N1126J	179	N1127J	180	N1128J	181	N1129J	182
N1130J	096	N1131J	097	N1132J	105	N1134J	045
N1135J	046	N1136J	071	N1542	016	N1544	018
N1545	019	N1546	020	N1547	041	N1548	042
N1549	043	N1550	044	N2111J	029		

Viaçao Aerea Sao Paulo SA - VASP, (VP), Sao Paulo, Brazil

Ordered two Srs.422EQs on 23Jun67 with an option on three more; the option was not taken up. Both aircraft were del in Dec67 in a 74 seat single class configuration and were operated on multi-sector schedules within Brazil until disposed of in May and Jun74. From Sao Paulo and Rio de Janeiro the aircraft operated to Belem, Fortaleza, Manaus, Recife and

Salvador in the north and to Porto Alegre in the south. During their last years of service they operated less densely travelled sectors out of Brasilia.

PP-SRT   119   PP-SRU   126

Victor Comptometers Inc, Chicago, Illinois, USA

This company ordered a Srs.410AQ through Page Airways International which was del in Sep66. The aircraft was fitted with an executive cabin forward and a 30 seat cabin to the rear and was operated as a company executive aircraft until sold in Oct72.

N3939V   054

Virgin Atlantic Airways Ltd, (VS), London, UK

Leased a Srs.432FD from British Island Airways from Jan to Apr85 for operation on the company's schedules from Gatwick to Maastricht. The aircraft's fin was painted in Virgin's colours, with the fuselage retaining British Island Airways colours but with Virgin Atlantic titling.

G-AXMU   157

Western Airways Ltd, Nassau, Bahamas

A Letter of Intent for eight to ten aircraft for delivery in 1965 was signed on 21Aug61 by East & West Steamship Co (1961), Karachi, on behalf of Western Airways. The contract, signed on 30Jan62, defined the order as eight Srs.202AD aircraft. On 08Nov62 Western Airways exercised an option on two further Srs.202AD units, making a total of ten aircraft, but on 03May63 Western advised BAC that they wished to sell four aircraft via Atomic Agencies (Aviation) Ltd, a UK representative for foreign airlines, and a further four aircraft directly via BAC. The first two aircraft built for Western Airways aircraft were offered by BAC to Tennessee Gas Corporation on 03Apr64; none was ever delivered to Western.

Westinghouse Electric Corporation, Baltimore, Maryland, USA

Obtained two used Srs.401AKs in Feb83 and Jan88; one has been extensively modified as a radar testbed and trials platform. It first flew on 17Jul89 with a Westinghouse/Texas Instruments radar, Martin Marietta electro-optical sensor and Westinghouse/TRW EW system as a testbed for the systems later to be installed in the McDonnell Douglas YF-23A Advanced Tactical Fighter. The aircraft have also been used for flight testing the Westinghouse/Honeywell MODAR (Modular Avionics Radar) MR-3000 windshear detection system.

N162W   087   N164W   090

Wirakris Udara, Kuala Lumpur, Malaysia

Leased a Srs.481FW from Air Malawi from Sep92, reportedly to operate cargo flights. The aircraft had been returned to the lessor by Mar93.

7Q-YKF   243

Wright Airlines Inc, (KC), Cleveland, Ohio, USA

Leased a Srs.203AE from Air Illinois from Jul to Sep84.

N1542   016

Zambia Airways Corporation Ltd, (QZ), Lusaka, Zambia

Took over an order placed by Central African Airways for two Srs.207AJs and leased the aircraft to British Eagle International Airways from new in Apr66 until Dec67. The aircraft were fitted with a single class 74 seat cabin and had uprated Rolls-Royce Spey Mk511-14 engines installed with provision for a water injection system, the only Srs.200s so built for commercial use. The type was then used on Zambia Airways schedules from Lusaka to Blantyre, Dar-es-Salaam, Kasama, Livingstone, Lubumbashi, Mauritius, Nairobi, Ndola and Antananarivo. One of the aircraft was leased to Air Malawi from Nov70 until Feb72. The aircraft were sold in Mar75.

9J-RCH   039   9J-RCI   040

SCHEDULED ROUTE MAPS

Section 1   North America

Section 2   Central and South America

Section 3   Asia and the Pacific

Section 4   Africa

Section 5   Europe

128

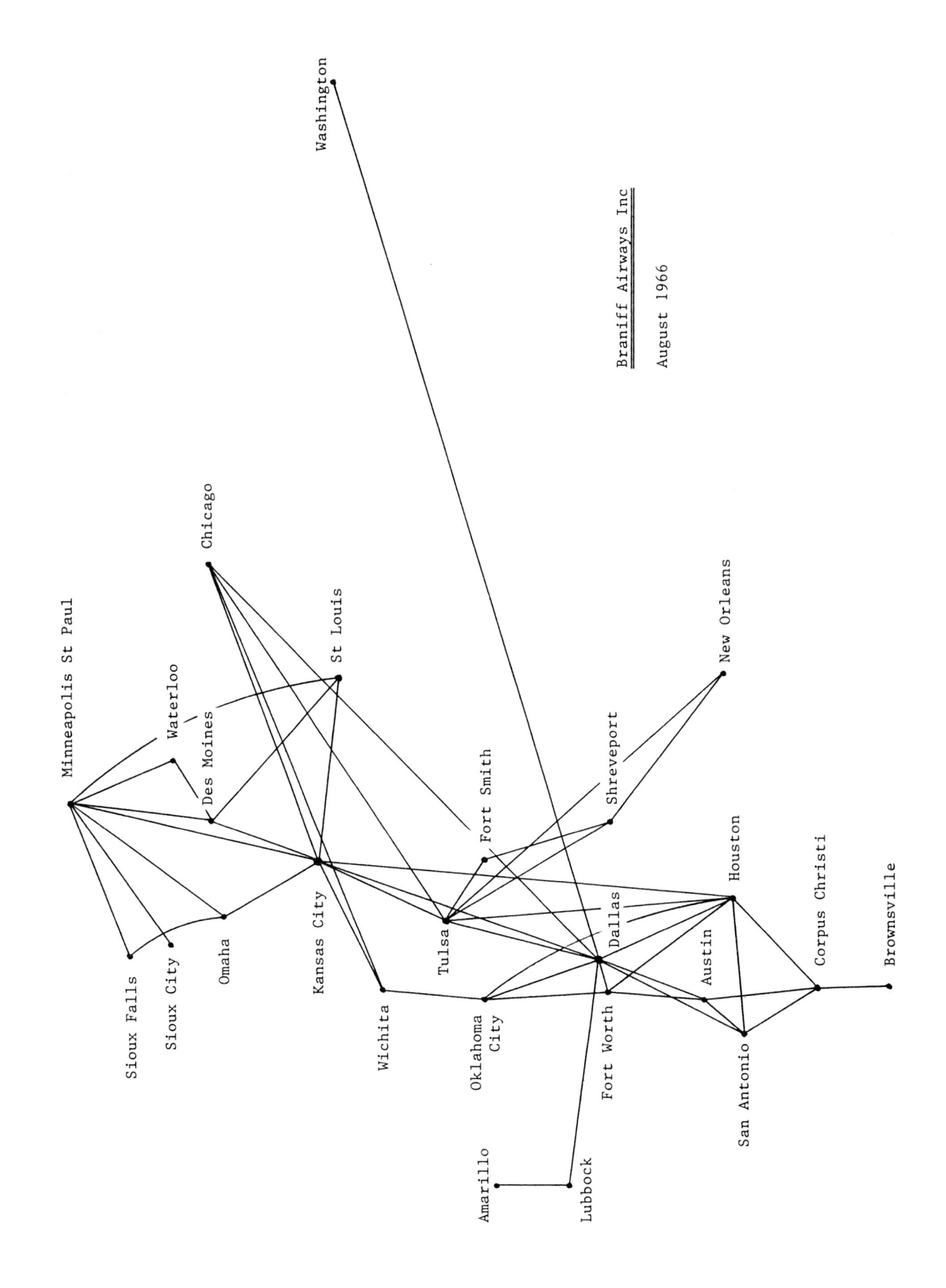

129

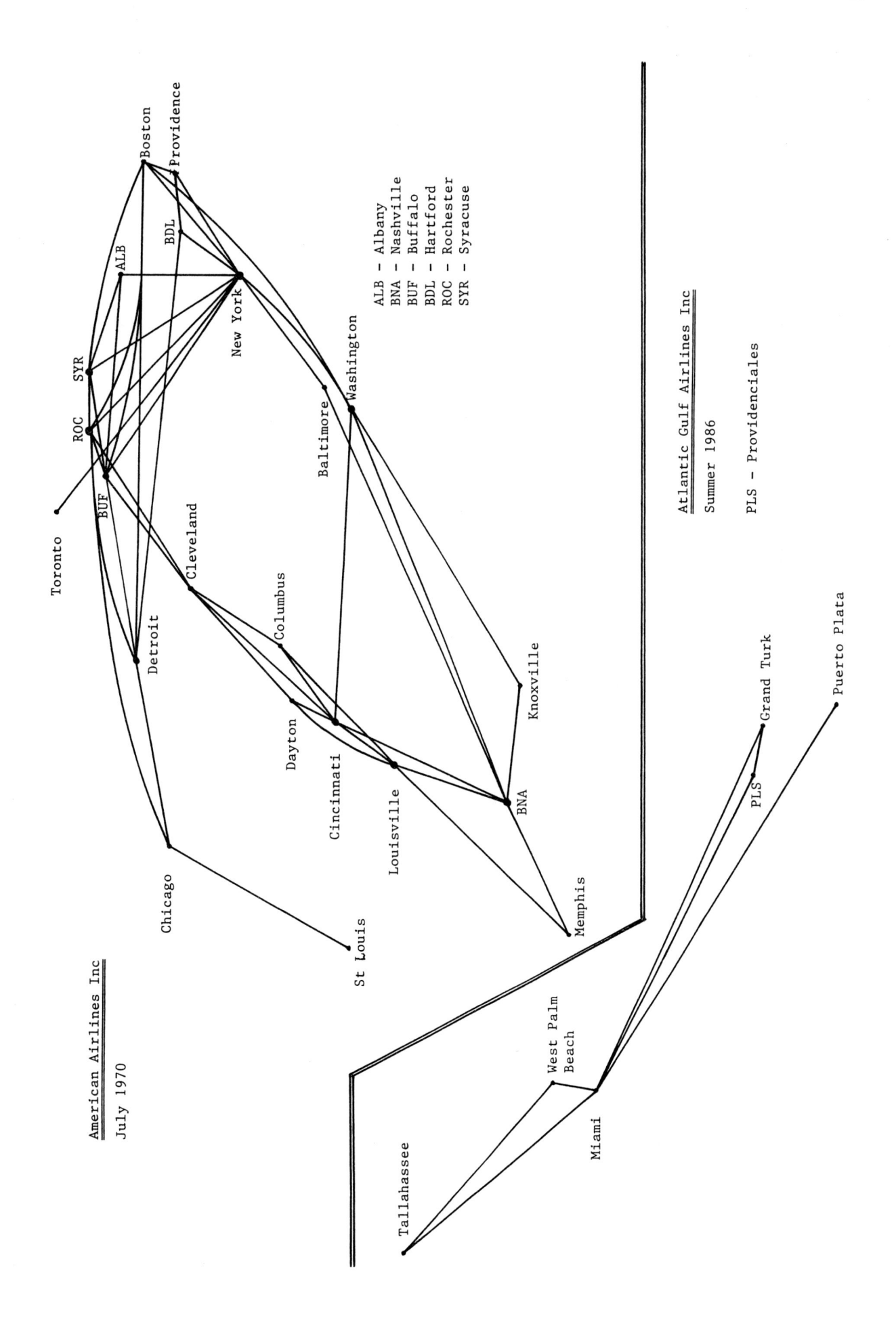

ALB — Albany
BNA — Nashville
BUF — Buffalo
BDL — Hartford
ROC — Rochester
SYR — Syracuse

American Airlines Inc
July 1970

Atlantic Gulf Airlines Inc
Summer 1986

PLS — Providenciales

Mohawk Airlines Inc — July 1970

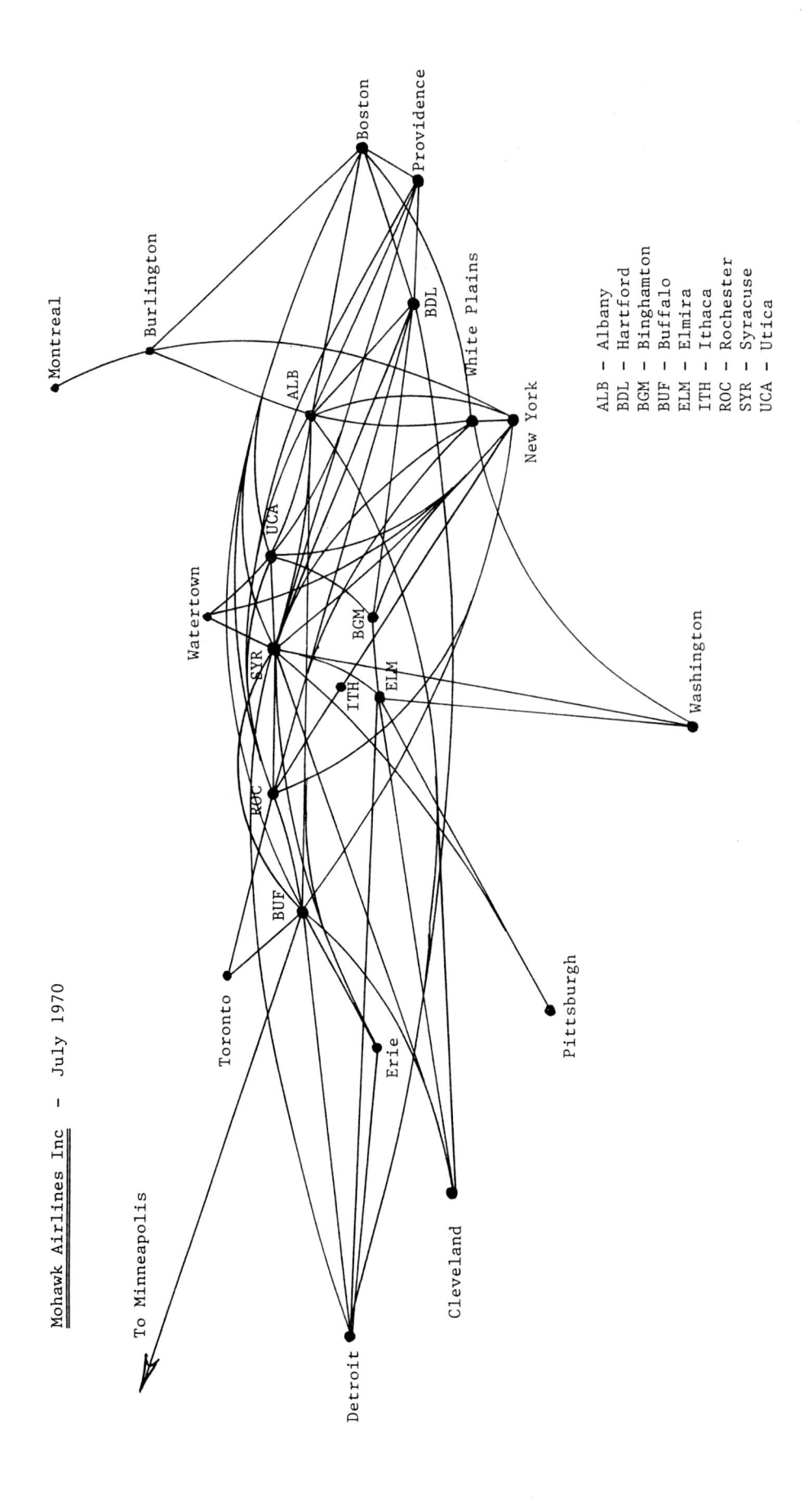

ALB — Albany
BDL — Hartford
BGM — Binghamton
BUF — Buffalo
ELM — Elmira
ITH — Ithaca
ROC — Rochester
SYR — Syracuse
UCA — Utica

Allegheny Airlines Inc — October 1976

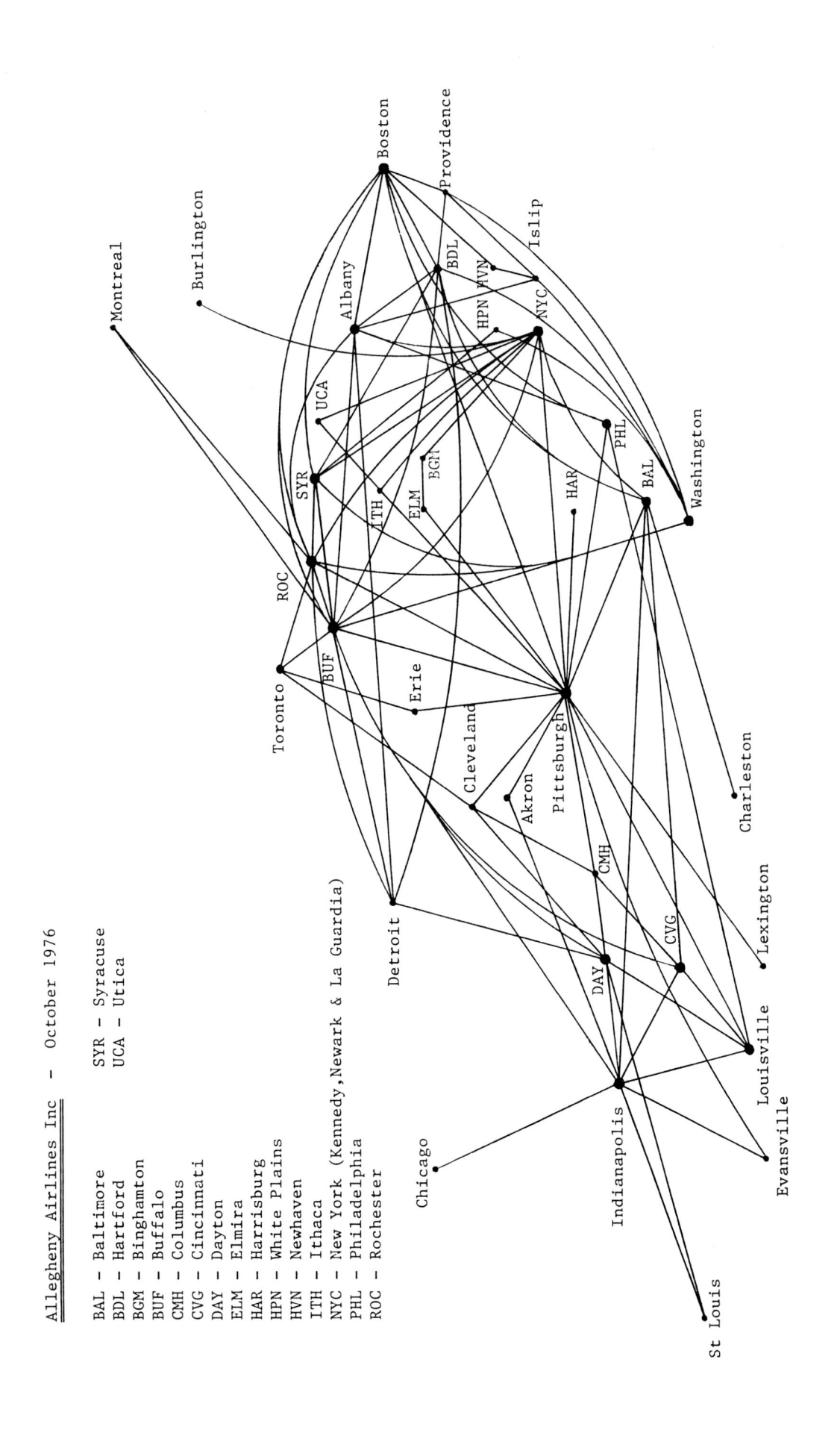

BAL – Baltimore
BDL – Hartford
BGM – Binghamton
BUF – Buffalo
CMH – Columbus
CVG – Cincinnati
DAY – Dayton
ELM – Elmira
HAR – Harrisburg
HPN – White Plains
HVN – Newhaven
ITH – Ithaca
NYC – New York (Kennedy, Newark & La Guardia)
PHL – Philadelphia
ROC – Rochester

SYR – Syracuse
UCA – Utica

132

Cascade Airways Inc – Summer 1985

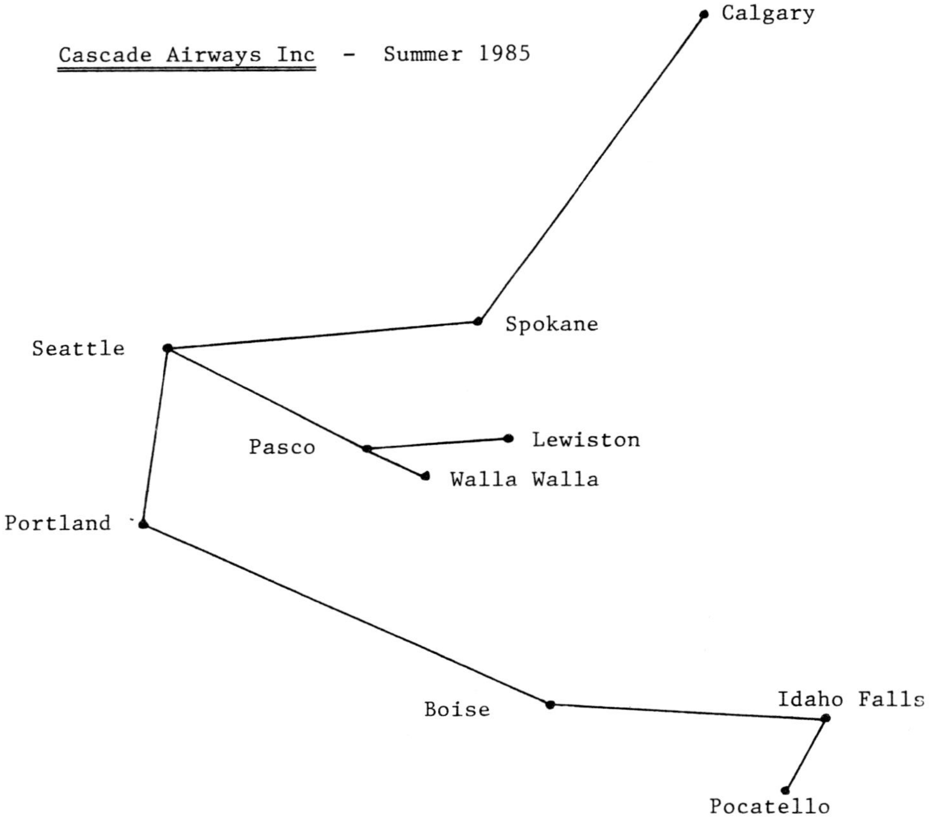

Pacific Express Inc – September 1983

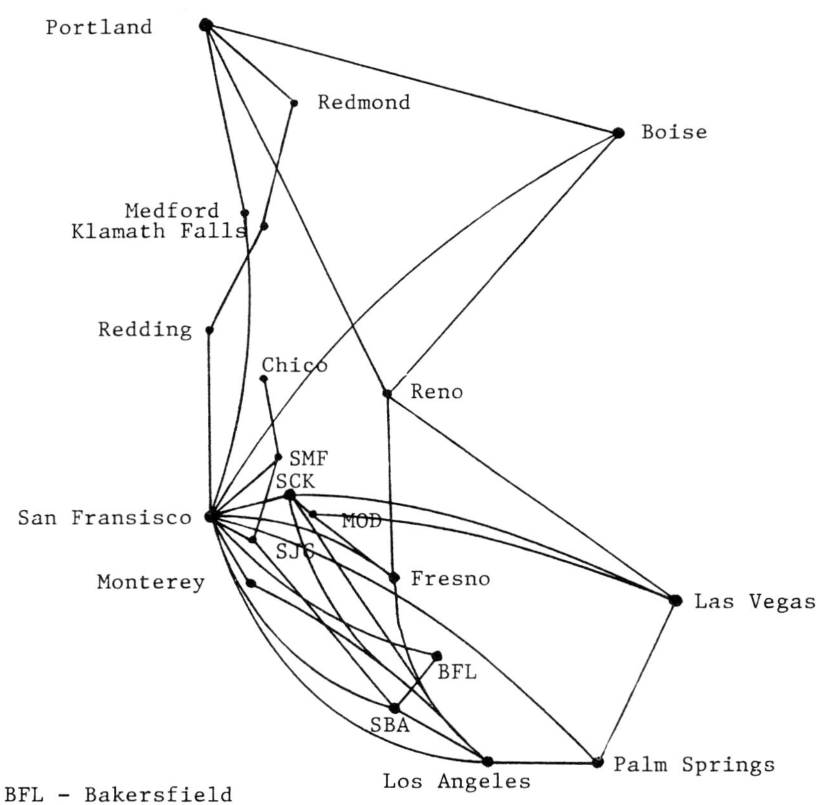

BFL – Bakersfield
MOD – Modesto
SCK – Stockton
SBA – Santa Barbara
SJC – San Jose
SMF – Sacramento

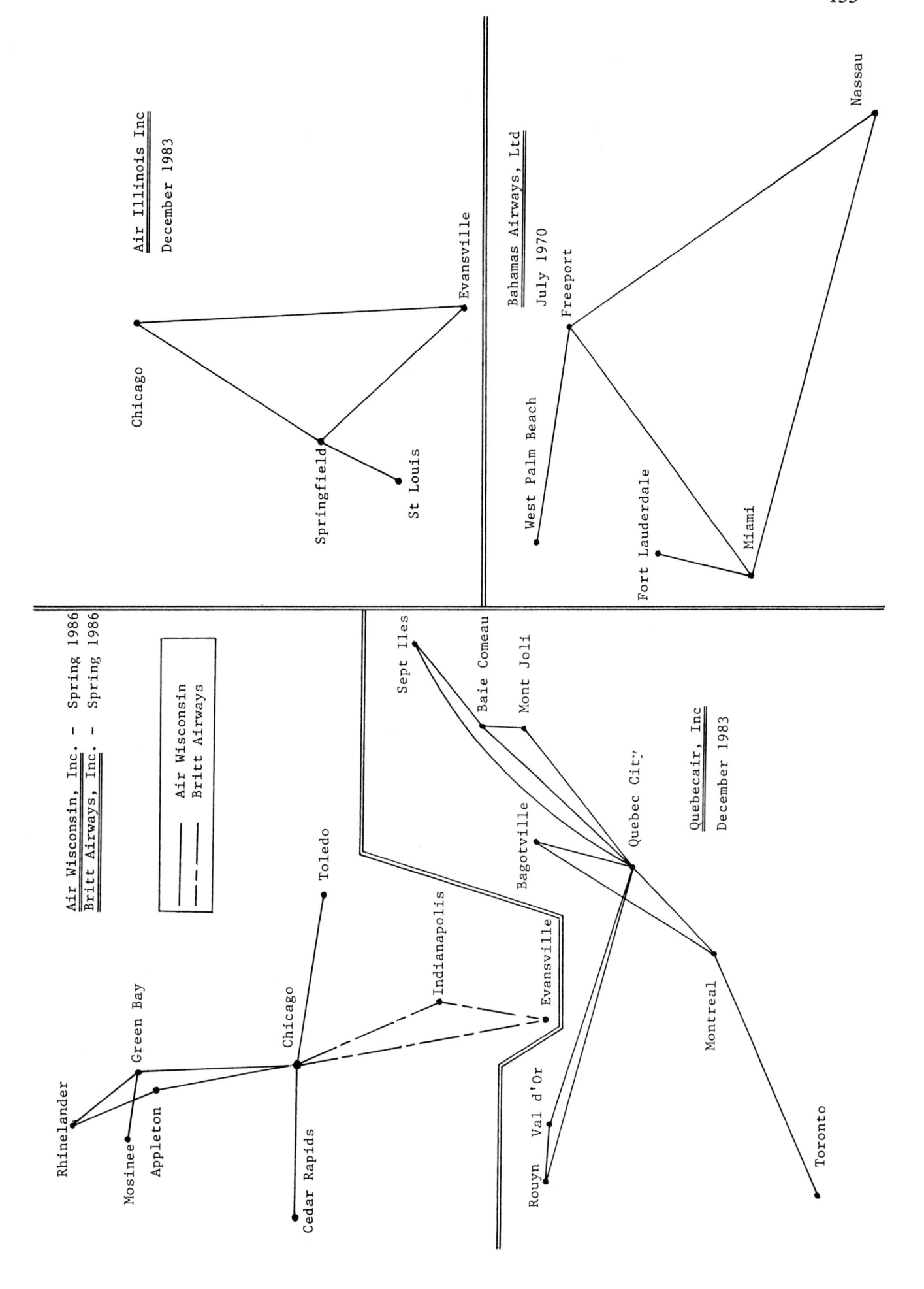

Air Illinois Inc
December 1983

- Chicago
- Springfield
- St Louis
- Evansville

Bahamas Airways, Ltd
July 1970

- West Palm Beach
- Freeport
- Nassau
- Fort Lauderdale
- Miami

Air Wisconsin, Inc. - Spring 1986
Britt Airways, Inc. - Spring 1986

| ——— | Air Wisconsin |
| - - - | Britt Airways |

- Rhinelander
- Mosinee
- Appleton
- Green Bay
- Chicago
- Cedar Rapids
- Toledo
- Indianapolis
- Evansville

Quebecair, Inc
December 1983

- Sept Iles
- Baie Comeau
- Mont Joli
- Bagotville
- Quebec City
- Rouyn
- Val d'Or
- Montreal
- Toronto

133

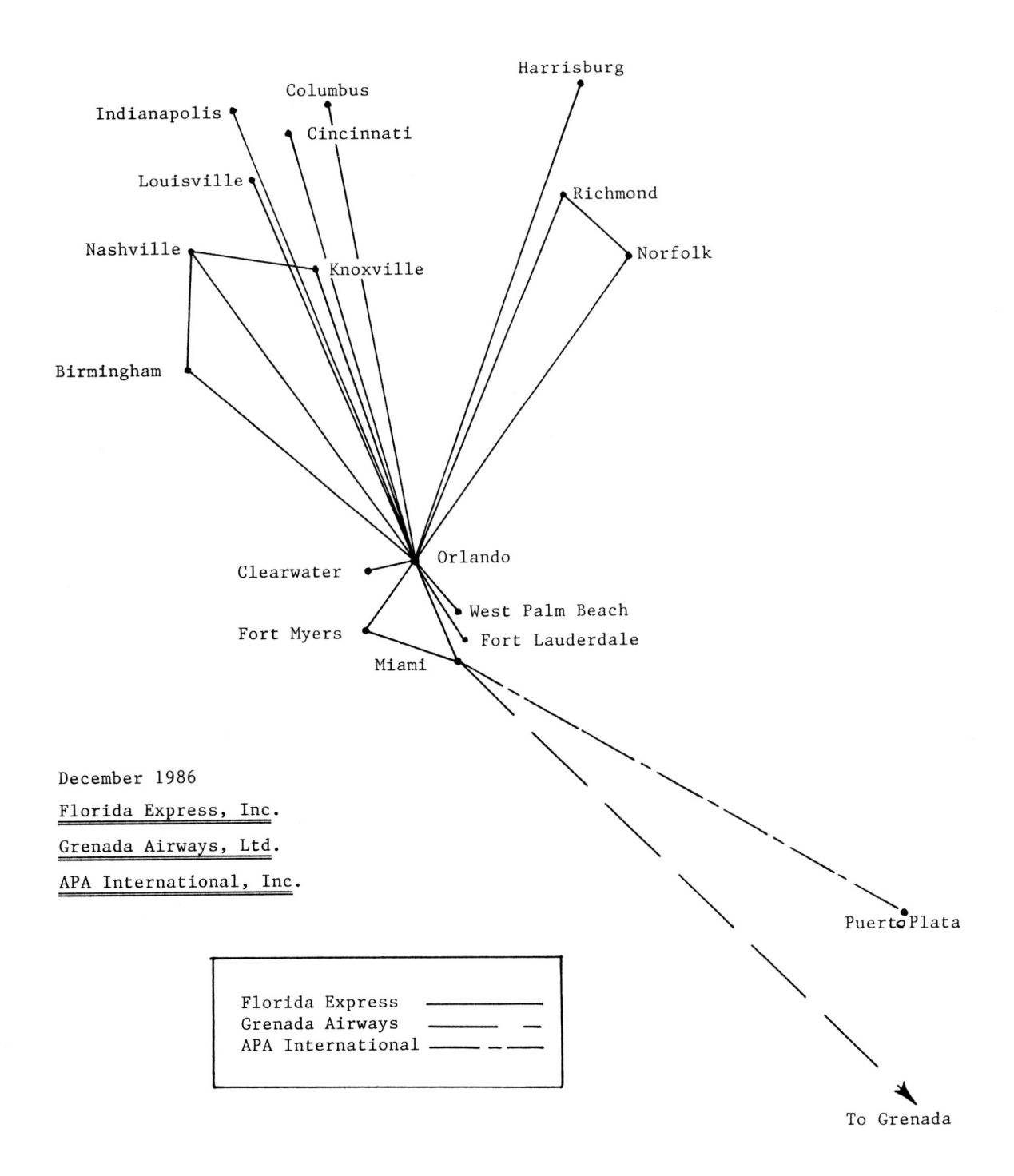

December 1986
Florida Express, Inc.
Grenada Airways, Ltd.
APA International, Inc.

The last year of scheduled One-Eleven operations in the United States
January 1989

———— US Air Inc
– – – Braniff Airways Inc

CLE – Cleveland
CMH – Columbus
CVG – Cincinnati
DAY – Dayton
GSO – Greensboro
HTS – Huntington
PIT – Pittsburgh
RIC – Richmond
TRI – Tri-City Airport

135

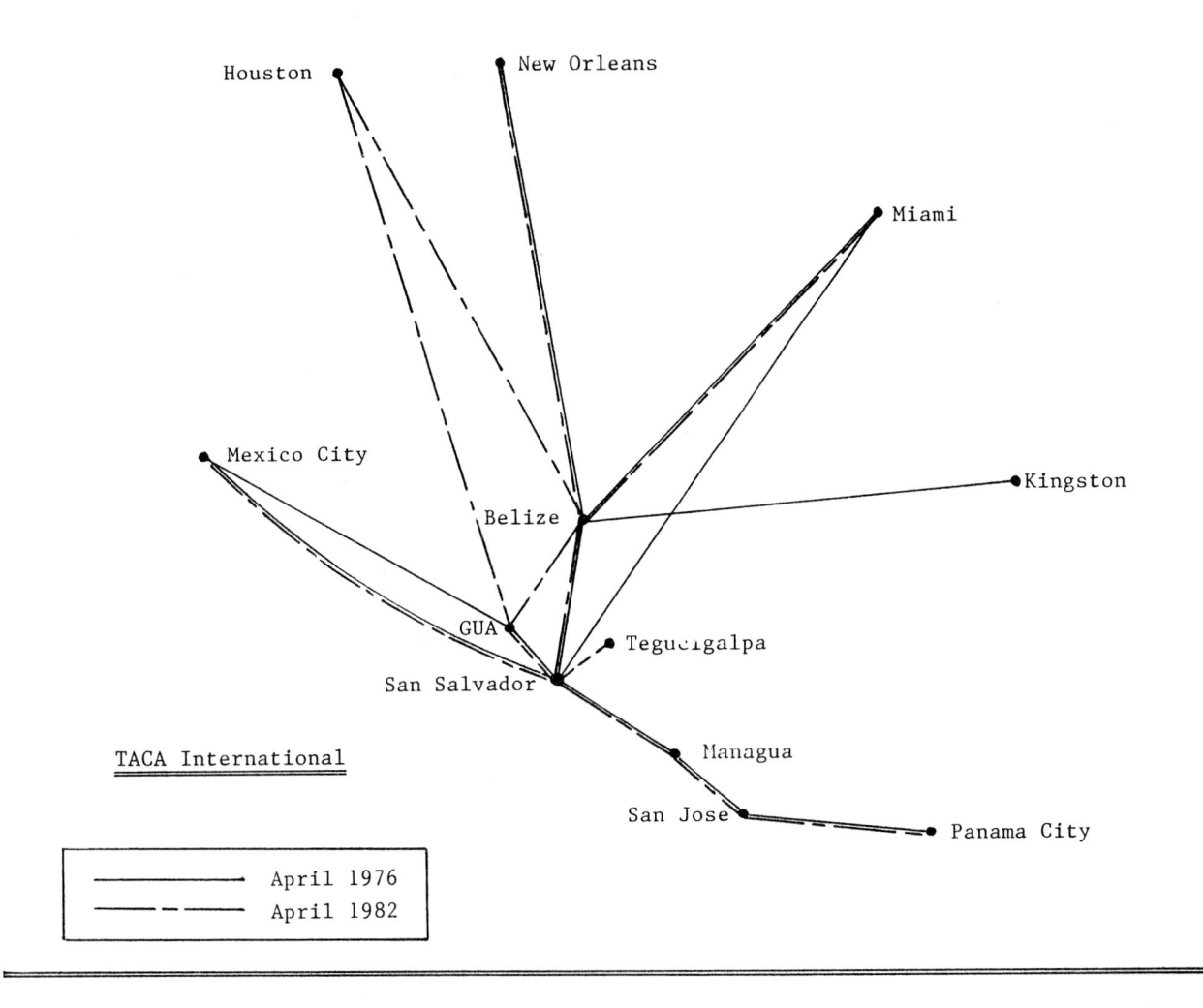

136

Houston •   • New Orleans   • Miami

• Mexico City   Belize   • Kingston

GUA   • Tegucigalpa
San Salvador
Managua
San Jose   • Panama City

TACA International

| ———————▶ | April 1976 |
| — — — — — | April 1982 |

LANICA — July 1970

Transportes Aereos Nacionales S.A. — July 1970

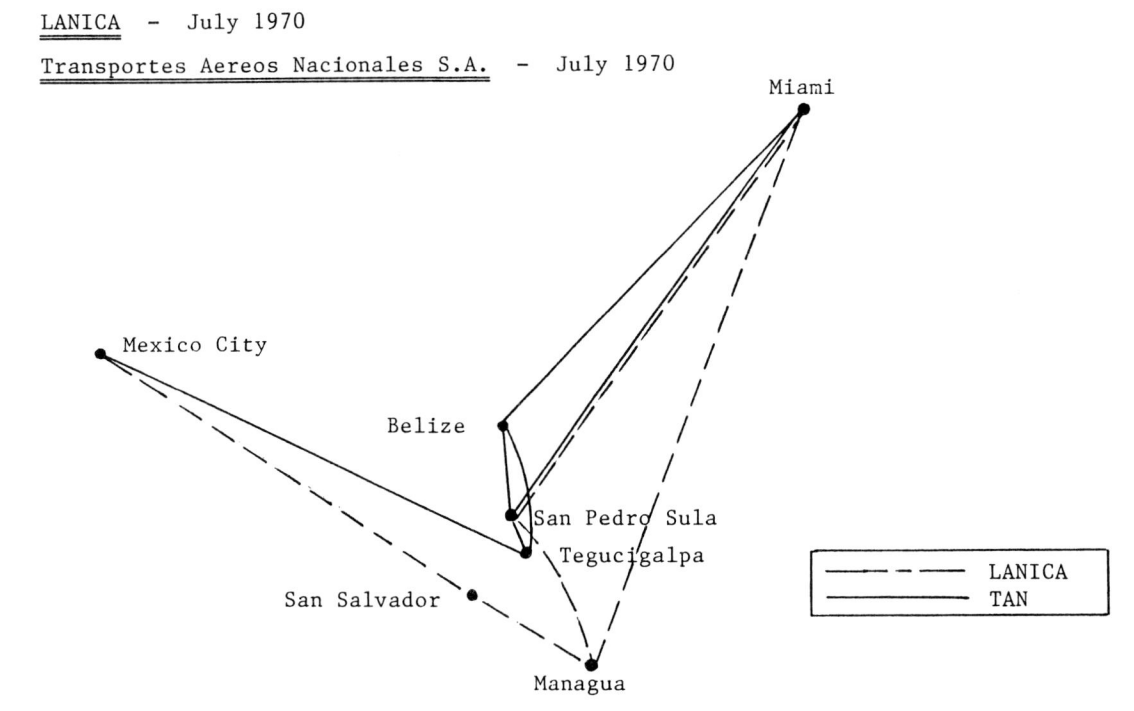

• Miami

• Mexico City

Belize

San Pedro Sula
Tegucigalpa
San Salvador •
Managua

| — — — — | LANICA |
| ———— | TAN |

LACSA - July 1977

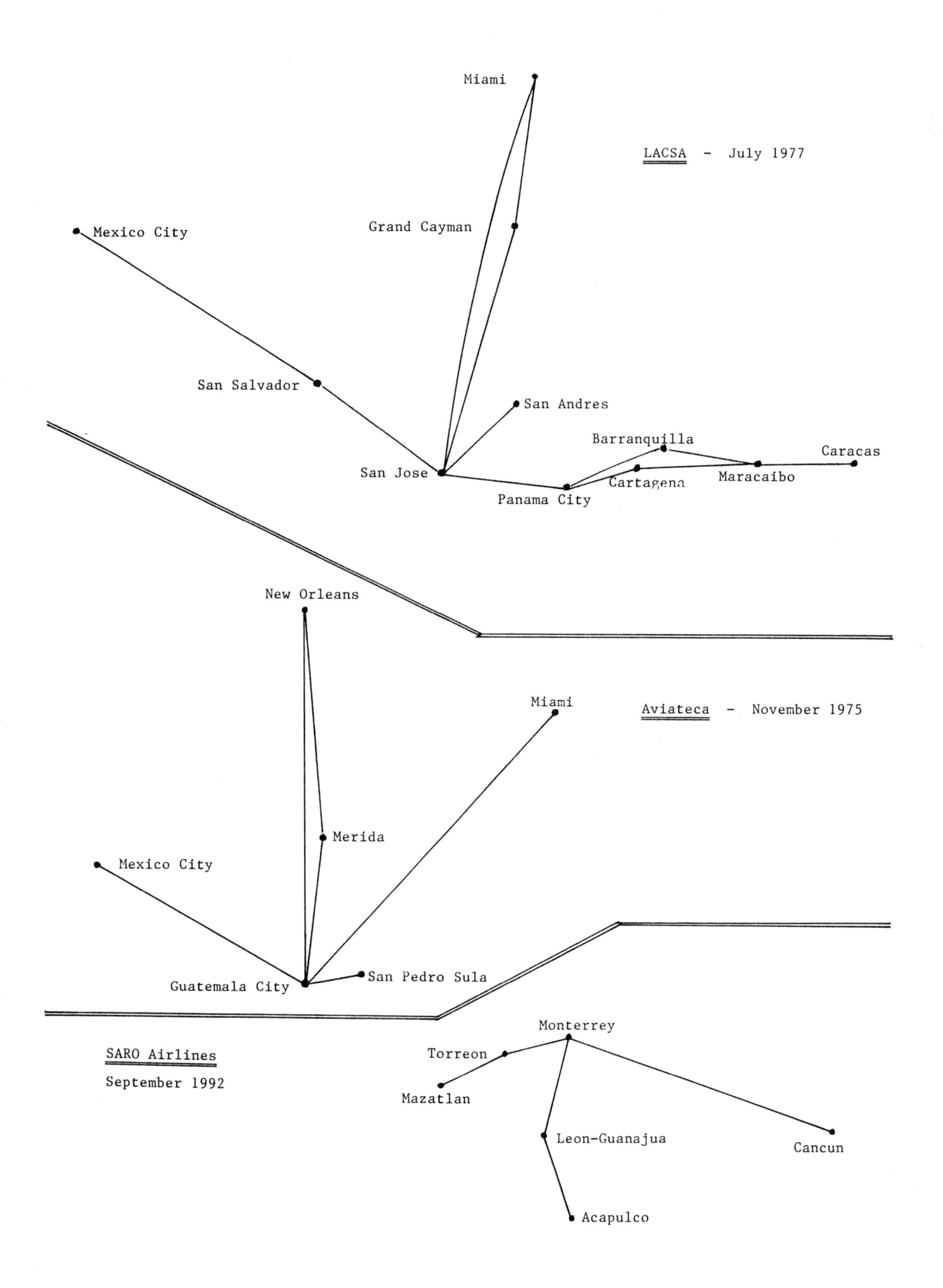

Aviateca - November 1975

SARO Airlines
September 1992

138

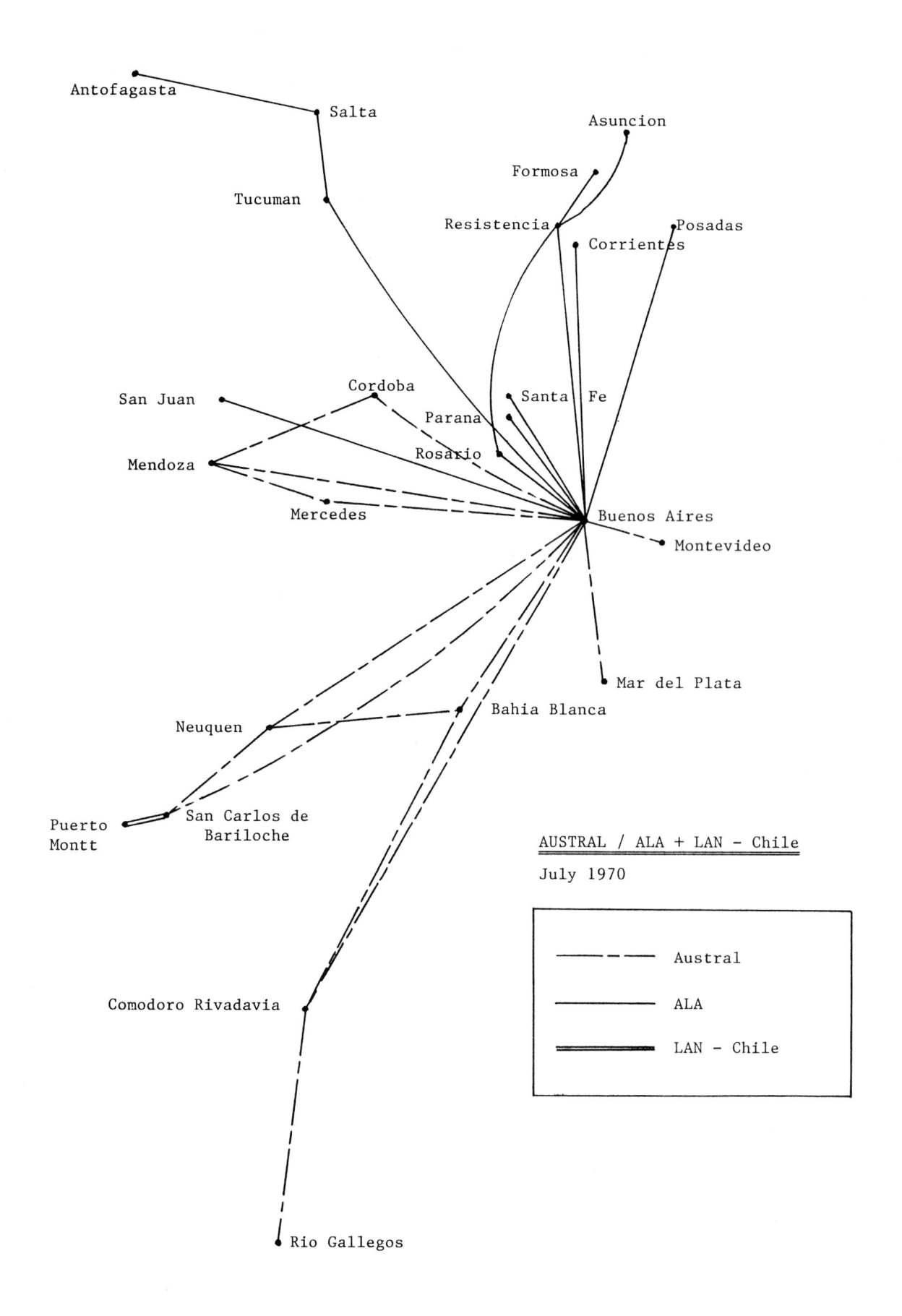

AUSTRAL / ALA + LAN - Chile

July 1970

line style	airline
— — —	Austral
————	ALA
════	LAN - Chile

139

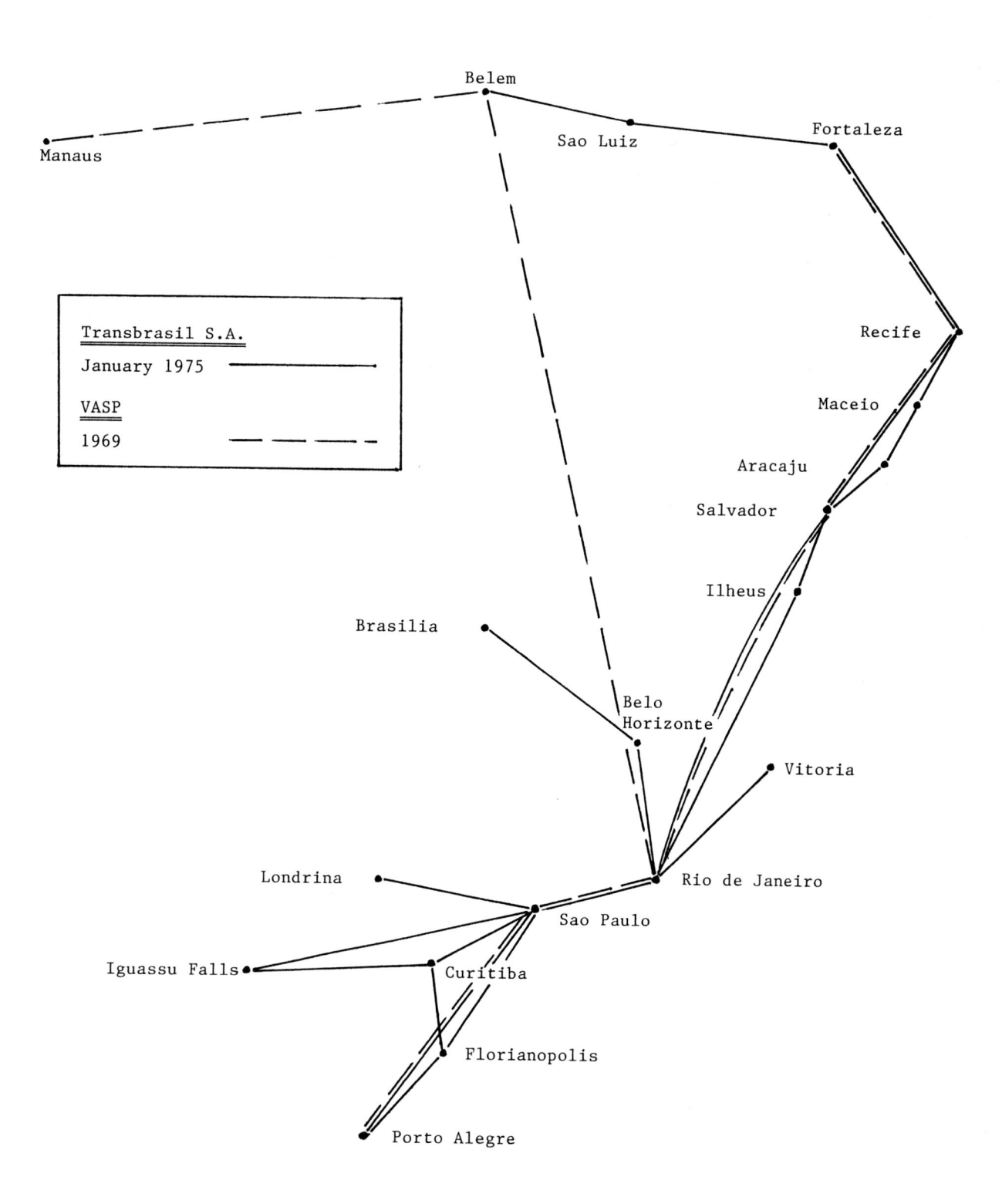

Compania de Aviacion Faucett, S.A.
November 1978

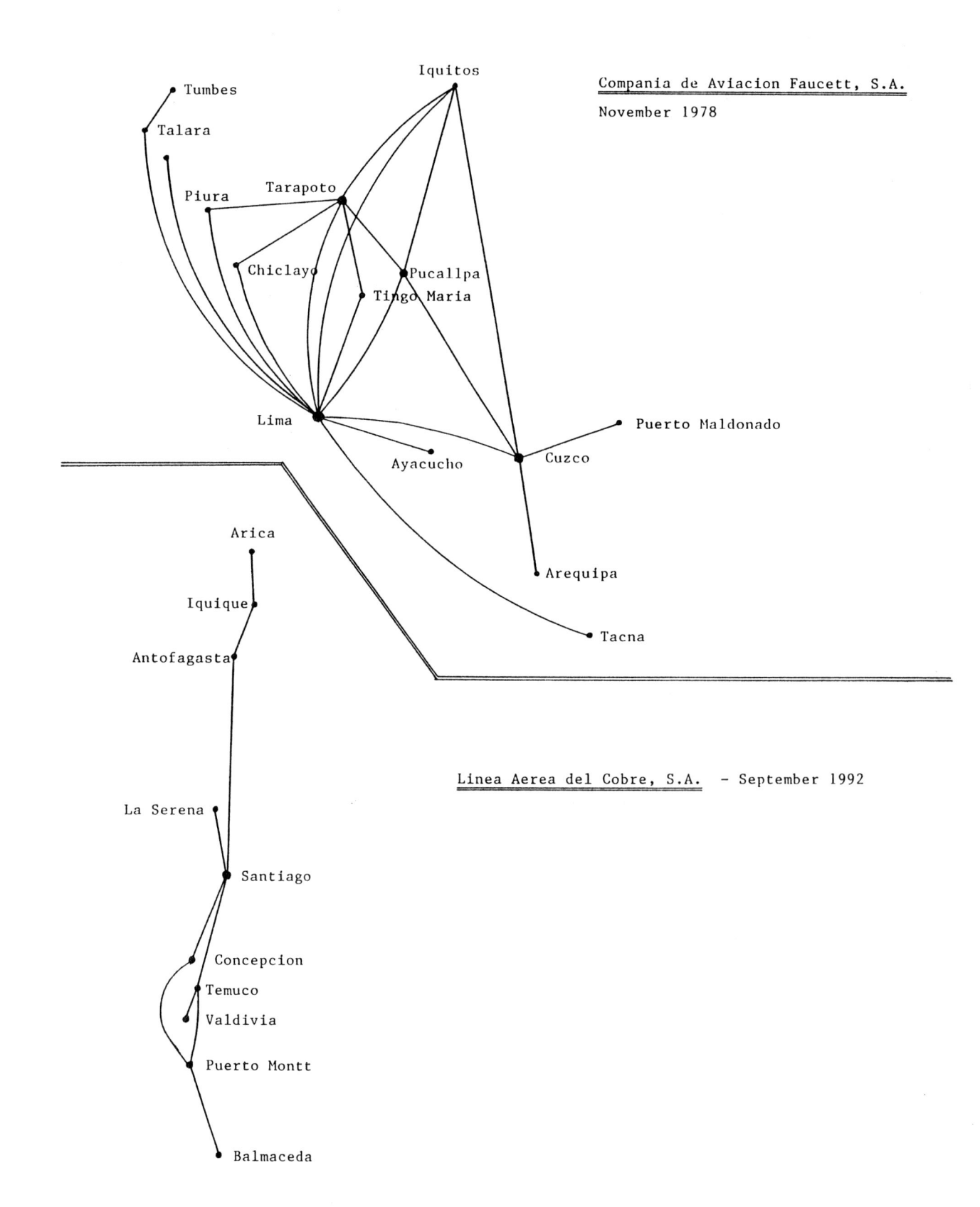

- Tumbes
- Talara
- Iquitos
- Piura
- Tarapoto
- Chiclayo
- Pucallpa
- Tingo Maria
- Lima
- Ayacucho
- Cuzco
- Puerto Maldonado
- Arequipa
- Tacna

Linea Aerea del Cobre, S.A. — September 1992

- Arica
- Iquique
- Antofagasta
- La Serena
- Santiago
- Concepcion
- Temuco
- Valdivia
- Puerto Montt
- Balmaceda

141

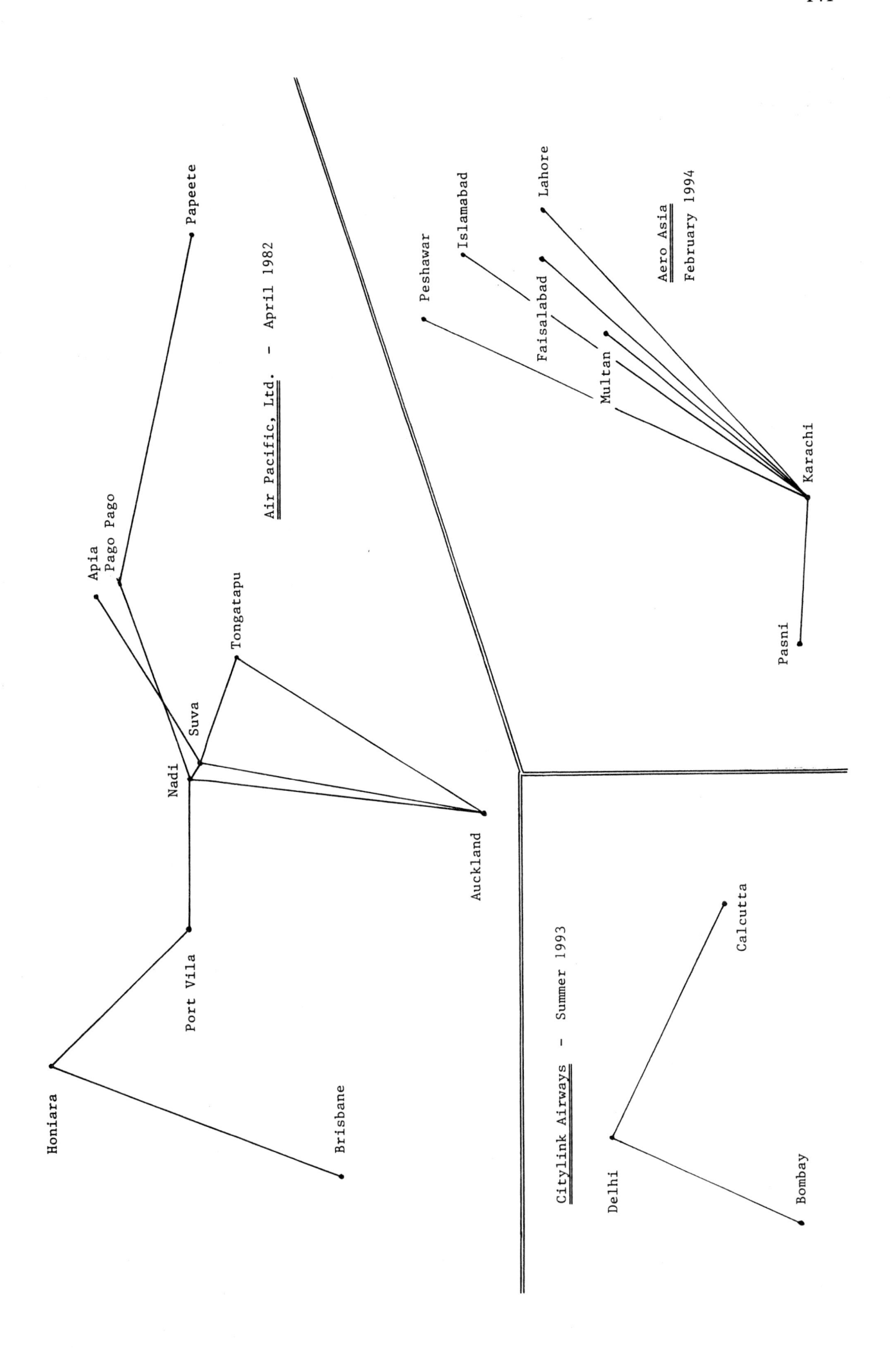

Air Pacific, Ltd. - April 1982

Aero Asia
February 1994

Citylink Airways - Summer 1993

DOMESTIC

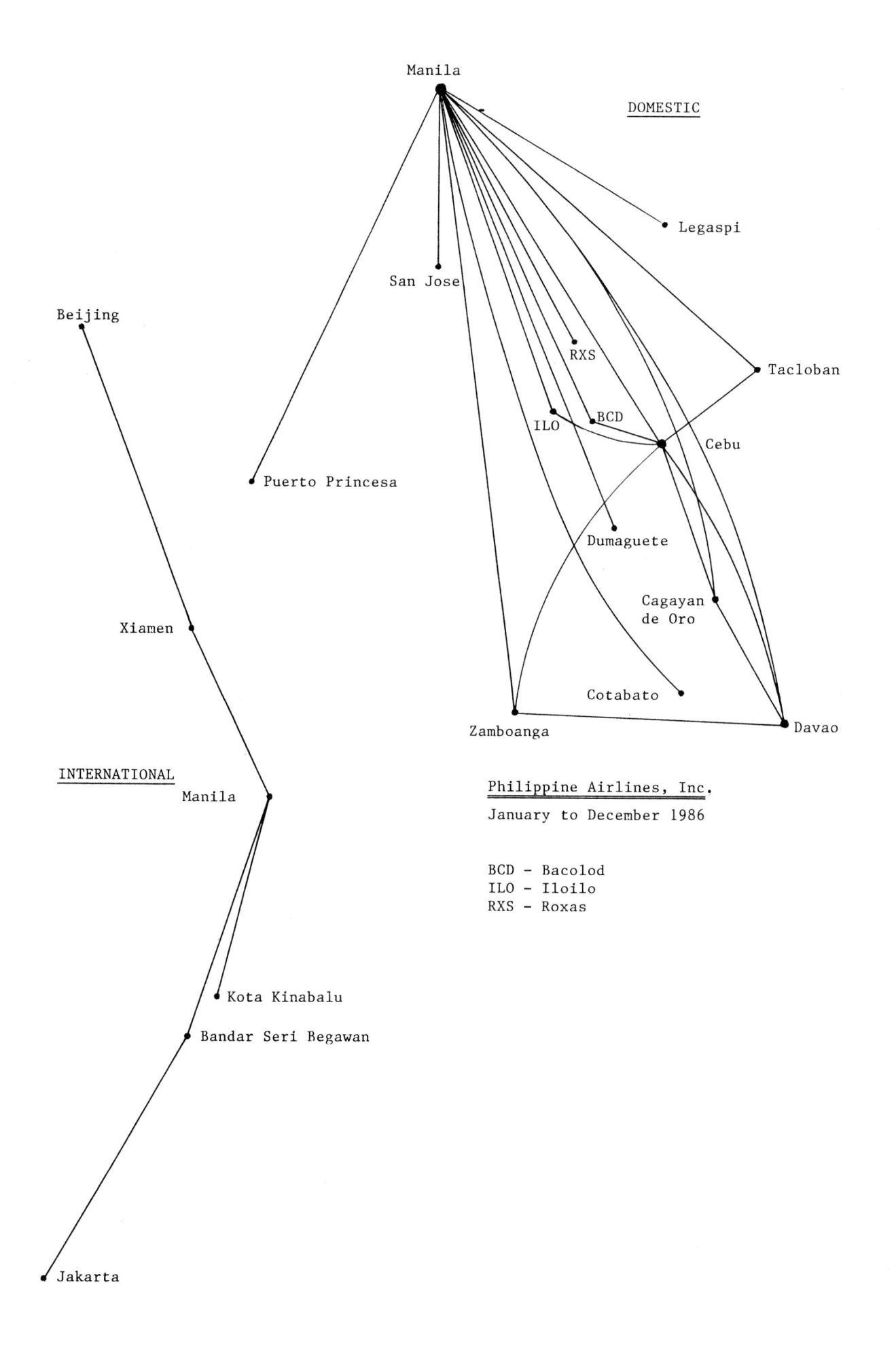

Manila
Legaspi
San Jose
RXS
Tacloban
ILO
BCD
Cebu
Puerto Princesa
Dumaguete
Cagayan de Oro
Cotabato
Zamboanga
Davao

Beijing

Xiamen

INTERNATIONAL
Manila

Kota Kinabalu
Bandar Seri Begawan

Jakarta

Philippine Airlines, Inc.
January to December 1986

BCD — Bacolod
ILO — Iloilo
RXS — Roxas

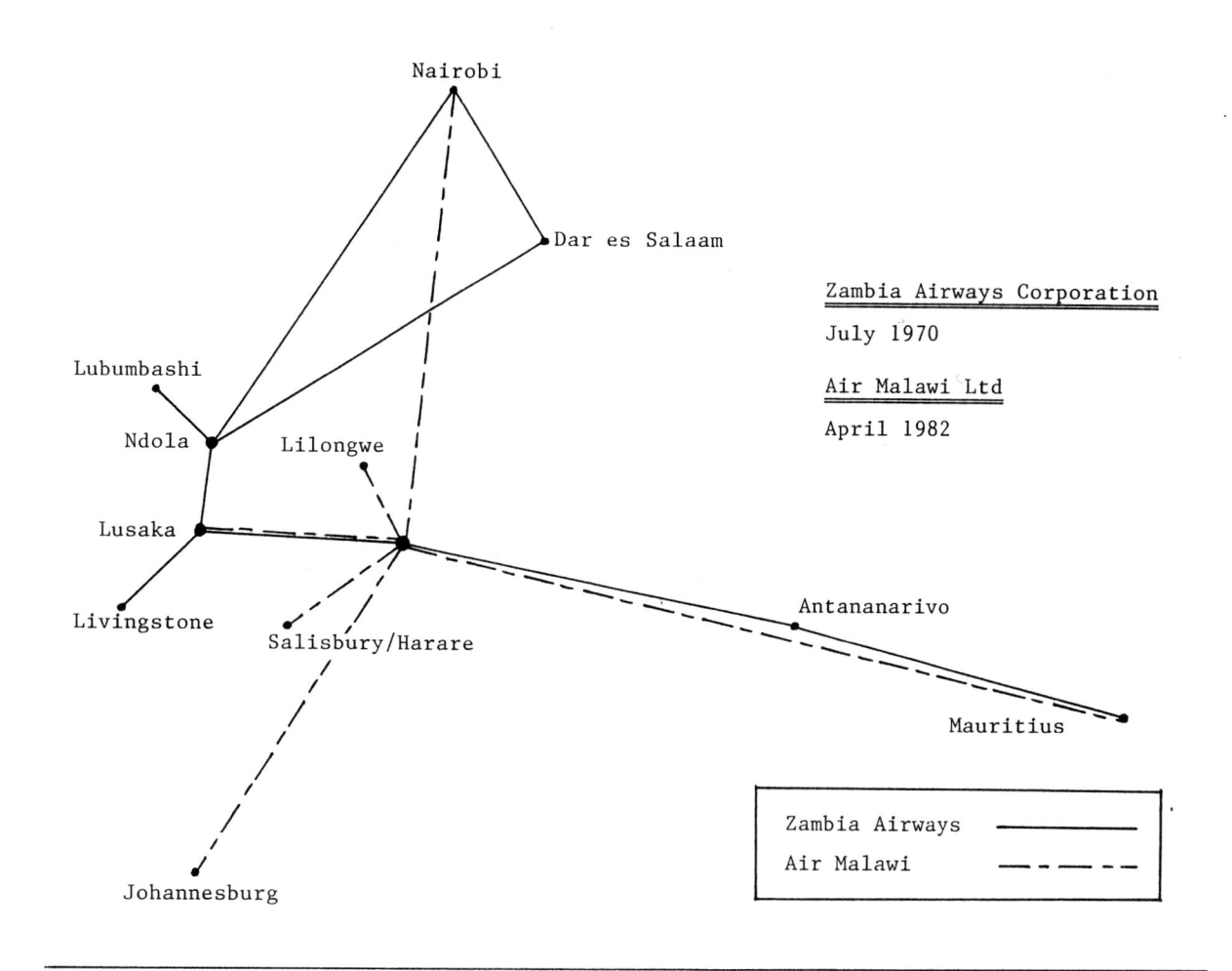

Zambia Airways Corporation
July 1970

Air Malawi Ltd
April 1982

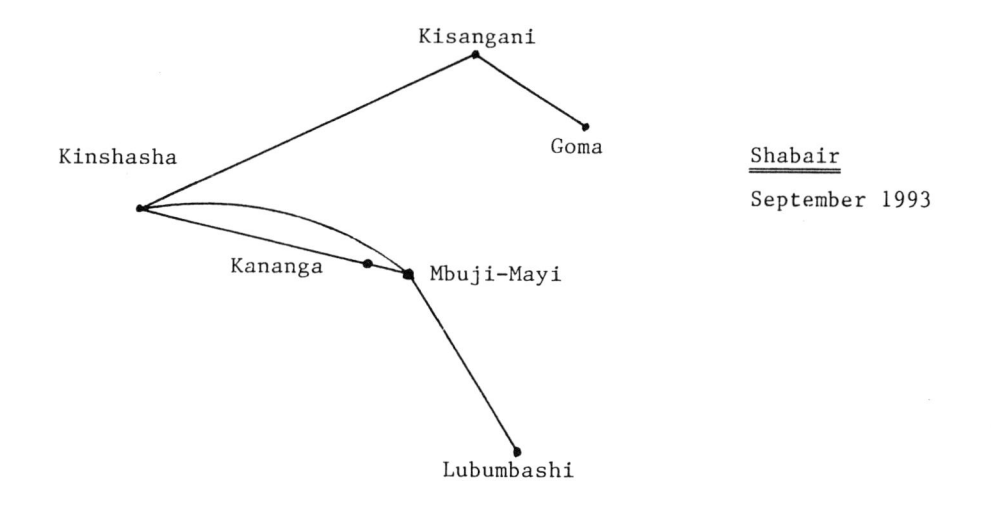

Zambia Airways ———
Air Malawi – – – –

Shabair
September 1993

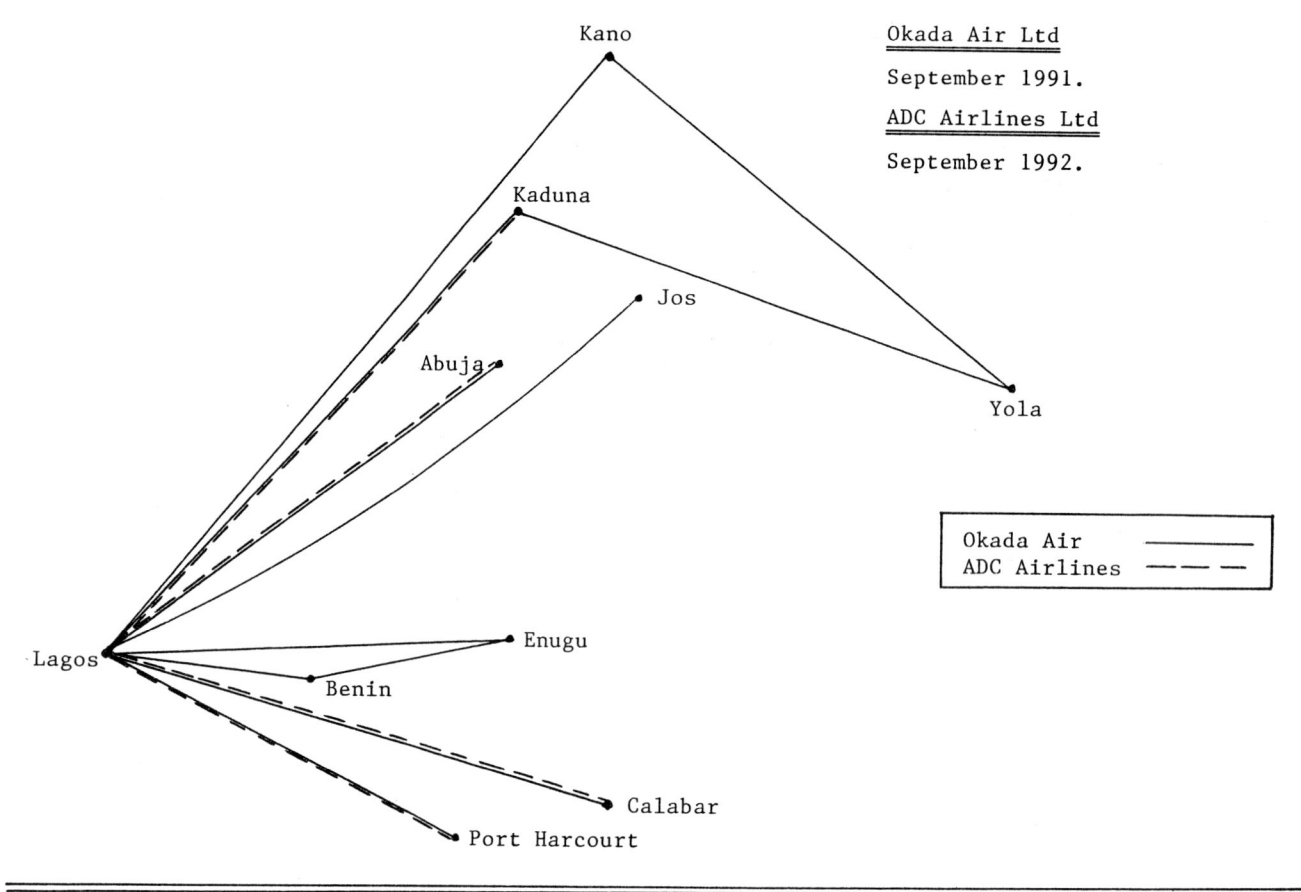

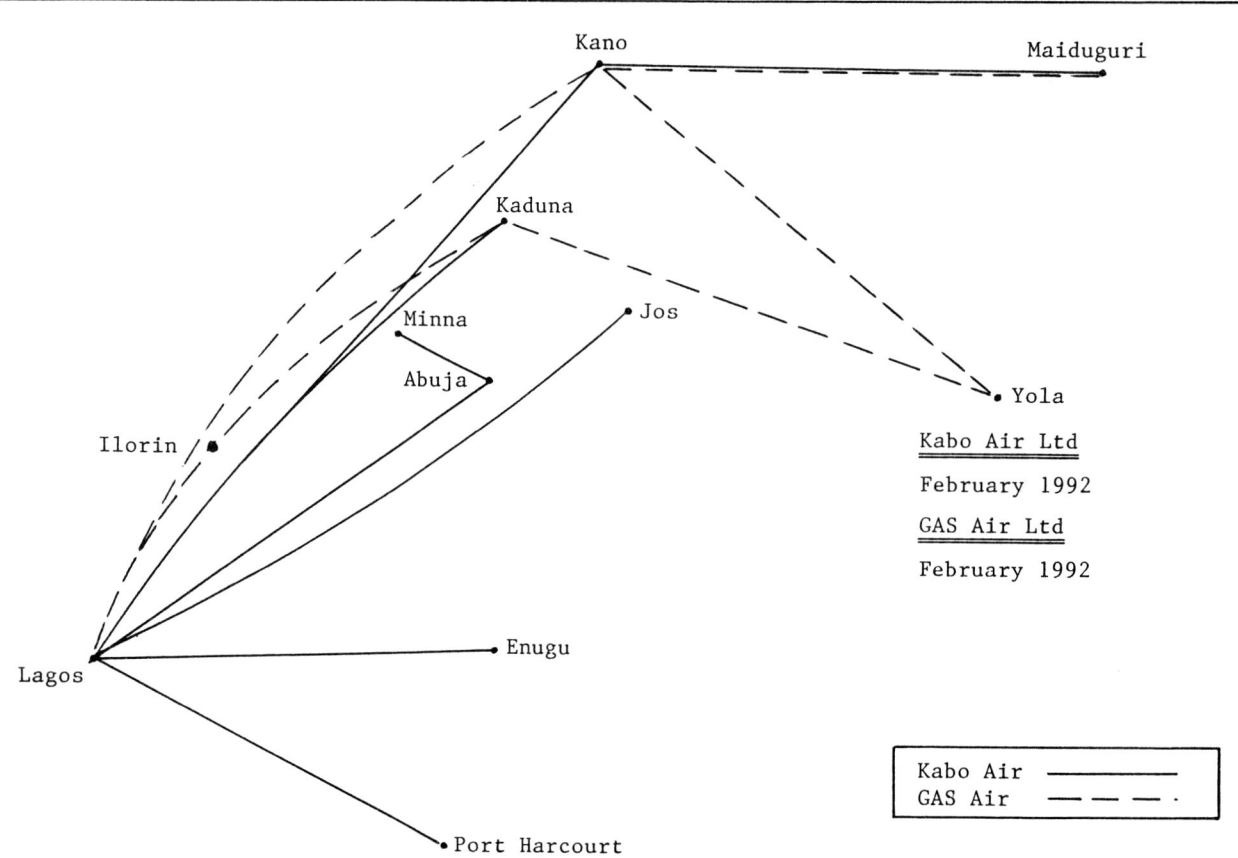

Okada Air Ltd
September 1991.
ADC Airlines Ltd
September 1992.

Okada Air ———
ADC Airlines – – –

Kabo Air Ltd
February 1992
GAS Air Ltd
February 1992

Kabo Air ———
GAS Air – – –

C/n 091 - Srs.402AP XX919 of the RAE in the "Raspberry Ripple" c/s in Jul83 (K Gaskell)

C/n 103 - Srs.204AF N1122J of USAir in Jul89 (Elliot Greenman)

C/n 110 - Srs.304AX G-BPNX ex Cymru/Dan-Air at Lasham in Jan89 (K Gaskell)

C/n 091 - Srs.402AP PI-C1131 of Philippine Air Lines (Brooklands Museum)

C/n 108 - Srs.409AY G-BGTU Rolls-Royce/Turbo-Union (Alan Miles)

C/n 111 - Srs.412EB AN-BBI of LANICA (Brooklands Museum)

C/n 102 - Srs.204AF N1120J of USAir in Jan84 (Elliot Greenman)

C/n 112 - Srs.304AX G-WLAD of Cymru but still with Manx cheatline, seen at Lasham in Aug88 (K Gaskell)

C/n 115 - Srs.408EF G-BBMG in British Airways early c/s at Heathrow in Mar81 (K Gaskell)

C/n 162 - Srs.409AY G-AXBB of British Island Airways (Brooklands Museum)

C/n 053 - G-ASYD as the prototype Srs.670; note the anti-deep stall/spin parachute housing behind the APU exhaust. Similar parachute housings were fitted to several of the early Srs.200s during pre-service flight testing (Brooklands Museum)

British Eagle International
Summer 1968

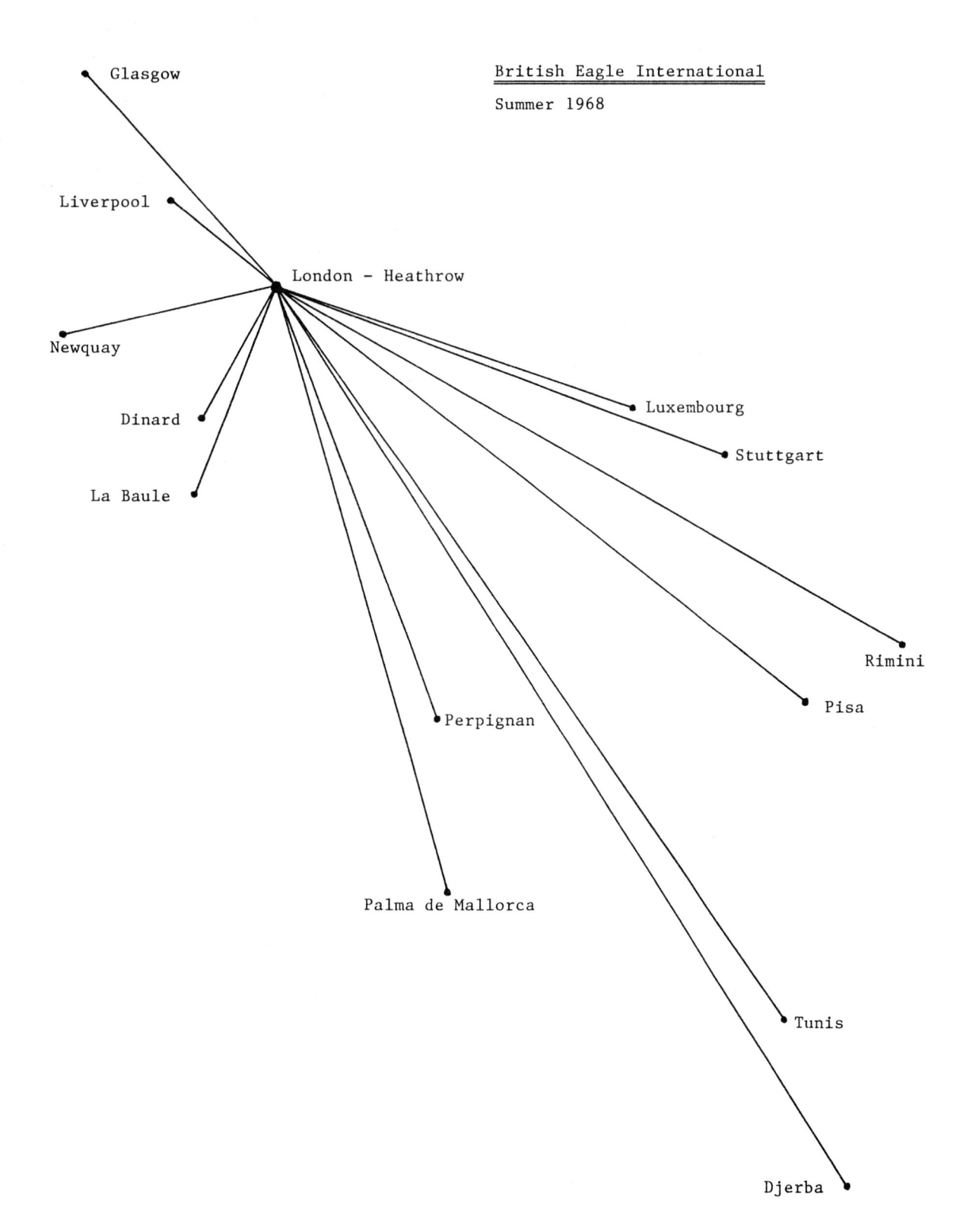

- Glasgow
- Liverpool
- London – Heathrow
- Newquay
- Dinard
- La Baule
- Luxembourg
- Stuttgart
- Rimini
- Pisa
- Perpignan
- Palma de Mallorca
- Tunis
- Djerba

145

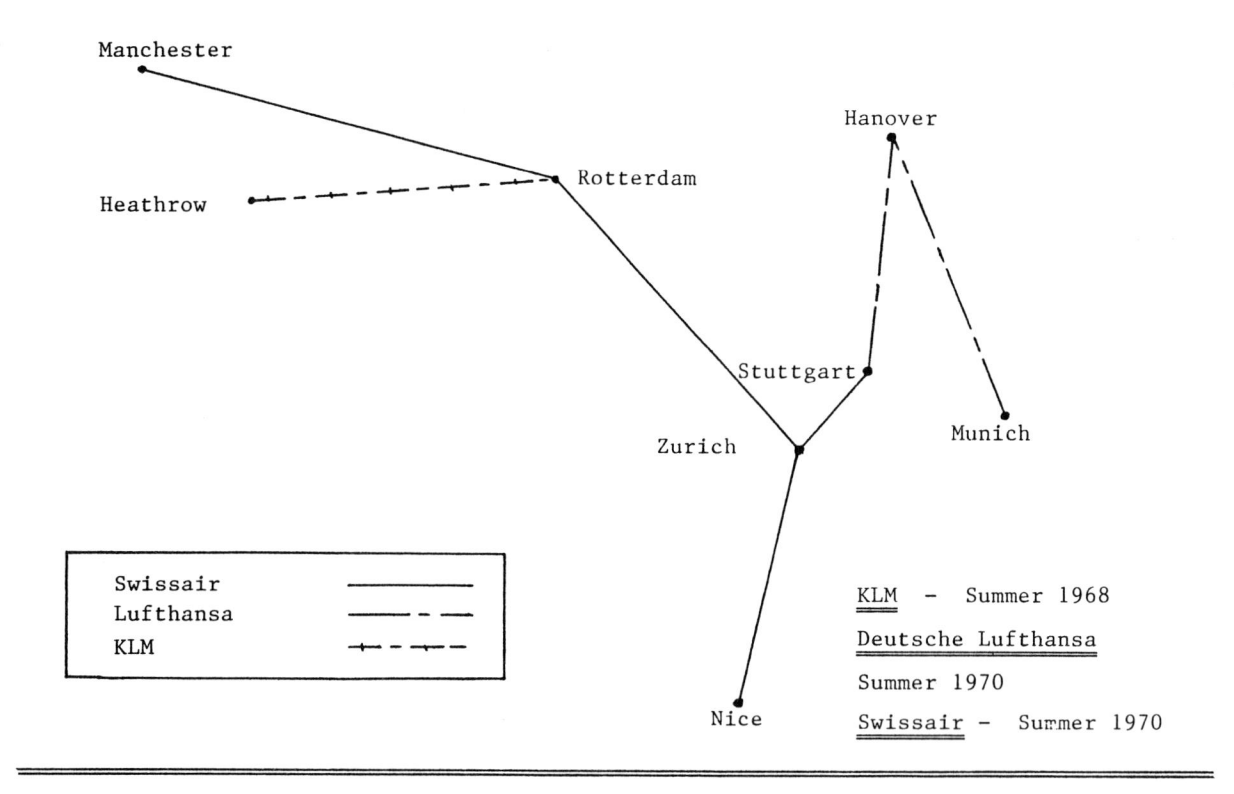

Manchester

Hanover

Heathrow •-----•----- Rotterdam

Stuttgart

Zurich

Munich

Swissair	———————
Lufthansa	— — — —
KLM	—+—+—+—

KLM - Summer 1968

Deutsche Lufthansa
Summer 1970

Swissair - Summer 1970

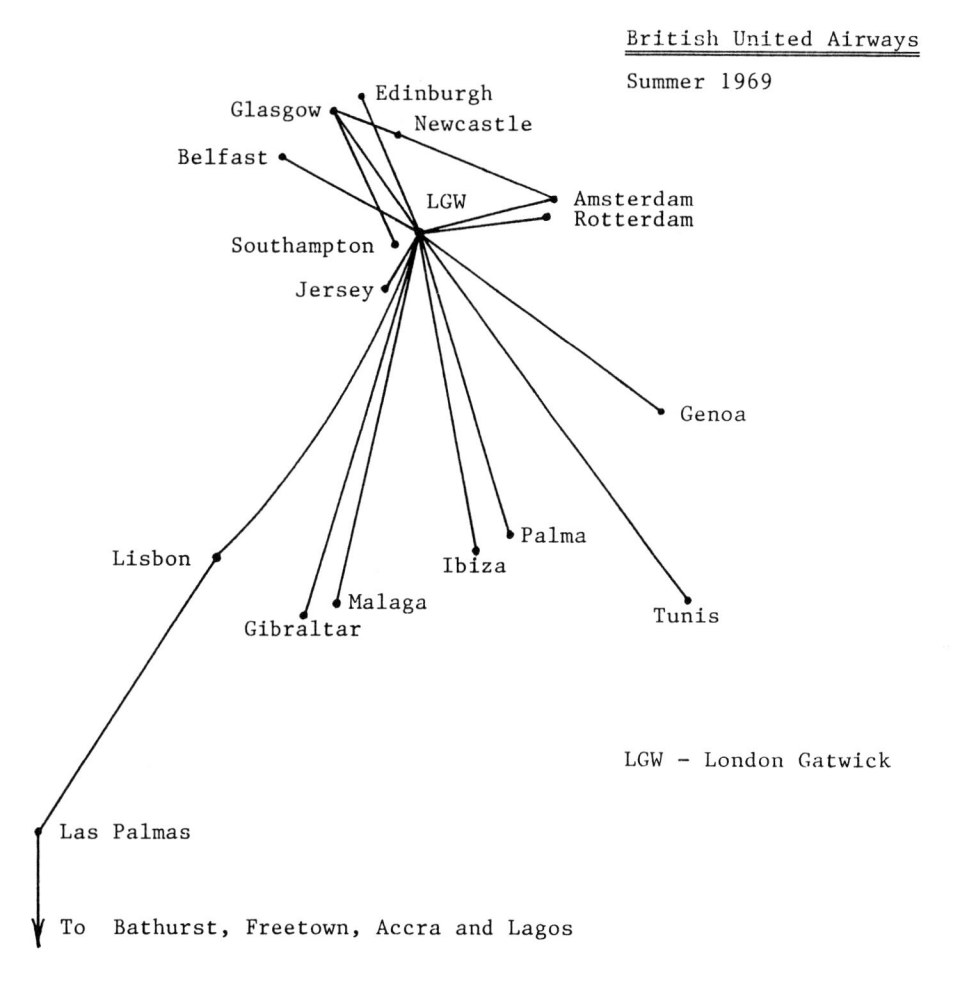

Nice

British United Airways
Summer 1969

Edinburgh
Glasgow
Newcastle
Belfast
LGW
Amsterdam
Southampton
Rotterdam
Jersey

Genoa

Palma
Lisbon
Ibiza
Malaga
Gibraltar
Tunis

LGW - London Gatwick

Las Palmas

↓ To Bathurst, Freetown, Accra and Lagos

Aer Lingus Teoranta - July 1970

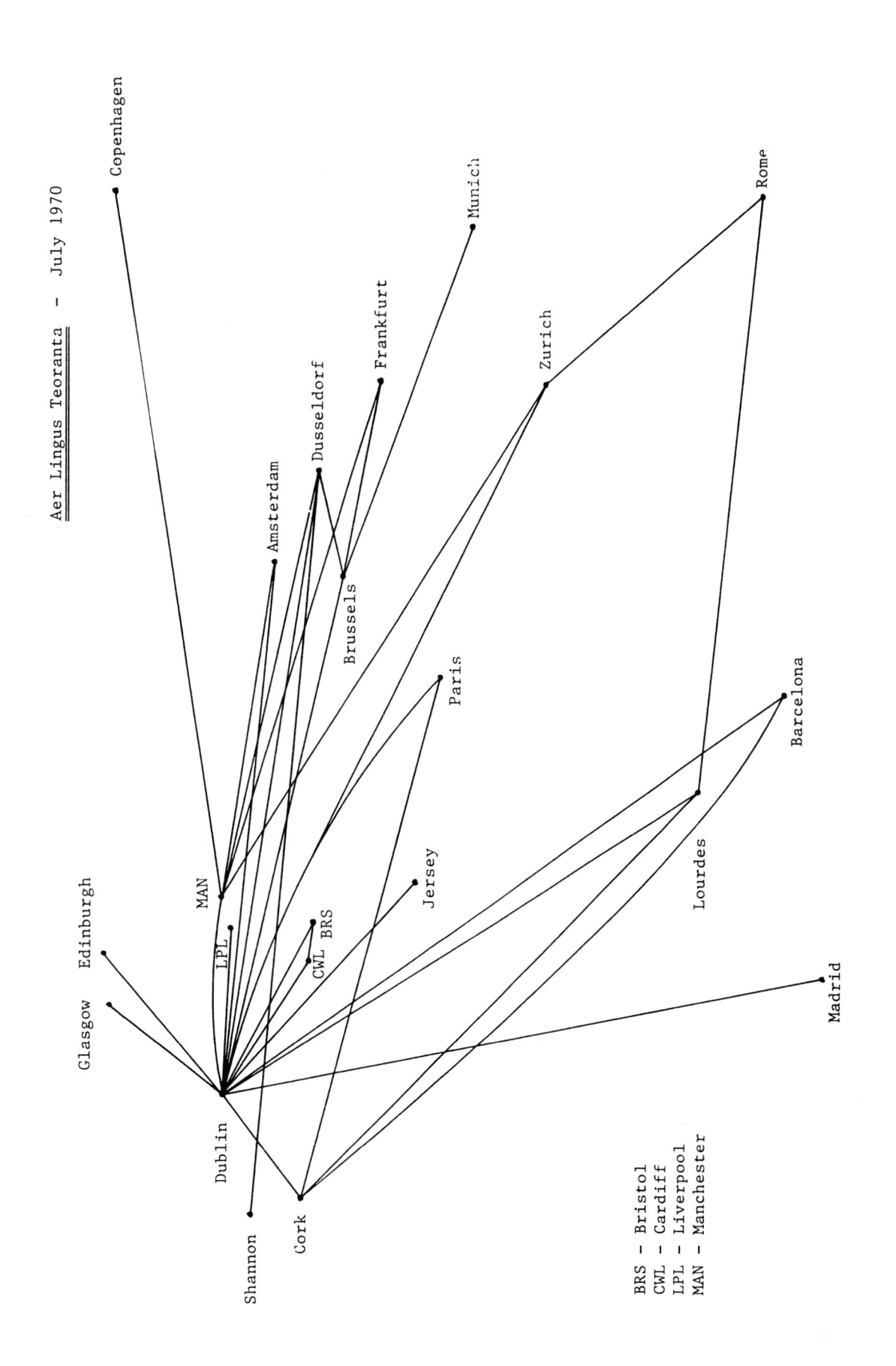

BRS - Bristol
CWL - Cardiff
LPL - Liverpool
MAN - Manchester

Copenhagen

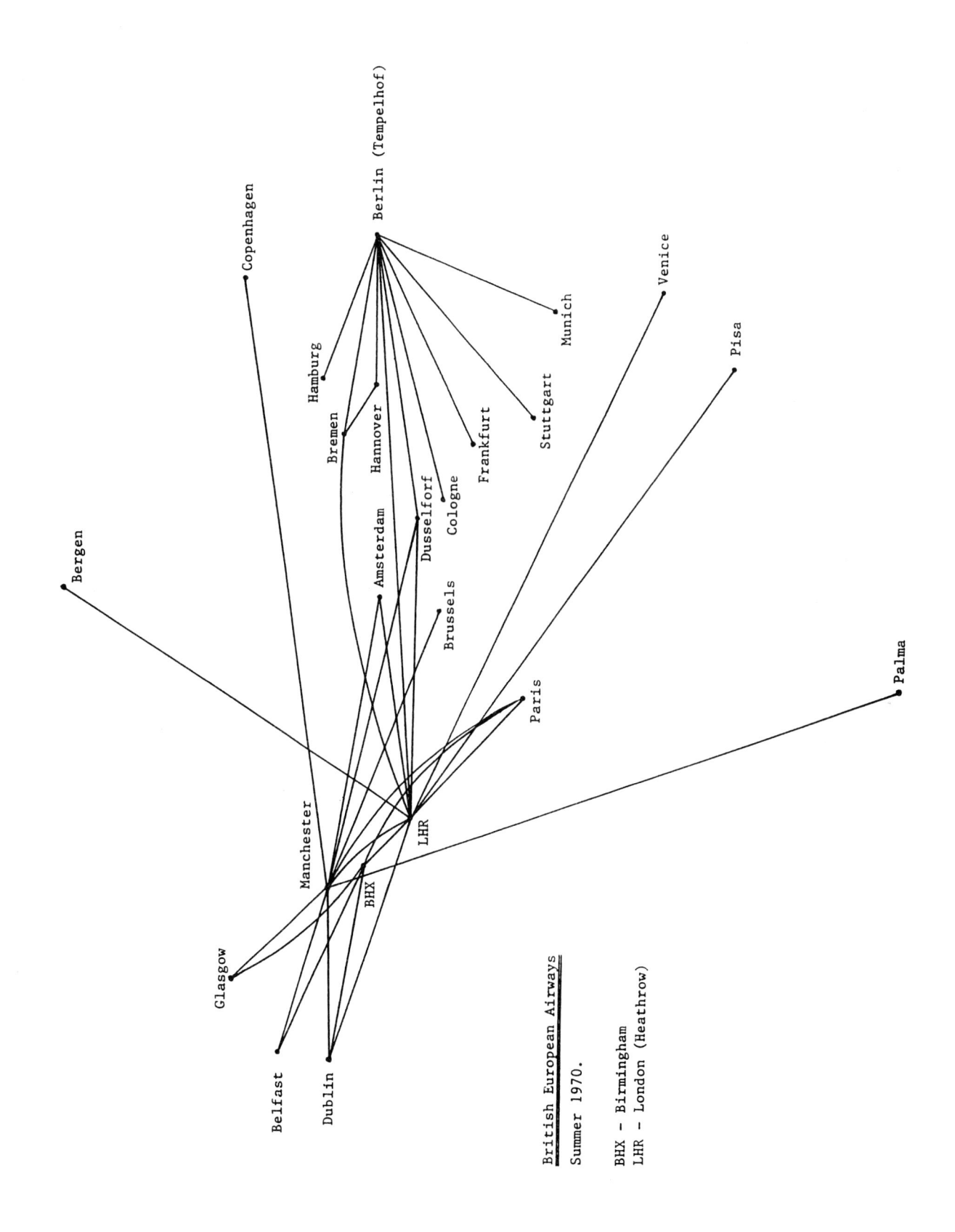

Berlin (Tempelhof)

Venice

Hamburg

Munich

Bremen

Hannover

Pisa

Frankfurt

Stuttgart

Bergen

Amsterdam

Dusseldorf

Cologne

Brussels

Palma

Paris

Manchester

LHR

BHX

Glasgow

Belfast

Dublin

British European Airways
Summer 1970.

BHX - Birmingham
LHR - London (Heathrow)

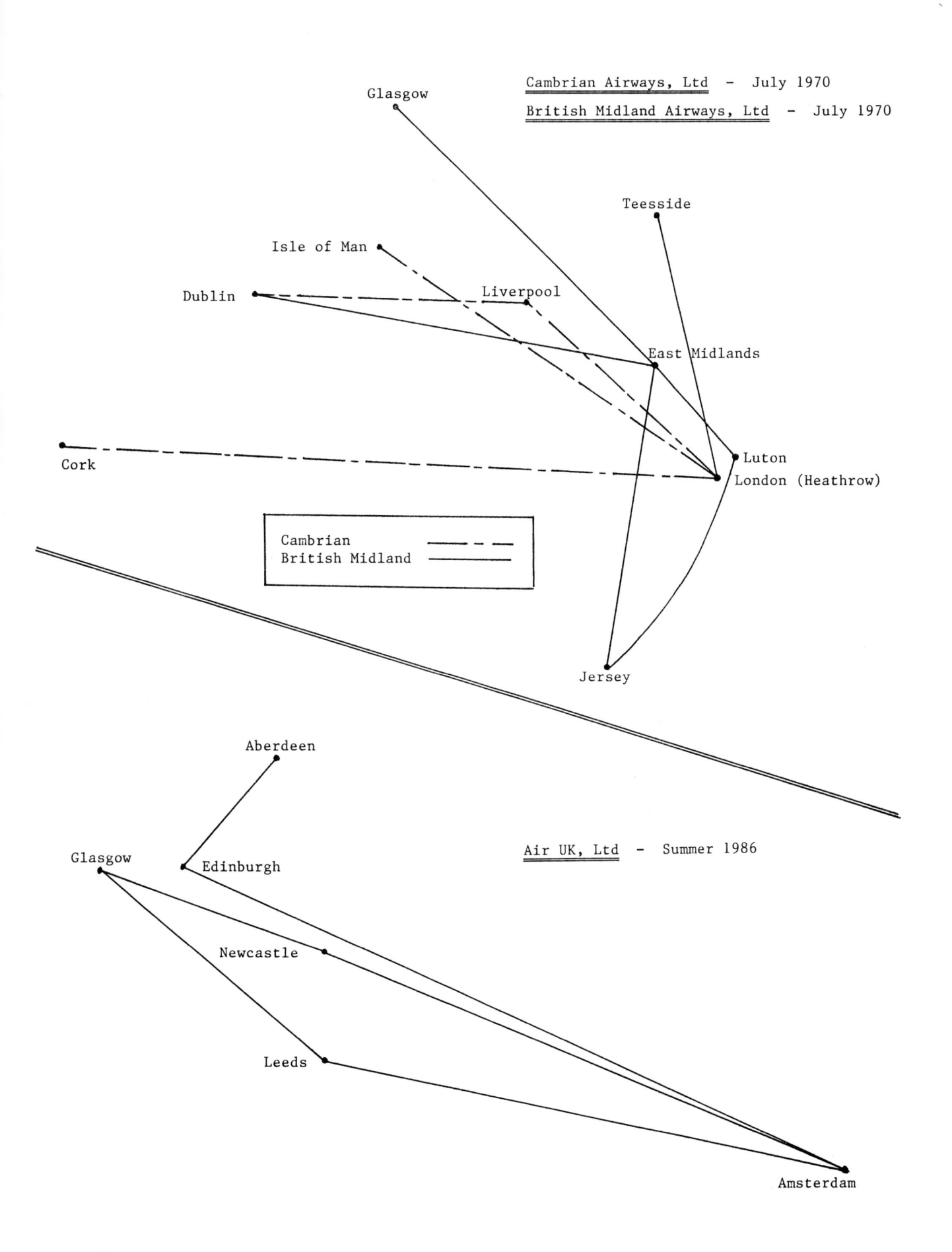

Cambrian Airways, Ltd - July 1970
British Midland Airways, Ltd - July 1970

Cambrian — — —
British Midland ———

Air UK, Ltd - Summer 1986

British Caledonian Airways Ltd
Summer 1987

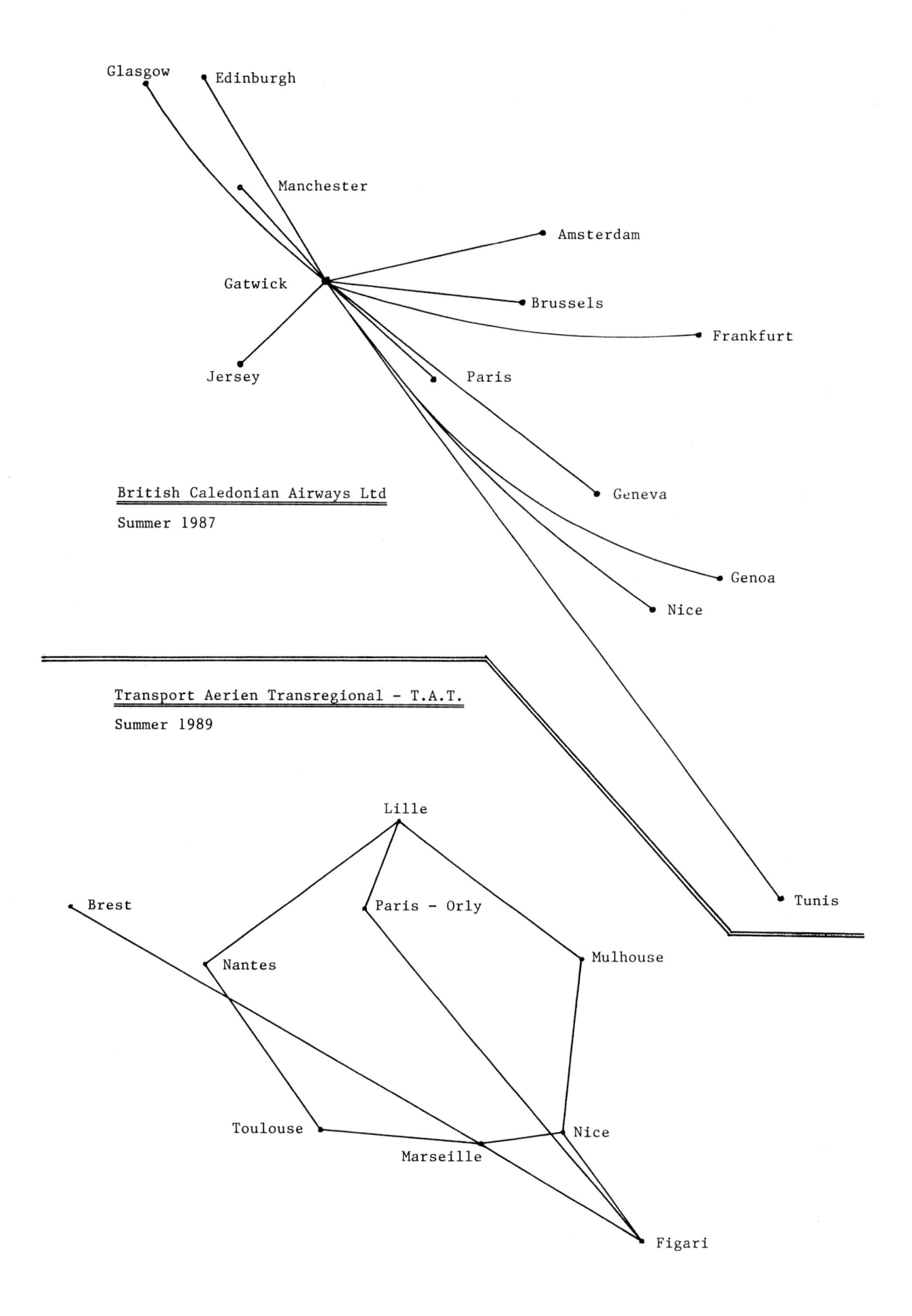

Transport Aerien Transregional – T.A.T.
Summer 1989

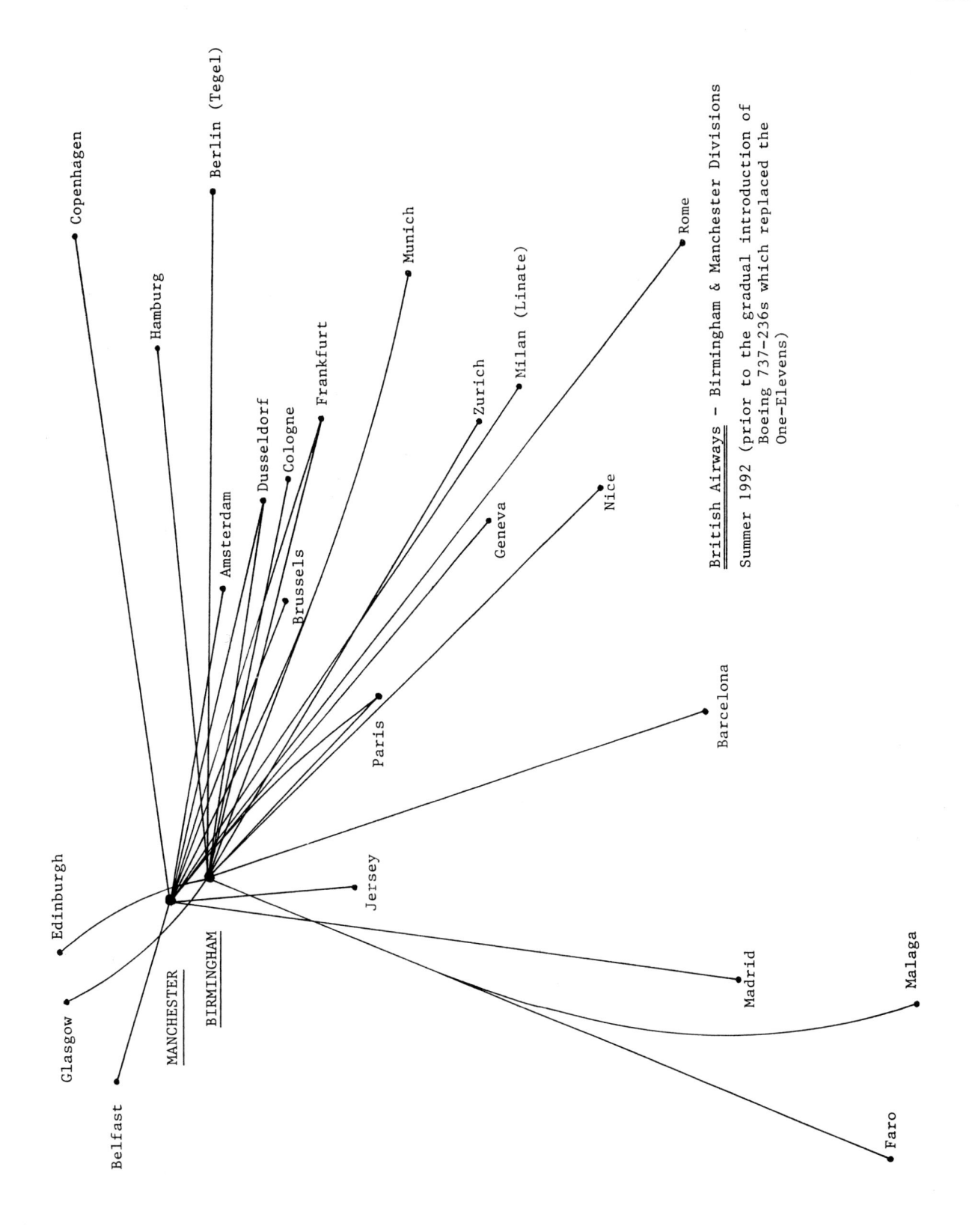

Belfast
Glasgow
Edinburgh
MANCHESTER
BIRMINGHAM
Copenhagen
Hamburg
Berlin (Tegel)
Amsterdam
Dusseldorf
Cologne
Frankfurt
Brussels
Munich
Zurich
Milan (Linate)
Geneva
Nice
Rome
Paris
Jersey
Barcelona
Madrid
Malaga
Faro

British Airways - Birmingham & Manchester Divisions
Summer 1992 (prior to the gradual introduction of Boeing 737-236s which replaced the One-Elevens)

152

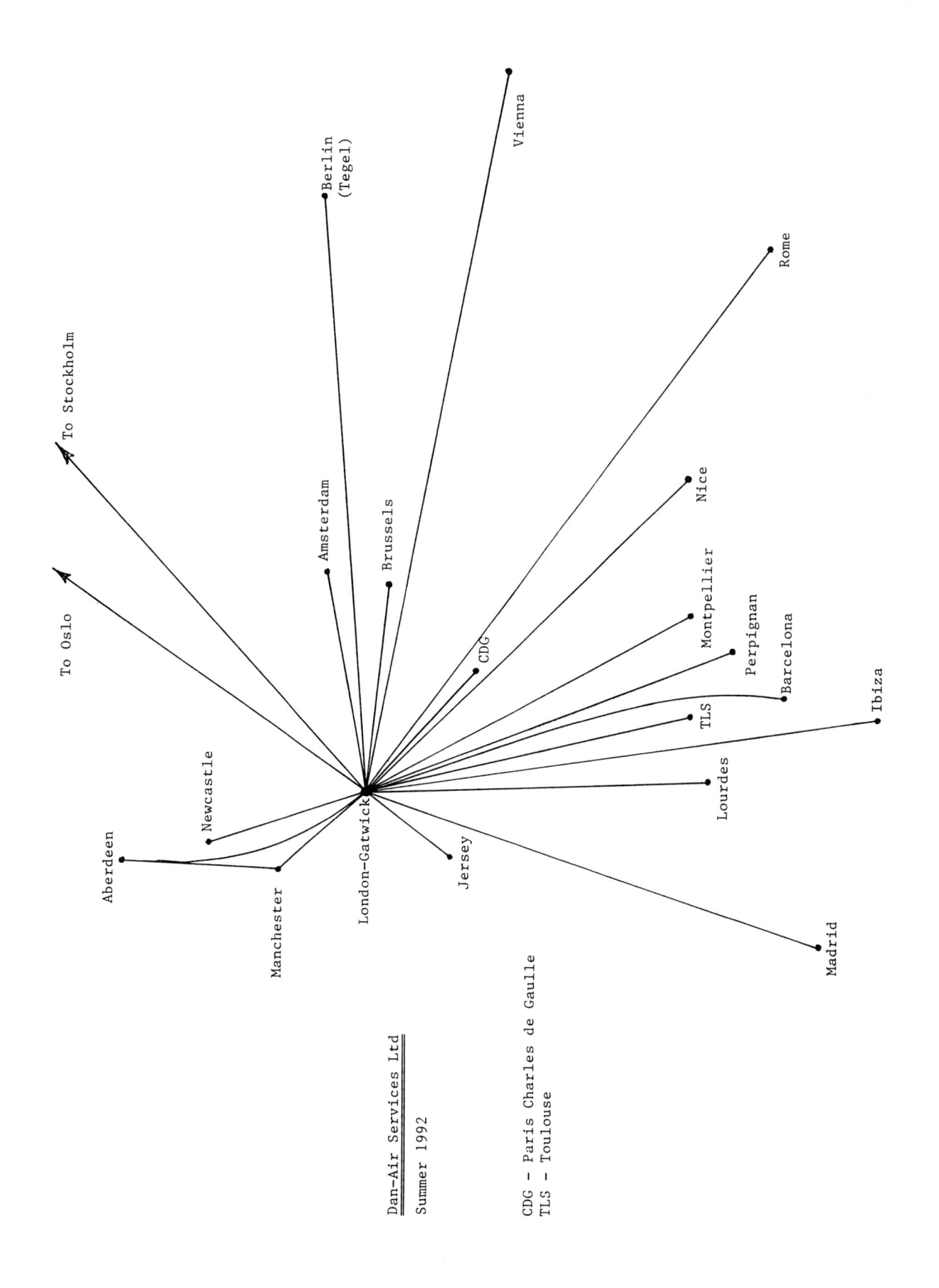

Vienna
Berlin (Tegel)
Rome
To Stockholm
Nice
Amsterdam
Brussels
Montpellier
To Oslo
CDG
Perpignan
Barcelona
TLS
Ibiza
Newcastle
Lourdes
Aberdeen
London-Gatwick
Manchester
Jersey
Madrid

Dan-Air Services Ltd
Summer 1992

CDG - Paris Charles de Gaulle
TLS - Toulouse

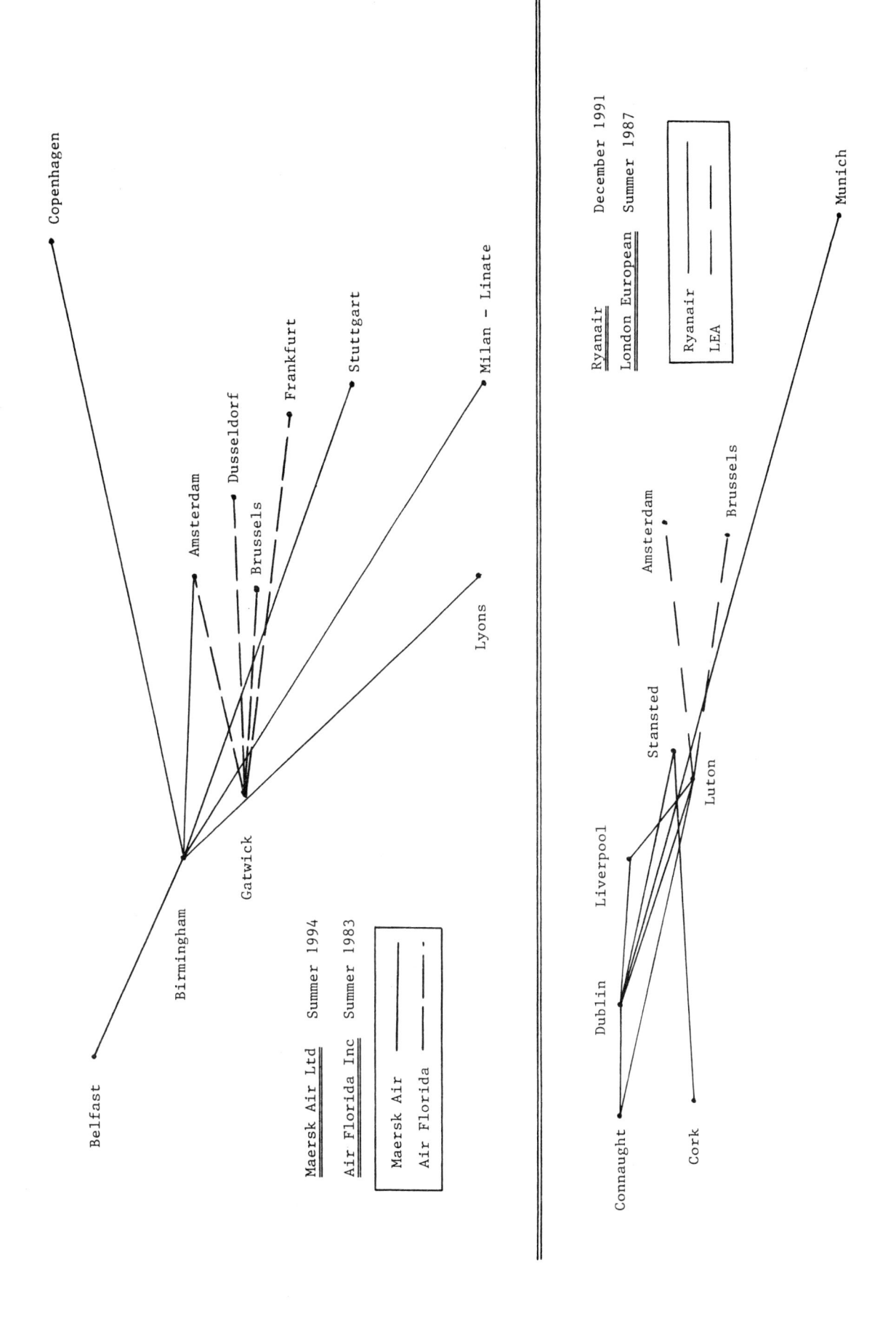

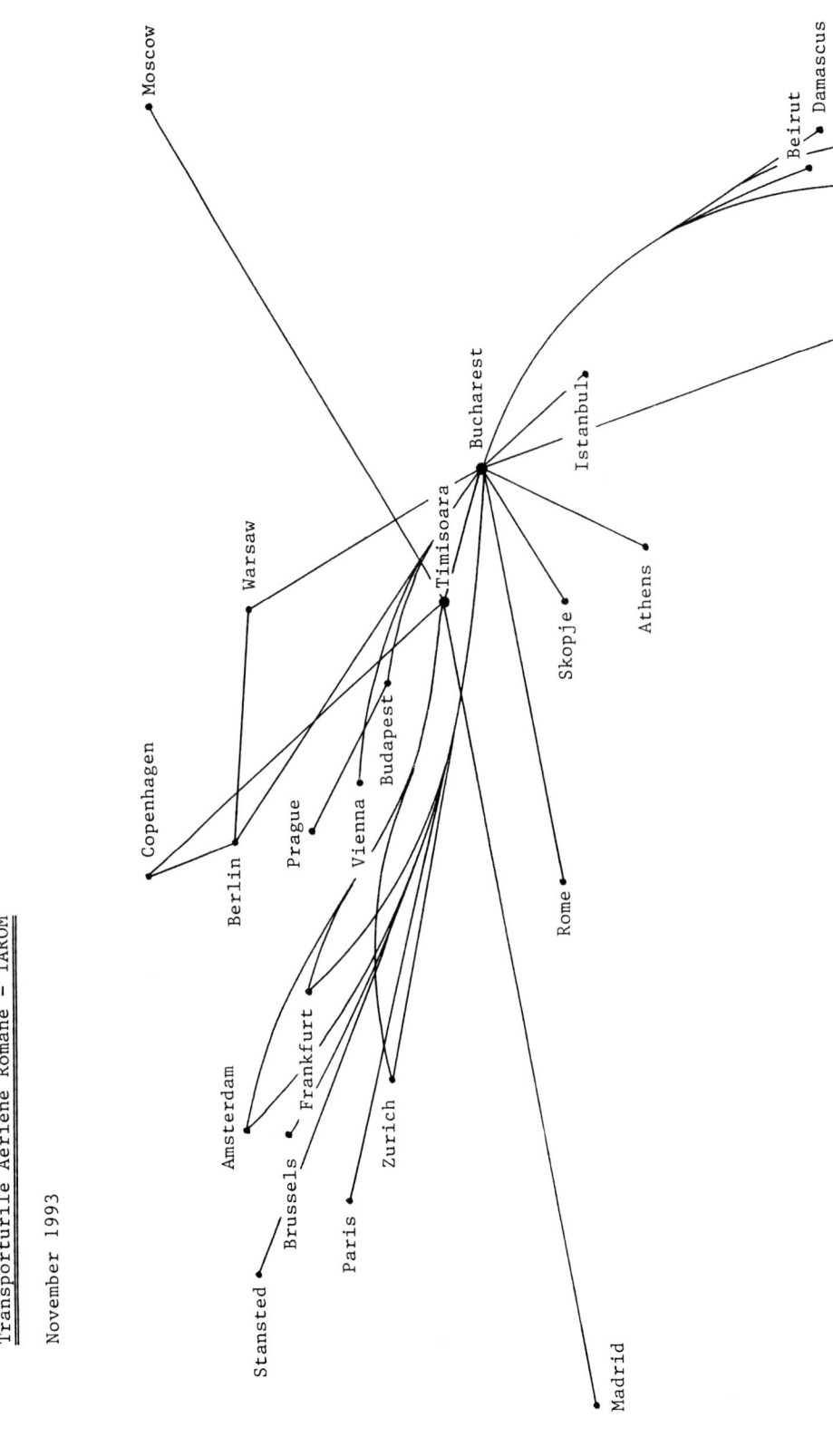

Transporturile Aeriene Romane - TAROM

November 1993

Cyprus Airways
Summer 1994

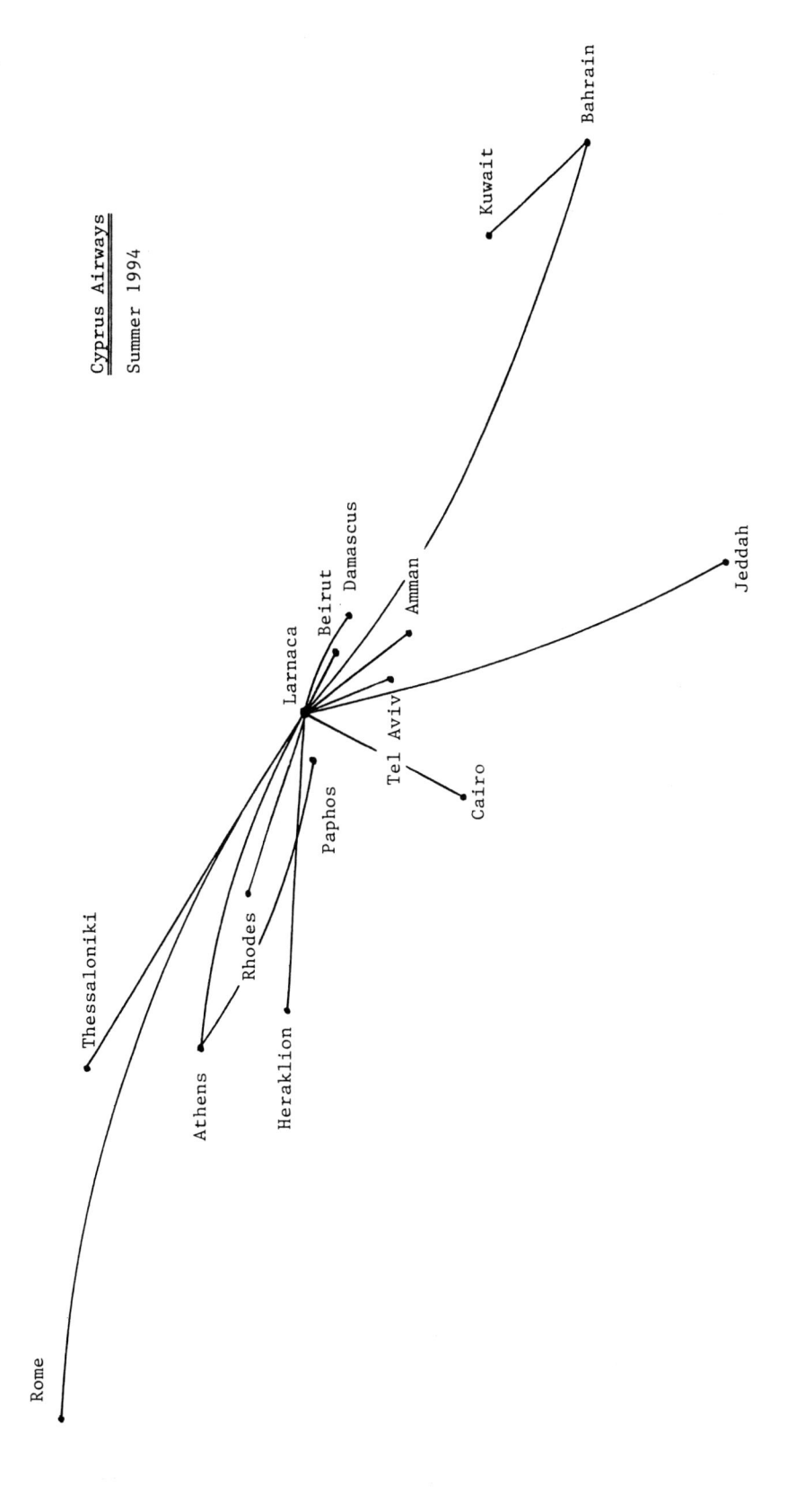

- Bahrain
- Kuwait
- Jeddah
- Amman
- Damascus
- Beirut
- Larnaca
- Tel Aviv
- Cairo
- Paphos
- Rhodes
- Heraklion
- Athens
- Thessaloniki
- Rome

INDIVIDUAL AIRCRAFT HISTORIES

Each aircraft built is listed in constructor's number order, first detailing UK production and second those aircraft produced in Romania. The letter 'W' appears in some cases after the constructor's number; this indicates that final assembly took place at Weybridge and that the aircraft was first flown from there. All other UK built aircraft were completed and first flown from Hurn. Following the constructor's number is shown the aircraft type as originally built and then the history of the aircraft where known. Any subsequent change of type is shown in the history. It has not always been possible to obtain precise details for some of the aircraft, this especially applying to Romanian produced examples. The most likely details are shown where conflicting information has appeared from various sources. Where possible the total airframe hours and landings are shown for an aircraft if it has been written off, permanently withdrawn from use or is in longterm storage. Accurate details of many Nigerian registered One-Elevens have been impossible to obtain; several Nigerian registered aircraft have been reported as seen which cannot be identified with known constructor's numbers.

004   200AB   First prototype. Regd as G-ASHG to British Aircraft Corp 25Mar63; rolled out 28Jul63; ff 20Aug63. W/o 22Oct63 Chicklade, Wilts, UK, after failing to recover from a deep stall during flight testing. Regn cx 06Dec63.
                                                                    TT 81 hrs, 78 ldgs.

005   201AC   Regd as G-ASJA to British United Airways 06Jun63; ff 19Dec63, CofA issued 29Feb64, del 11Oct65. Ferried to Cambridge for exec conversion 14Oct69 after sale to E T Barwick Inds; regn cx same date. Ff 07Mar70 as G-52-1 after conversion by Marshall of Cambridge (Engineering); del via Prestwick 02Apr70 as N734EB. Sold Kalib Lsg Co 29Apr70 and lsd back to E T Barwick Inds. Sold E T Barwick Inds 04Mar75. Sold Omni A/C Sales 15Apr75. Sold as XB-MUO to Mario Vasquez Rana 17Apr75. Lsd Estado Mayor Presidencial Jun76 and sublsd as TP-0201 to Mexican Govt 01Oct76 to Sep77 when restored as XB-MUO. Sold as VR-CAQ to Omni A/C Sales 04Sep78. Sold as N3756F to Kenny Rogers Ltd 24Apr80. Re-regd N97KR 20May80. Regd to Tracinda Corp Mar84. Regd to CBN Continental Broadcasting Network Mar85. Re-regd N88NB May85. Regd to Airplanes Inc Jun85. Regd to Calcutta A/C Lsg Oct88. Regn cx Aug89 after a/c reduced to spares Jul89.
                                                                    TT 15,095 hrs, 11,403 ldgs.

006   201AC   Regd as G-ASJB to British United Airways 06Jun63; ff 14Feb64. W/o 18Mar64 in heavy landing incident Wisley, Surrey, UK, flight test centre prior to del. Regn cx 18Mar64. Planned for rebuild at Weybridge as c/n 095 but not proceeded with.
                                                                    TT 17hrs, 16 ldgs.

007   201AC   Regd as G-ASJC to British United Airways 06Jun63; ff 01Apr64; CofA issued 18May64; del 06Nov65. Company merged with Caledonian Airways to form Caledonian//BUA 30Nov70; named "City of Glasgow". Regd to Caledonian-British United Airways 14Apr71. Co renamed British Caledonian Airways 01Nov71. Regd to British Caledonian Airways 04May72. Regn cx 04Dec81 after sale to Pacific Express. Regd as N101EX to Security Pacific Commercial Lsg Dec81 and del ex Gatwick in full Pacific Express c/s 10Dec81. Regd to British Jet A/C Co Mar84. Co ceased ops 02May84. Lsd Air Wisconsin in full c/s from Jan85 to Apr86. Regd to Jet Acceptance Corp Apr86. Sold to Florida Express and regd to them Jun86, having been painted in full c/s by 10Apr86. Co merged into Braniff Airways 01Mar88. Sold to Guinness Peat Avn and regd as EI-BWI to Air Tara 20Jul88 with CofA issued same date.

Lsd back to Braniff Airways.   Co ceased ops 06Nov89.   Del to Southend 18Apr90 ex Kansas City.   Regn cx ...   Restored as G-ASJC to British Air Ferries 26Oct90, but a/c remained in store still painted as EI-BWI in Florida Express c/s with Braniff titles for spares use only.   B/u 24/30Jan94; regn cx as dest 14Mar94.   TT 45,798 hrs, 46,711 ldgs.

008   201AC   Regd as G-ASJD to British United Airways 06Jun63;   ff 06Jul64.
                Force-landed 20Aug64 Salisbury Plain.   A/c dismantled and taken to Hurn by road for rebuild.   CofA issued 04Aug65;   del 05Aug65.   Co merged with Caledonian Airways to form Caledonian//BUA 30Nov70;   named "City of Edinburgh". Regd to Caledonian-British United Airways 14Apr71.   Sold 21Sep71 Royal A/C Establishment, Bedford, UK.   Regn cx 01Oct71 and regd XX105.   Del RAE 26Mar73 after mods at Hurn.   Op by Blind Landing Experimental Unit, Thurleigh, Beds.   RAE absorbed into Defence Research Agency Apr91.   A/c still painted with RAE titles Jan92.

009   201AC   Regd as G-ASJE to British United Airways 06Jun63;   ff 05May64;
                CofA issued 22May64.   Demonstrated at Farnborough Air Show Sep64.   Del 23Jul65.   First One-Eleven to visit Jersey 17Aug65.   Co merged with Caledonian Airways to form Caledonian//BUA 30Nov70;   named "City of Dundee".   Regd to Caledonian-British United Airways 14Apr71.   Co renamed British Caledonian Airways 01Nov71.   Regd to British Caledonian Airways 04May72.   Regn cx 01Jun82 after sale to Pacific Express.   Regd as N29967 to Security Pacific Commercial Lsg Jun82 but regn not used.   Del ex Gatwick as N102EX 10Jun82 in full Pacific Express c/s.   Regd as N102EX to Security Pacific Commercial Lsg Jul82.   Co ceased ops 02May84.   Regd to British Jet A/c Co Mar84.   Lsd Cascade Airways Sep84 to 20Dec85.   Sold to Florida Express and regd to them Jan86.   Co merged with Braniff Airways 01Mar88.   Sold Guinness Peat Avn and regd as EI-BWJ to Air Tara 30Aug88;   CofA issued same date.   Lsd back to Braniff Airways.   Co ceased ops 06Nov89.   Stored Kansas City.   Ferried Orlando 29Sep90.   Regn cx 14Jan91 and a/c reduced to spares Mar91.   TT 46,416 hrs, 47,320 ldgs.

010   201AC   Regd as G-ASJF to British United Airways 06Jun63;   ff 28Jul64;
                CofA issued 10Aug64;   del 22May65.   Co merged with Caledonian Airways to form Caledonian//BUA 30Nov70;   named "Burgh of Fort William".   Regd to Caledonian-British United Airways 14Apr71.   Co renamed British Caledonian Airways 01Nov71.   Regd to British Caledonian Airways 04May72.   Regn cx 26Apr82 after sale to Pacific Express.   Regd as N103EX to Security Pacific Commercial Lsg Apr82 and del ex Gatwick 30Apr82 in full Pacific Express c/s.   Co ceased ops 02May84.   Regd to British Jet A/c Co Mar84.   Lsd Cascade Airways 19Oct84 to Jan86.   Sold to Florida Express and regd to them Jan86.   B/u for spares Jan86;   regn cx Sep87.   TT 39,357 hrs, 40,987 ldgs.

011   201AC   Regd as G-ASJG to British United Airways 06Jun63;   ff 31Oct64;
                CofA issued 04Dec64;   del 06Jul65.   Co merged with Caledonian Airways to form Caledonian//BUA 30Nov70;   named "Burgh of Paisley".   Regd to Caledonian-British United Airways 14Apr71.   Co renamed British Caledonian Airways 01Nov71.   Regd to British Caledonian Airways 04May72.   Regn cx 24Mar82 after sale to Pacific Express.   Regd as N104EX to Security Pacific Commercial Lsg Mar82 and del ex Gatwick 27Mar82 in full Pacific Express c/s.   Co ceased ops 02May84.   Regd to British Jet A/c Co Mar84.   Lsd Air Wisconsin in full c/s 04Jan85 to Apr86.   Regd to Jet Acceptance Corp Apr86.   Sold to Florida Express and regd to them Jul86.   Co merged with Braniff Airways 01Mar88.   Sold Guinness Peat Avn and regd as EI-BWK to Air Tara 15Jul88; CofA issued same date.   Lsd back to Braniff Airways.   Co ceased ops 06Nov89.   Del Southend 28Mar90 in full Braniff c/s for lse to British Air Ferries.   Regn cx ...   Rolled out in full BAF c/s 15Jul90 as G-DBAF.   Regd as G-DBAF to British Air Ferries 17Jul90.

CofA issued 31Jul90.   Entered service Stansted to Mahon 03Aug90.   Flew last revenue flight 04Dec92 Stavanger to Southend and put into storage.

TT 47,854 hrs, 48,758 ldgs.

012   201AC   Regd as G-ASJH to British United Airways 06Jun63;   ff 17Sep64 and put into storage; CofA issued 16Apr65; del 17Apr65.   Co merged with Caledonian Airways to form Caledonian//BUA 30Nov70; named "Burgh of Hawick". Regd to Caledonian-British United Airways 14Apr71.   Co renamed British Caledonian Airways 01Nov71. Regd to British Caledonian Airways 04May72.   Sold to Pacific Express. Regd as N105EX to Security Pacific Commercial Lsg Feb82 and del ex Gatwick 24Feb82 in full Pacific Express c/s.   UK regn cx 01Mar82.   Co ceased ops 02May84.   Regd to British Jet A/c Co Mar84.   Lsd Air Wisconsin in full c/s with r/o Miami 28Jan85.   Lse completed Apr86.   Regd to Jet Acceptance Corp Apr86.   Sold to Florida Express and regd to them Jul86.   Co merged with Braniff Airways 01Mar88.   Sold Guinness Peat Avn and regd as EI-BWL to Air Tara 20Jul88; CofA issued same date.   Lsd back to Braniff Airways.   Co ceased ops 06Nov89.   Del Southend 14May90 in full Braniff c/s for lse to British Air Ferries.   Regn cx ...   Regd as G-OCNW to British Air Ferries 26Oct90.   CofA issued 02Nov90.   In service as BAF5183 Luton to Malta 24Nov90.   Flew last revenue flight 31Aug92 Geneva to Stansted.   Ferried Southend 02Dec92 and put into storage.

TT 47,567 hrs, 48,720 ldgs.

013   201AC   Regd as G-ASJI to British United Airways 06Jun63;   ff 22Dec64; CofA issued 21Jan65;   del 22Jan65 and carried out 200 hrs of route proving before return to BAC 14Feb65.   Del for service 15Apr65.   Co merged with Caledonian Airways to form Caledonian//BUA 30Nov70; named "Royal Burgh of Nairn". Regd to Caledonian-British United Airways 14Apr71.   Co renamed British Caledonian Airways 01Nov71. Regd to British Caledonian Airways 04May72. Regn cx 25Jan82 on sale to Pacific Express.   Regd as N106EX to Security Pacific Commercial Lsg Jan82 and del ex Gatwick 27Jan82 in full Pacific Express c/s.   Co ceased ops 02May84.   Regd to British Jet A/c Co Mar84.   Lsd Cascade Airways Sep84 to Jan86.   Sold to Florida Express and regd to them Jan86.   Co merged with Braniff Airways 01Mar88.   Sold Guinness Peat Avn and regd as EI-BWM to Air Tara 19Jul88; CofA issued same date.   Lsd back to Braniff Airways.   Co ceased ops 06Nov89.   Ferried Kansas City to Orlando 27Oct90 for storage. Regn cx Apr91.   Lsd Shabair Mar91 and regd 9Q-CSJ.

014   201AC   Regd as G-ASJJ to British United Airways 06Jun63;   ff 24Feb65, CofA issued 06Apr65; del 06Apr65.   Operated the world's first One-Eleven commercial service from Gatwick to Genoa 09Apr65.   Inaugurated British United jet service Gatwick to Belfast 04Jan66. W/o 14Jan69 soon after t/o from Milan-Linate, Italy. Regn cx 14Jan69.   TT 8,283 hrs, 6,128 ldgs.

015   203AE   R/o 24May64;   ff 09Jun64 as N1541;   regd as G-ASUF to British Aircraft Corp (Operating) Ltd 30Jun64; CofA issued 04Jul64.   British regd for demo flights and became first One-Eleven to visit London-Heathrow 06Jul64. Flown to Filton for refurbishment 23Feb65.   Regn cx 23Feb65.   Departed Filton as N1541 28Jul65.   Del Braniff Airways 10Aug65.   Lsd as N111QA to Qualitron Aero 29Jun71 and cvtd into exec config.   Returned Braniff 17Aug72 regd as N541BN.   Sold as N5LG to Omni Investments Corp 16Oct72.   Sold as N5LC(1) to Stewart Lumber Co 05Nov72.   Re-regd N8LG to Omni A/c Sales 19Nov75.   Sold Amway Corp 20Dec75.   Re-regd N523AC 18Feb76.   Regd as N583CC to Nationwide Advertising Services Sep91 for flying on behalf of the Cleveland Cavaliers.

016   203AE   Ff 30Oct64 as N1542. Put into storage until del Braniff Airways 20Apr65. Sold Allegheny Airlines 18Aug72. Co renamed USAir 28Oct79. Lsd Air Illinois Oct83; named "Frank Tudor". Sold Air Illinois, painted in full c/s and regd to them Jan84. Lsd Wright Airlines Jul84 to Sep84 in Air Illinois c/s with Wright titles. Lsd Atlantic Gulf Airlines Nov84 still named "Frank Tudor". Flown with APA International sticker on port side Apr86. Co suspended ops 01Sep86 and a/c returned lessor. Regd to Citizens Bank & Trust Co of Paducah Mar87. Regd to Capital Trade Services Sep87. Regn cx Jan88 after a/c b/u for spares 10Aug87.
                                                                            TT 51,092 hrs, 69,890 ldgs.

017   203AE   Ff 10Feb65 as N1543; del Braniff Airways 11Mar65. Lsd Flamingo Airlines Jul71 to May72. Cvtd to exec config by Aviation Traders at Southend, UK, after del 14Aug73 and re-del 22Dec73. Sold McCulloch International Airlines 31Mar77 and lsd Air Chariot Jul77. Sold Omni A/c Sales Jan78. Sold Bermuda Learjet and painted as VR-BAC at Heathrow 14Sep78 but reverted to N1543 the following day. Regd to Satellite Ltd Jul81, named "Bebeji". Regd to Cerro Industries Oct82. Sold Florida Express and regd to International Metals & Machinery Jul84. Regd to Finalco Aug85. Co merged with Braniff Airways 01Mar88. Co ceased ops 06Nov89. Regd to Ludlow Industries Jul90. Stored Orlando.   TT 33,594 hrs, 40,062 ldgs.

018   203AE   Ff 26Mar65 as N1544; del Braniff Airways 06Apr65. Sold Allegheny Airlines 03Mar72. Co renamed USAir 28Oct79. Sold Florida Express and regd to International Metals & Machines Feb84; named "Orlando 2". Regd to Finalco Aug85. Co merged with Braniff Airways 01Mar88. Co ceased ops 06Nov89. Regd to Ludlow Industries Jul90. Stored Orlando and later Hondo, TX. Regd to CRL Inc Dec92.   TT 61,251 hrs, 78,507 ldgs.

019   203AE   Ff 10May65 as N1545; del Braniff Airways 12May65.   Sold Allegheny Airlines 24Jul72.   Co renamed USAir 28Oct79.   Wfs 07Oct83. Sold Florida Express and regd to International Metals & Machines Mar84; named "Orlando 3". Regd to Finalco Aug85. Co merged with Braniff Airways 01Mar88. Co ceased ops 06Nov89. Regd to Ludlow Industries Jul90. Stored Orlando and later Hondo, TX. Regd to CRL Inc Dec92.   TT 59,950 hrs, 76,987 ldgs.

020   203AE   Ff 30May65 as N1546; del Braniff Airways 02Jun65. Sold Allegheny Airlines 07Sep72.   Co renamed USAir 28Oct79.   Sold Florida Express and regd to them Dec85. Co merged with Braniff Airways 01Mar88. Sold Guinness Peat Avn and regd as EI-BWN to Air Tara 13Jun88; CofA issued same date. Lsd back to Braniff. Co ceased ops 06Nov89. Stored Orlando. Regn cx 14Jan91 and a/c reduced to produce.   TT 56,796 hrs, 74,948 ldgs.

021-028 202AD   Cx order for Western Airways Ltd; not built.

029   204AF   R/o 27Mar65; ff 04May65 as N2111J; del Mohawk Airlines 15May65; named "New York" by Mrs Nelson Rockefeller 24May65. Co merged into Allegheny Airlines 12Apr72. Co renamed USAir 28Oct79. Wfu and stored Las Vegas. Regd to USAir Leasing & Services Nov88. Regd to USAir Dec88. Regd to McDonnell Douglas Corp May89. Regd to ALG Inc Sep89. Ferried 11May91 Las Vegas via Philadelphia, Goose Bay, Iqualuit and Keflavik to Southend 12May91 for spares use by British Air Ferries. Finally b/u Feb92.   TT 55,272 hrs, 79,360 ldgs.

030   204AF   Ff 19Jun65 as N1112J; del Mohawk Airlines 25Jun65; named "Ohio". Entered service 15Jul65. Co merged into Allegheny Airlines 12Apr72.

Co renamed USAir 28Oct79. Wfs ... and stored Las Vegas. Regd to USAir Leasing & Services Nov88. Regd to USAir Dec88. Regd to McDonnell Douglas Corp May89. Regd to ALG Inc Sep89. Ferried Bristol via Keflavik 22Dec90 and on to Algiers. Sold Kabo Air 21Feb91 for spares use with US regn cx Feb91. Reduced to spares Mar91.
TT 55,100 hrs, 79,040 ldgs.

031   204AF   Ff 03Aug65 as N1113J; del Mohawk Airlines 10Aug65; named "Pennsylvania". Co merged into Allegheny Airlines 12Apr72. Co renamed USAir 28Oct79. Wfs ... and stored Las Vegas. Regd to USAir Leasing & Services Nov88. Regd to USAir Dec88. Regd to McDonnell Douglas Corp May89. Regd to ALG Inc Sep89. Ferried Orlando and noted stored 09Apr91. Sold Kabo Air with del Luton 13Apr91. Regn cx Apr91. Painted as 5N-KBS and departed Luton 17Apr91; named "Hasiya Bayero".

032   204AF   Ff 26Sep65 as N1114J; del Mohawk Airlines 29Sep65; named "Massechusetts". Co merged into Allegheny Airlines 12Apr72. Co renamed USAir 28Oct79. Wfs ... and stored Las Vegas. Regd to USAir Leasing & Services Nov88. Regd to USAir Dec88. Regd to McDonnell Douglas Corp May89. Regd to ALG Inc Sep89. Ferried Orlando and noted stored 09Apr91. Regn cx Apr91. Ferried via Keflavik to Luton 02May91 on sale to Kabo Air. Painted as 5N-KBV and del via Palma 06May91; named "El-Kanemi of Borno".

033   W 301AG   Built to Kuwait Airways order with regn 9K-ACI res. Not del and lsd to British Eagle from new by Kuwait Finance Co. Regd as G-ATPJ to British Eagle International Airlines 16Feb66; ff 20May66; CofA issued 07Jun66; del 08Jun66 named "Stalwart". Lsd Scandinavian Airlines System 05Dec67 to Mar68. Lsd KLM 29Mar68 to Aug68 in full c/s. Co ceased ops 06Nov68 and a/c flown to Weybridge for storage, later to Wisley. Regn cx 23Nov68 after a/c repossessed by Kuwait Finance Co. Restored as G-ATPJ to Shackleton Aviation 10Mar70. Sold Dan-Air Services to whom regd 20Apr70 after del to Lasham 20Mar70. Ferried Luton 01Jan71 and entered service following day. Regd to Dan-Air Engineering 19Feb76. Regd to Dan-Air Services 23Jan81. Sold International Lease Finance Corp 19Jan90 and lsd back by Dan-Air. Flew last revenue flight as DA875 Zurich to Gatwick 27Oct90. Ferried Manchester as DA79PJ 28Oct90 and returned lessor. Regn cx 19Nov90 and lsd LADECO as CC-CYF with del from Manchester 23Nov90, arriving Santiago 24Nov90. Entered service 07Dec90.

034 W 301AG   Built to Kuwait Airways order with regn 9K-ACJ res. Not del and lsd to British Eagle International Airlines from new by Kuwait Finance Co. Regd as G-ATPK to British Eagle International Airlines 16Feb66; ff 14Jun66; CofA issued 22Jun66; del 24Jun66 named "Spur". Lsd Swissair Nov67 to 29Apr68. Co ceased ops 06Nov68 and a/c flown to Weybridge for storage, later to Wisley. Regn cx 23Nov68 after a/c repossessed by Kuwait Finance Co. Sold Bahamas Airways as VP-BCP 15Mar70 and ff as such 11Apr70. Returned British Aircraft Corp and stored Wisley following del Hurn 16Oct70 after Bahamas Airways ceased trading 09Oct70. Sold Laker Airways and restored to them as G-ATPK 18Feb71. A/c ferried Lasham 26Feb81 on sale to Hughes International and regd to them 05Mar81. Never flown. Regd to Willowbrook International 29Mar82. Regd to Chemco Equipment Finance 17Jun82 for op by Bryan Aviation on exec charter work. Del Lasham 01Mar85 for conversion for lse to Dan-Air Services. Regd to Dan-Air Services 03Apr85 with del ex Lasham 07Apr85. Named "Highland Opportunity" at Inverness 28Mar88; renamed "Highland Enterprise" 1991. Flew last flight as DA133 Aberdeen to Gatwick via Manchester 02Apr91 and ferried Hurn as DA79PK same day on return to Chemco Equipment Finance. Regn cx 01May91. Sold Okada Air as 5N-OMO and del ex Southend via Ostend 11May91.

035   301AG   Built to Kuwait Airways order with regn 9K-ACK res. Not del and
                       lsd to British Eagle International Airlines from new by Kuwait Finance
Co. Regd as G-ATPL to British Eagle International Airlines 16Feb66; ff 13Jul66; CofA issued 22Jul66; del 22Jul66 named "Superb". Lsd Scandinavian Airlines System in full c/s named "Arnold Viking" 06Aug67 to Dec67. Co ceased ops 06Nov68 and a/c flown to Weybridge for storage, later to Wisley. Regn cx 23Nov68 after a/c repossessed by Kuwait Finance Co. Restored as G-ATPL to Shackleton Aviation 08Sep69. Regd Romanic Trading 14Oct69 for op by Dan-Air Services. Regd to Dan-Air Services 30Mar71. Sold International Lease Finance Corp 19Jan90 and lsd back by Dan-Air. Flew last revenue service as DA478 Jersey to Gatwick before ferry to Manchester as DA79PL 15Nov90 on return to lessor. Regn cx 17Dec90 and lsd LADECO as CC-CYI with del ex Manchester 17Dec90 arriving Santiago 24Dec90. Entered service 15Jan91. Wfs and stored Santiago.

036-038   206AH   Cx order for Bonanza Airlines; not built.

039   207AJ   Ff 19Feb66 as VP-YXA. Built and painted for Central African
                       Airways. Sold Zambia Airways before del with regn 9J-RCH res.
Del 22Apr66 and ferried Heathrow same day for lease to British Eagle International Airlines, to whom regd as G-ATTP 28Apr66. Painted in full British Eagle c/s, named "Swift" and r/o 30Apr66; CofA issued same day. Route proving started 02May66, initially to Glasgow. Entered service inaugurating jet service on British Eagle's Heathrow to Glasgow route 09May66. Withdrawn 17Nov67. Regn cx 14Dec67. R/o in full Zambia Airways c/s as 9J-RCH at Heathrow 13Dec67. Del ex Heathrow 15Dec67 at end of lease. Lsd Air Malawi as 7Q-YKE 03Nov70 when Zambian regn cx. Flew last service for Air Malawi 31Mar72 and restored as 9J-RCH 01Apr72. Withdrawn from Zambian service 25Mar75 and restored as G-ATTP to Dan-Air Services 26Mar75 on sale to them with del Gatwick via Bilbao 29Mar75. CofA re-issued 08May75 and entered service following day. Sold International Lease Finance Corp 19Dec89 and lsd back to Dan-Air Services. Flew last service as DA914 Toulouse to Gatwick 27Oct91. Returned lessor and ferried Gatwick to Hurn as DA79TP 28Oct91. Test flown 18Nov91 and handed over to LADECO following day on lease. Regn cx 19Nov91 and del as CC-CYM via Stornoway and Keflavik 21Nov91, arriving Santiago 24Nov91. Entered service 04Dec91.

040   207AJ   Ff 16Apr66 as VP-YXB. Built and painted for Central A f r i c a n
                       Airways. Sold Zambia Airways before del and painted in full c/s as
9J-RCI. Del 25Apr66 and flown Heathrow for publicity purposes 10May66. Seen Filton 11May66 and noted carrying out crew training Stansted on behalf of British Eagle 12May66. Flown to Zambia 14May66 for publicity before returning Heathrow 21May66 for lease to British Eagle. Regd as G-ATVH to British Eagle International Airlines 26May66. CofA issued 27May66 and entered service same day named "Serene". Sublsd Swissair 01Apr67 to 14Nov67. Regn cx 14Dec67. R/o in full Zambia Airways c/s as 9J-RCI 14Dec67. Del ex Heathrow 15Dec67 at end of lease. Restored as G-ATVH to Dan-Air Services 26Mar75 on sale to them and del Gatwick via Bilbao 29Mar75. CofA re-issued 22Apr75; named "City of Newcastle upon Tyne" 28Oct76. Sold International Lease Finance Corp 19Dec89 and leased back to Dan-Air Services. Flew last service as DA081 Aberdeen to Gatwick 11Nov91. Returned lessor and ferried Gatwick to Hurn as DA79VH 11Nov91. Test flown 03Dec91. Regn cx 04Dec91. Lsd LADECO as CC-CYL and del 05Dec91 via Stornoway, Keflavik and Sondre Stromfjord, arriving Santiago 09Dec91. Entered service 17Dec91.

041   203AE   Ff 18Jul65 as N1547; del Braniff Airways 20Jul65. Sold Allegheny
                       Airlines Apr72. Co renamed USAir 28Oct79. Sold Air Illinois and
painted in full c/s by 20Jul82. Regd to Air Illinois Aug82 named "Les Smith". Repossessed 18Apr84 and ferried Chicago-O'Hare to Indianapolis for storage. Regd to

USAir Jul84. Lsd Florida Express Oct84 to 30Apr85, when sold to them. Regn G-BLVO res for Air UK but ntu. Regd to Florida Express Jun85. Co merged with Braniff Airways 01Mar88. Sold Guinness Peat Avn and regd as EI-BWO to Air Tara 01Sep88; CofA issued same date. Lsd back by Braniff Airways. Co ceased ops 06Nov89. Stored Orlando. Regn cx Mar91 and lsd ADC Airlines as 5N-BAA with del via Keflavik, Hurn and Algiers 27Apr91.

042   203AE   Ff 15Aug65 as N1548; del Braniff Airways 18Aug65. Sold Allegheny Airlines 04May72. Co renamed USAir 28Oct79. Lsd Pacific Express 23May83 to 17Dec83. Sold Florida Express and regd to International Metals & Machines Feb84; named "Orlando 1". Entered service 27Jan84. Regd to Finalco Inc Aug85. Co merged with Braniff Airways 01Mar88. Co ceased ops 06Nov89. Regd to Ludlow Industries Jul90. Stored Hondo, Texas. Regd to CRL Inc Dec92.
TT 59,196 hrs, 76,162 ldgs.

043   203AE   Ff 20Sep65 as N1549; del Braniff Airways 24Sep65. Sold Allegheny Airlines 17Apr72. Co renamed USAir 28Oct79. Lsd Florida Express Jan84 until sold to them 29Jun85. Regn G-BLVP res for Air UK but ntu. Regd to Florida Express Jul85. Co merged with Braniff Airways 01Mar88. Sold Guinness Peat Avn and regd as EI-BWP to Air Tara 29Aug88; CofA issued same date. Lsd back by Braniff Airways. Co ceased ops 06Nov89. Stored Orlando. Regn cx 14Dec90. Ferried Ostend via Keflavik 16Dec90 on lse to ADC Airlines as 5N-AYY; named "The Magnificat".

044   203AE   Ff 01Oct65 as N1550; del Braniff Airways 04Oct65. Sold Allegheny Airlines Apr72. Damaged landing Rochester, New York, 09Jul78 and subsequently w/o.   TT 33,699 hrs, 48,220 ldgs.

045   203AE   Ff 03Nov65 as N1551; del Braniff Airways 08Nov65. Sold Mohawk Airlines as N1134J Sep70 and painted in the company's new c/s. Co merged into Allegheny Airlines 12Apr72. Co renamed USAir 28Oct79. Wfs ... and stored Las Vegas. Regd to USAir Leasing & Services Nov88. Regd to USAir Dec88. Regd to McDonnell Douglas Corp May89. Regd to ALG Inc Sep89. Regd to LCA Aircraft Jun90 and stored San Antonio, Texas.   TT 52,993 hrs, 73,302 ldgs.

046   203AE   Ff 22Nov65 as N1552; del Braniff Airways 24Nov65. Sold Mohawk Airlines as N1135J Sep70 and painted in the company's new c/s. Co merged into Allegheny Airlines 12Apr72. Co renamed USAir 28Oct79. Sold Florida Express and regd to International Metals & Machines Feb85. Co merged into Braniff Airways 01Mar88. Co ceased ops 06Nov89. Stored Orlando and later Hondo, Texas. Regd to CRL Inc Dec92.   TT 57,582 hrs, 75,587 ldgs.

047-048 202AD   Cx order for Western Airways Ltd; not built.

049   208AL   R/o 27Mar65 in full Aer Lingus Irish International c/s. Regd as EI-ANE to Aer Lingus 31Mar65; ff 28Apr65 as EI-ANE; CofA issued 14May65; del 14May65 named "St Mel". Carried out a pre-service six day tour of Europe 27May65 to 01Jun65. Entered service 06Jun65 as EI824 Dublin to Paris via Cork. Lsd British Aircraft Corp for crew training 23Nov67 to 30Nov67. Flew last service for Aer Lingus 04Jan91 from Paris-Charles de Gaulle to Dublin via Manchester as EI525. Ferried Shannon for storage 10Jan91 as EI991. Positioned Dublin as EI999 19Jul91. Sold Guinness Peat Aviation and lsd Hold-Trade Air Services as 5N-HTC with del ex Dublin via Faro in full c/s 20Sep91.

050   208AL   Regd as EI-ANF to Aer Lingus 31Mar65;   ff 09Jun65 as EI-ANF; CofA issued 11Jun65;   del 12Jun65 named "St Malachy/Maolmhaodhog".   Lsd LANICA with del ex Dublin 29Oct66 via Goose Bay to Miami in Aer Lingus c/s with LANICA titling. Regn cx 30Oct66 and regd AN-BBS. Entered service 01Nov66 on Miami to Managua route.   Returned Aer Lingus Apr67 and restored as EI-ANF 27Apr67.   Flew last service for Aer Lingus 30Nov90 from Frankfurt to Dublin.   Ferried Shannon for storage 02Dec90 as EI993.   Positioned Dublin as EI999 26Jul91. Sold Guinness Peat Aviation and lsd Hold-Trade Air Services as 5N-HTD with del ex Dublin in full c/s 10Mar92.

051   208AL   Regd as EI-ANG to Aer Lingus 31Mar65;   ff 24Jul65 as EI-ANG; CofA issued 31Jul65; del 31Jul65 named "St Declan/Deaglan". Flew last scheduled One-Eleven service for Aer Lingus as EI699 Dusseldorf to Dublin 28Feb91 and flew last revenue service for Aer Lingus 03Mar91 Liverpool to Dublin. Ferried Shannon for storage 05Mar91 as EI993.   Returned Dublin 22Mar91.   Regn cx 1991.   Sold Guinness Peat Aviation and lsd Hold-Trade Air Services as 5N-HTA with del ex Dublin via Faro 12Jun91.   Skidded of runway landing Kaduna, Nigeria, 29Aug92 and severely damaged, leading to w/o.   TT in excess of 46,550 hrs, 46,180 ldgs.

052   208AL   Regd as EI-ANH to Aer Lingus 31Mar65;   ff 27Aug65 as EI-ANH; CofA issued 09Sep65;   del 09Sep65 named "St Ronan" and entered service same day Dublin to Rome.   Flew last service for Aer Lingus 22Feb91 Dusseldorf to Dublin.   Ferried Shannon for storage 03Mar91 as EI991.   Returned Dublin 25Mar91. Sold Guinness Peat Aviation and lsd Hold-Trade Air Services as 5N-HTB with del ex Dublin via Faro 15Jul91.

053   400AM   Regd as G-ASYD to British Aircraft Corp (Operating) Ltd 09Nov64. Srs.400 prototype and development a/c. Ff 13Jul65 unpainted; CofA issued 14Aug65.   Carried out tropical trials at Madrid-Torrejon from 11Sep65. Demonstrated at Farnborough Air Show 1966 and to Autair International Airways at Luton 03Jan67.   Conversion to Srs.500 prototype started Hurn after del 04Feb67.

       500AM   R/o 22Jun67; regd as a Srs.500AM 27Jun67; ff 30Jun67. Positioned Wisley 03Jul67 to commence development flying;   CofA issued 13Feb68. Regd to British Aircraft Corp (Holdings) Ltd 04Feb69. Later cvtd to the Srs.475 prototype.

       475AM   Regd as a Srs.475AM 11May70; ff 27Aug70.   Shown at Farnborough Air Show Sep70.   CofA issued 10Feb71.   Fitted with Rolls-Royce Spey 512 hushkits and ff as such 14Jun74.   Later cvtd to the Srs.670 prototype.

       670AM   Ff 13Sep77 as a Srs.670AM but never regd as such. Regd to British Aerospace 21Aug78.   Displayed Farnborough 1978.   Evaluated by Queen's Flight of the Royal Air Force 09Apr80 to 15Apr80. Later demodified back to a Srs.475AM and retained by British Aerospace as a development airframe and company corporate a/c.   Retired from service Oct93; donated to Brooklands Museum, Weybridge, and was flown there 14Jul94 for preservation.   Regn cx as wfu 25Jul94.
                                                            TT in excess of 6,787 hrs, 6,325 ldgs.

054   400AQ   Regd as G-ASYE to British Aircraft Corp (Operating) 09Nov64. Built as second Srs.400 prototype and srs development a/c. Ff 16Sep65; CofA issued 23Sep65.   Ferried to Marshalls of Cambridge (Engineering) at Cambridge for fitting of exec interior 05Nov65 to 12Nov65.   Departed Wisley 17Nov65 on sales tour of

USA, Mexico, Guatemala, Honduras, Nicaragua, El Salvador and Costa Rica, returning 08Jan66.　Lsd American Airlines for crew training Dec65.　Second sales tour started 21Jan66 to Australia, New Zealand, Philippines, Taiwan, Japan, Thailand, Burma, Ceylon, India, Iran, Turkey and West Germany, returning 08Mar66.　Third tour to all South American countries and the Bahamas took place 05Apr66 to 01May66.　In these three tours the a/c covered 160,000 miles in 334 flights taking 396 flying hrs and was demonstrated in 40 countries.　Regn cx 13Apr66.　Sold to Page Airways International, sales agents for exec versions of the One-Eleven in the USA, for which regn N4111X was res but not used.　Cvtd to a Srs.410AQ and del to Victor Comptometers 08Sep66 as N3939V.　Sold as N77CS to Chesapeake & Ohio Railroad 26Oct72.　Regd to Chessie Systems ...　Re-regd N77QS 12Dec77.　Ferried Gander to Luton 14Mar79.　Re-regd HZ-AMK for Sheikh Abdul Maksoud Khotah 09Apr79.　Ferried Luton to Keflavik 18Apr84 on sale in the USA. Restored as N77QS to AMK Ltd Jun84.　Regd to Concord Avn May85.　Regd to Concord Promotions Dec85.　Re-regd as N8007U Aug86 for op by Undercover Avn.　Regd to Duncan A/c Sales of Florida Sep87.　Regd to Executive Air Lsg May88 and lsd Rodina Jet Service.　Painted as N17VK at Heathrow 14Mar89 although not officially regd as such until Jul89.　Re-regd N17MK Jul90.　Regd to Yukaipa Management Co Feb94.

<u>055</u>　　401AK　　　R/o Hurn 30Oct65 in full American Airlines c/s; ff 04Nov65 as N5015; del American Airlines 23Dec65.　Wfs 31Oct71.　Sold National A/c Lsg 24Jan73.　Del San Antonio 20Jun73.　Cvtd to exec configuration as first NAL One-Eleven (NAL1).　Re-regd N111NA(1).　Lsd Ryder Systems as N1JR 26Feb74. Regd as N56B to Sharon Steel Corp Jan75 and op by Beckett Avn.　Regd NPC Lsg Corp Jan87.　Regd NVF Co May91.　Sold Avn Resources 28Jun91.　Reduced to spares Aug91.　　　　　　　　　　　　　　　　　　　　　　　TT 14,493 hrs, 17,701 ldgs.

<u>056</u>　　401AK　　　Ff 08Dec65 as N5016; del American Airlines 22Jan66.　Wfs 22Nov71.　Sold National A/c Lsg 02Apr75.　Lsd Aeroamerica 03May76 for ops out of Berlin-Tegel, West Germany.　Returned National A/c Lsg Oct76. Lsd Pacific American Airlines Jan77 to 07Jul77.　Cvtd to exec configuration as a NAL One-Eleven (NAL14).　Re-regd N120TA Jul78.　Regd to Congoleum Avn Dec82.　Re-regd N12CZ May83, although seen Heathrow with these marks 02Feb83.　Sold and regd to Florida Express Sep86.　Re-regd N172FE Feb87.　Sold and regd to Flightway Inc Apr87. Regd to Flightways US May87.　Regd to Flightways Inc Aug87 and noted operating schedules on behalf of Flightway Air Services of Perth, Australia, between Singapore and Christmas Island in Jan/Feb88.　Regd to Calcutta A/c Lsg Jun89.　Re-regd N491ST Sep89.

<u>057</u>　　401AK　　　Ff 03Jan66 as N5017; del American Airlines 29Jan66.　Wfs 17Jan72. Sold National A/c Lsg 15Apr73.　Del San Antonio 20Jun73.　Cvtd to exec configuration as a NAL One-Eleven (NAL3).　Lsd Norton Simon 01Dec73 as N277NS.　Sold and regd to Norton Simon 12Jan81.　Sold and regd to CAW Inc Jan83. Del Lasham 10May83.　Sold to Bryan Avn/International Generics as VR-CBI and r/o as such 26May83.　Del ex Lasham 31May83.　US regn cx Jun83.　Regn cx 20Mar86. Painted in full Florida Express c/s at Manchester as N170FE by 17Jul86.　Regd as N170FE to Florida Express Aug86.　Co merged into Braniff Airways 01Mar88.　Sold Guinness Peat Avn and regd as EI-BWQ to Air Tara 21Jul88; CofA issued same date.　Lsd back by Braniff Airways; co ceased ops 06Nov89.　Lsd Shabair as 9Q-CUG and ferried Maastricht via Bangor and Rekjavik 19/20Sep90 in Florida Express c/s.　Repainted as 9Q-CEH and dep 27Sep90 in full Shabair c/s.

<u>058</u>　　401AK　　　Ff 15Jan66 as N5018; del American Airlines 15Feb66.　Wfs 11May71.　Sold Jet Travel as N711ST 17Apr73.　Lsd Sahara Hotel, Lake Tahoe, by May73 flying with Sahara Tahoe titles.　Dam on t/o 09Feb75 Lake Tahoe

hitting snowbank and sustaining port wing and undercarriage damage; nose section removed and used to make c/n 117 airworthy (see c/n 117 for details). Fuselage remained stored Burbank still as N711ST. Regd to Gulfstream American Corp as N97GA Jun86. Regd to Transworld Avn Systems Corp Jun89. Regd to TABAC Sep89. (Although history as shown after accident, it is believed a/c was not made airworthy again.)

TT at time of t/o accident 11,236 hrs, 14,939 ldgs.

059   401AK   Ff 29Jan66 as N5019; del American Airlines 24Feb66.   Wfs 08Nov71.   Sold National A/c Lsg 02Jul73.   Del San Antonio 20Jun73. Cvtd to exec configuration as a NAL One-Eleven (NAL2). Re-regd N112NA(1). Restored as N5019 to same owner and lsd First National Bank of Chicago 18Feb74. Lsd Hilton Hotels Jan76. Sold Coastal States Gas Corp and re-regd N100CC May77. Regd to Luqa Inc ...   Regd to Janmar Avn Corp Aug82.   Re-regd N700JA Feb83.   Regd to General Electric Credit Corp Nov84.   Regd to River City Investments Feb85.   Re-regd N650DH May90.   Ff 21Jun90 as prototype One-Eleven 2400 with Rolls-Royce Tay 650 engines. Demonstrated Farnborough Air Show 1990. Sold Dee Howard Co Sep92. Regn cx Oct92 and aircraft stored.   TT in excess of 15,878 hrs, 18,155 ldgs.

060   401AK   Ff 06Feb66 as N5020; del American Airlines 13Mar66.   Wfs 08Nov71.   Sold National A/c Lsg 15Apr74.   Cvtd to exec configuration as a NAL One-Eleven (NAL10). Re-regd N111NA(3) May75. Shown Paris Air Show Jun75.   Regd N102GP to Dr Ghaith Pharaon 21Oct75.   Sold as HZ-GRP(1) to Saudi Research & Development Corp 26Oct75.   Re-regd HZ-GP2 01Jan77.   Sold as HZ-NB3 to Commercial Bank of Saudi Arabia and del Hurn to Geneva 18Oct79.   Sold as HZ-MAA to Sheikh Al Amoudi Oct79 and reportedly operated on behalf of the President of Algeria.   Stored Hurn from 20Dec89.   Re-regd HZ-AMB2 with ff as such ex Hurn 04Jun93 and used by Saudi Arabian Presidential Flight.

061   401AK   Ff 16Feb66 as N5021; del American Airlines 04Mar66.   Wfs 13Sep71.   Sold Tristar Western 08Aug73.   Sold The Williams Companies 01Jan75. Sold Omni A/c Sales 11Jan78. Lsd Hustler Magazine Feb78 as N69HM.   Sold Aviation Equipment Lsg Mar78.   Restored as N5021 for lease to Consolidated Productions Dec78. Sold and re-regd N40AS to American Standard 07Feb79. Sold and regd to Florida Express Jun86. Re-regd N171FE Sep86. Co merged with Braniff Airways 01Mar88.   Sold Guinness Peat Avn and regd EI-BWR to Air Tara 22Jul88; CofA issued same date.   Lsd back by Braniff Airways.   Co ceased ops 06Nov89.   Regn cx Jun90 and sold as N682RW to Detroit Red Wings Jul90.

062   401AK   Ff 03Mar66 as N5022; del American Airlines 17Mar66.   Wfs 31Oct71. Sold Bahamasair 29Nov73 as VP-BDN. Re-regd C6-BDN Feb75.   Sold and restored as N5022 to the Garrett Corp; del 04Oct76.   Regd to Personal Way Aviation Jul84.   Re-regd N800MC(2) Aug85.   Sold Okada Air; del Southend 06May87 as N800MC.   Painted as 5N-AYU and del ex Southend 12May87.   US regn cx Jun87.   Ops in exec configuration for private use of the owner of Okada Air.

063   401AK   Ff 05Mar66 as N5023; del American Airlines 21Mar66.   Wfs 15Nov71.   Sold Bahamasair 20Dec73 as VP-BDP.   Re-regd C6-BDP Feb75. Ferried Dublin via Keflavik for maint by Aer Lingus 05Sep76. Returned by same routing 26Oct76. Wfs by Aug81 and stored San Jose, Costa Rica, by Apr82. Sold Beech A/c Corp 25Jun84 for lease to Cascade Airways.   Regd N217CA to Beech Aircraft Corp Aug84 and painted in full Cascade c/s. Regd to Cascade Airways Nov84. Lsd Air Illinois May86 for op on behalf of Atlantic Gulf Airlines. Latter company suspended ops 01Sep86. Returned Beech Acceptance Corp Mar87 and stored Tallahassee.   Regd to AJ Walter

International Aug88. Regd to Zircon Aviation Corp Dec89. Regd as G-BSXJ to Aviation Finance & Lsg Co (Jersey) 01Nov90. Regn cx 28Mar91 as sold in USA, never having adopted UK marks. Restored as N217CA to Zircon Aviation Corp Apr91. Lsd to National Aviation Company of Egypt by Jul92 and flown with both English and Arabic titles.

064   401AK   Ff 24Mar66 as N5024; del American Airlines 15Apr66. Wfs 14Sep70. Sold National A/c Lsg 28Feb75. Cvtd to exec configuration as a NAL One-Eleven (NAL12). Lsd TAG International 29Aug76 to Dec77. Sold National Commercial Bank of Saudi Arabia as HZ-NB2 and ferried Gander to Hurn 18Feb78.

065   401AK   Ff 25Mar66 as N5025; del American Airlines 07Apr66. Wfs 15Nov71. Sold National A/c Lsg 09Sep73. Del San Antonio 27Sep73. Cvtd to exec configuration as a NAL One-Eleven (NAL5). Re-regd N111NA(2) Feb74. Shown Farnborough Air Show Sep74. Restored as N5025 on sale to First National Bank of Chicago Mar75. Regd to First Chicago Corp ... Re-regd N76GW Feb76; named "Trust the People" for Governor George Wallace's election campaign. Sold Allis Chalmers Corp Jun76 as N825AC. Re-regd N825AQ to McMoran Properties Apr82. Re-regd N117MR May82. Regd to Freeport Indonesia Jul87. Regn cx Nov87 and regd PK-PJF to Freeport Indonesia for op on behalf of Dirgantara Air Services. Painted in Pertamina c/s and based Cairns, Australia, primarily for carriage of mining personnel between Timika in West Irian and Cairns. Flew last service on this contract 28Jan92.

066   401AK   Ff 08Apr66 as N5026; del American Airlines 23Apr66. Regd G-AZMI to Orientair 20Jan72 on sale to them and ferried Gander to Hurn 29Jan72. Painted in Orientair's yellow and black c/s for op out of Berlin; named "City of Berlin". CofA issued 05Oct72. Company never started ops. Regn cx 19Feb73 as sold in USA, but a/c remained stored Hurn. Regd G-16-19. Sold British Airways Board and del 07Sep73. Regd to British Airways Board as G-BBME 22Mar74 for op by Regional Division. CofA renewed 09Apr74. Later named "County of Shropshire". Regd to British Airways 01Apr84. Flew last service for British Airways 31Oct88 as BA5366 Glasgow to Birmingham. Positioned Hurn for storage as BA9664P 01Nov88. Sold Birmingham European Airways and regd to them 04Jan90. CofA renewed 30Jan90. Ferried Hurn to Birmingham 31Jan90; named "City of Nottingham". Entered service 01Feb90 Birmingham to Amsterdam. Co merged with Brymon Airways to form Brymon European Airways 25Oct92. Brymon European Airways de-merged 01Aug93 and co renamed Maersk Air. Painted in British Airways c/s.

067   401AK   Ff 16Apr66 as N5027; del American Airlines 29Apr66. Wfs 14Sep70. Sold National A/c Lsg 28Jul75. Cvtd to exec configuration as the last NAL One-Eleven (NAL16). Sold Saudi Research & Development Corp 01Mar77 as N5027. Re-regd HZ-GRP(2) Jun77. Regd N909CH to Hemmeter Investment Corp 10Dec80. Del Zurich to Hurn 08Jan81. Sold American Continental Corp Aug83. Regd to The Citizens' Southern National Bank Feb84. Re-regd N102ME Jun84. Regd to HT 109 Inc Mar90. Re-regd N109TH Jul90. Regd to Jack Prewitt & Assocs May92. Re-regd N765B Jul92. Regd to Calumet Inc Nov92.

068   401AK   Ff 26Apr66 as N5028; del American Airlines 10May66. Wfs 26Apr71. Sold National A/c Lsg 16Dec74. Cvtd to exec configuration as a NAL One-Eleven (NAL11). Sold Cameron Iron Works 01May76 as N3E. Restored as N5028 to Luqa Inc ... Lsd Air Charter 15Nov78 as N200CC. Re-regd N18HH to Luqa Inc 21Sep81. Regd to Helmsley Spear Mar82. Re-regd N18HD Nov88. Regd to Louisiana Pacific Corp Feb89. Re-regd N111LP Sep89.

069   401AK   Ff 03May66 as N5029; del American Airlines 21May66.   Wfs 25Oct70.   Sold National A/c Lsg 01Apr74.   Cvtd to exec configuration as a NAL One-Eleven (NAL9).   Sold LLG Corp with del to Johannesburg 25Mar75.   Regd 3D-LLG to same group of companies.   Sold Omni A/c Sales as VR-CAM Nov77.   Sold Sheikh Abdul Mohammed Baroom 08Apr78.   Painted HZ-AMB named "Nawaf" at Hurn 29Apr78.   Sold Sheikh Salem bin Laden Jul87.   R/o Hurn as VR-CCS 22Jul91.

070   203AE   Ff 05Dec65 as N1553; del Braniff Airways 08Dec65.   W/o 06Aug66 11 miles north-east of Falls City, Nebraska;   42 killed.
                                                                      TT 2,318 hrs, 2,942 ldgs.

071   203AE   Ff 19Dec65 as N1554; del Braniff Airways 22Dec65.   Sold Mohawk Airlines Sep70 as N1136J and painted in the company's new c/s.   Co merged into Allegheny Airlines 12Apr72.   Co renamed USAir 28Oct79.   Sold Florida Express and regd to International Metals & Machines Feb85 with del 08Feb85.   Co merged into Braniff Airways 01Mar88.   Co ceased ops 06Nov89.   Stored Orlando and later Hondo, Texas.   Regd to CRL Inc Dec92.   TT 56,483 hrs, 73,732 ldgs.

072   401AK   Ff 12May66 as N5030; del American Airlines 27May66.   Wfs 31Aug71.   Sold National A/c Lsg 25Oct73.   Del San Antonio 01Nov73.   Cvtd to exec configuration as a NAL One-Eleven (NAL6).   Sold Eli Lilly International Corp 25Apr77 as N310EL.   Sold and re-regd N119GA to SS Aviation Jul90 for use by the Seattle Supersonics basketball team.

073   401AK   Ff 21May66 as N5031; del American Airlines 09Jun66. Wfs and sold Magnolia Homes 21Apr69 as N111FL.   Fitted with a 22 seat corporate interior and longrange tanks.   Name changed to Farmland Corp Apr70.   Sold Stewart Lumber Co 29Oct75.   Re-regd N5LC(2) Nov76.   Regd to James Stewart Apr77.   Regd to Lone Star Industries Mar84.   Regd to Lukenbill Enterprises Aug89.   Re-regd N401SK Nov90.

074   401AK   Regd as G-ATVU to British Aircraft Corp (Operating) 02Jun66; ff 06Jun66 as G-ATVU; CofA issued 09Jun66.   British regn used for demo flights to Sweden.   Returned via Gatwick 09Jun66.   Regn cx 13Jun66 and painted as N5032.   Del American Airlines 21Jun66.   Lsd Merpati Nusantara Airlines and del via Heathrow 13Aug71 in full c/s but returned from Jakarta when import licence not granted by Indonesian Govt.   Ferried via Prestwick 15Nov71 on return USA.   Lsd LANICA as AN-BHN Mar72 to ...72.   Restored as N5032.   Sold Out Island Airways as VP-BDI 15Mar73.   Co merged with Flamingo Airlines to form Bahamasair 01Jul73.   Sold British Airways Board and del as VP-BDI Keflavik to Hurn 18Dec73.   Regd G-BBMF to British Airways Board 08May74 for op by Regional Division.   CofA issued 30Jul74; named "County of Worcestershire".   Made emergency landing on foam at Hurn after nose leg failed to extend 05Dec74; repaired.   Wfs 14Nov83 over winter period.   Regd to British Airways 01Apr84.   Returned to service Apr84.   Flew last service for British Airways 31Oct88 as BA5383 Dusseldorf to Birmingham.   To Hurn for storage 02Nov88 as BA9666P.   Sold Birmingham European Airways and regd to them 02Apr90.   Ferried Manchester to Birmingham 12Apr90 and entered service same date Birmingham to Frankfurt; named "City of Leicester".   Ferried Southend 31Jul91.   R/o in Okada Air c/s as 5N-EHI 05Aug91.   Sold Okada Air and del ex Birmingham 09Aug91.   UK regn cx ...

075   401AK   Ff 10Jun66 as N5033; del American Airlines 27Jun66.   Wfs 08Nov71.   Sold as N55JT to Jet Travel 16Jan74.   Restored as N5033

to Dresser Industries 09Mar75.   Sold Govt of Sharjah and ferried Naples to Luton 05May84.   Regn cx and painted as A6-SHJ with del via Larnaca 25Jun84.   Sold Florida Express and regd to them as N179FE Dec86.   Del as such ex Manchester 23Dec86.   Regn cx Jan88 after a/c b/u without ever seeing service with Florida Express.
TT 16,215 hrs, 19,503 ldgs.

076   401AK   Ff 25Jun66 as N5034;   del American Airlines 09Jul66.   Wfs 17Jan72.   Sold National A/c Lsg 16Apr75.   Cvtd to exec configuration as a NAL One-Eleven (NAL15).   Sold and regd to TAG A/c Services Jun77.   Regn cx and regd VR-BHS to Air Hanson/Air St George May83.   Co name changed to Air Hamilton May84.   Regn cx 17Mar86.   Sold HM Holdings Apr86 as N333GB.   Regd to HM Industries Feb88.   Cvtd to Srs.2400 with Rolls-Royce Tay engines and also fitted with a glass cockpit.   Flown as such but put into store after certification abandoned.

077   401AK   Ff 01Jul66 as N5035;   del American Airlines 22Jul66.   Sold TAROM with del to Hurn 11Jun72.   Painted in full c/s and del ex Hurn as YR-BCG 20Jun72.   Wfs at   TT 26,945 hrs, 23,796 ldgs.

078   401AK   Ff 23Jul66 as N5036;   del American Airlines 04Aug66.   Wfs 17Jan72.   Sold National A/c Lsg 08Aug73.   Cvtd to exec configuration as a NAL One-Eleven (NAL4).   Lsd Commonwealth Oil Refining 18Jul74 to Mar76.   Lsd Norton Simon ... with regn N111NS.   Regd N9WP to Walter F Probst Jun76.   Regn officially cx Jan82, but a/c continued to fly as such.   Regd to Personal Way Avn Apr84.   Re-regd N800MC(1) Apr85.   Restored as N9WP May85.   Re-regd N800PW Aug85.   Co name changed to Jet Fleet Dec85.   Sold Prince Talal as HZ-TA1, being painted as such in Brussels and del 28Apr87.   Sold Southern A/c Services as N62WH Oct89 and op by Huizenga Holdings.

079   401AK   Ff 06Aug66 as N5037;   del American Airlines 19Aug66.   Wfs 17Jan72.   Sold Dresser Industries 04Nov73.   Regd to Personal Way Avn Feb83.   Re-regd N800DM Mar83.   Co name changed to Jet Fleet Dec85.   Regd to Tower Acquisition Corp Jun87.   Re-regd N880DP to Round Ball One Corp Oct87.

080   401AK   Ff 23Aug66 as N5038;   del American Airlines 08Sep66.   Wfs 17Jan72.   Sold Jet Travel 17Jan73.   Lsd Cimaron Industries 19Jan73 as N10HM.   Sold Rogers Brothers Jun74 as N22RB.   Sold Oral Roberts Evangelistic Assoc ...   Sold Omni A/c Sales 24Mar77 as N90TF.   Sold MF Bin Abdul Aziz Aug77 as HZ-MFA.   Sold Sheikh Salem Bin Laden Jan81.   Re-regd HZ-BL1 Jul82.

081   401AK   Ff 01Oct66 as N5039;   del American Airlines 12Oct66.   Wfs 17Jan72.   Sold National A/c Lsg 07Mar75.   Lsd Austral Lineas Aereas 09Dec76 to 15Apr77; entered service 31Dec76.   Cvtd to exec configuration as a NAL One-Eleven (NAL13).   Del Hurn via Gander as HZ-RH1 27Jul80 for Al Jabalain Trading & Investment Co.   Co name changed to Saudi-Oger Aug80.   Re-regd HZ-HR1 21Jul83.   Sold ATM Aviation Sep85 as VR-CTM.   Sold Gazelle Jan88 as VR-CCG.

082   204AF   Ff 19Nov65 as N1115J; del Mohawk Airlines 21Nov65;   named "Michigan".   Co merged into Allegheny Airlines 12Apr72.   Co renamed USAir 28Oct79.   Wfs ...   Regd to McDonnell Douglas Corp May85.   Stored Las Vegas.   Regd to ALG Sep89.   Ferried Luton via Keflavik 03Jul91.   Sold Kabo Air and incorrectly painted as 5N-KGB.   Repainted as 5N-KBG and del from Luton via Palma and Tamanrasset to Kano 05Jul91.   Bellylanded Port Harcourt, Nigeria, 15Sep91 and subsequently w/o.   TT 48,522 hrs, 70,457 ldgs.

083   W   212AR   Ff 02Mar66 as N502T.   Ferried Cambridge 10Mar66 for fitting out.
                              Returned 25Mar66.   Del Tenneco 05Apr66.   Sold First National Bank
of Chicago Sep70 and lsd back to Tenneco.   Sold Chaffinch Ltd Feb87 as VR-CBZ.   Regd
N70611 to Calcutta A/c Lsg Feb89.   Re-regd N490ST Mar89.

084   W   211AH   Ff 15Jan66 as D-ABHH; del Helmut Horten 29Jan66;   German CofA
                              issued 02Feb67.   Sold Tenneco through Omni A/c Sales and painted
as N504T at Zurich 12Sep75.   Ferried to USA following day.   Sold ARAVCO and flown
Heathrow 23Jan87.   Painted as VR-CBX 25Jan87.   Op by Insight Aviation from Dec87.
Painted as A6-RAK Southend 26Apr88 but regn taped over as VR-CBX and continued to fly
as such until del Manchester 03Aug88.   R/o Manchester as A6-RAK on sale to Govt of Ras
Al Khaimah and del via Larnaca 24Aug88.   Sold Roan Selection Trust International as S9-
TAE and painted as such Manchester 27Nov90.   Del ex Manchester 30Nov90.   Sold
Aliendros de la Cruz Mar93 and regd XA-ADC.

085   201AC   Regd as G-ASTJ to British United Airways 27May64;   ff 25Oct65;
                              CofA issued 29Oct65;   del 09Nov65.   Co merged with Caledonian
Airways to form Caledonian//BUA 30Nov70; named "Royal Burgh of Dunfermline".   Regd
to Caledonian-British United Airways 14Apr71.   Co renamed British Caledonian Airways
01Nov71.   Regd to British Caledonian Airways 04May72.   Regn cx 30Dec81 after sale to
Pacific Express.   Regd N107EX to Security Pacific Commercial Lsg Dec81 and del ex
Gatwick 03Jan82.   Co ceased ops 02May84.   Regd to British Jet A/c Co Mar84.   Lsd Air
Wisconsin in full c/s Feb85.   Ferried Manchester via Reykjavik for maint 24Jul85, returning
the same way 27Aug85 in Air Wisconsin c/s.   Sold Florida Express and regd to them
May86, having previously been r/o Maimi in full c/s 28Apr86.   Co merged into Braniff
Airways 01Mar88.   Sold Guinness Peat Avn and regd EI-BWS to Air Tara 19Jul88; CofA
issued same date.   Lsd back to Braniff Airways.   Co ceased ops 06Nov89.   Ferried Kansas
City to Hondo via Orlando 22Sep90.   Lsd SARO from 11Jan91.   Regn cx 14Jan91 and
regd XA-RTN.   Ferried Hondo to Tampico 25Jan91 and on to San Jose, Costa Rica,
following day.   Del Monterrey 11Mar91 and entered service 18Mar91 Monterrey to Ciudad
Juarez and Culiacan before returning Monterrey.   Wfs and stored Monterrey by Jul93.
                              TT in excess of 47,765 hrs, 47,912 ldgs.

086   401AK   Ff 14Oct66 as N5040;   del American Airlines 28Oct66.   Wfs
                              31Oct71.   Sold National A/c Lsg 05Mar74.   Cvtd to exec
configuration as a NAL One-Eleven (NAL8).   Re-regd N111NA(4) Dec75.   Shown
Farnborough Air Show Sep76.   Lsd Coastal States Gas Corp as N500CS 14Dec76.   Sold
Coastal States Gas Corp 31Mar81.   Sold ABCO Lsg Nov82 and lsd back to Coastal States
Gas Corp.   Re-regd N950CC to ABCO Aviation Dec86.   Regn cx Jul92 and regd HR-
AMO.

087   401AK   Ff 29Oct66 as N5041; del American Airlines 10Nov66.   Sold Dan-Air
                              Services with del Gatwick 14Mar69.   Regd G-AXCP to Dan-Air
Services 26Mar69.   CofA issued 04Apr69.   Lsd British Midland Airways 25Oct82 to
10Jan83.   Sold British Aerospace and stored Manchester from 27Oct86. Regn cx 01Dec86.
Sold Florida Express and regd to them as N173FE Feb87.   Sold Westinghouse Electric Corp
Jan88.   Re-regd N162W Aug89.

088   401AK   Ff 09Nov66 as N5042;   del American Airlines 19Nov66.   Wfs
                              18Oct71.   Sold National A/c Lsg May74 as N112NA(2).   Restored
as N5042 and lsd First National Bank of Chicago May74.   Lsd Austral Lineas Aereas
09Dec76 to 25Apr77; entered service 29Dec76.   Cvtd to exec configuration as a NAL One-
Eleven (NAL7).   Sold Rashid Engineering as HZ-NIR with del Gander to Hurn 09Oct79;

named "Nourah". Ferried onwards via Athens 16Oct79. Painted as HZ-MAJ at Luton 14Jun83 on sale to Jarallah Inc and then flown for a while with both HZ regns.

089   401AK   Ff 21Nov66 as N5043; del American Airlines 10Dec66. Wfs 17Jan72. Sold Out Island Airways as VP-BDJ 22Jun73. Co merged with Flamingo Airlines to form Bahamasair 01Jul73. Re-regd C6-BDJ Feb75. Wfu by Aug81 and stored San Jose, Costa Rica, by Apr82. Regd N218CA to Beech A/c Corp Nov84 on sale to them for lse to Cascade Airways. Regd to Cascade Airways Feb85 and painted in their full c/s. Lsd Atlantic Gulf Airlines for op on behalf of Grenada Airways and entered service as GG103 Miami to Grenada 11Jun86. Regd to Beech Acceptance Corp Mar87 and stored in Cascade Airways c/s Tallahassee. Regd to AJ Walter International Aug88. Regd to Zircon Aviation Corp Dec89. Regd G-BSXK to Aviation Finance & Lsg Co (Jersey) 01Nov90. Regn cx 28Mar91 as sold in USA, never having adopted UK marks. Regd N97JF to Zircon Aviation Corp Mar91 and op by the Jetfleet Corp. Regn cx Jun94 and reportedly regd TG-TJF.

090   401AK   Ff 06Dec66 as N5044; del American Airlines 16Dec66. Sold Dan-Air Services, to whom regd as G-AXCK 24Mar69; del Gatwick 26Mar69; CofA issued 24Apr69. Ferried Lasham 04Jan83 for prep for sale to Westinghouse Electric Corp. Departed Lasham on del 03Feb83. Regn cx 04Feb83. Regd N164W to Westinghouse Electric Corp Apr85. Used as radar testbed and trials a/c.

091   W 402AP   Ff 07Apr66 as PI-C1121; del Philippine Airlines 19Apr66; entered service 01May66. Returned British Aircraft Corp 08Feb72. Sale to Aeroflug as D-AFWC not completed. Sold Royal A/c Establishment, Farnborough, as XX919 16May74. RAE absorbed into Defence Research Agency Apr91.

092   402AP   Ff 17Sep66 as PI-C1131; del Philippine Airlines 24Sep66. Lsd by British Aircraft Corp for demonstrations to East-West Airlines, Australia, Jun69. W/o 12Sep69 Manila after flying into high ground.
TT 7,208 hrs, 6,445 ldgs.

093   407AW   Ff 05Dec66 as YS-17C; del TACA International 14Dec66; entered service 28Dec66; later named "El Centroamericano". Wfu 02Oct87 and stored San Salvador. Regd G-BSXU to Winchester A/c Financing 01Nov90 but remained stored San Salvador as YS-17C. Painted in Kabo Air c/s and test flown San Salvador as YS-17C 03Nov91 following sale to Kabo Air. Ferried Miami 22Nov91 where painted as 5N-KBR. Del via Gander and Palma 24Nov91. UK regn cx 04Dec91, never having adopted these marks. Reduced to spares Aug93. TT 43,136 hrs, 45,414 ldgs.

094   402AP   Originally built for Philippine Airlines as PI-C1141. Ff 03Jan67 as G-16-1 in full Bavaria c/s. Regd G-AVEJ to British Aircraft Corp (Operating) 23Jan67. Ff as such 02Feb67; CofA issued 15Feb67. Noted crew training Teesside 18Mar67. Lsd Bavaria Fluggesellschaft with del 23Mar67. Returned British Aircraft Corp at Hurn at end of lse 30Oct67. Repainted for Philippine Airlines as PI-C1141 15Nov67. Regn cx 28Nov67 and del Philippine Airlines 30Nov67. Returned British Aircraft Corp 11Jan72. Sale to Aeroflug as D-AFWB not completed. Sold Quebecair and painted CF-QBR in full c/s with first flight as such 06Mar73. Del ex Hurn 12Mar73. Wfs May85. Del Gatwick 08Dec85 as C-FQBR on sale to Okada Air. Painted as 5N-AOW in full c/s by early Jan86. Force-landed in scrubland 6km from Sokoto Airport, Nigeria, at Dutsin-Maigara 26Jun91 and w/o following diversion from Kano due bad weather. Due Sokoto Airport closed and no lights available, captain elected to force-land in bush due low fuel; three killed. TT 35,860 hrs, 39,057 ldgs.

095 200AT   Regd as G-ASVT to British Aircraft Corp (Operating) 19Aug64. Planned rebuild at Weybridge of c/n 006 but not proceeded with. Regn cx 20Jul71.

096 W 215AU   Ff 06Apr66 as N11181; del Aloha Airlines 15Apr66; named "Queen Kapiolani". Entered service 27Apr66. Sold Mohawk Airlines as N1130J 13Mar69. Co merged into Allegheny Airlines 12Apr72. Co renamed USAir 28Oct79. Wfu ... and stored Las Vegas. Regd to USAir Lsg & Services Nov88. Regd to USAir Dec88. Regd to McDonnell Douglas Corp May89. Regd to ALG Inc Sep89 and stored Hondo, Texas. Sold Hellenic Air and ferried Southend via Keflavik 13Sep92 and on to Athens 14Sep92. Regn cx Nov92 and painted in full Hellenic c/s by 19Jan93. Regd SX-BAR Nov93.

097 215AU   Ff 30May66 as N11182; del Aloha Airlines 07Jun66, arriving Honolulu 08Jun66; entered service 11Jun66. Sold Mohawk Airlines as N1131J 27Mar69. Co merged into Allegheny Airlines 12Apr72. Co renamed USAir 28Oct79. Wfs 01Nov83 and stored Las Vegas. Regd to USAir Lsg & Services Nov88. Regd to USAir Dec88. Regd to McDonnell Douglas Corp May89. Regd to ALG Inc Sep89. Ferried Orlando for further storage by 23Nov91.   TT 46,749 hrs, 71,901 ldgs.

098 204AF   Ff 01Aug66 as N1116J; del Mohawk Airlines 05Aug66; named "Discover America". W/o nr Blossburg, Pennsylvania, 23Jun67.
                                                                     TT 2,259 hrs, 4,052 ldgs.

099 204AF   Ff 26Aug66 as N1117J; del Mohawk Airlines 30Aug66; named "Ontario". Co merged into Allegheny Airlines 12Apr72. Co renamed USAir 28Oct79. Lsd Quebecair May82 to Jan83 in USAir c/s with Quebecair titles. Wfs ... and stored Las Vegas. Regd to McDonnell Douglas Corp May89. Regd to ALG Inc Sep89. Ferried Orlando for further storage by 23Nov91.
                                                                     TT 51,745 hrs, 73,759 ldgs.

100 204AF   Ff 20Sep66 as N1118J; del Mohawk Airlines 26Sep66; named "Vermont". Co merged into Allegheny Airlines 12Apr72. Co renamed USAir 28Oct79. Wfs ... and stored Las Vegas. Regd to McDonnell Douglas Corp May89. Regd to ALG Inc Sep89. Ferried Southend 28May91. Sold to GAS Air and r/o in Gas Airlines c/s as 5N-SKS 05Jun91. Not del and repainted as 5N-KBT in Kabo Air c/s after sale to them with r/o Southend 21Oct91; named "Sir Abubakar 111".

101 204AF   Ff 11Oct66 as N1119J; del Mohawk Airlines 15Oct66; named "Connecticut". Co merged into Allegheny Airlines 12Apr72. Co renamed USAir 28Oct79. Regd to USAir Lsg & Services Nov88. Regd to USAir Dec88. Wfs ... and stored Las Vegas. Regd to McDonnell Douglas Corp May89. Regd to ALG Inc Sep89. Regd to Comtran International Mar90. Ferried Hurn 05Apr90 in USAir c/s without titles. Robbed of all useful parts by Jaffe Group and finally b/u 11Mar91. Regn cx Jul93.   TT 52,792 hrs, 75,158 ldgs.

102 204AF   Ff 06Jan67 as N1120J; del Mohawk Airlines 24Jan67; named "New Jersey". Renamed "Discover America" late 1967. Repainted in the company's new c/s and renamed "Robert E Peach" 1971. Co merged into Allegheny Airlines 12Apr72. Co renamed USAir 28Oct79. Lsd Pacific Express 08Nov82 to 31Dec83, all white with Pacific Express titles. Flew last service for Pacific Express 22Nov83 and then sublsd Emerald Air for the last month of the period. Wfs by USAir ... Regd to McDonnell Douglas Corp May89. Regd to ALG Inc Sep89. Lsd Classic Air ...90

to ...90. Ferried Luton from Keflavik 24Mar91. Regd 5N-KBD and del via Palma as QNK101F 31Mar91 on sale to Kabo Air; named "Adamu Gutus Mutkai".

<u>103</u>   204AF   Ff 10Aug67 as N1122J; del Mohawk Airlines 17Aug67; named "Quebec".   Co merged into Allegheny Airlines 12Apr72.   Co renamed USAir 28Oct79. Wfs ... and stored Las Vegas. Regd to McDonnell Douglas Corp May89. Regd to ALG Inc Sep89. Ferried Luton via Keflavik 06Jun91. Del from Luton via Palma for spares use by Kabo Air 08Jun91. Reduced to spares Mar92.
TT 51,564 hrs, 72,780 ldgs.

<u>104</u>   204AF   Ff 19Dec67 as N1123J; del Mohawk Airlines 30Dec67; named "Rhode Island". This was the 100th One-Eleven del. Co merged into Allegheny Airlines 12Apr72. Co renamed USAir 28Oct79. Wfs ... and stored Las Vegas. Regd to McDonnell Douglas Corp May89. Regd to ALG Inc Sep89. Ferried Luton 13Feb91. Painted as 5N-KBC and del Kano ex Luton via Palma and Tamanrasset to Kabo Air 16Feb91; named "Alhaji Bara Waiman".

<u>105</u>   215AU   Ff 26May67 as N11183. Displayed Paris Air Show May67 in full Aloha c/s.   Del Aloha Airlines 31May67;   named "Queen Kaahumanu". Lsd Mohawk Airlines as N1132J 15Apr69. Lse carried over to Allegheny Airlines when co merged into that co 12Apr72. Co renamed USAir 28Oct79. Sold USAir 12Feb81. Wfs ... and stored Las Vegas. Regd to USAir Lsg & Services Nov88. Regd to USAir Dec88. Regd to McDonnell Douglas Corp May89. Regd to ALG Inc Sep89. Ferried Luton via Keflavik 27Sep91. Sold Kabo Air as 5N-KBM and del via Agadir 01Oct91; named "Mahammadu Dikko".

<u>106</u>   407AW   Ff 03Feb67 as YS-18C; del TACA International 21Feb67; later named "El Salvador". Wfu 01Jun88 and stored San Salvador. Regd G-BSXV to Winchester A/c Financing 01Nov90 but remained stored San Salvador as YS-18C without adopting UK marks, Painted in Kabo Air c/s and test flown San Salvador as YS-18C 31Jan92 following sale to Kabo Air. Painted as 5N-KBW and ferried Miami 11Feb92. UK regn cx 12Feb92. Del via Keflavik and Palma 13Feb92.

<u>107</u>   320L-AZ   Regd as G-AVBW to Laker Airways (Lsg) 15Nov66; ff 17Feb67; CofA issued 25Feb67; del 25Feb67 on lse. Sublsd Air Congo Feb68 to May68. Purchased by Laker Airways 02Apr72. Regd to Laker Airways (International) 02Apr73. Co ceased all ops 25Feb82. Lsd British Caledonian Airways by Nordic Finance 31Mar82. Regd G-BKAU to British Caledonian 06Apr82. Painted in Air Manchester c/s Jun82 for lse to them but not del. Regd to OBS Ltd 01Nov83, same date sold to Okada Air. Regn cx 16Nov83 and regd 5N-AOZ. Reported wfu and engineless Benin, Nigeria, Aug88.

<u>108</u>   409AY   R/o 28Feb67 in LACSA c/s; ff 06Mar67 as TI-1056C; del LACSA 14Apr67; named "El Tico"; entered service 14May67 San Jose to Miami. Sold TACA International Airlines as YS-01C 11Apr73; named "El Izalco". Regd G-BGTU to British Aerospace 06Jan79 for onward sale to Turbo Union. Regd to Turbo Union 16Feb79. Painted with these marks same date. Cvtd with large forward main deck cargo door. CofA issued 11Aug79. Was due to become the third Srs.2400 conversion fr a Srs.400 until the programme was abandoned. Sold Nationwide Air Charter (Pty) Ltd with del Lanseria 29Apr94 as G-BGTU. Regn cx 03May94, having been regd ZS-NNM 05Apr94.

<u>109</u>   320L-AZ   Regd as G-AVBX to Laker Airways (Lsg) 15Nov66; ff 28Mar67; CofA issued 07Apr67; del 08Apr67 on lse. Purchased by Laker

Airways 02Apr72. Regd to Laker Airways (International) 02Apr73. Co ceased all ops 25Feb82. Lsd British Caledonian Airways by Nordic Finance 31Mar82. Regd G-BKAV to British Caledonian 22Apr82. R/o in British Caledonian c/s 12Aug82 and entered service 15Aug82 as BR894 Gatwick to Paris-Charles de Gaulle. Regd to OBS Ltd 27Sep83, same date sold Okada Air, and del ex Gatwick 26Sep83. Regd cx 04Oct83 and regd 5N-AOP. Stored Manchester 10Dec87 to 26Aug88.

110   304AX   Regd as G-ATPH to British Eagle International Airlines 16Feb66; ff 19Apr67; CofA issued 28Apr67; del 28Apr67; named "Salute". Co ceased ops 06Nov68 and a/c flown Weybridge from Liverpool for storage 18Nov68 and later positioned Wisley. Regn cx 01Apr69. Sold Quebecair 01Apr69 as CF-QBN, first flying as such 23Apr69; named "Le St Laurent". Re-regd C-FQBN. Sold Airways International Cymru, to whom regd as G-YMRU 17Mar84. Ferried Cardiff to Lasham 22Mar84. CofA issued 19Apr84; del ex Lasham 19Apr84. Lsd British Midland Airways in full c/s ... to 27Jan86. Repainted in Cymru c/s Mar86. Co ceased trading Jan88 and a/c repossessed by Havelet Lsg 19Jan88. Lsd Dan-Air Services, to whom regd as G-BPNX 27Apr88 and painted in these marks 12May88. CofA issued 13May88. Del Luton to Lasham 17May88 before ferry to Gatwick 20May88. Entered service 21May88 as DA775 Gatwick to Dublin. Position Lasham for storage at end of lse 29Nov88. Ferried Manchester 26Apr89 without titles for further storage. Ferried Southend 11Nov89. Sold Okada Air and del ex Southend via Ostend 22May91. Regn cx 29May91 and regd 5N-MZE.

111   412EB   Ff 08Apr67 as AN-BBI; del LANICA 20Apr67; entered service 01May67. Returned Hurn 31Jan72 for repairs after interior dam by fire during hijack attempt. Sold as N221CN to ICN Pharmaceuticals Corp 10Oct72. Departed Hurn 11Oct72, still as AN-BBI, for Burbank, USA, for fitment of exec interior and longrange tanks and was not flown by LANICA again. Reported Geneva 12Mar73 and Shannon 16Mar73 without titles, still painted AN-BBI. Regd N767RV to Revlon Corp Jan76. Regd to IASCO ... Regd N90AM to AMM Inc Apr79 and del as such ex Hurn to the USA for mods 24Aug79. Sold and regd HZ-JAM to Sheikh Abdul Momenah 15Oct79. Sold and regd N71MA to Maxfly Aviation Sep88. Regd to Worldwide Church of God Oct88. Re-regd N111AC Jan89 and op by the Ambassador College.

112   304AX   Regd as G-ATPI to British Eagle International Airlines 16Feb66; ff 12May67; CofA issued 22May67; del 25May67; named "Supreme". Co ceased all ops 06Nov68 and a/c flown Weybridge for storage, later positioning Wisley. Regn cx 01Apr69. Sold Quebecair as CF-QBO 01Apr69; named "Le Royaume du Chateau Sanguency"; del 15Apr69. Re-regd C-FQBO. Regd G-WLAD to Airways International Cymru 01Nov84 after sale to them and painted as such Montreal-Dorval 05Nov84. Arrived Lasham 08Nov84. CofA issued 30Nov84 and del ex Lasham same day. Lsd British Midland Airways in full c/s and del East Midlands 05Nov85. Entered service Leeds/Bradford to Heathrow 07Nov85. Lsd Manx Airlines and r/o East Midlands in full c/s 15May87. Entered service Isle of Man to Heathrow 16May87. Returned lessor early Dec87 after op last service for Manx Airlines 03Dec87. Noted in Manx c/s with Cymru titles by 15Dec87. Co ceased trading Jan88 and a/c repossessed by Havelet Lsg 19Jan88. Ferried Lasham for storage 06Jun88. Ferried Southend 31Oct90. Sold Okada Air and r/o in full c/s 07May91. Del Ostend same day, where painted as 5N-OVE and departed for Nigeria following day. UK regn cx 09May91.

113   320L-AZ   Regd as G-AVBY to Laker Airways (Lsg) 15Nov66; ff 01May67 as G-AVBY in Air Congo c/s; CofA issued 09May67; del Laker Airways 09May67 on lse and immediately sublsd to Air Congo. Entered service 15May67. Returned Laker Airways at Gatwick at end of lse 28Feb68 and repainted in Laker c/s.

Painted with large LADY DU PONT - THE MOST WANTED WOMAN ON EARTH titles May70 to promote a fashion competition. Purchased by Laker Airways 02Apr72. Regd to Laker Airways (International) 02Apr73. Co ceased ops 25Feb82. Regd G-BKAW to British Caledonian Airways 22Apr82. Regd to OBS Ltd 12Nov83, same date sold and del to Okada Air. Regn cx 16Nov83 and regd 5N-AOK. Noted Manchester 10Dec91 devoid of many parts. Sold AEA Reactor Services of Risley, Cheshire, for investigation into airframe NDT inspection techniques and del by road ex Manchester 31Jan92.

TT 44,989 hrs, 26,103 ldgs.

<u>114</u>   408EF   Regd as G-AVGP to Channel Airways 07Feb67; ff 09Jun67; CofA issued 14Jun67; del 14Jun67. Entered service 16Jun67 Southend to Rotterdam. Sold and regd to British Aircraft Corp 14May68 after op its last service for Channel Airways 13May68. Lsd Bavaria Fluggesellschaft in Channel Airways c/s with del 16May68. Entered service 17May68. Returned British Aircraft Corp at Hurn 27Jun68 and painted in full Dominicana c/s with r/o 16Jul68. Lsg deal not completed; regn HI-148 had been res. Lsd Autair International Airways in full c/s and del Luton 13Dec68 for weekend use only; named "Halcyon Cloud". Returned Hurn during week for crew training until lsd fulltime from 04Feb69. Regd to British Aircraft Corp (Holdings) 04Feb69 and lse to Autair continued. Returned British Aircraft Corp at Weybridge 10Feb70. Regd to Cambrian Airways 24Mar70 on sale to them. Del Liverpool 04Apr70. Co absorbed into British Airways 01Apr74. Inaugurated jet service to Inverness 01Apr75. Regd to British Airways Board 01Apr76; named "County of Nottinghamshire" 1983. Regd to British Airways 01Apr84. Flew last service for British Airways 31Oct88 as BA5356 Manchester to Birmingham. Positioned Hurn for storage as BA9663P 01Nov88. Regd to Birmingham European Airways 02Apr90 after sale to them and del 20Jun90; named "City of Coventry". Co merged with Brymon Airways to form Brymon European Airways 25Oct92. Brymon European de-merged 01Aug93 and co renamed Maersk Air and a/c painted in British Airways c/s.

<u>115</u>   408EF   Regd as G-AWEJ to Channel Airways 05Mar68; ff 01May68; CofA issued 07May68; del 10May68. Entered service 12May68. Wfs Stansted 15Feb72 following cessation of jet ops. Stored Southend from 09Aug72. Sold British Airways and ferried Southend to Cardiff as G-AWEJ 05Sep73. Regd G-BBMG to British Airways Board 26Sep73 for op by Regional Division. R/o Cardiff in British Airways c/s 17Oct73. CofA issued 18Oct73. Entered service 31Oct73 Glasgow to Paris via Birmingham; named "County of Gloucestershire" 1983. Regd to British Airways 01Apr84. Flew last service for British Airways as BA5383 Birmingham to Glasgow 31Oct88. Positioned Hurn for storage as BA9669P 03Nov88. Regd to Birmingham European Airways 27Feb90 on sale to them. Ferried Hurn to Birmingham 21Apr90. Entered service 22Apr90 Birmingham to Amsterdam; named "Stratford upon Avon". Co merged with Brymon Airways to form Brymon European Airways 25Oct92. Brymon European de-merged 01Aug93 and co renamed Maersk Air and a/c painted in British Airways c/s.

<u>116</u>   408EF   Regd as G-AWGG to Channel Airways 08Apr68. C/n amended to 128 from 16May68 to 11Jun68 before reverting to 116 again; Channel Airways order cx. Regd to British Aircraft Corp 19Apr68. R/o in full Bavaria Fluggesellschaft c/s 13Jun68. Designation changed to Srs.413FA 18Jun68. Ff 20Jun68 as G-AWGG; CofA issued 24Jun68. Lsd Bavaria Fluggesellschaft 25Jun68 to 08Nov68; named "Nymphenburg". Regd to Exporters' Refinance Corp 28Nov68. Lsd Austral Compania Argentina de Transportes Aereos on behalf of Aerotransportes Litoral Argentino 29Nov68, initially being retained in the UK for crew training. Entered service 04Dec68. Returned off lease with del ex Buenos Aires 10Apr69, arriving Hurn 13Apr69. Regn cx

26Apr69. Sold Bavaria Fluggesellschaft as D-ALLI and del ex Gatwick 25Apr69; named "Morits von Schwind" from 03Nov72. Lsd Gulf Aviation 13Nov75 in full Gulfair c/s after repainting Teesside. Bavaria merged with Germanair to form Bavaria/Germanair Fluggesellschaft 01Mar77. Returned ex Gulfair lse May77. Sold Air Pacific after preparation at Hurn. Del ex Hurn as DQ-FCR 25Jun78, arriving Nadi 01Jul78. Wfu 08Sep81 due corrosion and reduced to produce. TT 23,489 hrs, 18,381 ldgs.

117   420EL   R/o in Aerotransportes Litoral Argentino livery as LV-JGX; ff 10Aug68 as LV-PKB. Del ALA in ferry marks LV-PKB 25Sep68. Reverted to LV-JGX on arrival Argentina. Entered service 29Sep68. Co renamed Austral Lineas Aereas after complete merger with Austral Compania Argentina de Transportes Aereos 23Jun71. Cockpit area destroyed by oxygen fire Buenos Aires 27Jan78. Sold Omni Aviation 1978. (FAA records all show subsequent history refers to c/n 058 since the identity plate was located in the nose section of this airframe which was later used to rebuild c/n 117. However the manufacturer identifies the airframe as shown here.) Re-regd N128TA to Tigerair 02Feb79. Nose section of c/n 058 mated to airframe of c/n 117 at Buenos Aires and a/c flown to USA Apr79 as LV-JGX. Argentine regn cx 09Jun80. Regd to Gulfstream American Corp Oct81. Ff after overhaul and complete refit 21Feb84, still regd LV-JGX. Re-regd N128GA Dec85. Regd to Aviation Inc Jan86. Regd to Transworld Avn Systems Corp Jun89. Regd to TABAC Sep89 and reduced to spares.
TT 22,477 hrs, 23,427 ldgs.

118   423ET   Ff 12Oct67 as G-16-2. Ferried Cambridge for fitting out with exec interior by Marshall of Cambridge (Engineering). Ff as VC92-2111 from Cambridge 10Aug68 and ferried Hurn 28Aug68. Del Força Aerea Brasileira 15Oct68. Regd G-BEJM to Ford Motor Co 08Dec76 on sale to them. Del ex Rio de Janeiro 15Dec76 via Recife, Dakar, Tenerife and Lisbon to Stansted 17Dec76. CofA issued 22Feb77.

119   422EQ   Ff 18Oct67 as PP-SRT; del VASP 19Dec67. Returned Hurn via Rekjavik 30May74 after sale to Carver Aero regd N18814. After modifications ferried to USA ex Hurn 12Sep74 for op by Summit Aero. Sold as N114M to WA Moncrief Dec76. Sold Montex Drilling Co Jun77; named "Lucky Liz".

120   419EP   Ff 08Aug67 as N270E. Originally ordered by Page Airways International. Del Engelhard Industries 21Sep67. Sold Rockwell Manufacturing Co through Qualitron Aero as N44R 30Apr71. Sold Amway Corp as N524AC 30Mar77.

121   432FD   Ff 28Aug68 as G-16-5. Lsd Bahamas Airways as VP-BCY. H/o 09Nov68; del 11Nov68, arriving Nassau 12Nov68. Returned off lease Aug69. Sold Gulf Aviation and regd to them as G-AXOX 06Oct69. CofA issued 13Nov69; del Nov69. Regn cx 14Oct75 and regd A40-BX. Retired and ferried East Midlands via Rome 12Dec77. Restored as G-AXOX to British & Commonwealth Shipping (Aviation) 22Jun78. Del Hurn to Gatwick 06Jan79 in full British Island Airways c/s; named "Island Endeavour". Co merged with Air Anglia to form Air UK 16Oct79. Sold British Island Airways 01Jan82. Regd to British Island Airways 20May82. Lsd Air UK with del Norwich 02Nov85. R/o in full Air UK c/s 09Nov85. Sublsd British Airways with del Luton to Manchester 31Oct86. Entered service 03Nov86 as BA5492 Manchester to Belfast. Flew last service 30Apr87 as BA5485 Belfast to Birmingham and ferried Norwich as BA9710P same date at end of lse. Lsd TAT 27Mar89 to ... British Island Airways ceased ops 01Feb90. Regd to Tollhold Ltd 13Feb90. Del Southend 26May90 for painting in Okada Air c/s. Sold Okada Air and ferried Ostend 13Jun90. Painted as 5N-AXT 25Jun90. UK regn cx 11Jul90. Del ex Ostend 14Jul90.

122   420EL   R/o incorrectly painted LY-IZR 15Jul67; ff 21Jul67 as LV-IZR in full Austral c/s.   Regd G-AVTF to British Aircraft Corp 11Aug67 for demonstrations in Romania.   CofA issued 15Aug67.   Painted G-AVTF 15Aug67 and flown Bucharest 18Aug67.   Regn cx 29Sep67.   Painted with ferry marks LV-PID and del Austral Compania Argentina de Transportes Aereos via Gatwick 12Oct67.   Restored as LV-IZR on arrival Argentina.   Entered service 23Oct67.   Co renamed Austral Lineas Aereas after the complete merger with Aerotransportes Litoral Argentino 23Jun71.   Sold British Aerospace 27Feb81.   Ferried COOPESA at San Jose, Costa Rica, 14Jan82 for storage on behalf of British Aerospace.   Regn N3126H res Jun82 but ntu.   Sold Quebecair, arriving Montreal 28Sep82.   Regd C-GQBP.   Wfs May85.   Sold Okada Air.   Del Gatwick as C-GQBP 01Feb86.   Painted as 5N-AOM and departed Gatwick 06Feb86 via Algiers.   Wfu Lagos and reduced to spares Oct92.   TT in excess of 35,860 hrs, 39,057 ldgs.

123   420EL   Ff 05Sep67 as LV-IZS;   del Austral Compania Argentina de Transportes Aereos 08Nov67 via Gatwick, where departure was delayed until 10Nov67 in ferry marks LV-PIF after earlier h/o 12Oct67.   Restored as LV-IZS on arrival Argentina.   Co renamed Austral Lineas Aereas after the complete merger with Aerotransportes Litoral Argentino 23Jun71.   Sold British Aerospace 28Oct80.   Ferried COOPESA at San Jose, Costa Rica, 14Jan82 for storage on behalf of British Aerospace.   Regn N3126Q res Jun82 but ntu.   Sold Quebecair Sep82.   Regd C-GQBV.   Wfs May85.   Sold Okada Air;   del Gatwick as C-GQBV 01Nov85.   Del as 5N-AOS ...

124   217EA   Ff 03Nov67 as A12-124;   h/o 21Dec67;   del Royal Australian Air Force 12Jan68, arriving Fairbairn 18Jan68, for op by 34 Squadron.   Wfu and h/o to Hawker Pacific 28Feb90.   Sold Burtonwood Developments, to whom regd G-EXPM 05Mar90.   Stored Sydney-Mascot, Australia.   Regd to European Aviation 10Sep90.   Departed Sydney 30Aug91 via Alice Springs and Port Hedland, arriving Southend via Nice 01Sep91.   Sold Okada Air.   Regn cx 06Dec91 and painted as 5N-TOM.   Re-regd 5N-NRC and del via Ostend 06Dec91.   Used as a corporate a/c for charter and co use.

125   217EA   Ff 10Jan68 as A12-125;   h/o 31Jan68;   del Royal Australian Air Force 08Feb68 for op by 34 Squadron.   Wfu and h/o to Hawker Pacific 30Jan90.   Sold Burtonwood Developments, to whom regd G-KROO 05Mar90.   Ferried Hurn via Nice 22Apr90 for storage.   Regd to European Aviation 10Sep90.   Ferried Southend 25Oct91. Sold Okada Air and r/o regd 5N-SDP 15Dec91.   UK regn cx 24Jan92.   Del ex Southend via Ostend 27Jan92.   Used as a corporate a/c for charter and co use.

126   422EQ   Ff 08Nov67 as PP-SRU;   del VASP 19Dec67.   Returned Hurn via Reykjavik 23Jun74 on sale to Carver Corp.   Refurbished and r/o Hurn as N18813 09Oct74.   Del Hurn to Frankfurt 11Nov74 and then Nice through Hurn to Keflavik 17Nov74.   Re-regd N80GM to Groves Manufacturing Aug76.   Re-regd N809M to Air Chariot Jan78.   Regd to Tracinda Corp 05Jan79.   Re-regd N341TC 11Feb79 and flown Halifax to Luton as such 01Mar79.   Sold Geo Service 11Feb79.   Re-regd N111GS Jan81.   Del Manchester 04Oct84.   Sold Govt of Ras Al Khaimah and r/o as A6-RKT 17Oct84 with del following day (after earlier being incorrectly painted A6-KTH).   Ferried Southend 21Jun88 and painted as VR-CCJ for Aravco.   In longterm storage Manchester-Ringway.   Departed Manchester 29Nov91 for Filton on three month lse to Rolls-Royce.   Ferried from Filton via Keflavik 11Sep92 for Opa Locka and resale.   Regd N51387 to Aravco Inc Oct92.

127   414EG   Ff 06Dec67 as G-16-3;   del Bavaria Fluggesellschaft as D-ANDY 29Dec67;   named "Schwabing".   Crashed on t/o Gerona 19Jul70 at TT 4,400 hrs, 3,669 ldgs.   Wreckage flown to Hurn in CL-44-0 N447T 01Oct70 and a/c

C/n 166 - Srs.416EK HB-ITK of Aeroleasing SA (Brooklands Museum)

C/n 167 - Srs.424EU YR-BCC of Liniile Aeriene Romane (BAe)

C/n 227 - Srs.528FL D-AMUC of Bavaria Flug (Brooklands Museum)

C/n 175 - Srs.501EX G-AWYS in Caledonian//BUA c/s (via D Slack)

C/n 183 - Srs.212AR N503T of Tenneco Inc at Heathrow in Sep84 (K Gaskell)

C/n 183 - Srs.212AR HZ-AMH of Aravco at Lasham in Oct87 (K Gaskell)

One of Cyprus Airways' three Srs.537FGs (BAe)

C/n 230 - Srs.520FN 4X-BAR of Arkia Inland Airways (BAe)

C/n 191 - Srs.501EX G-AXJK of British Caledonian at Jersey in Oct84 (K Gaskell)

C/n 201 - Srs.518FG G-AXMG of Monarch at Luton in Aug78 (K Gaskell)

C/n 229 - Srs.515FB 5N-IMO of Oriental Airlines at Lasham in Apr94 (K Gaskell)

C/n 233 - Srs.518FG G-AYOP of Court Line at Luton in Apr72 (E W Sawyer)

C/n 235 - Srs.524FF 7Q-YKK of Air Malawi (S Codd)

Unidentified Srs.479FU of Air Pacific (D Collishaw Collection)

C/n 251 - Srs.485GD 1003 of the SOAF seen negotiating a roundabout in Bournemouth town centre on 23May76 while en route from Poole Quay to Hurn for repair after clearly evident cockpit damage following an oxygen fire (BAe)

The first fuselage to be shipped to Romania (c/n 268/401) being loaded aboard Aeromaritime's Guppy F-BPPA at Hurn on 26Jan80 (BAe)

C/ns 201/186 - Srs.518FG and 509EW EI-CDO and EI-CCW of Ryanair seen at Lasham in May94 after being withdrawn from service (K Gaskell)

A line-up of Dan-Air tails at Hurn on 12Nov92 following their withdrawal from service (K Gaskell)

A frustrated sale to Okada Air of Srs.510EDs by British Airways left seven aircraft stored at Hurn for a while; these two shots show lines of noses and tails on 12Nov92 (K Gaskell)

rebuilt on One-Eleven production line.   Regd G-AZDG to Dan-Air Engineering 19Aug71 and re-regd G-AZED same date (to avoid confusion with Comet 4 G-APDG) on sale to them. CofA issued 21Dec71 and del Hurn to Lasham via Luton same date.   Regd to Dan-Air Services 14Jul80.   Sold British Aerospace and stored Manchester 27Oct86.   Regn cx 01Dec86 on sale to Florida Express with regn N174FE res, but a/c remained in storage Manchester.   Restored as G-AZED to Dan-Air Services 13Apr87 on lse from Florida Express.   CofA re-issued 14Apr87.   Lse completed 31Oct87 and a/c painted all-white Southend.   Regn cx 15Mar88 and regd N174FE to Florida Express Mar88, although co had merged into Braniff Airways 01Mar88.   Del from Manchester via Keflalvik 19Mar88.   Sold Guinness Peat Avn and regd EI-BWT to Air Tara 22Jul88; CofA issued same day.   Lsd back to Braniff Airways.   Co ceased ops 06Nov89.   Stored Orlando.   Lsd ADC Airlines as 5N-BAB and del via Keflavik, Hurn and Algiers 11Apr91.

128   408EF   Regd as G-AWKJ to Channel Airways 11Jun68 (this c/n was taken up by G-AWGG 15May68 to 11Jun68);   ff 29Jan69;   CofA issued 05Feb69.   Lsd British United Airways in full c/s 03Apr69.   Del Channel Airways 08Oct69 Stansted at end of lse.   Ferried Stansted to Southend 11Oct71 for storage.   Airtested 10Dec71 and ferried Berlin same day.   Co put into receivership 01Feb72.   Stored Hurn from 09Feb72.   Sold Air Hanson and regd G-BIII to Air Hanson Helicopters 15Jan74;   ff as such 12Feb74;   CofA issued 15Feb74.   Ferried ex Hurn 18Feb74 to Newark via Prestwick and Goose Bay for exec conversion.   Regn cx 08Jul74 after del to Manila on same date on sale to Central Bank of the Philippines as RP-C1.   Op by Philippine Air Force 702 Squadron of 700th Special Mission Wing on Presidential and VIP flights from Nichols Air Base near Manila.   Ferried Gatwick 12Feb84 and stored.   Regd G-NIII to Bacone Ltd 15Apr85.   CofA issued ...   In longterm storage Manchester.   Sold Okada Air and r/o Manchester in full c/s as 5N-AYV 09Sep87.   Test flown as G-NIII 11Sep87 and departed Manchester 12Sep87.   Regn cx 14Sep87 and regd 5N-AYV.

129   416EK   Regd as G-AVOE to Autair International Airways 06Jun67;   ff 08Mar68;   CofA issued 18Mar68;   del 19Mar68;   named "Halcyon Days".   Regd to Cambrian Airways 12Jan70 on sale to them.   Del 19Jan70.   Co absorbed into British Airways 01Apr74.   Regd to British Airways Board 01Apr76.   Sold British Aerospace Dec78 and lsd back to British Airways Regional Division.   Flew last service for British Airways Brussels to Birmingham 30Jun80 and positioned Cardiff same day for storage.   Regn cx 01Feb82 as wfu Hurn.   Noted painted as G-SURE in Air Manchester c/s 01Apr82.   Regd G-SURE to Keydeck Ltd 13Apr82.   Del Air Manchester ex Hurn 18May82.   Painted with British Air Ferries titles 01Sep82.   Regd to Greyhound Equipment Finance 08Sep82.   In storage Cardiff by 01Nov82.   Ferried Cardiff to Lasham for storage 21Jan83.   Moved into hangar 29Apr83.   Restored as G-AVOE to Dan-Air Services 05May83 and r/o in Dan-Air c/s with an all-white tail as G-AVOE 11May83.   Returned Lasham 26Sep83 for storage.   Sold to and painted in Britt Airways c/s Apr84.   Regd N390BA to Britt Airways Jun84 and r/o Lasham as such 05Jun84.   UK regn cx 21Jun84 and a/c ferried Hurn following day.   Del Britt Airways ex Hurn via Keflavik 23Jun84.   Sold Okada Air and del Keflavik to Southend as N390BA 27Aug87.   Painted in Okada c/s as 5N-AYS and ferried Gatwick 03Sep87.   Reduced to spares Oct92.
TT in excess of 32,746 hrs, 33,122 ldgs.

130   424EU   Ff 23Jan68 as G-16-4;   del TAROM as YR-BCA 14Jun68.   Entered service 20Jun68.   W/o Constanta, Romania, 07Dec70 on approach in bad visibility.   TT 4,255 hrs, 3,223 ldgs.

131   416EK   Regd as G-AVOF to Autair International Airways 06Jun67;   ff 18Jan68;   CofA issued 29Jan68;   del 08Feb68;   named "Halcyon

Breeze". Regd to Cambrian Airways 10Dec69 on sale to them. Del 19Dec69. Co absorbed into British Airways 01Apr74. Lsd Gulf Air 30Oct74 to Nov74. Regd to British Airways Board 01Apr76. Sold British Aerospace Dec78 and lsd back to British Airways Regional Division. Flew last service for British Airways as BA981 Milan-Linate to Birmingham 31Aug80 and positioned Cardiff same day for storage as BA9629M. Regn cx 01Feb82 as wfu at Hurn. R/o as G-BMAN in Air Manchester c/s 06Sep82. Regd G-BMAN to Air Manchester 10Sep82. Test flown as G-16-32 13Sep82. CofA issued 15Sep82. Not del Air Manchester and stored Hurn. Restored as G-AVOF to British Aerospace 18Mar83. Lsd British Island Airways and del Liverpool 05May83, still in basic Air Manchester c/s. Entered service 06May83. Returned British Aerospace 03Nov83. Lsd British Caledonian Airways with del Filton to Gatwick 16Nov83, still in Air Manchester c/s with British Caledonian titles. Entered service 29Nov83 Gatwick to Brussels. Lse completed 31Jan84. Regd to Dan-Air Services 25May84 when lsd by them until 15Oct84, when positioned Lasham. Sold to and painted in full Britt Airways c/s; r/o 25Jan85. Painted as N392BA 05Feb85. UK regn cx 15Mar85. Regd N392BA to Britt Airways Mar85. Ferried Manchester 20Mar85. Del from Manchester via Keflavik 21Mar85. Entered service as RU930 Terre Haute via Champaign to Chicago-O'Hare 27Mar85. Sold Okada Air and del Southend via Keflavik 12May87 as N392BA. Regd cx Aug87. Regd 5N-AYT.

<u>132</u>   416EK   Regd as G-AWBL to Autair International Airways 17Jan68; ff 22Apr68; CofA issued 30Apr68; del 01May68; named "Halcyon Dawn". Entered service 03May68. Regd to Court Line Aviation 05Dec69 and painted in Court Line's turquoise c/s, the only Srs.400 to be painted in the new Court c/s. Ferried Wisley from Luton 11Jan71 for overhaul. Regd to Cambrian Airways 20Jan71 on sale to them. Del Cardiff 12Feb71. Lsd Gulf Air Oct73 to 30Jun74. Co absorbed into British Airways 01Apr74. Regd to British Airways Board 01Apr76. Named "County of Leicestershire" 1983. Regd to British Airways 01Apr84. Flew last service for British Airways as BA5023 Brussels to Manchester 30Oct88. Ferried Hurn for storage as BA9667P 02Nov88. Sold Birmingham European Airways, to whom regd 27Feb90 after ferrying Hurn to Manchester 07Jan90. Named "City of Birmingham". Entered service 12Mar90. Co merged with Brymon Airways to form Brymon European Airways 25Oct92. Brymon European de-merged 01Aug93 and co renamed Maersk Air. A/c painted in British Airways c/s.

<u>133</u>   302L-AZ   Regd as G-AVYZ to Laker Airways (Lsg) 29Nov67; ff 08Apr68; CofA issued 11Apr68; del 11Apr68 on lease. Purchased by Laker Airways 02Apr72. Regd to Laker Airways (International) 02Apr73. Co ceased all ops 25Feb82. Regd G-BKAX to British Caledonian Airways 22Apr82. Sold Okada Air and del ex Gatwick 26Sep83, being regd to OBS Ltd following day. Regn cx 04Oct83 and regd 5N-AOT. Later named "The Archbishop Idahosa". W/o Port Harcourt, Nigeria, 07Sep89 after a heavy landing.   TT 42,449 hrs, 24,256 ldgs.

<u>134</u>   204AF   Regd as G-AWDF to British Aircraft Corp 13Feb68; r/o as such and ff 04Mar68 in Mohawk Airlines c/s. CofA issued 05Mar68. UK regn used for braking trials Torrejon, Spain. Regn cx 15Mar68; del Mohawk Airlines 25Mar68 as N1124J; named "New Hampshire". Co merged into Allegheny Airlines 12Apr72. Co renamed USAir 28Oct79. Wfs. Regd to McDonnell Douglas Corp May89. Regd to ALG Inc Sep89. Stored Waco, Texas. Reduced to spares Jan91.
   TT 50,254 hrs, 70,402 ldgs.

<u>135</u>   204AF   Ff 11Jun68 as N1125J; del Mohawk Airlines 17Jun68; named "New Jersey" (has also been quoted as "Maine"). Co merged into Allegheny

Airlines 12Apr72. Co renamed USAir 28Oct79. Sold ONA Export Corp 19May80. Painted Hurn as HZ-MOI 27Mar81 for Saudi Wings. Departed Manchester 27May82 after six months' storage. Regd N4550T to First United Air Nov83. Sold Federal Deposit Insurance Corp 25Feb89. Regd to Donald B Matheson Jul89 after sale 19Jun89. Regd to Southern A/c Sales Sep90. Reduced to spares Oct90. Regn cx Dec93.

TT 29,157 hrs, 43,598 ldgs.

136   510ED   Regd as G-AVMH to British European Airways 11May67. First production Srs.500. Ff 07Feb68 and positioned Wisley following day. CofA issued 11Jun69; del 12Jun69. Regd to British Airways Board 01Apr74, same day co merged with BOAC; named "County of Cheshire". Regd to British Airways 22Mar84. Flew last revenue flight as BA5357 Hamburg to Birmingham 23Nov92. Ferried Hurn for storage as BA9707E 24Nov92. Sold European Aviation 07May93 and ferried Filton as BA9662P 25Jun93. Regd to European Aviation 16Aug93. Painted in European Aircharter c/s Nov93. Lsd European Aircharter and entered service 16Feb94 between Bristol and Lyons.

137   510ED   Regd as G-AVMI to British European Airways 11May67; ff 13May68; CofA issued 07Jun68; del 02Apr69. Co merged with BOAC to form British Airways 01Apr74. Regd to British Airways Board 01Apr74; named "County of Merseyside". Regd to British Airways 22Mar84. Flew last revenue flight as BA5368 Glasgow to Birmingham 14Nov92. Ferried Hurn for storage as BA9706E 18Nov92. Sold European Aviation 07May93 and ferried Filton as BA9693P 01Jul93. Regd to European Aviation 16Aug93; r/o Hurn 27Jan94 in European Aircharter c/s named "The Rome Express". Lsd European Aircharter and entered service 23Feb94.

138   510ED   Regd as G-AVMJ to British European Airways 11May67; ff 15Jul68; CofA issued 09Aug68; del 29Aug68. Entered revenue service 01Sep68 ex Berlin-Tempelhof. Co merged with BOAC to form British Airways 01Apr74. Regd to British Airways Board 01Apr74; named "Strathclyde Region". Regd to British Airways 22Mar84. Flew last revenue flight as BA4575 Belfast to Heathrow before positioning back to Belfast as BA4630P 06Jan92. Ferried Belfast to Hurn for storage as BA9731E 13Jan92. Painted in Okada Air c/s; sale not finalised. Sold European Aviation 07May93 and ferried Filton as BA9663P 25May93 with "European" titles for storage. Regd to European Aviation 30Jun93. Being reduced to spares Filton Jun94.

TT 40,484 hrs, 45,721 ldgs.

139   510ED   Regd as G-AVMK to British European Airways 11May67; ff 08Aug68; CofA issued 12Sep68; del 16Sep68 with official handover at Farnborough Air Show two days later. Co merged with BOAC to form British Airways 01Apr74. Regd to British Airways Board 01Apr74; named "County of Kent". Regd to British Airways 22Mar84. Flew last scheduled British Airways service from Heathrow by a One-Eleven as BA5954 to Newcastle, returning as BA5955 12Jan92. Flew last revenue flight as BA5382 Glasgow to Birmingham 02Dec92. Ferried Hurn for storage as BA9742E 04Dec92. Sold European Aviation 07May93 and painted in co's red and white c/s. Ferried Filton as BA9665P 03Jun93; named "The Paris Express". Regd to European Aviation 30Jun93. Lsd European Aircharter and entered service 03Apr94.

140   510ED   Regd as G-AVML to British European Airways 11May67; ff 30Aug68 and displayed Farnborough Air Show Sep68. CofA issued 30Sep68; del 04Oct68. Co merged with BOAC to form British Airways 01Apr74. Regd to British Airways Board 01Apr74; named "County of Surrey". Regd to British Airways 22Mar84. Flew last revenue flight as BA5135 Dusseldorf to Manchester before positioning Hurn as

BA9726E for storage 13Jan92. Painted in Okada Air c/s; sale not finalised. Sold European Aviation 07May93 and ferried Filton for storage as BA9725P 14May93. Regd to European Aviation 30Jun93.   TT 40,003 hrs, 45,103 ldgs.

141   510ED   Regd as G-AVMM to British European Airways 11May67;   ff 28Sep68;   CofA issued 04Oct68;   del 25Oct68.   Co merged with BOAC to form British Airways 01Apr74.   Regd to British Airways Board 01Apr74;   named "County of Gloucestershire";   later named "County of Antrim".   Regd to British Airways 22Mar84.   Flew last revenue flight as BA5601 Paris-Charles de Gaulle to Glasgow before positioning Hurn as BA9730E for storage 13Jan92.   Painted in Okada Air c/s;   sale not finalised.   Sold European Aviation 07May93 and ferried Filton for storage as BA9665P 25May93.   Regd to European Aviation 30Jun93.   TT 39,713 hrs, 44,447 ldgs.

142   510ED   Regd as G-AVMN to British European Airways 11May67;   ff 14Oct68;   CofA issued 12Nov68;   del 20Nov68.   Co merged with BOAC to form British Airways 01Apr74.   Regd to British Airways Board 01Apr74;   named "County of Essex".   Regd to British Airways 22Mar84.   Flew last revenue flight as BA5153 Frankfurt to Manchester 09Aug92.   Ferried Hurn as BA9697E for storage 10Aug92.   Sold European Aviation 07May93 and ferried Cambridge for storage as BA9661P 11Aug93.   Regd to European Aviation 03Sep93.   Ferried Hurn for painting and pre-service mods 17May94.   Painted in European Aircharter c/s and del Filton 22Jun94.   Lsd European Aircharter and entered service 23Jun94 ex Stansted on a Ryanair schedule;   named "The Dublin Express".

143   510ED   Regd as G-AVMO to British European Airways 11May67;   ff 29Oct68;   CofA issued 19Nov68;   del 27Nov68.   Co merged with BOAC to form British Airways 01Apr74.   Regd to British Airways Board 01Apr74;   named "Lothian Region".   Regd to British Airways 22Mar84.   Flew last revenue flight as BA5601 Paris-Charles de Gaulle to Glasgow 18Dec92.   Positioned Manchester as BA9717P 19Dec92.   Ferried Hurn as BA9720E for storage 29Dec92.   Donated Cosford Museum and ferried Cosford as BA9665P 22Mar93.   Regn cx as wfu 12Jul93.
                                                                TT 41,413 hrs, 45,857 ldgs.

144   510ED   Regd as G-AVMP to British European Airways 11May67;   ff 05Nov68;   CofA issued 03Dec68;   del 11Dec68.   Co merged with BOAC to form British Airways 01Apr74.   Regd to British Airways Board 01Apr74. Hijacked en route Manchester to Heathrow 07Jan75;   flown Stansted where hijacker was overpowered.   Named "Bailiwick of Jersey".   Regd to British Airways 22Mar84.   Flew last revenue flight as BA5107 Copenhagen to Manchester 07Oct92.   Ferried Hurn for storage as BA9734E 09Oct92.   Sold European Aviation 07May93 and h/o Hurn 11Aug93.   Regd to European Aviation 03Sep93.   Painted in European Aircharter c/s Oct93;   named "The Madrid Express".   Remains in storage Hurn.   TT 41,747 hrs, 47,451 ldgs.

145   510ED   Regd as G-AVMR to British European Airways 11May67;   ff 28Nov68;   CofA issued 10Feb69.   Retained for autoland trials Wisley. Del 05May70.   Co merged with BOAC to form British Airways 01Apr74.   Regd to British Airways Board 01Apr74;   named "County of Tyne & Wear".   Regd to British Airways 22Mar84.   Flew last revenue flight as BA5129 Dusseldorf to Manchester before positioning Hurn for storage as BA9745E 13Jan92.   Painted in Okada Air c/s;   sale not finalised.   Sold European Aviation 07May93 and ferried Filton for storage as BA9664P 25May93.   Regd to European Aviation 30Jun93.   TT 37,823 hrs, 42,554 ldgs.

146   510ED   Regd as G-AVMS to British European Airways 11May67;   ff 14Dec68;   CofA issued 20Dec68;   del 13Jan69.   Co merged with BOAC to form British Airways 01Apr74.   Regd to British Airways Board 01Apr74; named "County of West Sussex".   Regd to British Airways 22Mar84.   Flew last revenue international flight by a Srs.510ED Paris-Charles de Gaulle to Glasgow as BA5601 followed by last revenue flight by a Srs.510ED Glasgow to Birmingham as BA5382, both on 31Dec92. Ferried Hurn for storage as BA9734E 05Jan93.   Sold European Aviation 07May93 and h/o Hurn 11Aug93.   Regd to European Aviation 03Sep93 and painted in their c/s the same month.   Due to enter service with European Aircharter Oct94.

147   510ED   Regd as G-AVMT to British European Airways 11May67;   ff 10Jan69;   CofA issued 15Mar69;   del 28Mar69.   Co merged with BOAC to form British Airways 01Apr74.   Regd to British Airways Board 01Apr74; named "County of Glamorgan"; later named "County of Berkshire".   Regd to British Airways 22Mar84.   Flew last revenue flight as BA5007 Paris-Charles de Gaulle to Manchester 30Sep92.   Ferried Hurn for storage as BA9729E 01Oct92.   Sold European Aviation 07May93 and ferried Filton as BA9664P 01Jul93.   Regd to European Aviation 16Aug93. Lsd Air Bristol and painted in their c/s Sep93.

148   510ED   Regd as G-AVMU to British European Airways 11May67;   ff 29Jan69;   CofA issued 17Mar69;   del 19Mar69.   Co merged with BOAC to form British Airways 01Apr74.   Regd to British Airways Board 01Apr74; named "County of Dorset".   Regd to British Airways 22Mar84.   Flew last revenue flight as BA5383 Dusseldorf to Birmingham 16Oct92.   Positioned Manchester as BA9745P 17Oct92. Ferried Hurn for storage as BA9680E 29Oct92. Donated Duxford Avn Society Museum and ferried Duxford as BA9379P 04Mar93.   Regn cx as wfu 12Jul93.
                                                                        TT 40,280 hrs, 45,541 ldgs.

149   510ED   Regd as G-AVMV to British European Airways 11May67;   ff 21Mar69;   CofA issued 02Apr69;   del 21Apr69.   Co merged with BOAC to form British Airways 01Apr74.   Regd to British Airways Board 01Apr74; named "County of Powys"; later named "Greater Manchester County".   Regd to British Airways 22Mar84.   Flew last revenue flight as BA5153 Frankfurt to Manchester 31Jul92.   Ferried Hurn for storage as BA9699E 01Aug92.   Sold European Aviation 07May93 and ferried Cambridge for storage as BA9660P 11Aug93.   Regd to European Aviation 03Sep93. Ferried back to Hurn 02Aug94 for further storage.   TT 40,512 hrs, 45,564 ldgs.

150   510ED   Regd as G-AVMW to British European Airways 11May67;   ff 27Apr69;   CofA issued 02May69;   del 02May69.   Co merged with BOAC to form British Airways 01Apr74.   Regd to British Airways Board 01Apr74; named "Grampian Region".   Regd to British Airways 22Mar84.   Flew last scheduled flight as BA5287 Belfast to Manchester 15Dec92.   Last revenue flight was as BA9396C on local flying Christmas air experience charter from Manchester 24Dec92.   Ferried Hurn for storage as BA9721E 30Dec92.   Sold European Aviation 07May93 and painted in European red and white c/s; named "The European Express".   Ferried Filton as BA9660P 03Jun93. Regd to European Aviation 30Jun93.   Ferried Hurn 01Oct93 for repaint in Air Bristol c/s. R/o 04Oct93 and ferried Filton 05Oct93.   Lsd Air Bristol.

151   510ED   Regd as G-AVMX to British European Airways 11May67;   ff 02Jun69;   CofA issued 09Jun69;   del 20Jun69, the 150th One-Eleven to be del.   Belly landed Teesside 21Feb73 while crew training; repaired.   Co merged with BOAC to form British Airways 01Apr74.   Regd to British Airways Board 01Apr74; named "County of Nottinghamshire".   Later named "County of East Sussex".   Regd to British

Airways 22Mar84. Flew last revenue flight as BA5059 Milan-Linate to Manchester before positioning Hurn for storage as BA9729E 13Jan92. Painted in Okada Airways c/s and test flown 16May92. Noted wearing 5N-USE 05Jun92 but later reverted to G-AVMX; sale not finalised. Sold European Aviation 07May93 and ferried Filton for storage as BA9722P 14May93. Regd to European Aviation 30Jun93. TT 38,020 hrs, 42,550 ldgs.

152   510ED   Regd as G-AVMY to British European Airways 11May67; ff 09Jul69; CofA issued 16Jul69; del 21Jul69. Co merged with BOAC to form British Airways 01Apr74. Regd to British Airways Board 01Apr74; named "County of Derbyshire". Regd to British Airways 22Mar84. Main undercarriage collapsed while taxying Copenhagen 12Nov86; repaired. Flew last revenue flight as BA5383 Dusseldorf to Glasgow via Birmingham 08Jan92. Ferried Hurn for storage as BA9725E 13Jan92. Painted in Okada Airways c/s; sale not finalised. Sold European Aviation 07May93 and ferried Filton for storage as BA9724P 14May93. Regd to European Aviation 30Jun93. TT 38,357 hrs, 42,923 ldgs.

153   510ED   Regd as G-AVMZ to British European Airways 11May67; ff 05Aug69; CofA issued 13Aug69; del 15Aug69. Co merged with BOAC to form British Airways 01Apr74. Regd to British Airways Board 01Apr74; named "County of Lancashire". Regd to British Airways 22Mar84. Flew last revenue flight as BA5383 Dusseldorf to Edinburgh via Birmingham 31Oct91. Positioned Glasgow 01Nov91. Ferried Glasgow to Hurn for storage as BA9746P 04Nov91. Painted in Okada Airways c/s and noted with 5N-OSA taped over; sale not finalised. Sold European Aviation 07May93 and ferried Filton for storage as BA9723P 14May93. Regd to European Aviation 30Jun93.
TT 38,376 hrs, 42,291 ldgs.

154   423ET   R/o 07Oct68; ff 09Oct68 as VC92-2110. Ferried Cambridge 11Oct68 for fitting out with exec interior by Marshall of Cambridge (Engineering). Del ex Weybridge to Força Aerea Brasileira 13May69. Sold as G-BEJW to Ford Motor Co, to whom regd 08Dec76. Del ex Rio de Janeiro 15Dec76 via Recife, Dakar, Tenerife and Lisbon to Stansted 18Dec76 as G-BEJW in FAB c/s. CofA issued 23Mar77. Sold Kabo Air and regn cx 26Jul93; del Norwich the same day for painting. Del via Palma 01Aug93 as QNK617A, regd as 5N-KKK; named "Malam Barnabas".

155   420EL   R/o unregd in Aerotransportes Litoral Argentino-ALA c/s 04Nov68. Painted as LV-JGY 06Nov68. Ff 08Nov68 as LV-PKA. Del Aerotransportes Litoral Argentino in ferry marks LV-PKA 17Dec68. Reverted to LV-JGY on arrival Argentina. Entered service 23Dec68. Co renamed Austral Lineas Aereas after complete merger with Austral Compania Argentina de Transportes Aereas 23Jun71. W/o nr San Carlos de Bariloche 21Nov77 when it flew into mountains; 45 killed, 34 injured.
TT 21,284 hrs, 22,229 ldgs.

156   424EU   Ff 11Dec68 as YR-BCB; del TAROM 17Dec68. B/u for spares 1988. TT 25,154 hrs, 14,947 ldgs.

157   432FD   Ff 27Nov68 as VP-BCZ. Lsd Bahamas Airways 04Dec68 to Aug69. Regd G-AXMU to British Aircraft Corp (Holdings) 19Aug69. CofA issued 21Aug69. Lsd Laker Airways in Bahamas Airways c/s with Laker Airways titles 21Aug69 to Sep69. Regn cx 09Oct69. Lsd Philippine Airlines as PI-C1151 with del ex Gatwick 14Oct69 until returned Hurn 19Feb71. Painted as G-16-14 by 22Feb71, still in full Philippine Airlines c/s. Sold Gulf Aviation 18Jun71 and restored to them as G-AXMU the same date. Painted in full c/s and ff as such 09Oct71. CofA re-issued 01Nov71; del Gulf Aviation 03Nov71. Painted in new Gulf Air c/s Stansted 22Nov74 to 03Dec74. Regn cx

10Oct75 and regd A40-BU. Lsd British Airways from del Heathrow 18Aug77 to 17Nov77, when ferried Cardiff to East Midlands. Restored as G-AXMU to British & Commonwealth Shipping Co (Avn) 22Jun78 after sale to them for op by British Island Airways. Ferried Hurn 29Jun78 for pre-service mods and painting. Del British Island Airways 09Feb79; named "Island Esprit". Co merged with Air Anglia to form Air UK 16Oct79. Sold British Island Airways 01Jan82. Regd to British Island Airways 20May82. Painted with Air Ecosse titles 21Jan84 for wet lse to Air Ecosse 23-25Jan84 for publicity purposes. Lsd Airways International Cymru from del Cardiff 30Mar84 to 04Nov84. Painted with Virgin Atlantic tail colours and lsd Virgin Atlantic Airways Jan85 to Apr85 still named "Island Esprit". Lsd Air UK and painted in full c/s Lasham before del Norwich 14May85. Del Southend at end of lse 28Apr88 and painted in British Island Airways c/s. Lsd TAT 25Apr89 to 06Feb90, when ferried Lille to Luton. British Island Airways ceased all ops 01Feb90. Regd Tollhold Ltd 13Feb90. Ferried Luton to Southend on sale to Okada Air 21Jul90. Painted in Okada Air c/s and del Ostend 05Oct90. Regd cx 08Oct90 and regd 5N-AXQ.

158 W 414EG   Ff 17Apr70 as D-AISY, having originally been allcoated D-ANDI but these marks not used. Del Bavaria Fluggesellschaft Schwabe & Co 22Apr70; named "Frans von Lenbach" from 03Nov72. Co merged with Germanair to form Bavaria/Germanair Fluggesellschaft 30Mar77. Del Hurn for exec conversion 28Nov77. Ferried USA 05Mar78. Regd HZ-MF1 to Aravco Mar78. Sold Kuwait Real Estate Centre Oct78. Sold Muburak Al Hassawi & Co as HZ-AMH with del ex Heathrow after repainting as such 02Jan79. Sold as HZ-AB1 to Sheikh Abdul Aziz al Ibrahim Oct82. Re-regd HZ-KB1 Jun94.

159 W 424EU   Ff 22Jul69 as YR-BCD; del TAROM 30Jul69. Lsd Liniile Aeriene Romane-LAR 15Dec75 to ... Sold GAS Airlines as 5N-AXV Nov89; named "Solomon".

160 W 414EG   Originally allocated as a Srs.402AP for Trabajos Aereos y Enlaces-TAE but order cx. Ff 19Dec70 as D-ANNO. Del Bavaria Fluggesellschaft Schwabe & Co 22Dec70; named "Carl Spitsweg" from 03Nov72. Co merged with Germanair to form Bavaria/Germanair Fluggesellschaft 30Mar77. Sold Ford Motor Co and regd G-BFMC 15Nov77 with ferry to Stansted same day. Ferried USA for exec fitting out 20Nov77. CofA issued 08Mar78. Sold Kabo Air and regn cx 27Jul93 following del to Norwich the previous day for painting. Del via Palma 01Aug93 as QNK617B, regd as 5N-GGG; named "Muhammadu Sbubakar Rimi".

161 402AP   Ff 20Sep68 as PI-C1151 in full Philippine Airlines c/s. Order not finalised and ferried Wisley late Nov68. Repainted for Trabajos Aereos y Enlaces-TAE and ferried Gatwick 01Mar69, still as PI-C1151. Painted as EC-BQF and del ex Gatwick 15Mar69 on lse; named "Nervion". Repossessed and del Weybridge 16Feb70. Regd G-AYHM to British Aircraft Corp 22Jul70. CofA issued 01Aug70. Lsd Bavaria Fluggesellschaft Schwabe & Co 01Aug70 to 04Jan71. Used by British Aircraft Corp for crew training. Stored Hurn from 28Feb71. Proposed sale Aeroflug as D-AFWA not finalised. Regn cx 02Aug72. Sold TAROM as YR-BCH and del 11Aug72 after ff as such in TAROM c/s 03Aug72. Wfs at   TT 22,375 hrs, 13,740 ldgs.

162 409AY   Ff 14Feb69 as G-16-6. Regd G-AXBB to British Aircraft Corp (Holdings) 06Mar69. CofA issued 10Mar69. Accepted by LACSA but retained by British Aircraft Corp. Lsd Quebecair for crew training 13Mar69 to 11Apr69. Demonstration to Gulf Aviation Bahrain 28Apr69. Regn cx 05May69. Lsd TAROM as YR-BCP 09May69. Restored as G-AXBB to British Aircraft Corp (Holdings)

05Aug69. Lsd Germanair Bedarfsluftfahrt in full c/s 14Aug69 to 23Oct69. Regn cx 05Nov69. Sold as TI-1055C with del to LACSA 05Nov69. Sold British Aircraft Corp and ferried Rekjavik to Hurn 24Jan74. Restored as G-AXBB to Gulf Aviation 26Feb74 on sale to them. Regd cx 09Oct75 and regd A40-BB. Ferried East Midlands 24Nov77 for storage/resale. Restored as G-AXBB to British & Commonwealth Shipping Co (Avn) 22Jun78 after sale to them for op by British Island Airways. Co merged with Air Anglia to form Air UK 16Oct79. Sold British Island Airways 01Jan82. Regd to British Island Airways 20May82; named "Island Envoy". Del Southend 11Oct89 for painting in Okada Air c/s after sale to them. R/o in full c/s 18Oct89. Regn cx 24Oct89 and del Ostend as 5N-AYR same day.

163 W 414EG   Ff 26Jan70 as D-AILY; del Bavaria Fluggesellschaft Schwabe & Co 26Feb70; named "Dominikus Zimmermann" from 03Nov72. Sold Hilton Hotels Corp and del via Prestwick 06Dec75. Regn cx 12Dec75 and regd N123H to Hilton Hotels Corp Nov75. Regd to BAC 1-11 Corp Jul85.

164   Not built.

165 W 424EU   Ff 29Sep69 as YR-BCE; del TAROM 23Nov69. Lsd GAS Airlines by 18Jul87 to ...89. Sold Liniile Aeriene Romane-LAR ...89. Wfs at   TT 23,935 hrs, 15,362 ldgs.

166   416EK   Regd as G-AWXJ to British Aircraft Corp (Holdings) 22Jan69; ff 27Feb69; CofA issued 18Mar69. Lsd Autair International Airways 20Mar69; named "Halcyon Sun". Returned British Aircraft Corp (Holdings) Nov69 and cvtd to exec configuration for sale to Aeroleasing SA as HB-ITK. Regn cx 10Jun70 on sale to Switzerland; deal not finalised and restored as G-AWXJ to British Aircraft Corp 19Aug70. Painted in Nigeria Airways c/s for demonstration with del via Gatwick 26Aug70. Returned 10Sep70. Regn cx 17Sep71. Sold Robin Loh and del as 9V-BEF 03Nov71. Lsd Air-Siam Air Co May72 to Dec72. Sold Pertamina Oil/Pelita Air Service as PK-PJC Jan73 and ferried Hurn 03Apr73 for maintenance. Re-del Pertamina Oil/Pelita Air Service 15May73; named "Aron". Operated a once weekly Denpasar to Darwin schedule on behalf of Merpati Nusantara Airlines mid 1977 to May78. Del Hurn via Naples 04Jun79 and painted as G-16-24 following day. Regd G-CBIA to British & Commonwealth Shipping Co (Avn) 28Jun79 for op by British Island Airways. Co merged with Air Anglia to form Air UK 16Oct79. CofA issued 13Dec79. Del Air UK 17Dec79 to Gatwick; named "Island Ensign". Sold British Island Airways 01Jan82. Regd to British Island Airways 20May82. Del Southend 05Oct89 on sale Okada Air. R/o in full Okada Air c/s 10Oct89. Ferried Ostend 11Oct89, where painted as 5N-AYW. UK regn cx 13Oct89.

167   424EU   Ff 26Jun69 as YR-BCC; del TAROM 03Jul69. Lsd Liniile Aeriene Romane 15Dec75; named "Bacau". Damaged by fire Bucharest 22Sep77; repaired. Sold GAS Airlines as 5N-AVX Apr89. Painted in GAS Airlines c/s Ostend and departed 30Nov90; named "David".

168 W 424EU   Ff 18Nov69 as YR-BCF; del TAROM 13Dec69. Lsd Liniile Aeriene Romane Apr76; named "Arad". Sold Okada Air as 5N-OKA May91.

169-173   Not built.

174   501EX   Regd as G-AWYR to British United Airways 11Feb69; ff 25Mar69; CofA issued 10Apr69; del 11Apr69. Entered service 14Apr69. Co

merged with Caledonian Airways to form Caledonian//BUA 30Nov70; named "Isle of Tiree" 19Feb71. Regd to Caledonian-British United Airways 14Apr71. Co renamed British Caledonian Airways 01Nov71. Regd to British Caledonian Airways 04May72. Co merged into British Airways 14Apr88. Regd to British Airways 14Apr88; named "County of Suffolk". Flew last revenue flight as BA5407 Paris-Charles de Gaulle to Birmingham 28May93. Ferried Manchester as BA9661P 01Jun93. Regn cx 04Jun93 and regd EI-CID. Lsd Ryanair 04Jun93 and ferried Dublin same date. Ferried Dublin to Filton for storage 24Mar94 as FR002P at end of lease. Restored to British Airways as G-AWYR 28Mar94. R/o as G-AWYR 07May94. Ferried from Filton to Hurn 29Jul94 prior to painting in British Airways c/s. Ferried Birmingham 18Aug94 to lse to Maersk Air Ltd; h/o 26Aug94. Entered service 22Sep94 as BA8358 from Birmingham to Amsterdam.

175   501EX   Regd as G-AWYS to British United Airways 11Feb69; ff 16Apr69; CofA issued 23Apr69; del 24Apr69. Entered service 28Apr69. Lsd Swissair in British United c/s with Swissair titles with del 23Apr70. Entered service 24Apr70. Flew last service 31Oct70 and returned Gatwick same day. Returned to service with British United 08Nov70. Co merged with Caledonian Airways to form Caledonian//BUA 30Nov70; named "Isle of Bute" Feb71. Regd to Caledonian-British United Airways 14Apr71. Co renamed British Caledonian Airways 01Nov71. Regd to British Caledonian Airways 04May72. Damaged Corfu after over-running runway into sea 19Jul72. Ferried Hurn 12Aug72 for repair; re-del Gatwick 15Dec72. Co merged into British Airways 14Apr88. Regd to British Airways 14Apr88; named "County of Norfolk". Flew last revenue flight as BA5379 Dusseldorf to Birmingham 05Feb93 and positioned Hurn as BA9665P same date for painting in Brymon European c/s. Lsd Brymon European Airways and ferried Hurn to Birmingham 07Mar93. Regd to Birmingham European Airways 17May93. Brymon European Airways de-merged 01Aug93 and co renamed Maersk Air. A/c painted in British Airways c/s.

176   501EX   Regd as G-AWYT to British United Airways 11Feb69; ff 06May69; CofA issued 13May69; del 13May69. Entered service 16May69. Co merged with Caledonian Airways to form Caledonian//BUA 30Nov70; named "Isle of Barra". Regd to Caledonian-British United Airways 14Apr71. Co renamed British Caledonian Airways 01Nov71. Regd to British Caledonian Airways 04May72. Co merged into British Airways 14Apr88. Regd to British Airways 14Apr88; named "County of Gwynedd". Flew last revenue flight as BA5383 Dusseldorf to Birmingham 30May93. Ferried Manchester as BA9660P 01Jun93. Regn cx 04Jun93 and regd EI-CIE. Lsd Ryanair 04Jun93 and ferried Dublin same date. Ferried Dublin to Filton for storage as FR001P 15Jan94 at end of lease. Restored as G-AWYT to British Airways 18Jan94. R/o as G-AWYT 25Mar94. Sold to Cargostar and due for del to Zaire Oct94.
                                                                    TT 47,861 hrs, 42,073 ldgs.

177   501EX   Regd as G-AWYU to British United Airways 11Feb69; ff 10Jun69; CofA issued 17Jun69; del 17Jun69. Entered service 19Jun69. Co merged with Caledonian Airways to form Caledonian//BUA 30Nov70; named "Isle of Colonsay". Regd to Caledonian-British United Airways 14Apr71. Co renamed British Caledonian Airways 01Nov71. Regd to British Caledonian Airways 04May72. Co merged into British Airways 14Apr88. Regd to British Airways 14Apr88; named "County of Avon". Flew last revenue flight as BA5364 Glasgow to Birmingham 30Apr93. Ferried Hurn as BA9721E for storage 14May93. Positioned Manchester as BA9661P 04Jun93. Lsd Ryanair 10Jun93. Regn cx 10Jun93 and regd EI-CIC. Ferried Dublin to Filton for storage as FR002P 17Mar94 at end of lease. Regn cx 18Mar94 and restored to British Airways as G-AWYU 21Mar94. R/o as G-AWYU 07May94. Sold to Cargostar and due for del to Zaire Oct94.   TT 48,339 hrs, 43,220 ldgs.

178   501EX   Regd as G-AWYV to British United Airways 11Feb69; ff 20Jun69; CofA issued 25Jun69; del 26Jun69.   Entered service 27Jun69.   Co merged with Caledonian Airways to form Caledonian//BUA 30Nov70; named "Isle of Harris" 05Mar71.   Regd to Caledonian-British United Airways 14Apr71.   Co renamed British Caledonian Airways 01Nov71.   Regd to British Caledonian Airways 04May72.   Co merged into British Airways 14Apr88.   Regd to British Airways 14Apr88; named "County of Powys".   Flew last revenue flight as BA5329 Brussels to Birmingham 11Mar93.   Ferried Hurn as BA9664P for storage 22Mar93.   Sold European Aviation and h/o Hurn 07Jul94; storage continues.   Regd to European Aviation 16Aug94.   TT 47,160 hrs, 41,757 ldgs.

179   204AF   Ff 15Jul68 as N1126J; del Mohawk Airlines 02Aug68; named "District of Colombia" (has also been quoted as "Minnesota").   Co merged into Allegheny Airlines 12Apr72.   Co renamed USAir 28Oct79.   Wfs ...   Regd to McDonnell Douglas Corp May89.   Regd to ALG Inc Sep89.   Lsd Classic Air ...90 to ...90. Ferried Bristol via Keflavik 01Dec90.   Sold Kabo Air 21Feb91.   US regn cx Feb91.   Regd 5N-KBA; named "Barnabas".   Overshot landing Sokoto, Nigeria, 23Aug92.   Damage sustained to starboard wing and undercarriage and subsequently w/o.
TT 50,656 hrs, 70,079 ldgs.

180   204AF   Ff 10Dec68 as N1127J; del Mohawk Airlines 31Dec68.   Co merged into Allegheny Airlines 12Apr72.   Co renamed USAir 28Oct79.   Wfs ...   Regd to McDonnell Douglas Corp May89.   Regd to ALG Inc Sep89.   Regd to Comtran International Mar90.   Lsd Classic Air ... and noted Phoenix 14Apr90 in Classic Air c/s. Ferried Southend 02Nov90.   Del Kabo Air ex Southend 10Nov90, being officially sold to them 21Feb91.   US regn cx Feb91.   Regd 5N-KBO; named "Gwamna Awan".

181   204AF   Ff 10Jan69 as N1128J; del Mohawk Airlines 21Jan69; named "Captain Joe Donnelly".   Co merged into Allegheny Airlines 12Apr72. Co renamed USAir 28Oct79.   Wfs ...   Regd to McDonnell Douglas Corp May89.   Regd to ALG Inc Sep89.   Regd to Comtran International Mar90.   Ferried Keflavik to Hurn in USAir c/s 30Mar90.   Robbed of all useful parts by Jaffe Group and finally b/u 18Mar91. Regn cx Apr93.   TT 48,416 hrs, 67,137 ldgs.

182   204AF   Ff 12May69 as N1129J; del Mohawk Airlines 17May69.   Co merged into Allegheny Airlines 12Apr72.   Co renamed USAir 28Oct79.   Wfs ...   Regd to McDonnell Douglas Corp May89.   Regd to ALG Inc Sep89.   Lsd Classic Air ...90 to ...90.   Reduced to spares 1990.   TT 47,529 hrs, 65,306 ldgs.

183 W 212AR   Ff 07Jun69 as N503T.   Ferried Marshall of Cambridge (Engineering) 11Jun69 for fitting out, returning 05Jul69.   Del Tenneco 08Jul69. Regd to Commonwealth Plan Mar87.   Regn cx Mar87.   Ferried Heathrow 14Mar87 and repainted as VR-CBY 15Mar87 for Aravco.   Re-regd HZ-AMH Jul87.   Sold Kuwait Real Estate Centre Feb88.   A/c remained in longterm storage Manchester as VR-CBY from 17May89, never having adopted Saudi marks.   Painted VR-CMI 14Jan92 on sale to Ashmawi Aviation.   Regn HZ-ND1 allocated but ntu.   Flown via Hurn to Malaga in overall buff c/s 29Feb92.   Later painted white with rainbow cheatline; named "Sabah".

184   509EW   Regd as G-AWWX to Caledonian Airways (Prestwick) 15Jan69; ff 11Feb69; CofA issued 12Mar69; del 29Mar69 after being earlier named "Flagship Isle of Skye" at a ceremony Prestwick 24Mar69.   Regd to CCT (A/c Lsg) 15Aug69 for continued op by Caledonian Airways.   Co merged with British United Airways to form Caledonian//BUA 30Nov70.   Co renamed British Caledonian Airways 01Nov71. Regd to Caledonian Airways (Lsg) 14Dec73. Regd to British Caledonian Airways 25Apr74.

Regd to Dan-Air Services 03Oct75 after sale to them.   Entered service 08Oct75 in British Caledonian c/s with Dan-Air titles.   R/o Lasham in full Dan-Air c/s 25Nov75.   Sold ILFC and lsd back to Dan-Air Services.   Flew last flight as DA910 Toulouse to Gatwick 03Nov92 before ferrying Hurn as DA89WX same date.   Lsd British Air Ferries and regd to them 12Nov92.   Ferried Southend 29Nov92 for storage.   Co renamed British World Airlines 06Apr93 and regd to them as G-OBWG 07Apr93.   Remains in store painted as G-AWWX.
TT 54,122 hrs, 34,292 ldgs.

185   509EW   Regd as G-AWWY to Caledonian Airways (Prestwick) 15Jan69; ff 11Mar69; CofA issued 31Mar69; del 31Mar69; named "Isle of Iona".   Regd to CCT (A/c Lsg) 15Aug69 for continued op by Caledonian Airways.   Co merged with British United Airways to form Caledonian//BUA 30Nov70.   Co renamed British Caledonian Airways 01Nov71.   Regd to Caledonian Airways (Lsg) 14Dec73.   R/o Gatwick as LV-PSW 31Dec73 for lse to Austral Lineas Aereas.   UK regn cx 31Dec73.   Del 05Jan74 ex Gatwick.   (Unconfirmed reports indicate regn LV-JNU may have been carried for a short while at this time.)   Restored as G-AWWY to Caledonian Airways (Lsg) 07Feb74 for lse to Austral Lineas Aereas under British registry.   Entered service 17Feb74. Regd to British Caledonian Airways 25Apr74.   Regn cx 13Oct75 after sale to Austral Lineas Aereas as LV-LHT 09Oct75.   One time named "Isla Gran Malvina".   Wfs after op last flight 24Sep92 and used as research airframe.   TT 50,410 hrs, 46,120 ldgs.

186   509EW   Regd as G-AWWZ to Caledonian Airways (Prestwick) 15Jan69; ff 18Apr69; CofA issued 28Apr69; del 28Apr69; named "Isle of Eriskay".   Regd to CCT (A/c Lsg) 15Aug69 for continued op by Caledonian Airways.   Co merged with British United Airways to form Caledonian//BUA 30Nov70.   Co renamed British Caledonian Airways 01Nov71.   Regd to Caledonian Airways (Lsg) 14Dec73.   Lsd Monarch Airlines with del Gatwick to Luton 14Nov75.   Painted in Monarch c/s and entered service 11Dec75 Luton to Vienna.   Sold Monarch Airlines and regd to them 17Jan77.   Flew last service for Monarch as OM675 Alicante to Luton 20Oct85.   Regd to British Island Airways 18Oct85 on sale to them and del Stansted 21Oct85; named "Island Express".   Lsd British Caledonian Airways early 1986 with all-white fin and no titles.   Ferried Lasham 22Jan90.   British Island Airways ceased all ops 01Feb90.   Regd to Tollhold Ltd 13Feb90. R/o Lasham in full Dan-Air Services c/s 06Apr90 when lsd to them, painted as G-BSYN. Regd as G-BSYN to Dan-Air Services 09Apr90 and ferried Gatwick 13Apr90.   In service 15Apr90 Gatwick to Faro as DA1722.   Flew last service as DA4589 Alicante to Manchester via Cardiff 28Oct90.   Regd Tollhold Ltd 01Nov90 at end of lse and flown Luton 26Nov90. Ferried Luton to Hurn as LON100P 06Dec90 for preparation for lse to Ryanair.   Regn cx 12Apr91 and regd EI-CCW to Ryanair with del Dublin as RYR003P same date.   CofA issued 12Apr91.   Entered service 14Apr91 Dublin to Stansted via Liverpool as RYR296. Wfs and ferried Lasham 11Apr94, where Irish marks removed.   Restored to Tollhold Ltd as G-AWWZ 29Apr94; stored.

187   515FB   Ff 22May69 as D-ALAT; regd to Germania-Airfonds; del Panair 13Jun69; named "Arno".   Co renamed Paninternational 01Jan70.   Co ceased ops 06Oct71.   Regd G-AZPY to British Aircraft Corp 21Mar72 and del Cologne to Hurn 25Mar72.   CofA issued ...   Regn cx 01May72 and sold Germanair Bedarfsluftfahrt as D-AMAS with del 25May72.   Co merged with Bavaria to form Bavaria/Germanair Fluggesellschaft 01Mar77.   Co merged into Hapag-Lloyd Fluggesellschaft Jan79.   R/o Frankfurt on sale to Austral Lineas Aereas as LV-PEW 20Nov79 with del 23Nov79.   Entered service 24Dec79.   Seen Buenos Aires 07Feb80 as such, still in Hapag-Lloyd c/s.   Re-regd LV-MZM.   One time named "Cabo de Hornos".   Wfu Buenos Aires Nov93.
TT in excess of 54,664 hrs, 42,880 ldgs.

188   517FE   Ff 17Jul69 as VP-BCN; del Bahamas Airways 23Jul69. Returned British Aircraft Corp at Hurn 16Oct70 following cessation of ops by Bahamas Airways 09Oct70 before positioning Wisley for storage. Regd G-AZEB to The Hong Kong & Shanghai Banking Corp 26Aug71. Sold Court Line Aviation, to whom regd 01Oct71. CofA issued 08Dec71, same day del Court Line in co's lilac c/s; named "Halcyon Bay". Entered service 17Dec71. Flew last flight for Court 18Nov72 and lsd Leeward Islands Air Transport Services with del ex Luton via Keflavik 28Nov72. Regn cx 01Dec72 and regd VP-LAP. Returned Luton via Keflavik at end of lse 07Mar74. Restored as G-AZEB to Court Line Aviation 18Mar74. Returned to service 02Apr74. Ferried Hurn 11Sep74 after collapse of Court Line Group 15Aug74. Regn cx 26Sep75 and sold Philippine Airlines with del ex Hurn via Brindisi 27Sep75 as RP-C1186, after ff as such 15Sep75. Arrived Manila 30Sep75 and painted in Philippine Airlines c/s. Entered service 06Oct75. Flew last flight as PR146 Iloilo to Manila 09Feb90 and stored.
TT 41,221 hrs, 46,942 ldgs.

189   517FE   Ff 21Jul69 as VP-BCO. Del Bahamas Airways 29Jul69. Returned British Aircraft Corp at Hurn 19Oct70 following cessation of ops by Bahamas Airways 09Oct70 before positioning Wisley for storage. Regd G-AZEC to The Hong Kong & Shanghai Banking Corp 26Aug71. Sold Court Line Aviation and del Luton in Bahamas Airways c/s 24Sep71. Regd Court Line Aviation 01Oct71. Ff 01Feb72 painted in Court Line's lilac c/s; named "Halcyon Cove". CofA issued 03Feb72. Entered service 04Feb72. Lsd Leeward Islands Air Transport Services with del ex Luton 01Dec73. Regn cx 03Dec73 and regd VP-LAR. Returned Luton at end of lse 26Mar74. Restored as G-AZEC to Court Line Aviation 01Apr74. Returned to service 06Apr74. Ferried Hurn 11Sep74 after collapse of Court Line Group 15Aug74. Regn cx 25Nov75 and sold Philippine Airlines with del ex Hurn via Athens 25Nov75 as RP-C1187. Arrived Manila 04Dec75 and painted in Philippine Airlines c/s. Entered service 09Dec75. Flew last flight as PR478 Cebu to Manila 08Apr90 and mothballed.   TT 40,721 hrs, 43,346 ldgs.

190   524FF   R/o 29Aug69 all white; ff 02Sep69 as D-AMIE; del Germanair Bedarfsluftfahft 17Oct69; named "Niedersachsen". Sold Philippine Airlines as RP-C1184 with del ex Hurn 12Apr74. Damaged in flight between Legaspi and Manila 03Jun75 after explosion in port toilet tore large hole in cabin roof; one passenger killed and five injured. Ferried Hurn via Nice for repairs 09Aug75. Re-del 22Feb76 from Hurn via Naples. Damaged 18Aug78 after bomb detonated in flight once again in port toilet between Cebu and Manila, killing one passenger and injuring three others. Ferried Hurn 09Oct78 for permanent repair. Re-del ex Hurn via Frankfurt 27Mar79, arriving Manila 04Apr79. Flew last flight as PR190 Roxas to Manila 03Jan92 and stored.
TT 42,023 hrs, 38,672 ldgs.

191   501EX   Regd as G-AXJK to British United Airways 18Jul69; ff 14Aug69. Used for development flying by British Aircraft Corp. CofA issued 04Mar70; del 05Mar70. Entered service 06Mar70. Co merged with Caledonian Airways to form Caledonian//BUA 30Nov70; named "Isle of Staffa". Regd to Caledonian-British United Airways 14Apr71. Co renamed British Caledonian Airways 01Nov71. Regd to British Caledonian Airways (Charter) 04May72. Flew last service 27Nov75. Lsd Austral Lineas Aereas with del Buenos Aires 09Dec75. Entered service 24Dec75. Flew last service 19Apr76 and returned off lse with del ex Buenos Aires 01May76, arriving Gatwick 03May76. Returned to service with British Caledonian Airways 06May76. Lsd Austrian Airlines with del 30Apr81. Entered service 02May81 in BCAL c/s with "Operated on behalf of Austrian" titles. Flew last service 31May81 and returned to service with British Caledonian Airways 04Jun81. Co merged into British Airways 14Apr88. Regd to British Airways 14Apr88; named "County of Hereford". Flew last revenue flight as BA5403

Paris-Charles de Gaulle to Birmingham 29Mar93.   Ferried Hurn for storage as BA9685P same date.   Positioned Manchester as BA9662P 04Jun93.   Lsd Ryanair 10Jun93.   Regn cx 10Jun93 and regd EI-CIB.   Ferried from Dublin to Filton for storage as FR001P 18Feb94 at end of lease.   Restored to British Airways as G-AXJK 18Feb94.   R/o as G-AXJK 12Mar94.   Sold to Cargostar and due for del to Zaire Oct94. TT 46,519hrs, 42,014 ldgs.

192   521FH   Ff 15Oct69 as G-16-7 in full Austral c/s; del Austral Compania Argentina de Transportes Aereos as LV-JNR 21Nov69.   Entered service 27Nov69.   Lsd Sadia Transportes Aereos as PP-SDP initially for crew training 17Sep70 to 08Jan71.   Lsd Court Line Aviation and del Luton via Seville as LV-JNR 17Apr71.   Regd G-AYXB to Court Line Aviation 22Apr71.   R/o as G-AYXB in a hybrid c/s named "Halcyon Bay" 28Apr71; CofA issued 30Apr71.   Regn cx 08Oct71 and del ex Luton as LV-JNR 14Oct71, arriving Buenos Aires 16Oct71 at end of lse to lessor, which had been merged with Aerotransportes Litoral Argentino 23Jun71 to form Austral Lineas Aereas. Damaged Bahia Blanca, Argentina, 04Dec73 after emergency landing following engine failure on takeoff.   Subsequently w/o.   TT 10,850 hrs, 10,292 ldgs.

193   523FJ   Regd as G-AXLL to British Midland Airways 29Jul69; ff 25Sep69 as G-16-8; CofA issued 10Dec69.   Ferried East Midlands 04Jan70 and h/o next day.   Returned Hurn for final fitting out and crew training; del 17Feb70.   Entered service 24Feb70 East Midlands to Jersey.   Flew last service 07Mar73.   Sold Transbrasil Linhas Aereas and del Hurn for preparation 12Mar73.   Cvtd to Srs.520FN.   Ff in Transbrasil c/s 03May73.   Regn cx 04May73.   Del Transbrasil as PP-SDT 04May73.   Sold British Aircraft Corp 03Aug77.   Lsd Faucett with del 08Aug77 regd OB-R-1137.   Sold Faucett and re-regd OB-R-1173 Sep79.   Wfu 01Jun82 and stored Lima until 14Sep83. Ferried Keflavik to Filton in full Faucett c/s without titles 31Oct83.   Restored as G-AXLL to British Aerospace 15Dec83.   Ferried Filton to Gatwick 19Dec83 in Faucett c/s after regn applied day before.   Regd to British Caledonian Airways 05Jan84.   CofA renewed 13Jun84 and entered service same day; named "City of Aberdeen".   Co merged into British Airways 14Apr88; named "County of Yorkshire".   Flew last revenue service as BA5325 Brussels to Birmingham before ferrying Hurn for storage as BA9708E 01Dec92.   Due for ferry to Filton and h/o to European Aviation Oct94.   TT 46,805 hrs, 44,042 ldgs.

194   521FH   Ff 08Oct69 as G-16-9; regd as G-AXPH to British Aircraft Corp (Holdings) 15Oct69.   UK regd for European demonstrations.   CofA issued 21Oct69.   Regn cx 13Nov69 and del Austral Compania Argentina de Transportes Aereos as LV-JNS 18Nov69.   Entered service 27Nov69.   Co renamed Austral Lineas Aereas after complete merger with Aerotransportes Litoral Argentino 23Jun71.   One time named "Islas Sandwich del Sur".   Flew last revenue flight 11Jan93; ferried to Quilmes Airport 14May93 and reduced to spares.   TT 52,919 hrs, 52,843 ldgs.

195   524FF   Ff 20Oct69 as D-AMUR; regd as G-AXSY to British Aircraft Corp (Holdings) 26Nov69; CofA issued 28Nov69.   UK marks applied for demonstration tour of Canada and USA.   Regn cx 12Dec69.   Del Germanair Bedarfsluftfahrt as D-AMUR 16Dec69.   Sold Philippine Airlines and del Frankfurt to Hurn 06Nov74 for preparation.   Regd RP-C1185; ff as such 19Nov74; del ex Hurn 27Nov74, still in Germanair c/s, arriving Manila 29Nov74.   Painted in Philippine Airlines c/s and entered service 05Dec74.   Flew Philippine Airlines' last revenue One-Eleven service 31May92 as PR278 Legaspi to Manila and put into storage. TT 46,038 hrs, 42,833 ldgs.

196   521FH   Ff 06Nov69 as G-16-10.   Painted in Aerotransportes Litoral Argentino-ALA c/s.   Del ALA as LV-JNT 25Nov69.   Entered service 24Dec69.   Co renamed Austral Lineas Aereas after complete merger with Austral Compania

Argentina de Transportes Aereos 23Jun71. One time named "Islas Georgias del Sur".

<u>197</u>   515FB   Ff 09Dec69 as G-16-11. Originally built for Paninternational but not del and painted in British Aircraft Corp c/s. Regd G-AXVO to British Aircraft Corp (Holdings) 05Jan70; CofA issued 09Jan70. Flown from Hurn via Brindisi 10Jan70 for hot weather trials and deomonstrations in BAC house c/s. Redesignated as a Srs.524FF. Regn cx 27Feb70. Painted for Germanair Bedarfsluftfahrt as D-AMOR and del 20Mar70. Co merged with Bavaria to form Bavaria/Germanair Fluggesellschaft 01Mar77. Co merged into Hapag-Lloyd Jan79. Sold Austral Lineas Aereas and del ex Frankfurt 23Jan80 as LV-PFR in Hapag-Lloyd c/s, arriving Buenos Aires 28Jan80. Re-regd LV-OAX and entered service 09Feb80. One time named "Puerto Argentino" and later "Isla Soledad". Wfu 06Sep93 and ferried Moron Airport for disposal.
                                                TT in excess of 52,784 hrs, 40,775 ldgs.

<u>198</u>   517FE   Ff 12Jan70 as G-16-12 Hurn to Wisley, painted overall white with grey undersides. Positioned Weybridge 15Jan70 and stored until ferried back to Wisley 12Oct70 for further storage. Painted for Bahamas Airways as VP-BCQ, first flying as such 12Nov70. Not del due Bahamas Airways ceasing ops 09Oct70. Ferried Hurn 15Apr71, still in Bahamas c/s as VP-BCQ, for further storage. Sold Court Line Aviation for op by Leeward Islands Air Transport Service and del Luton as VP-LAN 20Jun72 after CofA issued previous day. Ferried ex Luton 24Jun72 named "Halycon Beach" in Court Line's lilac c/s, arriving Antigua following day. Flew last service for LIAT 29Apr74. Del Luton via Reykjavik 30Apr74 at end of lse. Regd G-BCCV to Court Line Aviation 08May74. CofA issued 24May74. Entered service with Court Line 25May74 with LIAT tail markings and no Court titling. Flew last service for Court Line 15Aug74. Ferried Hurn 11Sep74 after collapse of Court Line Group 15Aug74. Regd G-BCXR to Monarch Airlines 28Feb75 and del Luton on lse 07Mar75; CofA issued same day. Wfs 03Mar83. Lsd Dan-Air Services with del Lasham 23Mar83 and regd to them same date. Entered service 25Mar83. Sold Dan-Air Services 31Oct83. Sold ILFC and lsd back to Dan-Air Services. Flew last flight as DA183 Manchester to Gatwick 02Nov92. Ferried Hurn as DA89XR 03Nov92. Lsd British Air Ferries and regd to them 12Nov92. Ferried Southend 26Nov92 for spares use only. Regn cx 30Mar93 as wfu. Regn G-OBWK res but ntu.   TT 47,506 hrs, 32,096 ldgs.

<u>199</u>   523FJ   Regd as G-AXLM to British Midland Airways 29Jul69. Ff 26Dec69; CofA issued 06Feb70; del 05Mar70. Op last service for British Midland 23Sep73 and del Court Line Aviation on lse following day. Entered service 26Sep73. Flew last service for Court Line 20Jan74. Returned British Midland Airways and ferried Hurn 04Feb74. Regn cx 10Apr74 and sold Transbrasil Linhas Aereas as PP-SDV with del ex Hurn 11Apr74. Purchased by British Aircraft Corp and del Hurn via Casablanca 06Dec76. Restored as G-AXLM 30Dec76. R/o Hurn in full Cyprus Airways c/s 17Jan77. CofA re-issued 27Feb77. Lsd Cyprus Airways with del from Hurn via Athens 28Feb77 until returned off lse 09Jan78. Regn cx 31Mar78. Sold Arkia Inland Airways, first flying in that company's c/s 15May78 as G-16-23. Del Arkia as 4X-BAS 20May78 Hurn to Tel Aviv via Athens. Returned British Aerospace with del Hurn via Salonica 14Sep79. Sold Philippine Airlines as RP-C1194 and del 14Jul80 in full c/s after ff as such 01Jul80. Arrived Manila 17Jul80. Flew last flight as PR292 Tacloban to Manila 10Jun90 and mothballed.   TT 42,249 hrs, 42,989 ldgs.

<u>200</u>   518FG   Regd as G-AXMF to Autair International Airways 14Aug69 as c/n 171; amended to c/n 200 26Aug69. Ff 25Nov69. Regd to Court Line Aviation 01Dec69; CofA issued 05Dec69; del Court Line same day; named "Halcyon Breeze" in the co's pink c/s. Ferried Manchester to Hurn 29Aug74 after collapse of Court

Line Group 15Aug74.   Regd to British Aircraft Corp 26Sep74.   Lsd Transbrasil Linhas Aereas with del via Las Palmas in basic Court Line c/s with British Aircraft Corp titles 06Dec74, arriving Sao Paulo following day.   Regn cx 10Dec74 and regd PT-TYV.   Lse terminated Nov77.   Restored as G-AXMF to British Aircraft Corp undated, but cx again 23Feb78 as not imported.   Sold Austral Lineas Aereas and regd to them as LV-MEX 28Jan78.   Entered service 09Feb78; one time named "Antardida Argentina".

201   518FG   Regd as G-AXMG to Autair International Airways 14Aug69 as c/n 173; amended to c/n 201 26Aug69.   Regd to Court Line Aviation 01Dec69; ff 08Dec69;   CofA issued 16Dec69;   del 18Dec69 named "Halcyon Sky" in Court Line's turquoise c/s.   R/o Luton in full Cyprus Airways c/s 03May74 regd 5B-DAF.   Regn cx 14May74 and lsd Cyprus Airways as 5B-DAF 15May74.   Entered service 01Jun74. Stranded Nicosia after Turkish invasion 22Jul74.   Court Line Group ceased trading 15Aug74.   Restored as G-AXMG to Lloyds Associated Air Lsg 24Nov75 and returned Hurn 11Dec75.   Lsd Bavaria Fluggesellschaft Schwabe & Co 30Apr76 to Sep76 with Cyprus Airways cheatlines and Bavaria titles and tail.   Lsd Monarch Airlines and r/o in their c/s 29Oct76.   Made a wheels-up landing Stansted 21Feb78 while crew training.   Ferried Hurn for repair 08Mar78.   Re-del Monarch Airlines 24May78 and returned to service following day.   Regd to British Island Airways 15May85 on sale to them;   del Luton to Stansted same date;   named "Island Emblem".   Co ceased all ops 01Feb90.   Regd to Tollhold Ltd 13Feb90.   Ferried Southend 04May90.   Regd G-FLRU to London European Airways 04May90.   R/o in Ryanair Europe c/s 08May90 for lease to them.   Entered service 10May90 Luton to Rome-Ciampino and Naples.   Regn cx 02May91 and regd to Ryanair as EI-CDO 03May91.   CofA issued 03May91.   Ferried Hurn to Dublin on lease 03May91. Entered service 08May91 Dublin to Liverpool.   Wfs and ferried Lasham 25Apr94, where Irish marks removed.   Restored as G-AXMG to Tollhold Ltd 06May94.   Stored.

202   518FG   Regd as G-AXMH to Autair International Airways 14Aug69 as c/n 176; amended to c/n 202 26Aug69.   Regd to Court Line Aviation 01Dec69; ff 12Jan70;   CofA issued 06Feb70;   del 11Feb70 named "Halcyon Sun" in Court Line's orange c/s.   Ferried Hurn 11Sep74 after collapse of Court Line Group 15Aug74.   Regd G-BDAS to Dan-Air Services 21Feb75.   Del Hurn to Lasham 28Feb75.   CofA issued 28Feb75.   Sold ILFC and lsd back to Dan-Air Services.   Flew last flight as DA484 Amsterdam to Gatwick 05Nov92 before ferrying Southend as DA89AS same date.   Lsd British Air Ferries and regd to them 12Nov92.   Re-regd G-OBWB 08Dec92.   Entered service 09Dec92 Southend to Amsterdam.   Co renamed British World Airlines 06Apr93.

203   518FG   Regd as G-AXMI to Autair International Airways 14Aug69 as c/n 177; amended to c/n 203 26Aug69.   Regd to Court Line Aviation 01Dec69; ff 27Jan70;   CofA issued 19Feb70;   del 24Mar70 named "Halcyon Days" in Court Line's pink c/s.   Ferried Hurn 11Sep74 after collapse of Court Line Group 15Aug74.   Regd G-BDAE to Dan-Air Services 21Feb75.   Del Hurn to Lasham 17Mar75.   CofA issued 28Mar75.   Entered service 30Mar75.   Nose wheel collapsed on landing Gatwick 29Dec79; repaired.   Sold ILFC and lsd back to Dan-Air Services.   Flew last flight as DA525 from Rome which diverted Heathrow in lieu of Gatwick 05Nov92.   Ferried Heathrow to Hurn as DA89AE 06Nov92.   Lsd British Air Ferries and regd to them 12Nov92.   Ferried Southend 27Nov92. Re-regd G-OBWD 14Jan93.   Positioned Stansted 05Feb93 and entered service 09Feb93 Stansted to Tarbes.   Co renamed British World Airlines 06Apr93;   named "City of Bucharest" and inaugurated scheduled service Stansted to Bucharest as VF300 28Jun93.

204   518FG   Regd as G-AXMJ to Autair International Airways 14Aug69 as c/n 180; amended to c/n 204 26Aug69.   Regd to Court Line Aviation 01Dec69;

ff 17Feb70; CofA issued 10Mar70; del 12Mar70 named "Halcyon Nights" in Court Line's turquoise c/s. Collided with Piper Aztec G-AYDE on landing Luton 18Apr74; repaired and air tested 09May74. Returned to service 11May74. Ferried Hurn 11Sep74 after collapse of Court Line Group 15Aug74. Regd G-BCWG to Monarch Airlines 03Feb75. Lsd Monarch Airlines with del Luton 28Feb75. Regd to British Aircraft Corp 25Oct76. Lsd Cyprus Airways in full co c/s 30Oct76 until returned Hurn 04Feb78 after ferry from Paris-Charles de Gaulle. Regn cx 14Jul78. Sold Philippine Airlines as RP-C1189 with del ex Hurn via Naples 10Aug78, arriving Manila 14Aug78. Painted in Philippine Airlines c/s and entered service 25Aug78. Flew last flight as PR239 Tuguegarao to Manila 11Aug91 and stored. TT 43,334 hrs, 35,477 ldgs.

<u>205</u>   518FG   Regd as G-AXMK to Autair International Airways 14Aug69 as c/n 185; amended to c/n 205 26Aug69. Regd to Court Line Aviation 01Dec69; ff 07Mar70; CofA issued 11Apr70; del 21Apr70 after acceptance 17Apr70 named "Halcyon Star" in Court Line's turquoise c/s. Later repainted in orange c/s. Lsd Aviateca with del 19Nov70, arriving Guatemala City 23Nov70. Regn cx 23Nov70 and regd TG-ARA (a/c remained in full Court c/s with Aviateca titling). Del Luton as TG-ARA at end of lse 03Apr71. Restored as G-AXMK to Court Line Aviation 06Apr71. CofA renewed 07Apr71. Lsd Leeward Islands Air Transport Services with del ex Luton 22Nov71, arriving Antigua 24Nov71. Regn cx 25Nov71 and regd VP-LAK. Entered service 01Dec71. Del Luton at end of lse as VP-LAK 02Jul72. Restored as G-AXMK to Court Line Aviation 05Jul72. Returned to service 08Jul72 after CofA renewed previous day. Lsd Germanair Bedarfsluftfahrt with del 21May74 in Court Line c/s with Germanair titling in silver. Regd to British Aircraft Corp 05Sep74 after collapse of Court Line Group 15Aug74 and lse to Germanair continued until 30Oct74. Regd G-BCWA to Dan-Air Services 22Jan75 on sale to them with r/o same day. Del Gatwick 29Jan75. Entered service 23Feb75. Sold ILFC and lsd back to Dan-Air Services. Flew last revenue Dan-Air One-Eleven flight when it arrived Gatwick from Toulouse as the DA910 at 0937 on 06Nov92. Ferried Hurn as DA89WA same date. Lsd British Air Ferries and regd to them 12Nov92. Ferried Southend 28Nov92 for spares use only. Regn cx 30Mar93 as wfu. Regn G-OBWI res but ntu. TT 56,498 hrs, 33,333 ldgs.

<u>206</u>   518FG   Regd as G-AXML to Autair International Airways 14Aug69 as c/n 187; amended to c/n 206 26Aug69. Regd to Court Line Aviation 01Dec69; ff 22Apr70; CofA issued 29Apr70; del 30Apr70 named "Halcyon Cloud" in Court Line's pink c/s. Ferried Hurn 16Dec71 for preparation for lse to LANICA. Flown in full Court Line c/s with additional LANICA titles. Del 22Dec71. Regn cx 23Dec71 and re-regd AN-BHJ. Returned Hurn at end of lse 17Mar72. Restored as G-AXML to Court Line Aviation 28Mar72. Del Luton following day and re-entered service same day. Ferried Hurn 11Sep74 after collapse of Court Line Group 15Aug74. Regd to British Aircraft Corp 26Sep74. Lsd Transbrasil Linhas Aereas with del ex Hurn 10Oct74. Regn cx 15Oct74 and re-regd PT-TYW in basic Court Line c/s with Transbrasil titles and fin emblem overpainted. Lsd Aviateca 02Sep75 named "Zaculeu" and regd TG-AVA. Sold Austral Lineas Aereas as LV-MRZ Mar79. Entered service 15Jun79. One time named "Bahia Agradable". Wfu Buenos Aires Nov93. TT in excess of 49,728 hrs, 41,848 ldgs.

<u>207</u>   515FB   Ff 01May70 as D-ALAR; regd to Germania-Airfonds; del Paninternational 13May70; named "Jorn". W/o Hamburg 06Sep71 soon after take-off. TT 4,325 hrs, 2,910 ldgs.

<u>208</u>   515FB   Ff 13May70 as D-ALAS; regd to Germania-Airfonds; del Paninternational 20Mar70. Co ceased ops 06Oct71 and a/c impounded Dubrovnik. Regd G-AZPE to British Aircraft Corp 09Mar72 and del Dubrovnik to Hurn

18Mar72. Ferried Bremen 25Apr72 and stored until returned Hurn 07Jul72. Lsd British Caledonian Airways with del Hurn to Gatwick 14Aug72. CofA issued 18Aug72. Regd to British Caledonian Airways 18Aug72. Returned British Aircraft Corp with del Gatwick to Hurn 18Oct72. Regn cx 17Oct73. Sold LACSA named "Arenal" as TI-LRK, being regd as such 27Nov73. Del ex Hurn via Keflavik 18Dec73. Lsd Dan-Air Services with del Gatwick 14Mar82 and then to Lasham following day. CofA issued 25Mar82. Regd to Dan-Air Services as G-BJYL 26Mar82. R/o in full c/s 24Mar82 and departed Lasham 26Mar82. Purchased by Dan-Air Services 28Oct82. Sold ILFC and lsd back to Dan-Air Services. Flew last flight as DA287 Jersey to Gatwick 01Nov92. Ferried Hurn as DA89YL 02Nov92. Lsd British Air Ferries and regd to them 12Nov92. Ferried Southend 27Nov92 for storage. Co renamed British World Airlines 06Apr93 and regd to them as G-OBWH 07Apr93. Remains in store painted as G-BJYL. TT 49,835 hrs, 31,334 ldgs.

209   501EX   Regd as G-AXJL to British United Airways 18Jul69; ff 20Feb70; CofA issued 02Mar70; del 05Mar70 or 03Mar70. Co merged with Caledonian Airways to form Caledonian//BUA 30Nov70; named "Isle of Mingulay" 26Feb71. Co renamed British Caledonian Airways 01Nov71. Sold Philippine Airlines and del Hurn 30Sep76 for preparation. Regn cx 11Nov76. Ff 06Dec76 in full Philippine Airlines c/s as RP-C1188. Del Philippine Airlines 01Mar77 ex Hurn via Naples, arriving Manila 04Mar77. Nose undercarriage collapsed Manila 29Aug84; repaired. Flew last flight as PR322 Kalibo to Manila 02Sep90 and mothballed. TT 43,068 hrs, 41,440 ldgs.

210   509EW   Regd as G-AXYD to CCT (Aircraft Lsg) 27Feb70; ff 06Mar70; CofA issued 16Mar70; del Caledonian Airways 18Mar70; named "Isle of Arran". Co merged with British United Airways to form Caledonian//BUA 30Nov70. Co renamed British Caledonian Airways 01Nov71. Regd to Caledonian Airways (Lsg) 14Feb73. Regd to British Caledonian Airways 25Apr74. Sold Dan-Air Services 20Apr76 and regd to them 05May76. Entered service 06May76. Lsd British Caledonian Airways 31Jan84 to ... Lsd British Caledonian Airways a second time in Dan-Air c/s 01Nov87. In service as BR977 Gatwick to Jersey same day. Returned lessor 20Apr88. Sold ILFC and lsd back Dan-Air Services. Flew last flight as DA680 Madrid to Gatwick 06Nov92 before ferrying Hurn as DA89YD same date. Lsd British Air Ferries and regd to them 12Nov92. Ferried Southend 29Nov92 for storage. Co renamed British World Airlines 06Apr93 and regd to them as G-OBWF 07Apr93. Remains in store painted as G-AXYD.
TT 50,496 hrs, 34,123 ldgs.

211   523FJ   Regd as G-AXLN to British Midland Airways 29Jul69; ff 04Feb70; CofA issued 12Mar70; del 12Mar70. Last service with British Midland 28Feb72 and lsd Court Line Aviation from following day. Entered service 03Mar72 in basic British Midland c/s with Court emblem and titles. Ferried Hurn 25Sep73 at end of lse after operating its last Court Line service previous day. Regn cx 07Nov73. Sold Transbrasil Linhas Aereas as PP-SDU and del ex Hurn 08Nov73, arriving Sao Paulo 09Nov73. Returned British Aircraft Corp and lsd Aviateca as TG-AYA with del Miami 22Apr78. Sold Cayman Airways with del Miami 29May78. R/o in full c/s named "Cayman Victory" 27Jun78 regd VR-CAL. In service 29Jun78. Wfu Miami 10Dec82. Ferried Luton via Shannon 03Feb84. Restored as G-AXLN to British Island Airways 11Apr84. Painted in full British Island c/s; named "Island Enterprise" and del Luton to Gatwick 17Apr84. Entered service following day Gatwick to Naples. Co ceased all ops 01Feb90. Regd to Tollhold Ltd 13Feb90 and del Southend 30Apr90. Regd G-EKPT to London European Airways 30Apr90. Painted in Ryanair Europe c/s and r/o 04May90 for lease to them. CofA issued ...90. Entered service 05May90 Luton and Manchester to Palma. Regn cx 17Dec90 on transfer of lease to Ryanair. Regd EI-CCX to Ryanair

18Dec90. CofA issued 18Dec90. Entered service 19Dec90 Luton via Manchester to Palma.

212   529FR   Ff 14May70 as G-16-13 painted overall white with grey undersides. Visited Birmingham 21Aug70. Del Phoenix Airways as HB-ITL 01Apr71. Stored Basle after collapse of Phoenix Airways 17Mar74. Sold Austral Lineas Aereas as LV-LOX with del ex Basle 18Jan75 in Phoenix c/s without titles. Entered service 29Jan75. W/o 07Mar81 in the Rio de la Plata, 8km south of Buenos Aires.
TT 21,729 hrs, 20,415 ldgs.

213   527FK   Ff 15Sep70 as PI-C1161; regd as G-AYOS to British Aircraft Corp (Holdings) 04Jan71 and painted as such 07Jan71. CofA issued ... Regn cx 19May71, reverting to PI-C1161 and stored Hurn. Del Philippine Airlines as PI-C1161 26Oct71, arriving Manila 29Oct71. Entered service 11Nov71. Re-regd RP-C1161 01Mar74. W/o 21May76; destroyed by fire and explosives on ground Zamboanga, Philippines, following hijacking which lasted two days.
TT 10,755 hrs, 11,145 ldgs.

214   501EX   Regd as G-AXJM to British United Airways 18Jul69; ff 17Mar70; CofA issued 24Mar70; del 25Mar70. Entered service 27Mar70. Co merged with Caledonian Airways to form Caledonian//BUA 30Nov70; named "Isle of Islay". Regd to Caledonian-British United Airways 14Apr71. Co renamed British Caledonian Airways 01Nov71. Regd to British Caledonian Airways 04May72. Flew last service 25Nov77 and lsd Air Malawi with del 26Nov77. Regd cx 27Nov77. Entered service regd 7Q-YKI 27Nov77. Flew last service 16Dec77. Restored as G-AXJM to British Caledonian Airways 18Dec77 and returned Gatwick 19Dec77. Returned to service with BCAL 21Dec77. Co merged into British Airways 14Apr88. Regd to British Airways 14Apr88; named "County of Durham". Flew last revenue flight as BA5329 Brussels to Birmingham 30Apr93. Ferried Hurn for storage as BA9662P 25May93. Sold Oriental Airlines of Nigeria and h/o 22Jul93. Regn cx 23Jul93 and regd 5N-OAL. Painted in Oriental c/s by 10Sep93. Del ex Hurn via Palma as OAL401 25Sep93.

215   527FK   Regd as G-AYKN to British Aircraft Corp (Holdings) 07Oct70; ff 09Oct70; CofA issued ...70. UK regd for demonstrations to TAROM 20/22Oct70 in full Philippine Airlines c/s. Regn cx 21Dec70 and regd PI-C1171. Restored as G-AYKN to British Aircraft Corp (Holdings) Apr71. Regn cx 19May71 and stored Hurn as PI-C1171 for Philippine Airlines. Del 29Oct71, arriving Manila 31Oct71. Entered service 15Nov71. Re-regd RP-C1171 01Mar74. Flew last flight as PR138 Bacolod to Manila 04Mar91 and stored.   TT 41,331 hrs, 45,427 ldgs.

216 to 225   Srs.500s Not built

226   527FK   Ff 03Nov70 as PR-C1181. Stored Wisley and later Hurn. Del Philippine Airlines 05Nov71, arriving Manila 09Nov71; the 200th One-Eleven delivery. Entered service 21Nov71. Re-regd RP-C1181 01Mar74. Flew last flight as PR130 San Jose to Manila 13Apr92 and stored.   TT 41,966 hrs, 46,261 ldgs.

227   528FL   Ff 28Oct70 as D-AMUC; del Bavaria Fluggesellschaft Schwabe & Co 03Dec70; named "Ludwig Thoma" from 03Nov72. Co merged with Germanair to form Bavaria/Germanair Fluggesellschaft 01Mar77. Co merged into Hapag-Lloyd Fluggesellschaft Jan79. Sold Austral Lineas Aereas as LV-OAY and del ex Frankfurt 29Jan80, arriving Buenos Aires 02Feb80. Entered service 17Feb80. One time named "Isla

Soledad" and later "Puerto Argentina".   Wfu Buenos Aires-Aeroparque 02Aug93.
TT in excess of 51,939 hrs, 41,071 ldgs.

228   520FN   Ff 21Sep70 as PP-SDQ; del Sadia Transportes Aereos 15Oct70. Co renamed Transbrasil Linhas Aereas Jun72. W/o 02Feb74 after heavy landing Sao Paulo-Congonhas; broke in two.   TT 10,518 hrs, 11,107 ldgs.

229   515FB   Ff 04Dec70 as D-ALAQ;   regd to Germania-Airfonds;   del Paninternational 04Mar71. Co ceased ops 06Oct71. Regd G-AZPZ to British Aircraft Corp 21Mar72 after Paninternational ceased trading. CofA issued 27Mar72. Ferried Cologne to Hurn 28Mar72. Regn cx 01May72 and del Germanair Bedarfsluftfahrt as D-AMAM 11May72. Co merged with Bavaria to form Bavaria/Germanair Fluggesellschaft 01Mar77. Co merged into Hapag-Lloyd Fluggesellschaft Jan79. Ferried Paris-Le Bourget for painting in Hapag-Lloyd c/s 28Jan80. Lsd Dan-Air Services with del Frankfurt via Luton to Lasham 10Apr81. CofA issued 29Apr81. Restored G-AZPZ to Dan-Air Services 30Apr81 and painted in their full c/s, entering service same date. Lse completed 28Feb82 after operating last service 23Feb82 and sold British Caledonian Airways with del 01Mar82. Regd to British Caledonian Airways 02Apr82 and entered service same date; named "City of Glasgow" 05Jan83. Co merged into British Airways 14Apr88. Regd to British Airways 14Apr88; named "Dumfries & Galloway Region". Flew last One-Eleven revenue flight for British Airways as BC306 Belfast to Birmingham 01Jul93 (a Brymon European flight). Ferried Lasham for storage as BA9664P 14Jul93. Sold Oriental Airlines of Nigeria and h/o 17Mar94; regn cx the same day. Noted at Lasham 18Apr94 in full Oriental c/s regd 5N-IMO. Del ex Lasham 04May94. W/o 18Sep94 after forced landing nr Tamanrasset, Algeria; four killed, 35 survived.   TT in excess of 44,524 hrs, 33,326 ldgs.

230   520FN   Ff 11Nov70 as PP-SDR; del Sadia Transportes Aereos 31Dec70. Co renamed Transbrasil Linhas Aereas Jun72. Regd G-BEKA to British Aircraft Corp 05Jan77 on sale to them and del Hurn via Casablanca and Nantes 08Jan77. CofA issued ... Regn cx 13Jul77. Sold Arkia Inland Airways and first flew in their c/s as G-16-22 12Jul77. Del Arkia ex Hurn via Athens regd 4X-BAR 18Jul77. Entered service 02Aug77. Flew last service for Arkia 11Sep79. Returned British Aerospace with del Hurn via Salonica 12Sep79. Sold Dan-Air Services 03Oct79 and del Manchester same date. Restored as G-BEKA to Dan-Air Services 10Oct79. CofA issued ...79 and entered service 11Oct79. Sold ILFC and lsd back to Dan-Air Services. Flew last flight as DA735 Oslo to Gatwick 03Nov92. Ferried Hurn as DA89KA 06Nov92. Lsd British Air Ferries and regd to them 12Nov92. Ferried Southend 28Nov92. Re-regd G-OBWC 08Dec92. Ferried Gatwick 18Feb93 and entered service following day Gatwick to Jersey. Co renamed British World Airlines 06Apr93.

231   527FK   Ff 16Dec70 as PI-C1191 in Philippine Airlines c/s. Order not finalised and modified to Srs.516FP for Aviateca. Del Empresa Guatemalteca de Aviacion-Aviateca as TG-AZA 25Mar71; named "Quetzel". Co renamed Aerolineas de Guatemala-Aviateca 1974. Regn cx 07Apr80. Sold Philippine Airlines and del Hurn via Casablanca as RP-C1193 25Apr80 for pre-service modifications. Del ex Hurn via Naples 07Jul80 after earlier test flight in full Philippine Airlines c/s 01Jul80. Arrived Manila 10Jul80. Entered service 29Jul80. W/o 21Jul89 after overrunning runway on landing Manila.   TT 39,644 hrs, 36,200 ldgs.

232   518FG   Regd as G-AYOR to Court Line Aviation 04Jan71; ff 29Jan71; CofA issued 05Feb71; del 18Mar71 named "Halcyon Dawn" in Court Line's orange c/s. Ferried Cardiff to Hurn 21Aug74 after collapse of Court Line Group 15Aug74.

Del Gatwick 31Jan75.   Regd G-BDAT to Dan-Air Services 25Feb75 after sale to them. CofA issued 25Feb75.   Sold ILFC and lsd back to Dan-Air Services.   Flew last flight as DA183 Manchester to Gatwick 05Nov92.   Ferried Southend as DA89AT 06Nov92.   Lsd British Air Ferries and regd to them 12Nov92.   Re-regd G-OBWA 01Dec92.   Entered service 07Dec92 Stansted to Istanbul.   Painted in British World c/s at Southend;   r/o 21Mar93.   Co renamed British World Airlines 06Apr93.

<u>233</u>   518FG   Built to British Caledonian Airways order for initial lse to Court Line Aviation.   Regd G-AYOP to Court Line Aviation 04Jan71;   ff 03Mar71;   CofA issued 26Mar71;   del 31Mar71 named "Halcyon Beach" in Court Line's orange c/s.   Entered service 02Apr71.   Flew last service 03Dec72 and returned Hurn 08Dec72 for modification to Srs.530FX.   Regd to British Caledonian Airways 16Mar73 and painted in their full c/s.   Del 15Mar73;   named "Isle of Hoy".   Entered service 19Mar73.   Lsd Air Malta in full c/s with del 30Apr75.   Entered service 05May75 Malta to Frankfurt and Amsterdam.   Lse completed 31Oct75.   Repainted in British Caledonian c/s and re-entered service 04Dec75.   Co merged into British Airways 14Apr88.   Regd to British Airways 14Apr88;   named "County of Humberside".   Flew last revenue flight as BA5405 Paris-Charles de Gaulle to Birmingham 31Dec92 before ferrying Hurn for storage as BA9665P same date.   Sold European Aviation and ferried Filton 07Jul94 for further storage after painting in European Aircharter c/s.   Regd to European Aviation 16Aug94.

TT 42,657 hrs, 37,338 ldgs.

<u>234</u>   528FL   Ff 08Feb71 as D-ALFA;   del Bavaria Fluggesellschaft Schwabe & Co 26Feb71.   Entered service 01Mar71;   named "Jakob Fugger".   Co merged with Germanair to form Bavaria/Germanair Fluggesellschaft 01Mar77.   Co merged into Hapag-Lloyd Fluggesellschaft Jan79.   R/o Paris-Le Bourget 28Jan80 in full Hapag-Lloyd c/s.   Sold British Caledonian Airways and del Frankfurt to Gatwick 29Oct81.   Regd G-BJRT to British Caledonian Airways 30Oct81.   R/o in British Caledonian c/s 31Jan82.   CofA issued 05Feb82.   Entered service 06Feb82;   named "New Town of East Kilbride".   Co merged into British Airways 14Apr88.   Regd to British Airways 14Apr88;   named "County of South Glamorgan".   Flew last revenue British Airways One-Eleven flight as BA5543 Edinburgh to Birmingham 23Jun93.   Ferried Lasham as BA9664P 25Jun93 for storage.   Sold Jaro International 01Oct93;   regn cx same day and regd YR-JBA;   del ex Lasham 05Oct93;   named "Traian Vuia".

<u>235</u>   524FF   Regd as G-AYSC as a Srs.518FG to Court Line Aviation 04Feb71.   Order not finalised and regn cx 30Mar71.   Redesignated a Srs.524FF.   Ff 17Apr71 as D-AMAT;   del Germanair Bedarfsluftfahft 08May71.   Co merged with Bavaria to form Bavaria/Germanair Fluggesellschaft 01Mar77.   Co merged into Hapag-Lloyd Fluggesellschaft Jan79. R/o Paris-Le Bourget 14Feb80 in Hapag-Lloyd new c/s.   Sold Air Malawi as 7Q-YKK and del ex Frankfurt 30Oct80.   Wfs Jun91.   Ferried ex Blantyre 22Jun92 via Nairobi, Addis Ababa, Luxor and Athens, arriving Hurn 25Jun92 before positioning Lasham same date.   Sold Okada Air and painted as 5N-USE in their c/s.   Del ex Southend via Palma 29Jul92.

<u>236</u>   525FT   Ff 30Apr71 as G-16-15.   Originally planned for sale to TAROM but deal not completed.   Converted to Srs.520FN and del Transbrasil Linhas Aereas as PP-SDS 23Sep72.   W/o Campinas, Brazil, 05Jan77.   Wreckage shipped Burbank, California, by 31Mar78 and stored.   Regn N110TA reserved to Tigerair Inc.

TT 12,671 hrs, 14,243 ldgs.

<u>237</u>   531FS   Originally built to British Caledonian Airways order for lse to LACSA through Court Line Aviation.   Regd G-AYWB to Court Line Aviation

14Apr71 as a Srs.500FS. Regn cx as not used 07May71. Ff 13May71 as TI-1084C; del LACSA 26May71, which purchased a/c outright in 1972; named "Miravalles". Re-regd TI-LRF ...74. Made heavy landing Santa Maria, Costa Rica, 03Sep75. Ferried Hurn 07Sep75 for repairs. R/o Hurn 27Oct75 re-regd TI-LRL, first flying as such 30Oct75. Re-del via Keflavik 01Nov75; named "Arenal". Sold Cayman Airways with del Miami 01Nov79. R/o as VR-CAB; named "Cayman Progress" 23Nov79. Entered service 01Dec79. Wfs Dec82. Ferried Shannon to Luton as VR-CAB 03Feb84. Restored as G-AYWB to British Island Airways 11Apr84; named "Island Envoy". CofA issued 22May84. Co ceased all ops 01Feb90. Regd Tollhold Ltd 13Feb90. Regd G-DJOS to London European Airways 25Apr90 and painted in Ryanair Europe c/s for lease to them. Entered service 28Apr90 Luton to Milan-Malpensa. Flew last service Madrid to Luton 06Dec90. Regn cx 17Dec90 and regd EI-CCU for lease to Ryanair 18Dec90. CofA issued 21Dec90. Entered service Luton to Connaught-Knock 21Dec90.

238   528FL   R/o 20Dec71; ff 28Feb72 as D-ANUE; del Bavaria Fluggesellschaft Schwabe & Co 15Mar72. Entered service 07Apr72; named "Albrecht Durer" from 03Nov72. Co merged with Germanair to form Bavaria/Germanair Fluggesellschaft 01Mar77. Co merged into Hapag-Lloyd Fluggesellschaft Jan79. R/o Paris-Le Bourget in full Hapag-Lloyd c/s 11Jan80. Sold British Caledonian Airways and del Frankfurt to Gatwick 29Oct81. Regd G-BJRU to British Caledonian Airways 30Oct81. CofA issued 08Mar92. Entered service 09Mar82; named "City of Edinburgh". Co merged into British Airways 14Apr88. Regd to British Airways 14Apr88; named "County of West Glamorgan". Flew last revenue flight as BA5385 Cologne to Birmingham 29Jan93. Ferried Hurn as BA9663P 01Feb93 for storage. Ferried Lasham 09Sep93. Sold Jaro International 04Oct93; regn cx, regd YR-JBB and del ex Lasham 04Oct93. Painted in JARO c/s and named "Aurel Vlaicu". Lsd Air Alfa of Turkey May94 and flown with their titles added.

239   476FM   First production Srs.475. Regd as G-AYUW to British Aircraft Corp 26Mar71; ff 05Apr71; CofA issued 02Jun71. Shown at Paris Air Show 1971. Regn cx 30Jun71. Repainted as G-16-17. Del Faucett as OB-R953 23Jul71, arriving Lima 26Jul71. Flew last service 31Dec82 and ferried Van Nuys for storage Mar83. Restored as G-AYUW to Macair Investments 04Mar87. Regd to Mediterranean Express 07Aug87. Del Luton 02Dec87 after ferry from USA. Regn cx 08Nov88 after overhaul abandoned. Fuselage sold AIM Aviation and del Hurn by road 29Jun89. Painted with AIM Aviation titles and used for watermisting fire retardant trials.

TT 28,200 hrs, 29,218 ldgs.

240   530FX   Regd as G-AZMF to Lloyds Associated A/c Lsg 14Jan72; ff 04Mar72; CofA issued 10Mar72; del British Caledonian Airways 14Mar72; named "Isle of Raasay". Entered service 17Mar72. Lsd Transbrasil Linhas Aereas with del 15Feb74 in basic BCAL c/s, arriving Sao Paulo 16Feb74. Regn cx 18Feb74 and entered service same day regd PT-TYY. Restored as G-AZMF to Lloyds Associated A/c Lsg 13Dec74 for op by British Caledonian Airways and del ex Sao Paulo same day, arriving Gatwick 15Dec74. CofA re-issued 23Jan75 and re-entered service following day. Lsd Austrian Airlines 31Mar75. Flew last Austrian service Munich to Vienna 06Sep75 and returned Gatwick 07Sep75 at end of lse. Regd to British Caledonian Airways 21Aug78. Lsd British Airways with del 24Oct78. Entered service 01Nov78. Returned British Caledonian Airways at end of lse 30Apr79. Lsd Air Malawi with del 21Oct79. Regn cx 25Oct79 and regd 7Q-YKJ. Restored as G-AZMF to British Caledonian Airways 24Apr80 at end of lse and del Gatwick 28Apr80. Returned to service with British Caledonian 14May80. Co merged into British Airways 14Apr88. Regd to British Airways 14Apr88; named "County of Northumberland". Flew last revenue flight as BA5363 Frankfurt to

Birmingham 22Dec92. Ferried Hurn for storage as BA9719E 23Dec92. To be sold to European Aviation and op by European Aircharter for exec charter work. Painted in European c/s Aug94 and h/o to European Aviation 20Sep 94.

<u>241</u>   476FM   Ff 07Jul71 as G-16-16. Built and painted as OB-R-1080 for Faucett. Regd G-AZUK to British Aircraft Corp 09May72 and repainted in BAC house c/s. Ff as G-AZUK 16May72. Special Category CofA issued 16May72. Carried out South American sales tour late May and early Jun72. Displayed Farnborough Air Show Sep72. Repainted in Faucett c/s. Regn cx 01Jul74. Del as OB-R-1080 18Jul74 but returned Hurn ex Keflavik same day. Re-del 19Jul74 via Keflavik, Goose Bay, Dorval, Miami and Panama City to Lima. Wfs 10Dec82. Ferried ex Lima via Talara, Barranquilla, Miami and Hobby to Van Nuys, California, 16Dec82 for storage. Restored as G-AZUK to Macair Investments 04Mar87. Painted as such and ferried to Heathrow 19Mar87 via Goose Bay for maintenance by British Airways. CofA re-issued 17Jun87. Del Luton from Heathrow 19Jun87 after painting in Mediterranean Express c/s. Regd to Mediterranean Express 07Aug87. Stored Luton by early Jan88. Sold Ryanair Europe and regd to Atlantic Computer Systems 31Mar89. CofA reissued 31Mar89. Lsd Baltic Airlines Sweden, entering service 31Mar89 Southend to Malmo; named "Nils Holgersson". Lse terminated after operating last Baltic service 31May89, having earlier been regd to London European Airways on 05May89. Lsd Loganair 05Jun89 to 03Oct89, when ferried Glasgow to Luton. Returned to service with London European Airways. Ferried Southend 15Feb91. R/o all white with British Air Ferries titles 03Apr91. Regd to British Air Ferries 26Jun91. A/c lsd from Mercurius Gruppen of Sweden. Entered service 30Jun91 with first revenue flight Vienna to Ankara. Flew last revenue service 11Nov92 Milan-Bergamo to Stansted. Ferried Southend and put in storage. Regd to Dawson Trading 10May93.
                                                                                                TT 23,397 hrs, 23,805 ldgs.

<u>242</u>   531FS   Ff 17Oct72 as TI-1095C; del LACSA 06Nov72; named "Poas". Periodic lse to Cayman Airways, when flown with their titles added. Re-regd TI-LRI Jan74. Lsd TACA International Nov81 to Mar82 in full new TACA c/s. Regd G-BJYM to Dan-Air Services 07May82 on sale to them. Del Gatwick 10May82 and ferried Lasham following day. CofA issued 17May82 and entered service same date. Sold ILFC and lsd back to Dan-Air Services. Flew last flight as DA4619 Pisa to Gatwick 30Oct92. Ferried Hurn as DA89YM 02Nov92. Lsd British Air Ferries and regd to them 12Nov92. Ferried Southend 25Nov92 and put into storage. Co renamed British World Airlines 06Apr93 and regd to them as G-OBWE 07Apr93. Airtested 27May93 and entered service Stansted to Pau 28May93.

<u>243</u>   481FW   Ff 20Jan72 as 7Q-YKF; del Air Malawi 23Feb72, arriving Blantyre 24Feb72. Wfs Jun91. Lsd Wirakris Udara of Malaysia and del via Muscat 09Sep92. Returned ex lease and sold GAS Airlines as 5N-SKS Mar93.

<u>244</u>   531FS   Ff 11May73 as TI-1096C; del LACSA 14May73. Lsd Cayman Airways in full c/s from ...73; named "Barracuda". Re-regd TI-LRJ 1974. Returned LACSA at end of lse Nov77; named "Chiripo". Ferried Gatwick to Lasham as TI-LRJ in full LACSA c/s 12Nov81. Regd G-BJMV to Dan-Air Services 26Nov81. Airtested 06Jan82, with CofA issued 07Jan82. Ferried Gatwick same day on lse to Dan-Air Services. Sold Dan-Air Services 28Oct82. Sold ILFC and lsd back to Dan-Air Services. Flew last flight as DA1601 Lisbon to Gatwick 01Nov92. Ferried Hurn as DA89MV 02Nov92. Lsd British Air Ferries and regd to them 12Nov92. Ferried Southend 26Nov92 and put into storage. Regn cx 30Mar93 as wfu. Regn G-OBWJ res but ntu.
                                                                                                TT 43,115 hrs, 28,582 ldgs.

245   479FU   R/o 26Jan72; ff 08Feb72 as DQ-FBQ; del Air Pacific ex Hurn 04Mar72, arriving Nadi 10Mar72; CofA issued 18Mar72.   Entered service 02Apr72.   Lsd Air Malawi in Air Pacific c/s with Air Malawi tail c/s and del 05Jul74.   Regn cx 09Jul74 and regd 7Q-YKG.   Restored as DQ-FBQ 16Nov75 at end of lse and returned to service with Air Pacific.   Wfs and ferried via Rome-Ciampino to Gatwick 22Mar84.   Sold Royal A/c Establishment, Bedford, as ZE433 early Jun84.   RAE absorbed into Defence Research Agency Apr91.   A/c nose modified Bedford to accommodate ECR90 radar due to be used in European Fighter Aircraft.   Ff after modification incorporated 08Jan93.   Transferred to GEC Ferranti Defence Systems Ltd in exchange for c/n 263 early 1994.

246   527FK   Ff 01Jun74 as RP-C1182; del Philippine Airlines 14Jun74, arriving Manila 18Jun74.   Nosewheel collapsed on landing Manila 19Nov78; repaired.   Damaged Manila 17Feb81 and repaired.   W/o 04Aug84 after overrunning runway into sea Tacloban, Leyte, Philippines.   TT 22,264 hrs, 23,704 ldgs.

247   485GD   Ff 21Nov74 as 1001; del Air Force of the Sultanate of Oman 18Dec74.   Returned Hurn 30Oct75 for fitting of maindeck forward cargo door.   Re-regd 551 Jul76.   Fitted with longrange tanks by Dan-Air Engineering at Lasham between 28Mar83 and 07Jul83.

248   527FL   Ff 29Jun74 as RP-C1183; del Philippine Airlines 05Jul74, arriving Manila 08Jul74.   Flew last flight as PR292 Tacloban to Manila 13Jun91 and stored.   TT 33,911 hrs, 37,314 ldgs.

249   485GD   Ff 20Dec74 as 1002; del Air Force of the Sultanate of Oman 29Jan75. Re-regd 552 Jul76.   Returned Hurn for fitting of maindeck forward cargo door.   Ff so fitted 02Aug77 and re-del 07Aug77.   Fitted with longrange tanks by Dan-Air Engineering at Lasham between Jul83 and 15Aug83.

250   479FU   Ff 16Jul73 as DQ-FBV; CofA issued 31Jul73; del Air Pacific 14Aug73.   Wfs and ferried Gatwick via Rome-Ciampino 12Mar84. Sold Empire Test Pilots School as ZE432.

251   485GD   Ff 19Mar75 as 1003.   Returned hangars for fitting of maindeck forward freight door and del Air Force of the Sultanate of Oman 01Nov75.   Severely damaged by oxygen fire 22Nov75.   Shipped by sea to Poole Quay and then by road to Hurn, arriving 23May76 for permanent repair.   Re-regd 553 Jul76.   Ff 07Feb77 after rebuild and re-del ex Hurn via Brindisi 26Feb77.   Fitted with longrange tanks by Dan-Air Engineering at Lasham between 07Feb83 and 19Mar83.

252   525FT   First production a/c to be fitted with hushkits installed.   R/o 08Dec76 in full TAROM c/s; ff 20Dec76 as YR-BCI; h/o 25Feb76; del TAROM 21Mar77.   Lsd Ryanair as YR-BCI 29Apr88 to 26May88 in TAROM c/s with Ryanair titles.

253   525FT   Ff 17Mar77 as YR-BCJ; del TAROM 04Apr77.   Returned Hurn 17Apr77 and re-del 11May77.   Painted in Marmara Air c/s for 1986 summer lse but co merged into Istanbul Hava Yollari.   Lsd Istanbul Hava Yollari as TC-ARI 15May86 to Jun86.   Restored as YR-BCJ to TAROM.   Lsd Anadolu Hava Yollari as TC-AKB named "Yelhan" 25Jun87 to Aug87.   Restored as YR-BCJ to TAROM.

254   525FT   Ff 28Apr77 as YR-BCK; del TAROM 14May77. Lsd Istanbul Hava Yollari as TC-JCP in Marmara Air's basic c/s ...86 to ...86.

255   525FT   Ff 17Jun77 as YR-BCL; del TAROM 09Jul77. Ferried Hurn 13Apr85 for preparation for lse to Lauda Air. R/o as OE-ILC named "Wolfgang Amadeus Mozart" 22Apr85. Del Hurn to Vienna 24Apr85. Returned TAROM at end of lse 30Nov85 and restored as YR-BCL. Lsd Istanbul Hava Yollari as TC-AKA ...86 to ...86 in full Istanbul Airways c/s. Returned TAROM and restored as YR-BCL. Lsd British Island Airways Jun87 to ...87. Regd EI-BVG to Ryanair 23Mar88. CofA issued 27Mar88. Del on lse to Ryanair Hurn to Dublin 27Mar88; named "The Spirit of Innisfree". Entered service 28Mar88. Ferried Hurn for painting in TAROM c/s at end of lse 06Mar91. Regn cx ...91. Painted as YR-BCL and ferried Hurn-Dublin-Bucharest as RO1502/RO1602 09Mar91. Lsd Ryanair for a second time and painted in full c/s with del Dublin 30Apr92. Restored as EI-BVG 01May92. Restored as YR-BCL, returned lessor 02Nov92 and ferried Dublin to Bucharest same date.

256   525FT   Ff 08Aug77 as YR-BCM; del TAROM 25Aug77. Ferried Hurn 21Mar85 for preparation for lse to Lauda Air. R/o as OE-ILD 29Mar85. Del Hurn to Vienna 29Mar85. Lse completed Jul86. Lsd British Island Airways, painted all white with black British Island Airways titles 09Apr87 to ...87 as YR-BCM. Regd EI-BVI to Ryanair 30May88 for lse to them. After pre-service modifications CofA issued 03Jun88 and del Hurn to Dublin 04Jun88; named "The Spirit of Connaught". Ferried Hurn 27Sep93 for repaint in TAROM c/s as YR-BCM. Ferried Bucharest at end of lease Oct93.

257   537GF   R/o 04Nov77 in Cyprus Airways c/s; ff 16Nov77 as 5B-DAG; h/o 24Nov77; CofA issued 01Dec77; del 08Dec77; named "Famagusta" Jun91.

258   537GF   R/o 09Jan78; ff 18Jan78 as 5B-DAH; CofA issued 26Jan78; del Cyprus Airways Hurn to Paris-Orly 28Jan78 and entered service same day Orly to Larnaca. Damaged Larnaca and ferried Hurn for repair. Re-del 19Apr78; named "Kyrenia" Jun91.

259   488GH   Ff 28Apr78 as HZ-MAM; h/o to Mr Mouaffak Al Midani 11May78. Ferried Long Beach, California, 19/20May78 via Keflavik, Dorval, Winnipeg and Los Angeles for fitting of exec interior and avionics package; this completed 16Dec78. Arrived Gatwick 01Dec85 and repainted as LX-MAM, departing 03Dec85. Regd to Al Tass Heel Liltijara SARL on Luxembourg Register. Ferried Hurn to Le Bourget 06Oct92 after long term storage. Sold Wind CI Ltd for operation on behalf of Abdul Aziz Ude of Nigeria. Regd 5N-UDE and ferried Hurn to Luton as such 07Jun93.

260   492GM   Regd as G-BLHD to British Aerospace 07Mar84; ff 01May84 as G-16-25; CofA issued 29May84. Ferried Hurn to Woodford 30May84 as G-BLHD for storage. Regd to McAlpine Aviation 09Jul84. Ferried via Keflavik 27Jul84 for exec fitting out Fort Lauderdale. Del Luton via Keflavik as RM936 23Apr86. Regd to Twinjet Aircraft Sales 15Mar90. Regn cx 21Feb91 after del ex Luton via Cairo 18Feb91 on sale to Luxmarine Ltd/Sheikh Kamal Adham. Regd HZ-KA7.

261   537GF   Ff 28Sep78 as 5B-DAJ; del Cyprus Airways 06Oct78; regd G-BFWN to British Airways Board 06Oct78; CofA issued 07Oct78 and lsd British Airways 07Oct78 with del Manchester via Milan. Flew last service 01Apr80 Edinburgh to Manchester and ferried Heathrow. Del Cyprus Airways 28Apr80 at end of

lse via Naples to Larnaca. Regn cx 28Apr80 and regd 5B-DAJ; named "Morphou" Jun91.

<u>262</u>   492GM   Regd as G-BLDH to British Aerospace as a Srs.475EZ 11Jan84; r/o 20Jan84; ff 02Feb84. Amended to Srs.492GM 07Mar84. CofA isused 28Mar84. Ferried Hurn to Woodford for storage 06Jun84. Regd to McAlpine Aviation 09Jul84. Del Fort Lauderdale via Rekjavik 17Jul84 for exec conversion. Del Luton 20Mar86. Regd to World Oil & Gas Resources 09Oct92. Regd to Twinjet Aircraft Sales Ltd 21Jun94. Sold Indonesian Air Transport Jul94.

<u>263</u>   539GL   Regd as G-BGKE to British Airways Board 30Jan80; ff 26Jan80; CofA issued 26Feb80; del Birmingham 03Mar80; named "County of Gwynedd"; later named "County of West Midlands". Regd to British Airways 01Apr84. Flew last service for British Airways as BA5139 Munich to Manchester 30Mar91 and stored. Ferried Hurn 18Apr91 as BA9680E for storage. Regd to GEC Ferranti Defence Systems 10Jun91 and painted in GEC Ferranti Aerospace Division c/s. Positioned Heathrow 21Jun91 for major check with British Airways. Ferried Thurleigh, Beds, 29Jul91. Transferred to Defence Research Agency through Ministry of Defence (Procurement Executive) in exchange for c/n 245. Regn cx 01Mar94 and regd ZH763.

<u>264</u>   539GL   Regd as G-BGKF to British Airways Board 11Feb80; ff 09May80; CofA issued 06Jun80; del 13Jun80; named "County of Warwickshire". Regd to British Airways 01Apr84. Flew last service for British Airways as BA5153 Frankfurt to Manchester 19Mar91 and stored. Ferried Hurn 22Apr91 as BA9684E for storage. Sold Okada Air 02Jul91 and r/o Hurn in full c/s as 5N-ORO 18Jul91. Del ex Hurn via Palma 19Jul91. UK regn cx 19Jul91.

<u>265</u>   539GL   Regd as G-BGKG to British Airways Board 11Feb80; ff 06Aug80; CofA issued 14Aug80; del 18Aug80; named "County of Staffordshire". Regd to British Airways 01Apr84. Flew last service for British Airways as BA5055 Rome to Manchester 30Mar91 and stored. Ferried Hurn 21Apr91 as BA9681E for storage. Sold Okada Air 02Jul91. Regn cx 19Jul91 and regd 5N-BIN. Del ex Hurn 27Jul91.

<u>266</u>   525FT   Ff 13Nov80 as YR-BCN; del TAROM 16Jan81. Lsd Inex Adria Airways summer 1985 as YU-AKN with Inex Adria titles and tail logo. Restored as YR-BCN. Lsd Adria Airways summer 1986 as YU-ANM. Restored as YR-BCN. Regd EI-BSY to Ryanair 02Mar87 for lse to them. After preparation for lse del Hurn to Dublin 14Mar87; named "The Spirit of Tipperary". Flew last service 02Nov89 Dublin to Luton. R/o Luton in new TAROM c/s 05Nov89 as YR-BCN. Irish regn cx 13Nov89. Returned TAROM at end of lse with del Luton to Bucharest as ROT1505 14Nov89.

<u>267</u>   487GK   Fitted with forward maindeck freight door. Ff 26Jun81 as YR-BCR; del TAROM 28Jul81. Lsd Anglo Cargo Airlines as YR-BCR with del Manston 17Mar86. Regd G-TOMO to Anglo Airlines 17Sep87 and lse continued. CofA issued 18Sep87. Anglo Cargo Airlines ceased trading 13Jan92 and a/c stored Luton. UK regn cx 09Jul92. Returned TAROM as YR-BCR.

<u>268</u>   561RC   Completed by ROMBAC as c/n 401

<u>269</u>   561RC   Completed by ROMBAC as c/n 402

<u>270</u>   561RC   Completed by ROMBAC as c/n 403

271   561RC   Completed by ROMBAC as c/n 404

272   525FT   Ff 15Feb82 as YR-BCO; del TAROM 12Mar82. Ferried Bucharest 20Mar82. Lsd Dan-Air Services and del Lasham 27Mar84. Regd G-TARO to Dan-Air Services 28Mar84. CofA issued 06Apr84 and departed Lasham same day. Initially flown in TAROM basic c/s with Dan-Air-London titles with white tail bearing Dan-Air emblem. Regn cx 24Dec85. Del ex Manchester as YR-BCO 28Dec85 on return TAROM at end of lse. Lsd Adria Airways as YU-ANN summer 1986. Restored as YR-BCO. Regd EI-BSZ to Ryanair 27Apr87 for lse to them. After pre-service maintenance del Hurn to Dublin 29Apr87; named "The Spirit of Dublin". CofA issued Apr87. Entered service 01May87. Flew last service Dublin to Luton 05Nov89. Regn cx 13Nov89. Restored as YR-BCO and ferried Luton to Bucharest 14Nov89 on return to TAROM at end of lse.

273   561RC   Completed by ROMBAC as c/n 405

274   561RC   Completed by ROMBAC as c/n 406

275   561RC   Completed by ROMBAC as c/n 407

276   561RC   Completed by ROMBAC as c/n 408

401/268 561RC   Fuselage ferried Hurn to Bucharest in Guppy F-BPPA 26Jan80. R/o Baneasa 27Aug82; ff 18Sep82 as YR-BRA; del TAROM 24Dec82. Lsd British Island Airways 01Jun86. Flew last service for British Island Airways as KD7542 Rome-Ciampino to Luton 01Nov86. Returned lessor as RO704 Luton to Bucharest 02Nov86. Lsd Adria Airways as YU-ANR 01May87 to 30Sep87. Restored as YR-BRA. Lsd Istanbul Hava Yollari as YR-BRA 01Jul88 to Oct88. Restored as YR-BRA. Lsd JAT in full c/s summer 1989 and again summer 1990. Lsd Aero Asia of Pakistan May93.

402/269 561RC   Ff 28Apr83 as YR-BRB. Displayed Paris Air Show 1983. Del TAROM Jul83. Lsd Dan-Air Services 03Apr85 to Oct85. Lsd Ryanair, to whom regd EI-BSS 17Nov88. CofA issued ...86. Del Hurn to Dublin 29Nov86 after preparation; named "The Spirit of Dublin". Entered service 01Dec86. Regn cx 13Nov89 and returned lessor as YR-BRB 14Nov89. Re-del Luton 14Dec89. Restored as EI-BSS 18Dec89 to Ryanair. Regn cx 02Nov90 and returned lessor as YR-BRB same date as ROT1502 Luton to Bucharest. Ferried Bucharest to Dublin 01Apr92 in new Ryanair c/s for renewed lse. Restored as EI-BSS to Ryanair 03Apr92. Entered service 03Apr82; named "The Spirit of Ireland". Returned TAROM Oct92 at end of lse. Regn cx ...92 and restored as YR-BRB. Lsd Ryanair yet again with del Hurn for preparation as YR-BRB 02Apr93. Restored as EI-BSS to Ryanair ...93. Regn cx ...93 and restored TAROM as YR-BRB Jun93. Lsd Aero Asia of Pakistan by early 1994.

403/270 561RC   Ff 26Apr84 as YR-BRC; del TAROM Aug84. Lsd Adria Airways as YU-ANS 29Apr87 to 01Nov87. Restored as YR-BRC.

404/271 561RC   Ff 02Apr85 as YR-BRD. Displayed Paris Air Show 31May85 to 09Jun85. Del TAROM Feb86. Lsd Adria Airways as YU-ANT 01May87 to Dec87. Restored as YR-BRD. Lsd Dan-Air Services 17Sep88 to 10Oct88 after operating last service 08Oct88. Lsd Dan-Air Services again 25Mar89. Entered service 26Mar89 Gatwick to Lisbon. Painted in full Dan-Air c/s Southend 18Apr89. Returned lessor 30Oct89 after operating last service for Dan-Air Services from Faro to Manchester the previous day. Lsd Aero Asia of Pakistan May93.

405/273 561RC   Ff 27Mar86 as YR-BRE; del TAROM Mar86. Lsd Dimex Mar90. Dimex renamed Romavia and lse continued.

406/274 561RC   Ff 30Sep86 as YR-BRF; del TAROM ...87. Lsd London European Airways and del Hurn to Luton 19May87; named "The Spirit of Europe". Entered service 22May87 Luton to Amsterdam. Regd G-BNIH to London European Airways 17Aug87. CofA issued 24Aug87. Lsd Loganair Apr89 to 31May89. Flew last service for Ryanair Europe 09May90 Turin to Luton. Regn cx 01Jun90 and regd EI-CAS to Ryanair 01Jun90 after r/o Luton 30May90. Entered service 01Jun90 Luton to Connaught/Knock. Del Luton to Bucharest as YR-BRF 07Oct90 at end of lse as RO799. Lsd Aero Asia of Pakistan by early 1994.

407/275 561RC   Ff 21Mar88 as YR-BRG; del TAROM ...88. Lsd Ryanair, to whom regd EI-BVH 31Mar88. CofA issued 01Apr88. Entered service Dublin to Manchester as RYR566 01Apr88; named "The Spirit of Tara". Ferried Hurn 25Sep93 for repaint in TAROM c/s as YR-BRG. Returned Dublin 29Sep93 and ferried Bucharest 01Oct93 at end of lease.

408/276 561RC   Ff 01Dec88 as YR-BRH; del TAROM ... Transferred Romavia. Lsd Citylink Airways of India Nov92. Co ceased ops Oct93 and aircraft returned Romavia. Lsd Aero Asia of Pakistan by early 1994.

409/277 561RC   Ff Apr89 as YR-BRI; del Romavia ...92. Lsd Citylink Airways of India Nov92. Co ceased ops Oct93 and aircraft returned Romavia.

410   475   Fitted with maindeck freight door. Originally built to the order of Romanian Army. Order cx and construction suspended.

411   2500   Originally allocated to Romavia as a Srs.561RC. Re-allocated as the first "Airstar 2500" for Kiwi International Airlines Inc.

412   2500   Second "Airstar 2500" for Kiwi International Airlines Inc.

413   2500   Third "Airstar 2500" for Kiwi International Airlines Inc.

414   2500   Fourth "Airstar 2500" for Kiwi International Airlines Inc.

REGISTRATION/CONSTRUCTOR'S NUMBER CROSS-REFERENCES

Registrations in this section enclosed within brackets were allocated but never used. Where registrations are duplicated, they are shown in date of use order, with initial use first.

CIVIL

NICARAGUA

AN-BBI	111
AN-BBS	050
AN-BHJ	206
AN-BHN	074

UNITED ARAB EMIRATES

A6-KTH	126
A6-RAK	084
A6-RKT	126
A6-SHJ	075

OMAN

A40-BB	162
A40-BU	157
A40-BX	121

CHILE

CC-CYF	033
CC-CYI	035
CC-CYL	040
CC-CYM	039

CANADA

CF-QBN	110
CF-QBO	112
CF-QBR	094
C-FQBN	110
C-FQBO	112
C-FQBR	094
C-GQBP	122
C-GQBV	123

BAHAMAS

C6-BDJ	089
C6-BDN	062
C6-BDP	063

GERMANY

D-ABHH	084
(D-AFWA)	161
(D-AFWB)	094
(D-AFWC)	091
D-AILY	163
D-AISY	158
D-ALAQ	229
D-ALAR	207
D-ALAS	208
D-ALAT	187
D-ALFA	234
D-ALLI	116
D-AMAM	229
D-AMAS	187
D-AMAT	235
D-AMIE	190
D-AMOR	197
D-AMUC	227
D-AMUR	195
(D-ANDI)	158
D-ANDY	127
D-ANNO	160
D-ANUE	238

FIJI

DQ-FBQ	245
DQ-FBV	250
DQ-FCR	116

SPAIN

EC-BQF	161

EIRE

EI-ANE	049
EI-ANF	050
EI-ANG	051
EI-ANH	052
EI-BSS	402
EI-BSY	266
EI-BSZ	272
EI-BVG	255
EI-BVH	407
EI-BVI	256
EI-BWI	007
EI-BWJ	009
EI-BWK	011
EI-BWL	012
EI-BWM	013
EI-BWN	020
EI-BWO	041
EI-BWP	043
EI-BWQ	057
EI-BWR	061
EI-BWS	085
EI-BWT	127
EI-CAS	406
EI-CCU	237
EI-CCW	186
EI-CCX	211
EI-CDO	201
EI-CIB	191
EI-CIC	177
EI-CID	174
EI-CIE	176

UNITED KINGDOM

G-16-1	094
G-16-2	118
G-16-3	127
G-16-4	130
G-16-5	121
G-16-6	162
G-16-7	192
G-16-8	193

G-16-9	194	G-AVMP	144	G-AYOP	233
G-16-10	196	G-AVMR	145	G-AYOR	232
G-16-11	197	G-AVMS	146	G-AYOS	213
G-16-12	198	G-AVMT	147	(G-AYSC)	235
G-16-13	212	G-AVMU	148	G-AYUW	239
G-16-14	157	G-AVMV	149	G-AYWB	237
G-16-15	236	G-AVMW	150	G-AYXB	192
G-16-16	241	G-AVMX	151	G-AZDG	127
G-16-17	239	G-AVMY	152	G-AZEB	188
G-16-19	066	G-AVMZ	153	G-AZEC	189
G-16-22	230	G-AVOE	129	G-AZED	127
G-16-23	199	G-AVOF	131	G-AZMF	240
G-16-24	166	G-AVTF	122	G-AZMI	066
G-16-25	260	G-AVYZ	133	G-AZPE	208
G-16-32	131	G-AWBL	132	G-AZPY	187
G-52-1	005	G-AWDF	134	G-AZPZ	229
G-ASHG	004	G-AWEJ	115	G-AZUK	241
G-ASJA	005	G-AWGG	116	G-BBME	066
G-ASJB	006	(G-AWGG)	128	G-BBMF	074
G-ASJC	007	G-AWKJ	128	G-BBMG	115
G-ASJD	008	G-AWWX	184	G-BCCV	198
G-ASJE	009	G-AWWY	185	G-BCWA	205
G-ASJF	010	G-AWWZ	186	G-BCWG	204
G-ASJG	011	G-AWXJ	166	G-BCXR	198
G-ASJH	012	G-AWYR	174	G-BDAE	203
G-ASJI	013	G-AWYS	175	G-BDAS	202
G-ASJJ	014	G-AWYT	176	G-BDAT	232
G-ASTJ	085	G-AWYU	177	G-BEJM	118
G-ASUF	015	G-AWYV	178	G-BEJW	154
(G-ASVT)	095	G-AXBB	162	G-BEKA	230
G-ASYD	053	G-AXCK	090	G-BFMC	160
G-ASYE	054	G-AXCP	087	G-BFWN	261
G-ATPH	110	G-AXJK	191	G-BGKE	263
G-ATPI	112	G-AXJL	209	G-BGKF	264
G-ATPJ	033	G-AXJM	214	G-BGKG	265
G-ATPK	034	G-AXLL	193	G-BGTU	108
G-ATPL	035	G-AXLM	199	G-BIII	128
G-ATTP	039	G-AXLN	211	G-BJMV	244
G-ATVH	040	G-AXMF	200	G-BJRT	234
G-ATVU	074	G-AXMG	201	G-BJRU	238
G-AVBW	107	G-AXMH	202	G-BJYL	208
G-AVBX	109	G-AXMI	203	G-BJYM	242
G-AVBY	113	G-AXMJ	204	G-BKAU	107
G-AVEJ	094	G-AXMK	205	G-BKAV	109
G-AVGP	114	G-AXML	206	G-BKAW	113
G-AVMH	136	G-AXMU	157	G-BKAX	133
G-AVMI	137	G-AXOX	121	G-BLDH	262
G-AVMJ	138	G-AXPH	194	G-BLHD	260
G-AVMK	139	G-AXSY	195	(G-BLVO)	041
G-AVML	140	G-AXVO	197	(G-BLVP)	043
G-AVMM	141	G-AXYD	210	G-BMAN	131
G-AVMN	142	G-AYHM	161	G-BNIH	406
G-AVMO	143	G-AYKN	215	G-BPNX	110

(G-BSXJ)	063	HZ-AMB	069	**LUXEMBOURG**	
(G-BSXK)	089	HZ-AMH	158		
(G-BSXU)	093	(HZ-AMH)	183	LX-MAM	259
(G-BSXV)	106	HZ-AMK	054		
G-BSYN	186	HZ-BL1	080		
G-CBIA	166	HZ-GP2	060	**ERRONEOUSLY**	
G-DBAF	011	HZ-GRP	060	**PAINTED**	
G-DJOS	237	HZ-GRP	067		
G-EKPT	211	HZ-HR1	081	LY-IZR	122
G-EXPM	124	HZ-JAM	111		
G-FLRU	201	HZ-KA7	260		
G-KROO	125	HZ-KB1	158	**UNITED STATES OF**	
G-NIII	128	HZ-MAA	060	**AMERICA**	
G-OBWA	232	HZ-MAJ	088		
G-OBWB	202	HZ-MAM	259	N1JR	055
G-OBWC	230	HZ-MFA	080	N3E	068
G-OBWD	203	HZ-MF1	158	N5LC	015
G-OBWE	242	HZ-MO1	135	N5LC	073
(G-OBWF)	210	HZ-NB2	064	N5LG	015
(G-OBWG)	184	HZ-NB3	060	N8LG	015
(G-OBWH)	208	(HZ-ND1)	183	N9WP	078
(G-OBWI)	205	HZ-NIR	088	N10HM	080
(G-OBWJ)	244	HZ-RH1	081	N12CZ	056
(G-OBWK)	198	HZ-TA1	078	N17MK	054
G-OCNW	012			N17VK	054
G-SURE	129			N18HD	068
G-TARO	272	**ARGENTINA**		N18HH	068
G-TOMO	267			N22RB	080
G-WLAD	112	LV-IZR	122	N40AS	061
G-YMRU	110	LV-IZS	123	N44R	120
		LV-JGX	117	N55JT	075
		LV-JGY	155	N56B	055
SWITZERLAND		LV-JNR	192	N58GA	117
		LV-JNS	194	N62WH	078
HB-ITK	166	LV-JNT	196	N69HM	061
HB-ITL	212	LV-JNU	185	N71MA	111
		LV-LHT	185	N76GW	065
		LV-LOX	212	N77CS	054
DOMINICAN		LV-MEX	200	N77QS	054
REPUBLIC		LV-MRZ	206	N80GM	126
		LV-MZM	187	N88NB	005
(HI-148)	114	LV-OAX	197	N90AM	111
		LV-OAY	227	N90TF	080
		LV-PEW	187	N97GA	058
HONDURAS		LV-PFR	197	N97JF	089
		LV-PID	122	N97KR	005
HR-AMO	086	LV-PIF	123	N100CC	059
		LV-PKA	155	N101EX	007
		LV-PKB	117	N102EX	009
SAUDI ARABIA		LV-PSW	185	N102GP	060
				N102ME	067
HZ-ABM2	060			N103EX	010
HZ-AB1	158			N104EX	011

N105EX	012	N583CC	015	N1553	070
N106EX	013	N650DH	059	N1554	071
N107EX	085	N682RW	061	N2111J	029
N109TH	067	N700JA	059	(N3126H)	122
(N110TA)	236	N711ST	058	(N3126Q)	123
N111AC	111	N734EB	005	N3756F	005
N111FL	073	N765B	067	N3939V	054
N111GS	126	N767RV	111	(N4111X)	054
N111LP	068	N800DM	079	N4550T	135
N111NA	055	N800MC	078	N5015	055
N111NA	065	N800MC	062	N5016	056
N111NA	060	N800PW	078	N5017	057
N111NA	086	N809M	126	N5018	058
N111NS	078	N825AC	065	N5019	059
N111QA	015	N825AQ	065	N5020	060
N112NA	059	N880DP	079	N5021	061
N112NA	088	N909CH	067	N5022	062
N114M	119	N950CC	086	N5023	063
N117MR	065	N1112J	030	N5024	064
N119GA	072	N1113J	031	N5025	065
N120TA	056	N1114J	032	N5026	066
N123H	163	N1115J	082	N5027	067
N128GA	117	N1116J	098	N5028	068
N128TA	117	N1117J	099	N5029	069
N162W	087	N1118J	100	N5030	072
N164W	090	N1119J	101	N5031	073
N170FE	057	N1120J	102	N5032	074
N171FE	061	N1122J	103	N5033	075
N172FE	056	N1123J	104	N5034	076
N173FE	087	N1124J	134	N5035	077
N174FE	127	N1125J	135	N5036	078
N179FE	075	N1126J	179	N5037	079
N200CC	068	N1127J	180	N5038	080
N217CA	063	N1128J	181	N5039	081
N218CA	089	N1129J	182	N5040	086
N221CN	111	N1130J	096	N5041	087
N270E	120	N1131J	097	N5042	088
N277NS	057	N1132J	105	N5043	089
N310EL	072	N1134J	045	N5044	090
N333GB	076	N1135J	046	N8007U	054
N341TC	126	N1136J	071	N11181	096
N390BA	129	N1541	015	N11182	097
N392BA	131	N1542	016	N11183	105
N401SK	073	N1543	017	N18813	126
N490ST	083	N1544	018	N18814	119
N491ST	056	N1545	019	(N29967)	009
N500CS	086	N1546	020	N51387	126
N502T	083	N1547	041	N70611	083
N503T	183	N1548	042		
N504T	084	N1549	043		
N523AC	015	N1550	044	**PERU**	
N524AC	120	N1551	045		
N541BN	015	N1552	046	OB-R-953	239

OB-R-1080	241	RP-C1182	246	**BAHAMAS**	
OB-R-1137	193	RP-C1183	248		
OB-R-1173	193	RP-C1184	190	VP-BCN	188
		RP-C1185	195	VP-BCO	189
		RP-C1186	188	VP-BCP	034
AUSTRIA		RP-C1187	189	VP-BCQ	198
		RP-C1188	209	VP-BCY	121
OE-ILC	255	RP-C1189	204	VP-BCZ	157
OE-ILD	256	RP-C1193	231	VP-BDI	074
		RP-C1194	199	VP-BDJ	089
				VP-BDN	062
PHILIPPINES				VP-BDP	063
		GREECE			
PI-C1121	091				
PI-C1131	092	SX-BAR	096	**ANTIGUA**	
PI-C1141	094				
PI-C1151	161			VP-LAK	205
PI-C1151	157	**SAO TOME ISLAND**		VP-LAN	198
PI-C1161	213			VP-LAP	188
PI-C1171	215	S9-TAE	084	VP-LAR	189
PI-C1181	226				
PI-C1191	231				
		TURKEY		**RHODESIA**	
		TC-AKA	255	VP-YXA	039
INDONESIA		TC-AKB	253	VP-YXB	040
		TC-ARI	253		
PK-PJC	166	TC-JCP	254		
PK-PJF	065			**BERMUDA**	
PK-T??	262				
				VR-BAC	017
		GUATEMALA		VR-BHS	076
BRAZIL					
		TG-ARA	205		
PP-SDP	192	TG-AVA	206	**CAYMAN ISLANDS**	
PP-SDQ	228	TG-AYA	211		
PP-SDR	230	TG-AZA	231	VR-CAB	237
PP-SDS	236	TG-TJF	089	VR-CAL	211
PP-SDT	193			VR-CAM	069
PP-SDU	211			VR-CAQ	005
PP-SDV	199	**COSTA RICA**		VR-CBI	057
PP-SRT	119			VR-CBX	084
PP-SRU	126	TI-1055C	162	VR-CBY	183
PT-TYV	200	TI-1056C	108	VR-CBZ	083
PT-TYW	206	TI-1084C	237	VR-CCG	081
PT-TYY	240	TI-1095C	242	VR-CCJ	126
		TI-1096C	244	VR-CCS	069
		TI-LRF	237	VR-CMI	183
PHILIPPINES		TI-LRI	242	VR-CTM	081
		TI-LRJ	244		
RP-C1	128	TI-LRK	208		
RP-C1161	213	TI-LRL	237		
RP-C1171	215				
RP-C1181	226				

MEXICO

XA-ADC	084
XA-RTN	085
XB-MUO	005

ROMANIA

YR-BCA	130
YR-BCB	156
YR-BCC	167
YR-BCD	159
YR-BCE	165
YR-BCF	168
YR-BCG	077
YR-BCH	161
YR-BCI	252
YR-BCJ	253
YR-BCK	254
YR-BCL	255
YR-BCM	256
YR-BCN	266
YR-BCO	272
YR-BCP	162
YR-BCR	267
YR-BRA	401
YR-BRB	402
YR-BRC	403
YR-BRD	404
YR-BRE	405
YR-BRF	406
YR-BRG	407
YR-BRH	408
YR-BRI	409
YR-JBA	234
YR-JBB	238

EL SALVADOR

YS-01C	108
YS-17C	093
YS-18C	106

YUGOSLAVIA

YU-AKN	266
YU-ANM	266
YU-ANN	272
YU-ANR	401
YU-ANS	403
YU-ANT	404

SOUTH AFRICA

ZS-NNM	108

SWAZILAND

3D-LLG	069

ISRAEL

4X-BAR	230
4X-BAS	199

CYPRUS

5B-DAF	201
5B-DAG	257
5B-DAH	258
5B-DAJ	261

NIGERIA

5N-AOK	113
5N-AOM	122
5N-AOP	109
5N-AOS	123
5N-AOT	133
5N-AOW	094
5N-AOZ	107
5N-AUS	???
5N-AVX	167
5N-AXQ	157
5N-AXT	121
5N-AXV	159
5N-AYR	162
5N-AYS	129
5N-AYT	131
5N-AYU	062
5N-AYV	128
5N-AYW	166
5N-AYY	043
5N-BAA	041
5N-BAB	127
5N-BIN	265
5N-EHI	074
5N-GGG	160
5N-HTA	051
5N-HTB	052
5N-HTC	049
5N-HTD	050
5N-HTP	???
5N-IMO	229
5N-IVE	112
5N-KBA	179
5N-KBC	104
5N-KBD	102
5N-KBE	???
5N-KBG	082
5N-KBM	105
5N-KBN	???
5N-KBO	180
5N-KBR	093
5N-KBS	031
5N-KBT	100
5N-KBV	032
5N-KBW	106
5N-KGB	082
5N-KKK	154
5N-MZE	110
5N-NRC	124
5N-OAL	214
5N-OKA	168
5N-OMO	034
5N-ORO	264
5N-OSA	153
5N-SDP	125
5N-SKS	100
5N-SKS	243
5N-TOM	124
5N-UDE	259
5N-USE	151
5N-USE	235

MALAWI

7Q-YKE	039
7Q-YKF	243
7Q-YKG	245
7Q-YKI	214
7Q-YKJ	240
7Q-YKK	235

ZAMBIA

9J-RCH	039
9J-RCI	040

KUWAIT

(9K-ACI)	033
(9K-ACJ)	034
(9K-ACK)	035

ZAIRE

9Q-CEH	057
9Q-CSJ	013
9Q-CUG	057

SINGAPORE

9V-BEF	166

MILITARY

AUSTRALIA

A12-124	124
A12-125	125

BRAZIL

VC92-2110	154
VC92-2111	118

MEXICO

TP-0201	005

SULTANATE OF OMAN

551	247
552	249
553	251
1001	247
1002	249
1003	251

UNITED KINGDOM

XX105	008
XX919	091
ZE432	250
ZE433	245
ZH763	263

ABBREVIATIONS

AC	Alternating Current
a/c	aircraft
ADF	Automatic Direction Finding equipment
APU	Auxiliary Power Unit
ARINC	United States Aeronautical Radio Inc
Assocs	Associates
ATC	Air Traffic Control
Avn	Aviation
BAC	British Aircraft Corporation
BAe	British Aerospace
BCAL	British Caledonian Airways
BCAR	British Civil Airworthiness Requirements
BCF	Bromochlorodifluoromethane
BEA	British European Airways
BOAC	British Overseas Airways Corporation
cx	cancelled or cancellation
cm	centimetres
c/n	constructor's number
Co	Company
CofA	Certificate of Airworthiness
CofG	Centre of Gravity
Corp	Corporation
c/s	colour scheme
dam	damaged
del	delivered or delivery
DC	Direct Current
demo	demonstration
DME	Direction Measuring Equipment
EAS	Equivalent Airspeed
exec	executive
FAA	United States Federal Aviation Agency/Administration
Ff	First flight
ft	feet
gall	gallons
Govt	Government
HD	Heavy Duty
HF	High Frequency
h/o	handed over
HP	High Pressure
Hrs	hours
HS	Hawker Siddeley
Hz	Hertz
ILFC	International Lease Finance Corporation
Imp	Imperial
in	inches
Inds	Industries
ISA	International Standard Atmosphere
kg	kilogrammes
km	kilometres
km/hr	kilometres per hour

kN	KiloNewton
kt	knots
kVa	Kilovolt-Amperes
lb	pounds
LCN	Load Classification Number
ldgs	landings
LP	Low Pressure
lsd	leased
lse	lease
Lsg	Leasing
m	metres
MLW	Maximum Landing Weight
mods	modifications
mph	miles per hour
MTOW	Maximum Take-Off Weight
MZFW	Maximum Zero Fuel Weight
NDT	Non-Destructive Testing
nm	nautical miles
ntu	not taken up
op	operated
ops	operations
psi	pounds per square inch
PVC	polyvinyl chloride
regd	registered
regn	registration
res	reserved
r/o	rolled out
Srs	Series
sublsd	subleased
TT	total time
TAS	True Airspeed
VHF	Very High Frequency
wfs	withdrawn from service
wfu	withdrawn from use
w/o	written off